1973

JOHN WILLIS'

THEATRE WORLD

1971-1972 SEASON

Volume 28

Crown Publishers, Inc.
419 Park Avenue South
New York, N.Y. 10016

TO

MALTIER CHAUNCEY HAGAN

whose life-long and zealous devotion to the creative arts as teacher, writer, and performer, has never diminished; and whose infectious zest for living, ardent interest in, and sincerely unselfish assistance to others has become a creative art in its own right.

Raul Julia, Jonelle Allen, Clifton Davis, Diana Davila
in "Two Gentlemen of Verona"
Winner of "Tony" and Drama Critics Circle Awards as Best Musical

CONTENTS

EDITOR: JOHN WILLIS
Assistant Editor: Stanley Reeves
Staff: Frances Crampon, Raymond Frederick, Lucy Williams
Staff Photographers: Bert Andrews, Scott Chelius, Louis Melancon,
Van Williams, Ted Yaple

THE SEASON IN REVIEW
June 1, 1971—May 31, 1972

This was another season with little cause for optimism from producers, actors, or audiences. Even though it was not distinguished, it was a slightly better year than anticipated. There were more productions on Broadway (26 new plays, 20 musicals, 10 revivals) than last season, and their quality was slightly more praiseworthy. The Pulitzer Prize committee, however, decided none merited its award. Boxoffice receipts dropped for several reasons: the economic recession, increased ticket costs, and unfavorable publicity relative to the Times Square and theatre district. Productions that received good reviews were unable to fill their houses, and the season had no "smash hits." Only the rock musical "Jesus Christ Superstar," and the comedy "Prisoner of Second Avenue" managed to sell out for a period. Peter Falk, Lee Grant, and Vincent Gardenia were excellent in the latter, and Mr. Gardenia won a "Tony" for his supporting performance, as did Mike Nichols for his direction.

Other "Tonys" for straight plays were awarded Sada Thompson ("Twigs") and Cliff Gorman ("Lenny") for best performances, and Elizabeth Wilson for best supporting actress in "Sticks and Bones," selected as best play. For excellence in musicals, "Tonys" went to Phil Silvers ("A Funny Thing Happened on the Way to the Forum") and Alexis Smith ("Follies") for best performers, Larry Blyden ("A Funny Thing . . .") and Linda Hopkins ("Inner City") for best supporting performers, and "Two Gentlemen of Verona" for best musical. "Follies" received six "Tonys" for best score, direction, choreography, sets, costumes, and lighting.

The New York Drama Critics Circle found itself in an embarrassing situation. After announcing "Sticks and Bones" its choice as best play, an error in tabulation was discovered making Off-Broadway's Public Theater's "That Championship Season" the winner by one vote. The loser received a special citation. Consequently, "Old Times," that had lost by one vote to Chelsea Theater Center's "Screens" as best foreign play, was also given a special citation. "Old Times," with stellar performances by Rosemary Harris, Mary Ure, and Robert Shaw, was the season's most controversial and enigmatic play. "Two Gentlemen . . ." added another honor with the Circle's award for best musical.

Productions that deserved greater support were "Vivat! Vivat Regina!" with laudable performances by Claire Bloom, Eileen Atkins, Douglas Rain, and Lee Richardson; "Country Girl" brilliantly played by Maureen Stapleton, Jason Robards, and George Grizzard; "On the Town" with delightful performances by Bernadette Peters, Ron Husmann, Jess Richards; "Promenade, All!" with bravura characterizations from Anne Jackson, Eli Wallach, Hume Cronyn, Richard Backus; "Lost in the Stars" poignantly performed by Brock Peters and Gilbert Price; "Moonchildren" with a memorable cast including Maureen Anderman, James Woods, and Cara Duff-MacCormick; "Unlikely Heroes" with Lou Jacobi, Michael Tolan, David Ackroyd praiseworthy; and the totally delightful "There's One in Every Marriage." Outstanding performers in other productions were Clifton Davis, Jonelle Allen, Raul Julia, Barbara Cook, Russ Thacker, Joan Hackett, Len Cariou, Keene Curtis, Donald Pleasence, Elaine Joyce, Robert Morse, George S. Irving, Richard Kiley, Julie Harris, Clive Revill, Gene Nelson, Frances Sternhagen, Ben Vereen, Paul Lipson, Joe Silver, Tom Aldredge, Mercedes McCambridge, and Beatrice Winde.

The healthiest aspect of the season was the increased number of "Black Theatre" productions—by and with black talent. They are not only evolving into a commercial art, but also developing new talent. For the first time in Broadway's history, three black musicals were presented—two by the multi-talented Melvin Van Peebles. His first production, "Ain't Supposed to Die a Natural Death," had an approach that for some was too angry, and drove patrons from the theatre. Succeeding productions, however, did not assault their audiences with messages, but provided pleasant entertainment. They also initiated new audiences to the magic of live theatre—a vitally necessary project if the stage is to survive television and inferior films with lower admission prices.

The Repertory Theater of Lincoln Center (still a misnomer) survived a tempestuous season. Agitation was provoked over the fate of its Forum, its financial survival, and its productions. Nevertheless, the progressively improving quality of its productions was evident in "Mary Stuart," "Twelfth Night," "The Crucible," and "Suggs." From its roster of actors, outstanding performers were Martha Henry, Blythe Danner, Robert Foxworth, Nancy Marchand, Salome Jens, Estelle Parsons, Les Roberts, Stephen Elliott, Lee Lawson, and Keene Curtis. The proposed plan for City Center to take over the Beaumont and convert its beautiful, almost-perfect Forum into twin film houses was fortunately defeated.

The perpetual action was at the seemingly indefatigable Joseph Papp's New York Shakespeare Festival Public Theater complex. Fourteen quality productions were presented, including the always-impressive Central Park festival. With its final offering of "Cymbeline," every play by Shakespeare had been presented in the park during its 15 seasons of free performances. Its up-dated "Two Gentlemen of Verona," and "Sticks and Bones" were transferred to Broadway and showered with awards. For the first time, it toured a company —"Basic Training of Pavlo Hummel." Mr. Papp's perception, fortitude, and perseverance were deservedly reaping rewards.

Off-Broadway had fewer productions and less quality than previously. There were 46 openings, and no financial hits except the 5 holdovers from other seasons. Its major disasters were "vanity productions"—financed by playwright or director for personal satisfaction. The most impressive Off-Broadway presentations were the unique "James Joyce Memorial Liquid Theatre," "Beggar's Opera," "One for the Money," "Hark!," "Leaves of Grass," "The Real Inspector Hound," Tennessee Williams' "Small Craft Warnings" (Mr. Williams substituted for a castmember in several performances), "Where Has Tommy Flowers Gone?" with exceptional performances by Robert Drivas and Marion Paone, and "Grease" with Adrienne Barbeau, Barry Bostwick, and Timothy Meyers noteworthy. Other Off-Broadway actors giving performances of merit were Marilyn Chris, Will Hare, Rue McClanahan, Terry Kiser, Joe Masiell, Carrie Nye, Lester Rawlins, Ed Evanko, David Rounds, Harold Gary, Ron Rifkin, Vinie Burrows, James Naughton, Lauren Jones, William Atherton, Hal Holbrook, Armand Assante, Christopher Walken, Catherine Burns, Gloria Foster, and the entire cast of "That Championship Season."

American Place Theatre opened its beautifully impressive new home in the lower depths of a new office building, becoming the first theatre built in New York since 1928. Three more in new office buildings are promised for next season. APT continued its non-profit, subscription series by living American playwrights. With the increased difficulty in securing production money, it's more apparent that the theatre's greatest hope for survival is support from grants and subsidies. Off-Off-Broadway (companies not under union contracts) had its most prolific and innovative year with more productions than Broadway and Off-Broadway combined. Gratefully, regional theatres continued to flourish, and hopefully, combined with Off-Off-Broadway's influence, will provide the much-needed new blood for an art that is struggling for its existence.

Additional observations relative to this season must be noted. Critics were seemingly exerting less influence on boxoffice receipts. "Twofers" (or reduced price tickets) were available for more productions, and prolonged their runs. More productions added extra matinees, eliminating one or two evening performances, and drawing larger audiences. The 7:30 P.M. curtain remained in effect, but some producers reverted to 8 P.M. Before it closed, "Hello, Dolly!" passed the record number of performances for musicals set by "My Fair Lady." It, however, became second longest when "Fiddler on the Roof" passed its record, and then continued playing until it broke that of the comedy "Life with Father," Broadway's longest run ever. As we close the records on another year, we beseech the muses to grant us a more rewarding 1972–73 season.

Peter Falk

Claire Bloom

BROADWAY CALENDAR

June 1, 1971 through May 31, 1972

Anne
Baxter

Richard Kiley

Alexis Smith

Keene Curtis

JOHN GOLDEN THEATRE

Opened Tuesday, June 1, 1971.*
Arthur Whitelaw and Gene Persson present:

YOU'RE A GOOD MAN, CHARLIE BROWN

Book, John Gordon; Based on comic strip "Peanuts" by
Charles M. Schulz; Music and Lyrics, Clark Gesner; Director,
Joseph Hardy; Sets and Costumes, Alan Kimmel; Lighting,
Jules Fisher; Musical Staging, Patricia Birch; Musical Super-
vision, Arrangements, and Additional Material, Joseph
Raposo; Associate Producer, Warren Lockhart; Musical Di-
rector, Jack Holmes; Original Cast Album by MGM Records.

CAST

Linus .... Stephen Fenning
Charlie Brown .... Dean Stolber
Patty.. Lee Wilson
Schroeder .... Carter Cole
Snoopy .... Grant Cowan
Lucy .... Liz O'Neal

UNDERSTUDIES: Linus, Charlie, Snoopy, Jason Holt;
Patty, Lucy, Merry Flershem

MUSICAL NUMBERS: "You're a Good Man, Charlie
Brown," "Schroeder," "Snoopy," "My Blanket and Me,"
"Kite," "Dr. Lucy," "Book Report," "The Red Baron,"
"T.E.A.M.," "Glee Club Rehearsal," "Little Known Facts,"
"Suppertime," "Happiness"

A Musical in two acts. An average day in the life of Charlie
Brown.

General Manager: Marvin A. Krauss
Company Manager: John Corkill
Press: Max Eisen, Warren Pincus, Milly Schoenbaum
Stage Managers: Barbara Tuttle, Jason Holt

* Closed June 26, 1971 after 31 performances and 15 previews. Original production opened Off-Broadway Mar. 7,
1967 and played 1597 performances. See THEATRE
WORLD, Vol. 23.

Martha Swope Photos

**Liz O'Neal, Carter Cole, Dean Stolber, Lee Wilson,
Stephen Fenning, Grant Cowan**

Lee Wilson, Grant Cowan

Stephen Fenning, Liz O'Neal

LYCEUM THEATRE

Opened Wednesday, June 2, 1971.*
Phoenix Theatre (T. Edward Hambleton, Managing Director) and Leland Hayward present:

THE TRIAL OF THE CATONSVILLE NINE

By Daniel Berrigan, S. J.; Director, Gordon Davidson; Setting, Peter Wexler; Costumes, Albert Wolsky; Lighting, Tharon Musser; Text prepared by Saul Levitt.

CAST

Daniel Berrigan	Colgate Salsbury
Philip Berrigan	Biff McGuire
David Darst	James Woods
John Hogan	Barton Heyman
Thomas Lewis	Sam Waterston
Marjorie Melville	Jacqueline Coslow
Thomas Melville	Joe Ponazecki
George Mische	Michael Moriarty
Mary Moylan	Ronnie Claire Edwards
Defense	Josef Sommer
Judge	Mason Adams
Witness	Helen Stenborg
Prosecution	Davis Roberts
Marshalls	Peter Gorwin, James O'Connell, Gerry Murphy

UNDERSTUDIES: Daniel, Prosecution, Defense, Jake Dengel; Philip, Hogan, Judge, Thomas, Arlen Snyder; Mary, Marjorie, Witness, Nancy Franklin; Mische, Lewis, Darst, Peter Gorwin

Presented without intermission.

General Manager: Marilyn S. Miller
Press: Sol Jacobson, Lewis Harmon, Ruth D. Smuckler
Stage Managers: Daniel Freuenberger, A. Robert Altshuler

* Closed June 26, 1971 after 29 performances. Opened Off-Broadway Sunday, Feb. 7, 1971 at Good Shepherd Faith Church where it played 130 performances before moving to Broadway. See THEATRE WORLD, Vol. 27.

Van Williams Photos

Barton Heyman, Jacqueline Coslow, Joe Ponazecki, Biff McGuire, Mason Adams (Judge), Colgate Salsbury, James Woods, Ronnie Claire Edwards, Michael Moriarty

MOROSCO THEATRE
Opened Thursday, September 9, 1971.*
Ashton Springer and Jeanne Warner present:

NO PLACE TO BE SOMEBODY

By Charles Gordone; Director, Mr. Gordone; Set, John Retsek; Lighting, Conrad Penrod.

CAST

Gabe Gabriel	Philip Thomas
Shanty Mulligan	Ian Sander
Johnny Williams	Terry Alexander
Dee Jacobson	Elaine Kerr
Evie Adams	Paulette Ellen Jones
Cora Beasley	Mary Alice
Melvin Smeltz	Henry Baker
Mary Lou Bolton	Terry Lumley
Sweets Crane	Julius W. Harris
Mike Maffucci	Nick Lewis
Louis	Jim Jacobs
Judge Bolton	Ed Van Nuys
Sergeant Cappaletti	Peter Savage
Harry	Malcolm Hurd

UNDERSTUDIES: Johnny, Frank Adu; Gabe, David Pendleton; Sweets, Lee Roy Giles; Dee, Mary Lou, Rebecca Nahas; Shanty, Cappaletti, Jim Jacobs; Maffucci, Peter Savage; Cora, Evie, Jeannie Jurgun; Melvin, Malcolm Hurd

A Drama in three acts. The action takes place in the past fifteen years in Johnny's Bar in West Greenwich Village, New York City.

Company Manager: Clayton Coots
Press: Howard Atlee, David Roggensack, Ellen Levine,
Irene Gandy, Joseph Allsopp
Stage Managers: Garland Lee Thompson, Malcolm Hurd

* Closed Oct. 9, 1971 after 37 performances and 15 previews. Winner of 1970 Pulitzer Prize originally opened Off-Broadway at the Public Theater on May 4, 1969 and played 572 performances. See THEATRE WORLD, Vol. 25.

Rik Lawrence, Nan White Photos

Left: Philip Thomas

Ian Sander, Mary Alice

Terry Alexander, Susan Spaulding

JOHN GOLDEN THEATRE

Opened Thursday, September 30, 1971.*
Gilbert Cates, Roy N. Nevans, and Albert J. Schiff present:

SOLITAIRE/DOUBLE SOLITAIRE

By Robert Anderson; Director, Arvin Brown; Sets, Kert Lundell; Costumes, Lewis Rampino; Lighting, Ronald Wallace.

CAST

"Solitaire"

Sam Bradley	Richard Venture
Madam	Ruth Nelson
Daughter	Patricia Pearcy
Brother	Will Fenno
Wife	Joyce Ebert
Father	John Cromwell
Captain	William Swetland

Intermission

"Double Solitaire"

Charley	Richard Venture
Barbara	Joyce Ebert
Mrs. Potter	Ruth Nelson
Mr. Potter	John Cromwell
Sylvia	Martha Schlamme
George	William Swetland
Peter	Will Fenno

UNDERSTUDIES: For Misses Ebert, Nelson, Schlamme, Alice Hirson; For Messrs. Cromwell, Swetland, Venture, William Countryman; Brother, Peter, Stephen Conrad; Daughter, Jean Weigel.

General Manager; Robert Kamlot
Press: Harvey B. Sabinson, Lee Solters, Sandra Manley
Stage Managers: Martin Gold, Stephen Conrad, Jean Weigel

* Closed Oct. 31, 1971 after 36 performances and 3 previews.

William L. Smith Photos

Top: Ruth Nelson (L) Richard Venture (R)

Joyce Ebert, Richard Venture Above: Will Fenno, Richard Venture, Patricia Pearcy 11

MARK HELLINGER THEATRE

Opened Tuesday, October 12, 1971.*
Robert Stigwood in association with MCA Inc. by arrangement with David Land presents:

JESUS CHRIST SUPERSTAR

Lyrics, Tim Rice; Music, Andrew Lloyd Webber; Conceived for the stage and directed by Tom O'Horgan; Associate Producers, Gatchell and Neufeld; Scenery, Robin Wagner; Costumes, Randy Barcelo; Lighting, Jules Fisher; Sound, Abe Jacob; Musical Direction, Marc Pressel; Orchestrations, Andrew Lloyd Webber; Production Supervisor, Charles Gray; Assistant Conductor, Seymour Miroff; Musical Supervisor, Mel Rodnon.

CAST

Judas Iscariot	Ben Vereen†1
Jesus of Nazareth	Jeff Fenholt
Mary Magdalene	Yvonne Elliman†2
First Priest	Alan Braunstein
Second Priest	Michael Meadows
Caiaphas	Bob Bingham
Annas	Phil Jethro
Third Priest	Steven Bell
Simon Zealotes/Merchant/Leper	Dennis Buckley
Pontius Pilate	Barry Dennen†3
Peter/Merchant/Leper	Michael Jason
Maid/Leper	Linda Rios
Soldier/Judas' Tormentor	Tom Stovall
Old Man/Apostle/Leper	Peter Schlosser
Soldier/Judas' Tormentor	Paul Sylvan
King Herod/Merchant/Leper	Paul Ainsley
Cured Leper/Temple Lady	Robin Grean
Cured Leper/Apostle/Merchant/Tormentor	James Sbano
Cured Leper/Temple Lady	Laura Michaels
Cured Leper/Apostle/Merchant/Tormentor	Clifford Lipson
Cured Leper/Temple Lady/Reporter	Bonnie Schon
Cured Leper/Apostle/Reporter	Pi Douglass
Cured Leper/Apostle Woman/Temple Lady	Celia Brin
Cured Leper/Apostle/Tormentor	Dennis Cooley
Reporter/Apostle Woman/Temple Lady/Leper	Anita Morris
Reporter/Leper	Ted Neeley
Reporter/Apostle Woman/Temple Lady/Leper	Kay Cole
Reporter/Leper	Kurt Yaghjian
Reporter/Leper	Margaret Warncke
Reporter/Apostle/Leper	Willie Windsor
Reporter/Apostle Woman/Temple Lady/Leper	Ferne Bork

Yvonne Elliman, Jeff Fenholt

Reporter/Apostle/Leper	Samuel E. Wright
Apostle Woman/Temple Lady/Leper	Denise Delapenha
Apostle/Merchant/Leper/Reporter	Robalee Barnes
Apostle/Leper/Reporter/Tormentor	Doug Lucas
Soul Girl/Leper	Charlotte Crossley
Soul Girl/Leper	Janet Powell
Soul Girl/Leper	Cecelia Norfleet
Judas' Tormentor/Soldier	Edward Barton
Judas' Tormentor/Soldier	Tony Gardner

and various Palm Sunday attendants, Alabaster monsters, the mob, and members of the crowd

UNDERSTUDIES: For Ben Vereen, Kurt Yaghjian; Jeff Fenholt, Ted Neeley, Dennis Cooley; Yvonne Elliman, Denise Delapenha; Bob Bingham, Peter Schlosser; Barry Dennen, Phil Jethro; Paul Ainsley, Michael Meadows; Phil Jethro, Michael Jason; Dennis Buckley, Robalee Barnes; Michael Jason, Willie Windsor; Michael Meadows, Alan Braunstein, Cliff Lipson; Steven Bell, Doug Lucas; Swing girl, Marsha Faye; Swing boy, Nat Morris.

MUSICAL NUMBERS: Overture, "Heaven on Their Minds," "What's the Buzz," "Strange Thing Mystifying," "Everything's All Right," "This Jesus Must Die," "Hosanna," "Simon Zealotes," "Poor Jerusalem," "Pilate's Dream," "The Temple," "I Don't Know How to Love Him," "Damned for All Time," "The Last Supper," "Gethsemane," "The Arrest," "Peter's Denial," "Pilate and Christ," "King Herod's Song," "Could We Start Again, Please," "Judas' Death," "Trial before Pilate," "Superstar," "The Crucifixion," "John 19:41"

A Musical in two acts. The action depicts the last seven days in the life of Jesus of Nazareth.

General Managers: Gatchell & Neufeld
Company Manager: John Corkill
Press: Merle Debuskey, Leo Stern
Stage Managers: Galen McKinley, Frank Marino

* Still playing May 31, 1972.
† Succeeded by: 1. Patrick Hude, 2. Marta Heflin, 3. Seth Allen

**Jeff Fenholt, Alan Braunstein, Paul Ainsley,
Michael Meadows**

Friedman-Abeles Photos

Jeff Fenholt (C), Ben Vereen (R)
Above: Jeff Fenholt (C)

ROYALE THEATRE
Opened Tuesday, October 19, 1971.*
Michael Abbott, Rocky H. Aoki, Jerry Hammer present:

THE INCOMPARABLE MAX

By Jerome Lawrence and Robert E. Lee; Based on Sir Max Beerbohm's trips beyond reality; Director, Gerald Freedman; Associate Producer, Donald Sheff; Settings, David Mitchell; Costumes, Theoni V. Aldredge; Lighting, Martin Aronstein; Special Sound, James Reichert.

CAST

Max Beerbohm	Clive Revill
Usher	Christina Gillespie
William Rothenstein	Michael Egan
Lewis, A Waiter	Louis Turenne
Enoch Soames	Richard Kiley
The Man	Martyn Green
Library Clerk	John Fitzgibbon
Girl Library Attendant	Fionnuala Flanagan
Theatre Goer	Claude Horton
Theatre Goer's Wife	Betty Sinclair
Usher	Fionnuala Flanagan
Young Man	John Fitzgibbon
Girl in a hurry	Christina Gillespie
A Frenchman	Louis Turenne
Hotel Clerk	Donald Marye
A. V. Laider	Richard Kiley
Maid	Christina Gillespie
Uncle Sydney	Donald Marye
Colonel Elbourne	Martyn Green
Mrs. Elbourne	Constance Carpenter
Mr. Blake	Rex Thompson
Mrs. Blake	Fionnuala Flanagan

UNDERSTUDIES: Mr. Kiley, Mr. Revill, Robert Stattel; Man, Rothenstein, Louis Turenne; Clerk, Young Man, Rex Thompson; Blake, John Fitzgibbon; Usher, Girl, Fionnuala Flanagan; Library Attendant, Mrs. Blake, Christina Gillespie; Theatregoer, Donald Marye; His Wife, Constance Carpenter; Elbourne, Michael Egan; Mrs. Elbourne, Betty Sinclair; Sidney, Claude Horton; Frenchman, Lewis, Stephen Schnetzer.

A Play in two acts: Act I: Max and Enoch Soames Act II: Max and A. V. Laider

General Manager: Al Goldin
Press: David Powers
Stage Managers: Alan Hall, Mary Porter Hall, Stephen Schnetzer

* Closed Nov. 6, 1971 after 23 performances and 10 previews.

Martha Swope Photos

Top: (L)Richard Kiley, Clive Revill (R) Revill, John FitzGibbon, Claude Horton

Constance Carpenter, Martyn Green, Fionnuala Flanagan, R Thompson, Richard Kiley (also above)

ETHEL BARRYMORE THEATRE

Opened Wednesday, October 20, 1971.*
(Moved to Ambassador on Nov. 17, 1971)
Eugene V. Wolsk, Charles Blackwell, Emanuel Azenberg, Robert Malina present:

AIN'T SUPPOSED TO DIE A NATURAL DEATH

Book, Words, and Music by Melvin Van Peebles; Director, Gilbert Moses; Scenery, Kert Lundell; Costumes, Bernard Johnson; Lighting, Martin Aronstein; Musical Direction and Supervision, Harold Wheeler; Sound, Jack Shearing; Associate Producer, Howard Friedman; Original Album by A & M Records.

CAST

Gloria Edwards	Dick Williams
Ralph Wilcox	Barbara Alston
Joe Fields	Marilyn B. Coleman
Arthur French	Carl Gordon
Madge Wells	Lauren Jones†
Clebert Ford	Sati Jamal
Jimmy Hayeson	Toney Brealond
Beatrice Winde	Albert Hall
Garrett Morris	Bill Duke
Gentry	

MUSICIANS: Harold Wheeler, Arthur Jenkins, Richard Pratt, Bill Salter, Lloyd Davis, Charles Sullivan, Robert Corten

MUSICAL NUMBERS: "Just Don't Make No Sense," "Coolest Place in Town," "You Can Get Up Before Noon Without Being a Square," "Mirror Mirror on the Wall," "Come Raising Your Leg on Me," "You Gotta Be Holdin' out Five Dollars on Me," "Sera Sera Jim," "Catch that on the Corner," "The Dozens," "Funky Girl on Motherless Broadway," "Tenth and Greenwich," "Heh Heh (Chuckle) Good Mornin' Sunshine," "You Ain't no Astronaut," "Three Boxes of Longs Please," "Lily Done the Zampoughi Every Time I Pulled Her Coattail," "I Got the Blood," "Salamaggis Birthday," "Come on Feet Do Your Thing," "Put a Curse on You"

"Tunes from Blackness" in two acts.

Press: Merle Debuskey, Faith Geer
Stage Managers: Nate Barnett, Helaine Head

* Closed July 30, 1972 after 325 performances.
† Succeeded by Cecelia Norfleet

Bert Andrews Photos

Madge Wells, Carl Gordon, Barbara Alston
Top Right: Clebert Ford, Sati Jamal, Toney Brealond

**Albert Hall Above: Marilyn B.
Coleman, Jimmy Hayeson**

15

HELEN HAYES THEATRE

Opened Thursday, October 21, 1971.*
(Moved to Lunt-Fontanne Jan. 10, 1972)
Leonard Soloway presents:

TO LIVE ANOTHER SUMMER
To Pass Another Winter

Written by Hayim Hefer; Music, Dov Seltzer; Additional Music, David Krivoshei, Alexander Argov, Naomi Shemer; Additional Lyrics, Naomi Shemer; Directed and Choreographed by Jonaton Karmon; Designed by Neil Peter Jampolis; Costumes, Lydia Pincus Gany; Music Arranged and Conducted by David Krivoshei; Musical Supervisor, Gary McFarland; Lyrics Translated mostly by David Paulsen; Sound, Anthony Alloy; Production Supervisor, Martin Herzer; Production Assistant, Carl F. Kugel; Original Cast Album by Buddah Records.

CAST

Rivka Raz
Aric Lavie
Yona Atari
Ili Gorlizki
Hanan Goldblatt

SINGERS: Abigail Atarri, Lisa Butbul, David Devon, Rafi Ginat, Sarah Golan, Ronit Goldblatt, Moses Goldstein, Lenore Grant, Mordechai Hamer, Yochai Hazani, Judith Rosenberg, Tslila Steren, Hillik Zadok

DANCERS: Zvulum Cohen, Constantin Dolgicer, Katya Dror, David Glazer, Nava Harari, Yuval Harat, Hana Kiviti, Ruth Lerman, Joseph Maimon, Ita Oren, Adam Pasternak, Hadassa Shachar, Ofira Tishler, Tuvia Tishler, Efraim Zamir, Miriam Zamir

MUSICAL NUMBERS: "Son of Man," "The Sacrifice," "What Are the Basic Things?," "The Grove of Eucalyptus," "The Tradition that Was Destroyed: Hasidic Medley," "The Boy with the Fiddle," "Can You Hear My Voice?," "Mediteranee," "When My Man Returns," "Better Days," "Tha'am Haze," "To Live Another Summer, To Pass Another Winter," "Hora Nora," "Noah's Ark," "Don't Destroy the World," "Give Shalom and Sabbath to Jerusalem," "Sorry We Won," "I'm Alive," "Give Me a Star," Finale.

A Musical from Israel in two acts.

Press: Betty Lee Hunt, Henry Luhrman, Harriett Trachtenberg, Maria Pucci
Stage Manager: Moshe Raz

* Closed March 19, 1972 after 173 performances and 14 previews; opened tour in Boston on April 4, 1972 and closed April 30, 1972 in the Forrest Theatre in Philadelphia, Pa.

Martha Swope Photos

**Top Right: Hillik Zadok,
David Glazer, Judith Rosenberg**

**Hanan Goldblatt, Yona Atari, Aric Lavie,
Rivka Raz, Ili Gorlizki**

**Hanan Goldblatt, Yona Atari, Aric Lavie,
Rivka Raz, Ili Gorlizki (also above)**

Anna Berger, Dori Brenner, Lou Jacobi, (R)
Jacobi, Alvin Kupperman

PLYMOUTH THEATRE
Opened Tuesday, October 26, 1971.*
Robert L. Livingston presents:

UNLIKELY HEROES

By Philip Roth; Adapted and Directed by Larry Arrick;
Scenery, Robert U. Taylor; Costumes, Frank Thompson;
Lighting, Roger Morgan; Music Researched and Edited by
Barbara Damashek.

CAST

"Defender of the Faith"
Sgt. Nathan Marx .... David Ackroyd
Capt. Paul Barrett .... Tom Rosqui
Pvt. Sheldon Grossbart .... Jon Korkes
LaHill.................................Stephen van Benschoten
Pvt. Larry Fishbein......................................Josh Mostel
Pvt. Michael Halpern .... Alvin Kupperman
Major Leo Ben Ezra .... George Bartenieff
Corporal Shulman ....Dori Brenner
Sergeant Philips...............................Stephen van Benschoten

"Epstein"
Epstein .... Lou Jacobi
Folk Singer ....Josh Mostel
Sheila ....Dori Brenner
Michael ....Alvin Kupperman
Goldie .... Anna Berger
Ida .... Rose Arrick
Mrs. Katz .... Lucille Patton
Doctor .... Jon Korkes
Ambulance Driver.......................Stephen van Benschoten

Intermission

"Eli, the Fanatic"
Eli...Michael Tolan
Tzuref.. Lou Jacobi
The Man ....David Ackroyd
Miriam .... Rose Arrick
Ted .... Lee Wallace
Artie ....George Bartenieff
Shirley .... Lucille Patton
Harry .... Tom Rosqui
Nurse ....Dori Brenner
Deliveryman....................................Alvin Kupperman
First Intern ....Josh Mostel
Second Intern .... Stephen Benschoten

General Manager: Diana Shumlin
Company Manager: David Hedges
Press: Merle Debuskey, Leo Stern
Stage Managers: Randall Brooks, Edmund Williams

* Closed Nov. 13, 1971 after 23 performances and 9 previews.

Henry Grossman Photos

**Michael Tolan, Lou Jacobi Above: Rose Arrick,
Lou Jacobi**

17

IMPERIAL THEATRE

Opened Sunday, October 31, 1971.*
Jerry Schlossberg-Vista Productions present:

ON THE TOWN

Book and Lyrics, Betty Comden, Adolph Green; Music, Leonard Bernstein; Based on idea by Jerome Robbins; Directed and Choreographed by Ron Field; Costumes, Ray Aghayan, Bob Mackie; Scenery, James Trittipo; Lighting, Tharon Musser; Musical Direction, Milton Rosenstock; Orchestrations, Leonard Bernstein, Hershy Kay; Assistant Choreographer, Michael Shawn; Musical Co-Ordinator, Dorothea Freitag; Associate Producers, Rick Mandell, Allen Litke, Makeup and Hairstyles, Ted Azar

CAST

Workman	David Wilder
Chip	Jess Richards
Ozzie	Remak Ramsay
Gabey	Ron Husmann
Flossie	Carol Petri
Flossie's friend	Marybeth Kurdock
Bill Poster	Don Croll
Little old lady	Zoya Leporska
Announcer	Orrin Reiley
Ivy Smith	Donna McKechnie
Hildy	Bernadette Peters
S. Uperman	David Wilder
Figment	Orrin Reiley
Claire	Phyllis Newman
Maude P. Dilly	Fran Stevens
Pitkin	Tom Avera
Lucy Schmeeler	Marilyn Cooper
Gina Henie	Gina Paglia
M. C. at Diamond Eddie's	Dennis Roth
Seniorita Dolores	Laura Kenyon
Bimmy	Larry Merritt
Coney Island Zoot Suiters	John Mineo, Tony Stevens

SINGERS: Martha Danielle, Sandra Dorsey, Bobbi Franklin, Laura Kenyon, Gail Nelson, Marie Santell, Don Croll, Richard Marr, Orrin Reiley, Dennis Roth, Luke Stover, David Wilder, Craig Yates

DANCERS: Carole Bishop, Eileen Casey, Jill Cook, Nancy Dalton, Marybeth Kurdock, Nancy Lynch, Gina Paglia, Pamela Peadon, Carol Petri, Andy Bew, Paul Charles, Larry Merritt, John Mineo, Jeff Phillips, Ken Scalice, Doug Spingler, Tony Stevens, Chester Walker

UNDERSTUDIES: Clair, Lucy, Laura Kenyon; Hildy, Marilyn Cooper; Ivy, Pamela Peadon; Gabey, Ozzie, Orrin Reiley; Chip, Andy Bew; Pitkin, Richard Marr; Maude, Bobbi Franklin; Old Lady, Nancy Lynch

MUSICAL NUMBERS: "I Feel Like I'm Not Out of Bed Yet," "New York, New York," "Miss Turnstiles Ballet," "Come Up to My Place," "Carried Away," "Lonely Town," "Do-Do-Re-Do," "I Can Cook Too," "Lucky To Be Me," "Times Square Ballet," "So Long Baby Ice Revue," "Nightclub Song," "You Got Me," "I Understand," "Playground of the Rich Ballet," "Some Other Time," "Coney Island Hep Cats."

A Musical in two acts and 29 scenes. The action takes place in New York City in June of 1944.

General Managers: George Thorn, Leonard A. Mulhern
Press: Betty Lee Hunt, Henry Luhrman, Harriett Trachtenberg, Maria Pucci
Stage Managers: Lee Murray, Martin De Martino

* Closed Jan. 1, 1972 after 65 performances and 4 previews. Original production opened Dec. 28, 1944 and ran for 462 performances. In the cast were Adolph Green, Cris Alexander, John Battles, Betty Comden, Nancy Walker, Sono Osato, and Alice Pearce. See THEATRE WORLD, Vol. 1

Friedman-Abeles Photos

**Top Left: Remak Ramsay, Phyllis Newman, Ron Husmann, Bernadette Peters, Jess Richards
Below: Marilyn Cooper, Tom Avera**

**Bernadette Peters, Jess Richards Above:
Donna McKechnie, Fran Stevens**

MARTIN BECK THEATRE

Opened Tuesday, November 2, 1971.*
Theatre 1972 (Richard Barr, Charles Woodward, Michael Harvey) presents:

THE GRASS HARP

Book and Lyrics, Kenward Elmslie; Based on novel and play by Truman Capote; Music, Claibe Richardson; Director, Ellis Rabb; Design and Lighting, James Tilton; Costumes, Nancy Potts; Musical Director, Theodore Saidenberg; Musical Arrangements, J. (Billy) Ver Planck; Choreography, Rhoda Levine; Additional Orchestrations, Jonathan Tunick, Robert Russell Bennett; Dance and Incidental Music, John Berkman; Associate Producer, Michael Kasdan; Assistant to the Producers, David Zimmerman; Production Assistant, Donald Snell; Technical Adviser, Frank Hauser; Hairstyles, Steven Deering

CAST

Dolly Talbo .... Barbara Cook
Collin Talbo.. Russ Thacker
Catherine Creek.. Carol Brice
Verena Talbo ....Ruth Ford
Maude Riordan .... Christine Stabile
Dr. Morris Ritz... Max Showalter
Judge Cool..John Baragrey
Babylove... Karen Morrow
Heavenly Pride and Joys ....Kelly Boa, Trudy Bordoff,
          Colin Duffy, Eva Grant, David Craig Moskin
Sheriff Amos Legrand .... Harvey Vernon

UNDERSTUDIES: Dolly, Verena, Laurie Franks; Catherine, Alyce Webb; Babylove, Travis Hudson; Collin, Walter Bobbie; Ritz, William Larsen; Sheriff, Allen Williams; Judge, Harvey Vernon; Maude, Ann Hodapp

MUSICAL NUMBERS: "Dropsy Cure Weather," "This One Day," "Think Big Rich," "If There's Love Enough," "Yellow Drum," "Marry with Me," "I'll Always Be in Love," "Floozies," "Call Me Babylove," "Walk into Heaven," "Hang a Little Moolah on the Washline," "Talkin' in Tongues," "Whooshin' Through My Flesh," "Something for Nothing," "Indian Blues," "Take a Little Sip," "What Do I Do Now?," "Pick Yourself a Flower," "The Flower Fortune Dance," "Reach Out"

A Musical in six scenes without intermission. The action takes place at the Talbo House in Joy City, and in River Woods in the past.

General Manager: Michael Kasdan
Company Manager: Oscar Abraham
Press: Betty Lee Hunt, Henry Luhrman, Harriett Trachtenberg, Maria Pucci
Stage Managers: Charles Kindl, Allen Williams

* Closed Nov. 6, 1971 after 7 performances and 5 previews. Original play opened Mar. 27, 1952 and ran for 36 performances. See THEATRE WORLD, Vol. 8.

Martha Swope Photos

Top Left: Max Showalter, Ruth Ford, Russ
Thacker, Barbara Cook, Carol Brice Below:
Carol Brice, John Baragrey, Russ Thacker,
Karen Morrow, Christine Stabile, Barbara
Cook, and children

Carol Brice, Barbara Cook, Russ Thacker

EUGENE O'NEILL THEATRE
Opened Thursday, November 11, 1971.*
Saint-Subber presents:

THE PRISONER OF SECOND AVENUE

By Neil Simon: Director, Mike Nichols; Setting, Richard Sylbert; Costumes, Anthea Sylbert; Lighting, Tharon Musser

CAST

Mel Edison	Peter Falk†1
Edna Edison	Lee Grant†2
Harry Edison	Vincent Gardenia†3
Pearl	Florence Stanley
Jessie	Tresa Hughes†4
Pauline	Dena Dietrich†5

UNDERSTUDIES: Harry, Mitchell Jason; Pearl, Jessie, Dietrich, Carol Morley

A Comedy in two acts. The action takes place at the present time in a New York City apartment building.

General Manager: C. Edwin Knill
Company Manager: James Turner
Press: Harvey B. Sabinson, Lee Solters, Cheryl Sue Dolby, Edie Kean

* Still playing May 31, 1972. Vincent Gardenia received "Tony" for Best Supporting Actor in a play, and Mike Nichols for Best Director.
† Succeeded by: 1. Art Carney, 2. Barbara Barrie, 3. Jack Somack, 4. Jean Baker, 5. Ruth Manning

Martha Swope Photos

Dena Dietrich, Florence Stanley, Tresa Hughes, Vincent Gardenia
Top: Lee Grant, Peter Falk

Peter Falk, Lee Grant Above: Dena Dietrich, Tresa Hughes, Florence Stanley, Vincent Gardenia, Peter Falk

BROADHURST THEATRE

Opened Sunday, November 14, 1971.*
(Moved Jan. 10, 1972 to Plymouth Theatre)
Frederick Brisson in association with Plum Productions,
Inc. presents:

TWIGS

By George Furth; Director, Michael Bennett; Settings, Peter Larkin; Costumes, Sara Brook; Lighting, David F. Segal; Hairstylist, Joe Tubens; Makeup, Joe Cranzano; Assistant to the Producers, Fred Hebert; Production Assistant, Bob Avian; Assistant to the Director, Larry Cohen.

CAST
"Emily"
Emily .... Sada Thompson
Frank .... Nicolas Coster
9 A.M. the day before Thanksgiving
"Celia"
Celia .... Sada Thompson
Phil .... Simon Oakland†1
Swede .... Conrad Bain†2
1 P.M. the same day
Intermission
"Dorothy"
Lou .... A. Larry Hines
Dorothy .... Sada Thompson
Ned .... Walter Klavun
6 P.M. that evening
"Ma"
Pa .... Robert Donley
Ma .... Sada Thompson
Priest .... MacIntyre Dixon
9 P.M. that evening

General Manager: Ben Rosenberg
Company Manager: James Awe
Press: Harvey Sabinson, Lee Solters, Marilynn LeVine, Edie Kean
Stage Managers: Jeff Chambers, Ned Farster

* Closed July 23, 1972 after 312 performances. Sada Thompson received "Tony" for Best Performance by an actress in a play.
† Succeeded by: 1. Mark Dawson, 2. Jack Murdock

Sada Thompson, and Top Right with A. Larry Haines

22

Robert Donley, Sada Thompson
Above: Sada Thompson, Nicolas Coster

BILLY ROSE THEATRE

Opened Tuesday, November 16, 1971.*
Roger L. Stevens in association with The Royal Shake-speare Company presents:

OLD TIMES

By Harold Pinter; Director, Peter Hall; Settings and Light-ing, John Bury; Costumes, Beatrice Dawson; Production Assistant, Bill Becker; A Dowling-Whitehead-Stevens Pro-duction

CAST

Deeley	Robert Shaw
Anna	Rosemary Harris
Kate	Mary Ure

A Play in two acts. The action takes place in a converted farmhouse in England on an autumn night.

General Manager: Oscar Olesen
Company Manager: Robert P. Cohen
Press: Seymour Krawitz, Patricia Krawitz, Vicki Stein
Stage Manager: Frederic de Wilde

* Closed Feb. 26, 1972 after 120 performances and 4 pre-views. Opened tour Feb. 28 in Eisenhower Theatre, Wash-ington, D.C., and closed April 1, 1972 at the Locust Theatre in Philadelphia.

Friedman-Abeles Photos

Rosemary Harris, Robert Shaw, Mary Ure
(also above)

23

ST. JAMES THEATRE

Opened Wednesday, December 1, 1971.*
The New York Shakespeare Festival (Joseph Papp, Producer) presents:

TWO GENTLEMEN OF VERONA

By William Shakespeare; Adapted by John Guare, Mel Shapiro; Lyrics, John Guare; Music, Galt MacDermott; Director, Mel Shapiro; Setting, Ming Cho Lee; Costumes, Theoni V. Aldredge; Lighting, Lawrence Metzler; Choreography, Jean Erdman; Musical Supervision, Harold Wheeler; Additional Musical Staging, Dennis Nahat; Sound, Jack Shearing; Associate Producer, Bernard Gersten; Original Cast Album by ABC/Dunhill Records.

CAST

Thurio	Frank O'Brien
Speed	Jose Perez
Valentine	Clifton Davis
Proteus	Raul Julia
Julia	Diana Davila
Lucetta	Alix Elias
Launce	John Bottoms
Antonio	Frederick Warriner
Crab	Phineas
Duke of Milan	Norman Matlock†
Silvia	Jonelle Allen
Tavern Host	Frederic Warriner
Eglamour	Alvin Lum

QUARTET: BLACK PASSION: Sheila Gibbs, Signa Joy, Kenneth Lowry, Sakinah Mahammud

CITIZENS OF VERONA AND MILAN: Loretta Abbott, Christopher Alden, Roger Briant, Douglas Brickhouse, Stockard Channing, Paul DeJohn, Nancy Denning, Richard DeRusso, Arthur Erickson, Georgyn Geetlein, Sheila Gibbs, Jeff Goldblum, Edward Henkel, Albert Insinnia, Jane Jaffe, Signa Joy, Kenneth Lowry, Sakinah Mahammud, Otis Sallid, Madeleine Swift

UNDERSTUDIES: Silvia, Signa Joy; Lucetta, Stockard Channing; Duke, Don Jay; Eglamour, Jeff Goldblum; Silvia, Hattie Winston

A Musical in two acts.

General Managers: Eugene Wolsk, Emanuel Azenberg
Company Manager: Michael Brandman
Press: Merle Debuskey, Faith Geer
Stage Managers: R. Derek Swire, D. W. Koehler, Anthony Neely

* Still playing May 31, 1972. Received both "Tony" and Drama Critics Circle awards for Best Musical of 1971–72 season, and "Tony" for Best Musical Libretto.
† Succeeded by Ellwoodson Williams

Friedman-Abeles Photos

John Bottoms Above: Clifton Davis, Jonelle Allen
Top: Diana Davila, Raul Julia

Jose Perez, John Bottoms, Raul Julia, Clifton Davis Top: (L) Signa Joy,
Alix Elias, Diana Davila (R) Jonelle Allen, Norman Matlock, Frank O'Brien

LYCEUM THEATRE

Opened Tuesday, December 7, 1971.*
Rick Hobard in association with Raymonde Weil presents:

WILD AND WONDERFUL

Book, Phil Phillips; From an original work by Bob Brotherton and Bob Miller; Music and Lyrics, Bob Goddman; Setting, Stephen Hendrickson; Director, Burry Fredrik; Dances and Musical Numbers Staged by Ronn Forella; Costumes, Frank Thompson; Lighting, Neil Peter Jampolis; Musical Direction, Vocal Arrangements, Dance Music Composed and Arranged by Thom Janusz; Orchestrations, Luther Henderson; Associate Producer, John C. O'Regan; Hairstylist, Nino Raffaello

CAST

Jenny	Laura McDuffie
Charlie	Walter Willison
Lionel Masters	Robert Burr
Brother John	Larry Small
Father Desmond	Ted Thurston

ENSEMBLE: Yveline Baudez, Pam Blair, Mary Ann Bruning, Carol Conte, Bob Daley, Anna Maria Fanizzi, Marcelo Gamboa, Adam Grammis, Patti Haine, Ann Reinking, Jimmy Roddy, Steven Vincent, Eddie Wright, Jr.

MUSICAL NUMBERS: "Wild and Wonderful," "My First Moment," "I Spy," "Desmond's Dilemma," "Moment Is Now," "Something Is Wonderful," "Chances," "She Should Have Me," "Jenny," "Fallen Angels," "Dance," "Petty Crime," "Come a Little Closer," "Little Bits and Pieces," "Is This My Town," "You Can Reach the Sun," "Wild and Wonderful"

A Musical in two acts. The action takes place in "The Big City."

General Manager: William Craver
Company Manager: Stanley Brody
Press: Max Eisen, Jeanne Gibson Merrick, Milly Schoenbaum
Stage Managers: Robert Keegan, Louis Pulvino, Philip Killian

* Closed Dec. 7, 1971 after one performance and 9 previews.

Right: Walter Willison, Laura McDuffie

Robert Burr, Walter Willison, Laura McDuffie

ETHEL BARRYMORE THEATRE

Opened Sunday, December 19, 1971.*
Joseph Kipness, Lawrence Kasha, Tom O'Horgan in association with RCA Records present:

INNER CITY

Music, Helen Miller; Lyrics, Eve Merriam; Based on book "The Inner City Mother Goose" by Eve Merriam; Conceived and Directed by Tom O'Horgan; Scenery, Robin Wagner; Costumes, Joseph G. Aulisi; Lighting, John Dodd; In association with Jane Reisman; Orchestrations and Arrangements, Gordon Harrell; Musical Direction, Clay Fullum; Vocal Arrangments, Helen Miller; Sound, Gary Harris; Associate Producers, Harvey Milk, John M. Nagel; Production Coordinator, Charlotte Dicker; Hairstylist, Nino Raffaello; Original Cast Album on RCA Records.

CAST

Joy Garrett	Paulette Ellen Jones
Carl Hall	Larry Marshall
Delores Hall	Allan Nicholls
Fluffer Hirsch	Florence Tarlow†
Linda Hopkins	

MUSICAL NUMBERS: "Fee Fi Fo Fum," "Now I Lay Me," "Locks/I Had a Little Teevee," "Hushabye Baby/My Mother Said," "Diddle Diddle Dumpling/Rub A Dub Dub," "You'll Find Mice," "Ding Dong Bell," "The Brave Old City of New York," "Urban Renewal," "The Nub of the Nation," "Mary, Mary," "City Life," "One Misty Moisty Morning," "Jack Be Nimble," "If Wishes Were Horses," Done Man/Deep in the Night," "Statistics," "12 Rooftops Leaping," "Take-A-Tour," "Congressman," "Simple Simon," "Poverty Program," "One, Two," "Tom, Tom," "Hickety, Pickety," "Half Alive," "This is the Way We Go to School," "The Spirit of Education," "Little Jack Horner," "Subway Dream," "Christmas Is Coming," "I'm Sorry Says the Machine," "Jeremiah Obadiah," "Riddle Song," "Shadow of the Sun," "Boys and Girls Come Out to Play," "Summer Nights," "Lucy Locket," "Winter Lights," "Wisdom," "The Hooker," "Wino Will/Man in the Doorway," "Starlight Starbright," "The Cow Jumped over the Moon," "The Dealer," "Taffy," "Numbers," "The Pickpocket," "Law and Order," "Kindness," "As I Went Over," "There Was a Little Man," "Who Killed Nobody," "It's My Belief," "Street Sermon," "The Great If," "On This Rock"

"A Street Cantata" in two acts and ten scenes. The action takes place at the present time in New York City.

General Manager: Philip Adler
Company Manager: Morry Efron
Press: Bill Doll, Dick Williams, Virginia Holden, Cindy Reagan
Stage Managers: Nicholas Russiyan, Daniel Landau, Joe Scott

Closed March 11, 1972 after 97 performances and 24 previews. Linda Hopkins received "Tony" for Best Supporting Actress in a musical.
Succeeded by Gretel Cummings

Bert Andrews Photos

Top Right: Linda Hopkins

Carl Hall, Delores Hall, Larry Marshall Back: Joy Garrett, Linda Hopkins, Florence Tarlow, Paulette Ellen Jones, Allan Nicholls, Fluffer Hirsch

MOROSCO THEATRE

Opened Sunday, January 2, 1972.*
Alexander H. Cohen and Rocky H. Aoki present:

FUN CITY

By Lester Colodny, Joan Rivers, Edgar Rosenberg; Director, Jerry Adler; Scenery, Ralph Alswang; Costumes, Ann Roth; Lighting, Jules Fisher; Production Associate, Hildy Parks; Associate Producer, Roy A. Somlyo; Production Assistant, Joan Barnet; Hairstylist, Graham Meech

CAST

Fritzie Ziroka	Renee Lippin
Paul Martino	Gabriel Dell
Jill Fairchild	Joan Rivers
Jose Rodriguez	Pierre Epstein
Mailman	Paul Ford
Hilly Martino	Victor Arnold
Mr. Ziroka	Louis Zorich
Estelle Fogelman	Rose Marie
Patrolman Toomey	Howard Storm
Patrolman McCarthy	J. J. Barry
Man	Noel Young

STANDBYS AND UNDERSTUDIES: Fritzie, Jill, Laura May Lewis; Estelle, Thelma Lee; Jose, Ziroka, Mailman, Gene Varrone; Toomey, McCarthy, Noel Young

A Comedy in two acts. The action takes place at the present time in Jill and Paul's New York City apartment.

Company Managers: Seymour Herscher, Robert Frissell
Press: James D. Proctor, Richard Hummler
Stage Managers: Robert L. Borod, Gene Varrone, Noel Young

* Closed Jan. 8, 1972 after 8 performances and 16 previews.

Friedman-Abeles Photos

Joan Rivers, Paul Ford, Gabriel Dell, Rose Marie
Top Left: Joan Rivers, Victor Arnold

ROYALE THEATRE

Opened Monday, January 3, 1972.*
David Merrick in association with Byron Goldman presents the Stratford National Theatre of Canada's production of:

THERE'S ONE IN EVERY MARRIAGE

Adapted by Suzanne Grossman and Paxton Whitehead from play by Georges Feydeau; Director, Jean Gascon; Designed by Alan Barlow; Lighting, Gil Wechsler; Associate Producer, Samuel Liff; Hairstylist, Hector Garcia

CAST

Lucienne	Roberta Maxwell
Pontagnac	Peter Donat
Vatelin	Richard Curnock
Jean	Wyman Pendleton
Roubillon	Jack Creley
Madame Pontagnac	Tudi Wiggins
Ulla	Marilyn Gardner
Soldignac	Donald Ewer
Armandine	Patricia Gage
Victor	Robin Marshall
Hotel Manager	John Cutts
Clara	Jeannette Landis
Pinchard	Tony Van Bridge
Madame Pinchard	Helen Burns
Hotel Guests	Stewart Robertson, Barbara Lester, Carol Jenkins, Luke Wymes, Eugene Brezany
Second Bellboy	Tom Alway
Commissioner	Hamish Robertson
Assistant Commissioner	Tom Alway
Second Commissioner	Wyman Pendleton
Gerome	Joseph Maher

UNDERSTUDIES: Lucienne, Armandine, Ulla, Jeannette Landis; Pontagnac, Roubillon, John Cutts; Vatelin, Hamish Robertson; Jean, Manager, Soldignac, Tom Alway; Mme. Pinchard, Barbara Lester; Mme. Pontagnac, Clara, Carol Jenkins; Victor, Bellboy, Commissioner, Stewart Robertson; Pinchard, Gerome, Wyman Pendleton

A Comedy in three acts. The action takes place in Paris at the beginning of this century in the salon of the Vatelin house, the Hotel Ultimus Room 39, and Roubillon's study.

General Manager: Jack Schlissel
Company Manager: Jay Kingwill
Press: Lee Solters, Harvey B. Sabinson, Marilynn Levine
Stage Managers: Elspeth Gaylor, Bob Bernard, Barbara Lester

* Closed Jan. 15, 1972 after 16 performances and 9 previews.

Martha Swope Photos

Patricia Gage, Jack Creley
Above: Jack Creley, Peter Donat

Patricia Gage, Jack Creley, Tudi Wiggins, Peter Donat, Roberta Maxwell, Richard Curnock, Marilyn Gardner

29

BROADHURST THEATRE

Opened Thursday, January 20, 1972.*
David Merrick and Arthur Cantor by arrangement with
H. M. Tennent Ltd. present:

VIVAT! VIVAT REGINA!

By Robert Bolt; Director, Peter Dews; Designed by Carl
Toms; Lighting, Lloyd Burlingame; Associate Producer, Sam-
uel Liff; Music Composed and Arranged by Richard Kayne;
Hairstylist, Ray Iagnocco

CAST

Catherine de Medici	Diana Kirkwood
Mary Queen of Scots	Claire Bloom
Francois II, King of France	Norman Allen
Cardinal of Lorraine	John Devlin
William Cecil	Douglas Rain
Elizabeth I of England	Eileen Atkins
Robert Dudley	Robert Elston
John Knox	Alexander Scourby
Claud Nau	Ralph Clanton
First Court Lady	Diana Kirkwood
Second Court Lady	Jane Singer
Bagpiper	Randy Levey
David Rizzio	Gaetano Bongiovanni
Lord Morton	Stephen Scott
Lord Bothwell	Lee Richardson†
Lord Bishop of Durham	Don McHenry
A Cleric	Norman Allen
Sir Francis Walsingham	John Devlin
de Quadra	Dillon Evans
Davison	Noel Craig
Henry Stuart, Lord Darnley,	Peter Coffield
Ruthven	Ian Sullivan
Lindsey	Joseph Hill
Scots Archbishop	Theodore Tenley
Lord Mor	Don McHenry
Ormiston	Norman Allen
Tala	Ralph Drischell
A Doctor	Theodore Tenley
A Prisoner	Ralph Drischell
Philip II, King of Spain	Brian Sturdivant
The Pope	Gaetano Bongiovanni
Jailers	Stephen Macht, Randy Levey
Brewer	Stephen Macht

COURTIERS, LAIRDS, CLERKS, SERVANTS, ETC.: Ian
Sullivan, Theodore Tenley, Stephen Macht, Brian Sturdivant,
Randy Levey

UNDERSTUDIES: Mary, Jane Singer; Elizabeth, Diana
Kirkwood; Cecil, Knox, Ralph Drischell; Morton, Joseph
Hill; Walsingham, Cardinal, Stephen Macht; Nau, Don
McHenry; Dudley, Darnley, Brian Sturdivant; Rizzio, Dau-
phin, John Handy; Bothwell, Ian Sullivan; de Quadra, Nor-
man Allen; Ormiston, Randy Levey

A Drama in two acts. The action takes place in France,
England, and Scotland.

General Manager: Jack Schlissel
Press: Arthur Cantor, Ellen Levene
Stage Managers: Mitchell Erickson, John Handy, Joseph
Hill

* Closed April 29, 1972 after 116 performances and 3 previews.
† Succeeded by John Cullum

Friedman-Abeles Photos

Top Right: Eileen Atkins

**Claire Bloom, Eileen Atkins, Stephen Macht, Theodore
Tenley Above: Claire Bloom, John Devlin**

LONGACRE THEATRE

Opened Wednesday, January 26, 1972.*
Robert Renfield presents:

THE SIGN IN SIDNEY BRUSTEIN'S WINDOW

By Lorraine Hansberry; Adapted by Robert Nemiroff, Charlotte Zaltzburg; Music, Gary William Friedman; Lyrics, Ray Errol Fox; Director, Alan Schneider; Musical Staging, Rhoda Levine; Scenery, William Ritman; Costumes, Theoni V. Aldredge; Lighting, Richard Nelson; Musical Director, Mack Schlefer; Music Orchestrated and Arranged by Gary W. Friedman; Associate Producer, Production Manager, Bruce Hoover; Assistant Director, Charles Haid; Production Assistant, Ewald M. Breuer; Hairstylist, Nino Raffaello

CAST

Singers	Pendleton Brown, Richard Cox, John Lansing, Arnetia Walker
Sidney Brustein	Hal Linden
Alton Scales	John Danelle
Iris Parodus Brustein	Zohra Lampert
Wally O'Hara	Mason Adams
Max	Dolph Sweet
Mavis Parodus Bryson	Frances Sternhagen
David Ragin	William Atherton
Gloria Parodus	Kelly Wood

STANDBYS: Sidney Gordon; Iris, Gloria, Kay Tornborgh; David, Alton, Gus Fleming; Max, Wally, Walt Wanderman

SONGS: "Can a Flower Think?," "In Another Life," "Mountain Girl," "To the People," "While There's Still Time," "Things as They Are," "Sweet Evenin' "

A Play with music in 3 acts and 8 scenes. The action takes place in the Brustein's apartment and adjoining courtyard in Greenwich Village, New York, in the early 1960's.

General Manager: Gatchell & Neufeld
Company Manager: G. Warren McClane
Press: Max Eisen, Milly Schoenbaum
Stage Manager: Richard Foltz

* Closed Jan. 29, 1972 after 5 performances and 9 previews. Original production opened Oct. 15, 1964 and played 99 performances. See THEATRE WORLD, Vol. 21.

Top Right: William Atherton, Kelly Wood, Hal Linden
Below: Hal Linden, Zohra Lampert

Zohra Lampert, Hal Linden

Frances Sternhagen, Hal Linden

HELEN HAYES THEATRE

Opened Thursday, January 27, 1972.*
Paul Alter presents:

WISE CHILD

By Simon Gray; Director, James Hammerstein; Sets, Peter Larkin; Costumes, Jane Greenwood; Lighting, Neil Peter Jampolis; Hairstylist, Hector Garcia

CAST

Mrs. Artminster .... Donald Pleasence
Jerry .... Bud Cort
Mr. Booker .... George Rose
Janice .... Lauren Jones

STANDBYS AND UNDERSTUDIES: Mrs. Artminster, Booker, Richard Neilson; Jerry, Tobias Haller; Janice, Peggy Kirkpatrick

A Comedy in two acts and three scenes. The action takes place in the Southern Hotel in Reading, England at the present time.

General Manager: Al Goldin
Press: Max Eisen, Milly Schoenbaum
Stage Managers: Robert Vandergriff, Tobias Haller

* Closed Jan. 29, 1972 after 4 performances and 13 previews.

Left: Lauren Jones, Donald Pleasence

George Rose, Donald Pleasence, Bud Cort

ANTA THEATRE

Opened Wednesday, February 9, 1972.*
Cheryl Crawford, Konrad Matthaei, Hale Matthews, Robert Weinstein in association with The American National Theatre and Academy present:

THE LOVE SUICIDE AT SCHOFIELD BARRACKS

By Romulus Linney; Director, John Berry; Setting and Costumes, Douglas W. Schmidt; Lighting, John Gleason; Sound, Paul Earls

CAST

The Commanding General	Robert Burr
Captain Martin	Earl Hindman
Military Police	Frank Geraci, Michael Landrum, John Straub, Edmund Williams
Major Cassidy	John P. Ryan
Private First Class Bowers	Mark Lamos
Master Sergeant Bates	Ralph Roberts
Patricia Bates	Katherine DeHetre
Katherine Nomura	Tina Chen
Warrant Officer Levandre	Matthew Tobin
Lieutenant General Evans	John Berry
Sergeant Major Ruggles	Alan Mixon
Lucy Lake	Mercedes McCambridge
Mrs. Norvel Bates	Del Green
Colonel Moore	William Redfield
Judith Borden	Lisa Richards
A Friend	David Stock
Edward Roundhouse	Jerome Dempsey
Voices	Lucille Patton, Michael Landrum
Mime	Frank Geraci, Michael Landrum

UNDERSTUDIES: Levandre, Cassidy, Frank Geraci; Judith, Katherine, Katherine deHetre; Friend, Michael Landrum; Evans, General, Moore, John Straub; Roundhouse, Ruggles, Bates, Edmund Williams; Martin, Bowers, David Yanowitz; Lucy, Mrs. Bates, Lucille Patton

A Drama in two acts. The action takes place just after Halloween of 1970 in the Officers' Club of Schofield Barracks in Hawaii.

General Manager: Marvin A. Krauss
Press: Max Eisen, Milly Schoenbaum
Stage Managers: Larry Whiteley, David Yanowitz

* Closed Feb. 12, 1972 after 5 performances and 7 previews.

Mercedes McCambridge, Tina Chen Top: William Redfield, Tina Chen, Robert Burr, Michael Landrum, Frank Geraci

ROYALE THEATRE

Opened Monday, February 21, 1972.*
David Merrick in association with Byron Goldman and
Max Brown by arrangement with Martin Rosen presents
the Washington Arena Stage Production of:

MOONCHILDREN

By Michael Weller; Director, Alan Schneider; Setting, William Ritman; Lighting, Martin Aronstein; Costumes, Marjorie Slaiman; Associate Producer, Samuel Liff; Hairstyles, Michel Kazan

CAST

Mike	Kevin Conway
Ruth	Maureen Anderman
Cootie (Mel)	Edward Herrmann
Norman	Christopher Guest
Dick	Stephen Collins
Kathy	Jill Eikenberry
Bob Rettie (Job)	James Woods
Shelly	Cara Duff-MacCormick
Ralph	Donegan Smith
Mr. Willis	Robert Prosky
Lucky	Ronald McLarty
Bream	Louis Zorich
Effing	Peter Alzado
Uncle Murry	Salem Ludwig
Cootie's Father	George Curley
Milkman	Michael Tucker

UNDERSTUDIES: Dick, Cootie, Effing, Donegan Smith; Bob, Milkman, Peter Alzado; Norman, Mike, Cootie's Father, Michael Tucker; Kathy, Ruth, Shelly, Gretchen Corbett; Bream, Ralph, Willis, Ronald McLarty; Uncle Murry, Lucky, George Curley

A Comedy in two acts and seven scenes. The action takes place in a student apartment in an American university town around 1965–66.

General Manager: Jack Schlissel
Press: Lee Solters, Harvey B. Sabinson, Marilyn LeVine, Edie Kean
Stage Managers: Alan Hall, George Curley

* Closed March 4, 1972 after 13 performances and 12 previews.

34   *Martha Swope Photos*

James Woods, Cara Duff-MacCormick, Christopher G
Top: Woods, Edward Hermann, Stephen Collins,
Maureen Anderman, Jill Eikenberry, Guest, Kevin Con

MOROSCO THEATRE

Opened Monday, February 28, 1972.*
George W. George and Barnard S. Straus present:

NIGHT WATCH

By Lucille Fletcher; Director, Fred Coe; Scenery, George Jenkins; Costumes, Donald Brooks; Lighting, Tharon Musser; Hairstylist, Ted Azar; Production Assistant, Carl F. Kugel, Nancy Rubin

CAST

Elaine Wheeler	Joan Hackett
John Wheeler	Len Cariou†
Helga	Jeanne Hepple
Vanelli	Martin Shakar
Curtis Appleby	Keene Curtis
Blanche Cooke	Elaine Kerr
Lt. Walker	William Kiehl
Dr. Tracey Lake	Barbara Cason
Sam Hoke	Rudy Bond

STANDBYS: Elaine, Linda Selman; John, Curtis, William Kiehl; Vanelli, Frank Hartenstein.

A Mystery in two acts and four scenes. The action takes place at the present time in a townhouse in the East Thirties in New York City.

General Managers: Leonard A. Mulhern, George Thorn
Press: Harvey B. Sabinson, Lee Solters, Cheryl Sue Dolby, Edie Kean
Stage Manager: Frank Hartenstein

* Closed June 11, 1972 after 120 performances and 17 previews.
† Succeeded by Edward Winter

Van Williams Photos

Top Left: Joan Hackett, Len Cariou

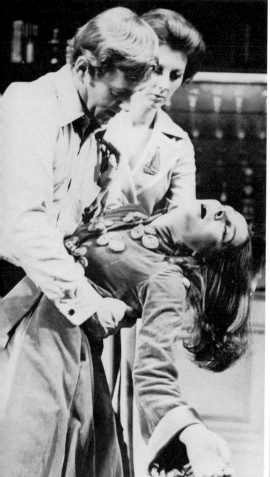

Len Cariou, Elaine Kerr, Joan Hackett

Joan Hackett, Keene Curtis

JOHN GOLDEN THEATRE

Opened Wednesday, March 1, 1972.*
New York Shakespeare Festival (Joseph Papp, Producer) presents:

STICKS AND BONES

By David Rabe; Director, Jeff Bleckner; Associate Producer, Bernard Gersten; Scenery, Santo LoQuasto; Costumes, Theoni V. Aldredge; Lighting, Ian Calderon; Song, Galt MacDermot, David Rabe

CAST

The Family:
Ozzie ....Tom Aldredge
Harriet ....Elizabeth Wilson†1
David ....Drew Snyder
Rick ....Cliff DeYoung†2
Others:
Sergeant Major .... Hector Elias
The Priest .... Charles Siebert
The Girl.. Asa Gim

STANDBYS: Ozzie, Priest, Tom Rosqui; Harriet, Ruth Manning; David, Peter Weller; Rick, Nathan Young; Sgt. Major, Walter McGinn; Girl, Lani Miyazaki.

A Drama in two acts. The action takes place in the family home in the autumn of 1968.

General Managers: Eugene Wolsk, Emanuel Azenberg
Company Manager: Michael Brandman
Press: Merle Debuskey, Leo Stern
Stage Managers: David Eidenberg, Tom Gardner

* Still playing May 31, 1972. Opened Sun., Nov. 7, 1971 at Public/Anspacher Theater and closed Feb. 20, 1972 after 129 performances. Received a "Tony" as Best Play, and a Special Citation from Drama Critics Circle after it was erroneously announced as Best Play of the 1971–72 season. Elizabeth Wilson received a "Tony" as Best Supporting Actress in a play.
† Succeeded by: 1. Rue McClanahan, 2. Alan Cauldwell

Friedman-Abeles Photos

Drew Snyder, Cliff DeYoung
Top Left: Elizabeth Wilson, Tom Aldredge

Drew Snyder, Tom Aldredge Top: Snyder, Hector Elias,
Cliff DeYoung, Aldredge, Elizabeth Wilson

Drew Snyder, Asa Gim

Josef Sommer, Elaine Hyman, Gwen Verdon, Elizabeth
Hubbard, Dennis Patrick

Gwen Verdon, Shawn Campbell, Ariane Munker,
Johnny Doran

RITZ THEATRE

Opened Tuesday, March 7, 1972.*
Arthur Whitelaw, Seth Harrison, in association with Ben
Gerard present:

CHILDREN! CHILDREN!

By Jack Horrigan; Director, Joseph Hardy; Designed and
Lit by Jo Mielziner; Costumes, Ann Roth; Assistants to the
Producers, John Clement, Dina Alkalay; Production Assistant, Steven Kronovek; Hairstylist, Romaine Greene; Portrait,
Stanley Roseman

CAST

Philip Collins	Dennis Patrick
Evelyn Collins	Elizabeth Hubbard
Peg Yaeger	Elaine Hyman
Dr. Karl Yaeger	Josef Sommer
Helen Giles	Gwen Verdon
Mark Collins	Shawn Campbell
Susan Collins	Ariane Munker
Bobby Collins	Johnny Doran

STANDBYS AND UNDERSTUDIES: Helen, Valerie
French; Philip, Karl, Philip Cusack; Mark, Brian Hall; Susan,
Susan Alpern; Bobby, Michael Kelley

A "Thriller" performed without intermission. The action
takes place in the Collins' duplex apartment off Gramercy
Park in New York City, at ten o'clock on New Year's Eve.

General Manager: Marvin A. Krauss
Business Manager: Michael Kasdan
Press: Max Eisen, Milly Schoenbaum
Stage Managers: Victor Straus, Philip Cusack

* Closed March 7, 1972 after one performance and 13 previews.

BILLY ROSE THEATRE

Opened Wednesday, March 15, 1972.*
The John F. Kennedy Center for the Performing Arts
presents:

THE COUNTRY GIRL

By Clifford Odets; Director, John Houseman; Settings and
Lighting, Douglas W. Schmidt; Costumes, Frank Thompson;
Produced for Kennedy Center by Roger L. Stevens in association with Hugh O'Brian; Supervised by Max Allentuck; Production Assistant, Carl Kugel

CAST

Bernie Dodd	George Grizzard
Larry	James Karem
Phil Cook	Roland Winters
Paul Unger	Joe Ponazecki
Nancy Stoddard	Eda Zahl
Frank Elgin	Jason Robards
Georgie Elgin	Maureen Stapleton
Ralph	William Shust

STANDBYS AND UNDERSTUDIES: Georgie, Jan Far-
rand; Frank, James Karen; Bernie, Larry, Phil, Paul, William
Shust; Ralph, Frank Hartenstein; Nancy, Julia Fremon

A Drama in two acts and eight scenes. The Action takes
place in a New York Theatre, a furnished room in New York,
and a Boston Theatre.

General Manager: Max Allentuck
Press: Michael Sean O'Shea, Leonard Traube
Stage Managers: Allen Leicht, Julia Fremon

* Closed May 6, 1972 after 62 performances and 4 previews.
Original production opened Nov. 10, 1950 with Paul Kelly,
Uta Hagen, and Steven Hill and played 235 performances.
See THEATRE WORLD, Vol. 7. Revived at City Center
Sept. 29, 1966 with Jennifer Jones, Rip Torn, and Joseph
Anthony for 24 performances. See THEATRE WORLD,
Vol. 23.

Bert Andrews, Fletcher Drake Photos

Maureen Stapleton, Jason Robards Top Right: Robards,
Stapleton, George Grizzard

George Grizzard, Maureen Stapleton

SHUBERT THEATRE
Opened Wednesday, March 22, 1972.*
John Flaxman in association with Harold Hastings and
Franklin Roberts presents:

THE SELLING OF THE PRESIDENT

Book, Jack O'Brien and Stuart Hample; Music, Bob James; Lyrics, Jack O'Brien; Based on book of same title by Joe McGinniss; Scenery, Tom John; Costumes, Nancy Potts; Lighting, Thomas Skelton; Musical Staging, Ethel Martin; Musical Direction, Harold Hastings; Orchestrations, Jonathan Tunick; Multi-media Designed by William Claxton, Mort Kasman, Gary Youngman, Jim Sant'Andrea; Production Supervisor, Arlene Caruso; Assistant Choreographer, Rick Atwell; Costume Coordinator, Steve Atha; Technical Adviser, Nicholas Johnson; Production Assistant, Harold Apter

CAST

Senator George W. Mason	Pat Hingle
Grace Mason	Barbara Barrie
Senator Hiram Robinson	Richard Goode
Sydney Wales	Robert Fitzsimmons
Irene Jantzen	Karen Morrow
Ted Bacon	Robert Darnell
Ward Nichols	John Glover
Johnny Olson	Johnny Olson
Arthur Hayes	John Bentley
Minister, Davey, Ralph Reeder	Tim Noble
Capt. Terror, Barney Zawicki	Steve Shochet
Timmy, Molly Kilgallen	Sheilah Rae
Creeply, Randall Phillips	Philip M. Thomas
Ghoulie, Franklin Douglass Pierce	Pi Douglass
Van Denisovich	Rick Atwell
Casey Steele	Jamie Carr
Bonnie Sue Taylor	Suellen Estey
Gloria Miller	Delores Hall
Linda Allington	Pamela Myers
Burgundy Moore	Trina Parks
Inga Brand	Deborah St. Darr
Dr. Loyd Blenheim	Bill Rienecke
Mrs. Pearline Gibbons	Lurlu Lindsay
Warren Stevenson	Peter Grounds
Fleetwing Horn	Vilma Vaccaro
Julie Milano	Pam Zarit

and George Andrew Robinson, Michael Serrecchia

STANDBYS AND UNDERSTUDIES: Mason, Leon B. Stevens; Ted, Ward, Jay Gerber; Grace, Irene, Christine Pickles; Olson, John Bentley

MUSICAL NUMBERS: "Something Holy," "If You Like People," "Sunset," "Little Moon," "Come-on-a-good Life," "I've Got to Trust You," "Mason Cares," "On the Winning Side," "Captain Terror," "He's a Man," "Stars of Glory," "Terminix," "Take My Hand," "A Passacaglia," "We're Gonna Live It Together," "America"

A Musical in two acts. The action takes place in 1976 in a television studio.

Company Manager: John Caruso
Press: Gifford/Wallace, Violet Welles
Stage Managers: Martha Knight, Larry Ziegler

* Closed March 25, 1972 after 5 performances and 6 previews.

Martha Swope Photos

Top Left: Pat Hingle

Pat Hingle, Barbara Barrie

ETHEL BARRYMORE THEATRE

Opened Monday, April 4, 1972.*
Jerry Schlossberg, Jerry Hammer and Adela Holzer present:

VOICES

By Richard Lortz; Director, Gilbert Cates; Designed and Lit by Jo Mielziner; Costumes, Theoni V. Aldredge; Original Music, Peggy Stuart Coolidge; Original Sound, Teijo Ito; Hairstyles and Make-up, Ted Azar; Production Associate, Seymour Gendal

CAST

Robert .... Richard Kiley
Claire .... Julie Harris
"Voices":
Mother .... Patricia Wheel
Jessica.. Lisa Essary
John .... Scott Firestone

STANDBYS AND UNDERSTUDIES: Robert, Robert Stattel; Claire, Laurie Franks; Mother, Laurie Franks; Jessica, Ivy Siegler; John, Steven Britt.

A mystery drama in 2 acts and 6 scenes. The action takes place in a country home at the present time.

General Managers: Leonard A. Mulhern, George Thorn
Press: Gifford/Wallace, Michael Gifford
Stage Managers: Martin Gold, Jean Weigel

* Closed April 8, 1972 after 8 performances and 8 previews.

Julie Harris, Richard Kiley (also above)
Top Right: Lisa Essary, Julie Harris

Friedman-Abeles Photos

LUNT-FONTANNE THEATRE

Opened Thursday, March 30, 1972.*
David Black in association with Seymour Vall and Henry
Honeckman presents:

A FUNNY THING
HAPPENED ON THE WAY
TO THE FORUM

Book, Burt Shevelove, Larry Gelbart; Based on plays of
Plautus; Music and Lyrics, Stephen Sondheim; Director, Burt
Shevelove; Choreography, Ralph Beaumont; Musical and Vo-
cal Direction, Milton Rosenstock; Settings, James Trittipo;
Costumes, Noel Taylor; Lighting, H. R. Poindexter; Produc-
tion Associate, Jose Vega; Produced by Larry Blyden; Produc-
tion Assistant, Richard F. Pardy; Orchestrations, Irwin
Kostal, Sid Ramin; Dance Music Arranged by Hal Schaefer,
Richard De Benidictis; Hairstyles, Dorman Allison.

CAST

Prologus	Phil Silvers†1
Senex	Jack Collins†2
Domina, his wife	Lizabeth Pritchett
Hero, his son	John Hansen
Hysterium, his slave	Larry Blyden
Pseudolus, slave to Hero	Phil Silvers
Lycus	Carl Ballantine
Erronius	Reginald Owen
Miles Gloriosus	Carl Lindstrom
Tintinabula	Lauren Lucas
Panacea	Gloria Mills
The Geminae	Trish Mahoney, Sonja Haney
Vibrata	Keita Keita
Gymnasia	Charlene Ryan
Philia	Pamela Hall
Proteans	Joe Ross, Bill Starr, Chad Block

UNDERSTUDIES: Courtesans, Domina, Patti Karr; Hero,
Bill Starr; Miles, Chad Block; Proteans, Patrick Spohn; Hys-
terium, Joe Ross

MUSICAL NUMBERS: "Comedy Tonight," "Farewell,"
"Love I Hear," "Free," "The House of Marcus Lycus,"
"Lovely," "Everybody Ought to Have a Maid," "I'm Calm,"
"Impossible," "Bring Me the Bride," "That Dirty Old Man,"
"Echo Song," "Dirge"

A Musical Comedy in two acts. The action takes place two
hundred years before the Christian era on a spring day, in
front of the houses of Lycus, Senex, and Erronius on a street
in Rome.

General Managers: Wolsk & Azenberg
Press: Betty Lee Hunt, Henry Luhrman, Harriett
Trachtenberg
Stage Managers: Scott Jackson, Patrick Spohn

* Closed Aug. 12, 1972 after 156 performances and 3 pre-
views. "Tonys" for Best Performance, and Best Supporting
Performance in a musical went to Phil Silvers and Larry
Blyden. For original production see THEATRE WORLD,
Vol. 18.
† Succeeded by: 1. John Bentley, Tom Poston, 2. Mort Mar-
shall

**Top Right: Keita Keita, Carl Ballantine, Phil
Silvers, John Hansen**

Phil Silvers, Larry Blyden

Charlene Ryan, Keita Keita, Sonja Haney, Trish Mahoney, Barbara Brown, Lauren Lucas, Phil Silvers Top: (L)Phil Silvers, Reginald Owen (R)Larry Blyden, Phil Silvers

LYCEUM THEATRE

Opened Wednesday, April 5, 1972*
Edgar Lansbury, Stuart Duncan, Joseph Beruh present:

ELIZABETH I

By Paul Foster; Director, John-Michael Tebelak; Scenery,
Robbie Anton; Lighting, Roger Morgan; Costumes, Susan
Tsu; Sound, Jack Shearing; Associate Producers, Edwin and
Michael Gifford; Production Assistant, Lucie D. Grosvenor

CAST

Jeff Chandler
Jerry Cunliffe
Tom Everett
Donald Forrest
Jerry Glover
Charles Haid
Jeanette Landis
Ruby Lynn Reyner
Dawn Siebel
Penelope Windust

(parts are interchangeable)

A play in two acts. The action takes place in the late 1500's,
the apogee of Elizabeth's reign. A touring company of Eliza-
bethan players perform their version of "Elizabeth I" on a
street platform in Shoreditch, London. They are thrown out
of London, then perform in a farm town on the backroads of
England, then at Cambridge University.

General Manager: Al Isaac
Press: Max Eisen, Milly Schoenbaum
Stage Manager: Gail Bell

* Closed April 9, 1972 after 5 performances and 11 previews.

Herve Villechaize, Penelope Windust, (Back) Jeanette Land
Jeff Chandler Top: Ruby Lynn Reyner, Villechaize,
Donald Forrest, Windust

MAJESTIC THEATRE

Opened Sunday, April 9, 1972.*
David Merrick presents:

SUGAR

Book, Peter Stone; Based on screenplay "Some Like It Hot" by Billy Wilder and I. A. L. Diamond that was based on story by Robert Thoeren; Music, Jule Styne; Lyrics, Bob Merrill; Directed and Choreographed by Gower Champion; Settings, Robin Wagner; Costumes, Alvin Colt; Lighting, Martin Aronstein; Musical Direction-Vocal Arrangements, Elliot Lawrence; Orchestrations, Philip J. Lang; Dance Music Arrangements, John Berkman; Associate Choreographer, Bert Michaels; Hairstylist, Joe Tubens; Make-up, Joe Cranzo; Production Associate, Samuel Liff; Production Assistant, Regina Lynn

CAST

Sweet Sue	Sheila Smith

Society Syncopaters:

Piano	Harriett Conrad
Drums	Linda Gandell
Bass	Nicole Barth
Trumpets	Leslie Latham, Marylou Sirinek
Trombones	Terry Cullen, Kathleen Witmer
Saxophones	Pam Blair, Eileen Casey, Debra Lyman, Sally Neal, Mary Zahn
Bienstock	Alan Kass
Joe	Tony Roberts
Jerry	Robert Morse
Spats Palazzo	Steve Condos
Dude	Gerard Brentte
Spat's Gang	Andy Bew, Roger Bigelow, Gene Cooper, Arthur Faria, Gene GeBauer, John Mineo, Don Percassi
Knuckles Norton	Dick Bonelle
First Poker Player	Igors Gavon
Knuckles' Gang	Ken Ayers, Richard Maxon, Dale Muchmore, Alexander Orfaly
Sugar Kane	Elaine Joyce
Cabdriver	Ken Ayers
Olga	Eileen Casey
Sunbathers	Nicole Barth, Pam Blair, Eileen Casey, Robin Hoctor, Debra Lyman, Peggy Lyman, Sally Neal, Pamela Sousa
Train Conductor	George Blackwell
Bellboy	Andy Bew
Osgood Fielding, Jr.	Cyril Ritchard
"Chicago" Singers	Ken Ayers, George Blackwell, Dick Bonelle, Igors Gavon, Hal Norman

MUSICAL NUMBERS: "Windy City Marmalade," "Penniless Bums," "Tear the Town Apart," "The Beauty that Drives Men Mad," "We Could Be Close," "Sun on My Face," "November Song," "Sugar," "Hey, Why Not!," "Beautiful Through and Through," "What Do You Give to a Man Who's Had Everything?," "Magic Nights," "It's Always Love," "When You Meet a Man in Chicago"

A musical comedy in 2 acts. The action takes place in 1931 in Chicago, Miami, and in between.

General Manager: Jack Schlissel
Company Manager: Vince McKnight
Press: Harvey B. Sabinson, Sandra Manley
Stage Managers: Charles Blackwell, Henry Velez, Bob St. Clair

* Still playing May 31, 1972

Martha Swope Photos

Top Right: Robert Morse, Tony Roberts, Sheila Smith

Robert Morse, Elaine Joyce Above:
Cyril Ritchard, Robert Morse

ALVIN THEATRE

Opened Sunday, April 16, 1972.*
Fred Coe, Arthur Cantor, Charles Taubman in association with Larc, Inc. present:

PROMENADE, ALL!

By David V. Robison; Director, Arthur Storch; Settings, David Chapman; Costumes, James Berton Harris; Lighting, Martin Aronstein; Associate to the Producers, Rose Teed

CAST

1895

Willie	Richard Backus
Mother H	Anne Jackson
Ollie H	Eli Wallach
Grandfather Huntziger	Hume Cronyn

1920

Wesley	Richard Backus
Willie	Hume Cronyn
Grandmother H	Anne Jackson
Ollie H	Eli Wallach

1945

Walter	Richard Backus
Wesley	Eli Wallach
Doris	Anne Jackson
Willie	Hume Cronyn

Approximately Now

Wendell	Richard Backus
Wesley	Eli Wallach
Doris	Anne Jackson
Joan	Anne Jackson
Willie	Hume Cronyn

STANDBYS: Mr. Cronyn, Mr. Wallach, Ben Kapen; Miss Jackson, Virginia Kiser; Mr. Backus, James Staley

A comedy in 2 acts and 4 scenes.

General Manager: Robert S. Fishko
Associate General Manager: John A. Prescott
Press: Arthur Cantor, Fred Weterick, Ellen Levene
Stage Managers: Ben Janney, James Staley

* Closed May 27, 1972 after 48 performances and 15 previews.

Friedman-Abeles Photos

Anne Jackson Top: Anne Jackson, Hume Cronyn, Eli Wallach, Richard Backus

Eli Wallach

ETHEL BARRYMORE THEATRE

Opened Monday, April 17, 1972.*
Roger L. Stevens and Arthur Cantor by arrangement
with H. M. Tennent Ltd. present:

CAPTAIN BRASSBOUND'S CONVERSION

By George Bernard Shaw; Director, Stephen Porter: Scenery, Michael Annals; Costumes, Sara Brook; Miss Bergman's costumes, Beatrice Dawson; Lighting, William H. Barchelder

CAST

Rankin	Leo Leyden
Drinkwater	Geoff Garland
Hassan	Yusef Bulos
Lady Cicely Waynflete	Ingrid Bergman
Sir Howard Hallam	Eric Berry
Marzo	Zito Kozan
Captain Brassbound	Pernell Roberts
Johnson	Jack Davidson
Osman	Leroy Lessane
Sidi El Assif	Manu Tupou
His Retinue	Joe Zaloom, Yusef Bulos
Cadi's Retinue	Richard Bowden, Calvin Culver, George Emch, Albert Sanders, John Scanlan
American Bluejacket	Ben Masters
Capt. Hamlin Kearney, USN	Jay Garner
American Officers	Richard Bowden, John Scanlan
American Armed Guard	Calvin Culver

UNDERSTUDIES: Brassbound, Michael Diamond; Rankin, Kearney, John Scanlan; Drinkwater, Hassan, Albert Sanders; Redbrook, Richard Bowden; Johnson, John Pavelko; Marzo, Louis Guss; Cadi, Osman, Joe Zaloom; Sidi, Steven Rosenthal; Bluejacket, Calvin Culver; Hallam, George Emch

A comedy in three acts. The action takes place in Morocco at the turn of the century.

General Manager: Robert S. Fishko
Company Manager: Marshall Young
Press: Arthur Cantor, Ellen Levene, Michael Sean O'Shea
Stage Managers: Bert Wood, David Taylor

* Closed April 29, 1972 after limited engagement of 16 performances. Last production Dec. 27, 1950 by NY City Center Theatre Co. with Edna Best and John Archer for 16 performances. See THEATRE WORLD, Vol. 7

Ingrid Bergman Top: in rehearsal Pernell Roberts, Geoff Garland, Eric Berry, Ingrid Bergman

IMPERIAL THEATRE

Opened Tuesday, April 18, 1972*
The John F. Kennedy Center for the Performing Arts
presents:

LOST IN THE STARS

Words, Maxwell Anderson; Based on Alan Paton's novel
"Cry, the Beloved Country"; Music, Kurt Weill; Director,
Gene Frankel; Settings, Oliver Smith; Costumes, Patricia
Quinn Stuart; Lighting, Paul Sullivan; Musical Direction,
Karen Gustafson; Choreography and Musical Staging, Louis
Johnson; Musical Arrangement-Orchestrations, Kurt Weill;
Producers, Roger L. Stevens, Diana Shumlin; Cast Album by
Columbia Records; Projections, Alec Nesbitt

CAST

Answerer	Lee Hooper
Dancer	Harold Pierson
Leader	Rod Perry
Drummer	Babafumi Akunyun
Stephen Kumalo	Brock Peters
Grace Kumalo	Rosetta LeNoire
Stationmaster	Adam Petroski
Young Man	Sid Marshall
The Woman	Ruby Freene Aspinall
Arthur Jarvis	Don Fenwick
James Jarvis	Jack Gwillim
Edward Jarvis	David Jay
Mrs. Jarvis	Karen Ford
John Kumalo	Leonard Jackson
Paulus	Leonard Hayward
William	Harold Pierson
Alex	Giancarlo Esposito
Foreman/Policeman	Mark Dempsey
Mrs. Mkize	Alyce Elizabeth Webb
Hlabeni	Garrett Saunders
Eland	Peter Bailey-Britton
Linda	Marki Bey
Johannes Pafuri	Autris Paige
Matthew Kumalo	Damon Evans
Absalom Kumalo	Gilbert Price
Rose	Judy Gibson
Irina	Margaret Cowie
Policeman/Guard	Roy Hausen
Servant	Richard Triggs
Burton	Alexander Reed
Judge	Staats Cotsworth†
McRae	Leonard Hayward

SINGERS: Lana Caradimas, Suzanne Cogan, Karen Ford,
Aleesaa Foster, Ruby Greene Aspinall, Amelia Haas, Edna
Husband, Urylee Leonardos, Rona Leslie Pervil, Therman
Bailey, Donald Coleman, Raymond Frith, Leonard Hayward,
Autris Paige, Mandingo Shaka, Richard Triggs

DANCERS: Michael Harrison, Wayne Stevenson Hayes,
Oba-Ya, Michael Oiwake

UNDERSTUDIES: Stephen/Leader, Clyde Walker; James/
Arthur, Mark Dempsey; Absalom, Harold Pierson; Irina/
Linda, Judy Gibson; John, Leonard Hayward; Grace, Lee
Hooper, Johannes, Matthew, Sid Marshall; Judge, Adam Pe-
troski; Answerer, Edna Husband; Eland, Alex Reed; Alex,
Douglas Grant; Edward, Riley Mills

MUSICAL NUMBERS: "The Hills of Ixopo," "Thousands
of Miles," "Train to Johannesburg," "The Search," "Little
Grey House," "Stay Well," "Trouble Man," "Murder in
Parkwold," "Fear," "Lost in the Stars," "Wild Justice," "O
Tixo, Tixo, Help Me," "Cry, the Beloved Country," "Big
Mole"

A musical play in 2 acts and 18 scenes. The action takes
place in Ndotsheni, a small village in South Africa, and in
Johannesburg.

Company Manager: David Hedges
Press: Seymour Krawitz, Patricia Krawitz,
Martin Shwartz
Stage Managers: Frank Hamilton, Robert Keegan,
Leonard Hayward

* Closed May 21, 1972 after 39 performances and 8 previews.
Original production opened Oct. 30, 1949 and played 281
performances with Todd Duncan, Gertrude Jeannette,
Julian Mayfield, and Inez Matthews. See THEATRE
WORLD, Vol. 6.
† Succeeded by Ian Martin

Top Right: Jack Gwillim, Brock Peters

Margaret Cowie, Gilbert Price Above:
Brock Peters

CORT THEATRE
Opened Thursday, April 20, 1972*
(No producers listed)

ALL THE GIRLS CAME OUT TO PLAY

By Richard T. Johnson, Daniel Hollywood; Director, John Gerstad; Settings and Lighting, Leo B. Meyer; Costumes, Joseph G. Aulisi; Production Supervisor, Wally Peterson

CAST

Barbara Duryea	Bette Marshall
Claude Duryea	Michael (M.P.) Murphy
Betty Ryals	Peg Shirley
Jean Fowler	Susan Bjurman
Mary Lou Richards	Charlotte Fairchild
Ken Fowler	Conard Fowkes
Joe Ryals	Fred Nassif
Fred Richards	Bill Britten
Ronnie Ames	Dennis Cole
Angel Rodriguez	Jay Barney
Susan	Christine Jones
Bruce	Don Simms

UNDERSTUDIES: Ronnie, Donn Whyte; Fred, Jack Aaron; Joe, Ken, Claude, Don Simms; Barbara, Jean, Claire Malis, Christine Jones

A comedy in 2 acts and 6 scenes. The action takes place at the present time in Pleasant Valley, a typically middle class suburban community some seventy miles from New York City, in the homes of the Duryeas, and Ronnie Ames.

General Manager: Victor Samrock
Company Manager: John Caruso
Press: Mary Bryant, Stanley F. Kaminsky
Stage Managers: Wally Peterson, Don Simms

* Closed April 22, 1972 after 4 performances and 15 previews.

Martha Swope Photos

Charlotte Fairchild, Bette Marshall, Bill Britten, Susan Bjurman
Top Right: Dennis Cole, Michael Murphy

HELEN HAYES THEATRE
Opened Tuesday, April 25, 1972*
Arthur Cantor presents:

THE LITTLE BLACK BOOK

By Jean-Claude Carriere; American version by Jerome
Kilty; Director, Milos Forman; Scenery, Oliver Smith; Costumes, Sara Brook; Lighting, Martin Aronstein

CAST

A Man ....Richard Benjamin
A Woman .... Delphine Seyrig
Standbys: Dean Santoro, Kathleen Miller

A comedy in 2 acts and 6 scenes. The action takes place at
the present time in a bachelor's apartment on West Twelfth
Street, in New York City.

General Manager: Robert S. Fishko
Associate General Manager: John A. Prestcott
Company Manager: Alfred Fischer
Press: Arthur Cantor Associates, Ellen Levene
Stage Managers: Robert L. Borod, Bryan Young

* Closed April 29, 1972 after 7 performances and 9 previews.

Delphine Seyrig, Richard Benjamin

MARTIN BECK THEATRE

Opened Saturday, April 29, 1972*
Jacqueline Babbin and Jay Wolf present:

RING ROUND THE BATHTUB

By Jane Trahey; Director, Harold Stone; Scenery, Ed Wittstein; Costumes, Joseph G. Aulisi; Lighting, Roger Morgan; Sound, Gary Harris; Hairstylist, Joe Tubens; Production Assistant, Ellen Siegel Perkiss

CAST

Darcy Train	Eileen Kearney
Mrs. Hanlon (Gran)	Carmen Mathews
Maggie Train	Elizabeth Ashley
Dan Train	Richard Mulligan
Esme Train	Carol Kane
Bea Rockosy	Kathleen Maguire
Louis Rockosy	Louis Turenne
Cousin Esther	Margaret Linn
Mr. Enright	Alek Primrose
Captain Harfeather	James Greene
Nurse Samson	Kate Wilkinson
Radio Commentator	John Cannon

UNDERSTUDIES AND STANDBYS: Maggie, Susan Bay; Dan, Ted Kazanoff; Darcy, Esme, Diana Bero; Gran, Kate Wilkinson; Captain, Enright, Louis, Joel Wolfe

A comedy in 3 acts and 6 scenes. The action takes place in the Train home in Chicago between October and Christmas of a year in the 1930's when the depression was in full swing.

General Manager: Victor Samrock
Company Manager: Morry Efron
Press: Shirley Herz
Stage Managers: Steven Zweigbaum, Joel Wolfe

* Closed April 29, 1972 after 1 performance and 3 previews.

Martha Swope, Carl Samrock Photos

**Left: Elizabeth Ashley, Carmen Mathews,
Richard Mulligan**

**Margaret Linn, Carol Kane, Alek Primrose,
Louis Turenne, Eileen Kearney**

Cathleen Maguire, Louis Turenne

51

SAM S. SHUBERT THEATRE

Opened Sunday, April 30, 1972*
Hillard Elkins presents:

AN EVENING WITH RICHARD NIXON AND...

By Gore Vidal; Director, Edwin Sherin; Scenery, William Ritman; Costumes, Joseph G. Aulisi; Lighting, H. R. Poindexter; Make-up, Bob O'Bradovich; Masks, Jane Stein; Visuals, Marjorie Morris; Music arranged and conducted by Charles Gross; Sound, Jack Shearing; Projection Consultant, William Batchelder; Production Supervisor, Michael Thoma; Associate Producer, George Platt

CAST

Pro .... Gene Rupert
Con .... Humbert Allen Astredo
George Washington .... Stephen D. Newman
Colonial/Eisenhower Aide/Caddy/Soldier Robert Christian
Dwight D. Eisenhower .... Philip Sterling
John F. Kennedy .... Robert King
Hannah Nixon/Pat Nixon .... Dorothy Dorian James
Henrietta Shockney/Evelyn Dorn/Gloria Steinem/Interviewer .... Maureen Anderman
Richard M. Nixon .... George S. Irving
Reporter/Frank Nixon/Campaign Worker/Lt. Calley/Herbert Klein .... William Knight
Jessamyn West/A Splendid Girl/
Interpreter/Tricia Nixon .... Susan Sarandon
Football Coach/Nixon Aide/Senator Knowland/Sam Rayburn/Gov. Pat Brown/Lyndon B. Johnson/
Spiro Agnew .... Robert Blackburn
Student/Jerry Voorhis/Dana Smith/Thomas E. Dewey/Frank Waters/Kennedy Mask .... Alex Wipf
Don Nixon/Nikita Khrushchev/Pres. Diem/Hubert Humphrey/Pvt. Meadlo .... Chet Carlin
Albert Upton/Harry Truman/Adlai Stevenson/Caddy/Noah Dietrich/Southern Senator/Barry Goldwater/Dr. Hutschnecker/Howard K. Smith .... George Hall

AMERICAN PEOPLE: Maureen Anderman, Robert Blackburn, Chet Carlin, Robert Christian, George Hall, Dorothy Dorian James, William Knight, Susan Sarandon, Alex Wipf

UNDERSTUDIES: Kennedy, Alex Wipf; Washington/Eisenhower, William Knight; Pro, Chet Carlin; Con, George Hall; Women, Jill Andre; Men, Tom Tarpey

A comedy in two acts. The action takes place during the present and in the past.

General Manager: Bill Liberman
Company Manager: G. Warren McClane
Press: Samuel J. Friedman
Stage Managers: John Actman, Victor Straus

* Closed May 13, 1972 after 16 performances and 16 previews

Henry Grossman Photos

Stephen D. Newman, Philip Sterling

George S. Irving, Susan Sarandon Above: Irving, George F
William Knight, Robert Blackburn, Alex Wipf, Chet Car

ANTA THEATRE

Opened Monday, May 1, 1972*
Bowman Productions, Inc. (Arthur C. Twitchell, Jr., President) with William L. Witt and William J. Gumperz presents:

DIFFERENT TIMES

Written and Directed by Michael Brown; Dances and Musical Numbers Staged by Tod Jackson; Audio, Jack Shearing; Scenery and Costumes, David Guthrie; Lighting, Martin Aronstein; Orchestrations, Norman Paris, Arthur Harris, Ted Simons; Musical Direction-Dance and Vocal Arrangements, Rene Wiegert; Production Assistant, Michael Brown, Jr.

CAST

Stephen Adams Levy	Sam Stoneburner
Margaret Adams	Barbara Williams
Gregory Adams	Jamie Ross
Mrs. Daniel Webster Hepplewhite/Kaiser/Hazel Hughes/Lady Ffenger/Mrs. Callahan/Josie	Mary Jo Catlett
Mrs. Hepplewhite's Mother/Kimberley Langley	Patti Karr
Nelle Harper	Joyce Nolen
Larry Lawrence Levy/Stan	Joe Masiell
Angela Adams	Candace Cooke
Doughboys	Terry Nicholson, Ronnie DeMarco, David K. Thome
Officer/Bobby/Frank	Ronald Young
Marianne/Marilyn/Linda	Dorothy Frank
Columbia	Karin Baker
Elsie/Abigail	Mary Bracken Phillips
Hazelnuts	Candace Cooke, Dorothy Frank, Karin Baker, Joyce Nolen
Hattie, Pauline and Mae Verne	Dorothy Frank, Candace Cooke, Karin Baker
Keynoters	Terry Nicholson, Mary Bracken Phillips, David K. Thome, Ronald Young
Joe	Terry Nicholson
Don	David K. Thome
Mel	Ronnie DeMarco

UNDERSTUDIES: Marilyn, Karin Baker; Abigail, Candace Cooke; Mrs. Hepplewhite, Hazel, Patti Karr; Mother, Kimberley, Lady Ffenger, Margaret, Dorothy Frank; Bobby, Terry Nicholson; Elsie, Josie, Angela, Marianne, Kaiser, Columbia, Hattie, Pauline, Mae Verne, Joyce Nolen; Stephen, Jamie Ross; Mrs. Callan, Barbara Williams; Gregory, Larry, Ronald Young

MUSICAL NUMBER: "Different Times," "Seeing the Sights," "The Spirit is Moving," "Here's Momma," "Everything in the World Has a Place," "I Wish I Didn't Love Him," "Forward into Tomorrow," "You're Perfect," "Marianne," "Daddy, Daddy," "I Feel Grand," "Sock Life in the Eye," "I'm not Through," "I Miss Him," "One More Time," "I Dreamed about Roses," "The Words I Never Said," "The Life of a Woman," "He Smiles," "Genuine Plastic," "Thanks a Lot," "When They Start Again"

A musical in 2 acts and 15 scenes with prologue and epilogue. The action takes place between 1905 and 1970.

General Manager: Virginia Snow
Press: David Powers, Michael Ewell
Stage Managers: Jack Timmers, Mary Porter Hall, Terry Nicholson

* Closed May 20, 1972 after 24 performances and 9 previews.

Top Right: Mary Jo Catlett Below: Ronald Young, Sam Stoneburner, Patti Karr, Mary Bracken Phillips

Joe Masiell, Dorothy Frank

ROYALE THEATRE
Opened Thursday, May 4, 1972*
Sandy Farber and Stanley Barnett in association with Jules Love and Roy Rubin present:

TOUGH TO GET HELP

By Steve Gordon; Director, Carl Reiner; Scenery, Ed Wittstein; Costumes, Joseph G. Aulisi; Lighting, John Gleason; Associate Producer, Larry Rosen; Assistant to the Producers, Ken Burros; Production Assistant, Ron Cummins

CAST

Luther Jackson	John Amos
Beulah Jackson	Lillian Hayman
Elaine Grant	Billie Lou Watt
Clifford Grant	Dick O'Neil†
Leroy Jackson	John Danelle
Carlotta	Chip Fields
Abe Lincoln	Abe Vigoda
Young Luther	John Danelle
Young Beulah	Chip Fields
Pee Wee	Jimmy Pelham
Mr. Charlie	Anthony Palmer
Boy Ghost	Ralph Carter

A comedy in two acts. The action takes place at the present time in and around the home of the Grants in Larchmont, N. Y.

General Manager: Elias Goldin
Press: Seymour Krawitz, Martin Shwartz
Stage Managers: Lee Murray, Stephen P. Pokart

* Closed May 4, 1972 after 1 performance and 22 previews.
† Succeeded Jack Cassidy during previews.

Friedman-Abeles Photos

Top: John Amos

Dick O'Neill
Top: Lillian Hayman

ETHEL BARRYMORE THEATRE
Opened Tuesday, May 16, 1972*
Melvin Van Peebles presents:

DON'T PLAY US CHEAP

Book, Words, Music, Direction, Melvin Van Peebles; Scenery, Kurt Lundell; Costumes, Bernard Johnson; Lighting, Martin Aronstein; Musical Supervision, Harold Wheeler; Original Cast Album by Stax Records

CAST

Mr. Percy	Thomas Anderson
Mrs. Washington	Joshie Jo Armstead
Harold Johnson/Rat	Nate Barnett
Mr. Johnson/Cockroach	Frank Carey
Mr. Bowser	Robert Dunn
Earnestine	Rhetta Hughes
Trinity	Joe Keyes, Jr. †1
Mrs. Bowser	Mabel King
David	Avon Long
Mr. Washington	George "Ooppee" McCurn
Miss Maybell	Esther Rolle†2
Mrs. Johnson	Jay Vanleer

MUSICAL NUMBERS: "Some Days It Seems That It Just Don't Even Pay to Get Out of Bed," "Break that Party," "8 Day Week," "Saturday Night," "I'm a Bad Character," "You Cut Up the Clothes in the Closet of My Dreams," "It Makes No Difference," "Quittin' Time," "Ain't Love Grand," "The Book of Life," "Know Your Business," "Big Future," "Feast on Me," "The Phoney Game," "Smash Him"

A comedy musical in two acts. The action takes place in Miss Maybell's apartment in Harlem "a coupla days before tomorrow."

General Managers: Eugene Wolsk, Emanuel Azenberg
Company Manager: David Payne
Press: Michael Alpert, Arthur Rubine
Stage Managers: Charles Blackwell, Charles Briggs, Jerry Laws

* Still palying May 31, 1972
†Succeded by 1. David Connell, 2. Theresa Merritt

Top Right: Rhetta Hughes, Esther Rolle
Below: Mabel King

Esther Rolle, Robert Dunn, Joshie Jo Armstead,
Thomas Anderson

Joe Keyes, Jr., Avon Long, Thomas Anderson

Russ Thacker, Yolande Bavan,
Edward Rambeau

BILLY ROSE THEATRE
Opened Sunday, May 21, 1972*
Leonard J. Goldberg and Ken Gaston in association with
R. Paul Woodville present:

HEATHEN!

Book, Robert Helpmann, Eaton Magoon, Jr.; Music and
Lyrics, Eaton Magoon, Jr.; Director, Lucia Victor; Choreog-
raphy, Sammy Bayes; Setting, Jack Brown; Lighting, Paul
Sullivan; Costumes, Bruce Harrow; Make-up and Hairstyles,
Ted Azar; Orchestrations, Larry Fallon; Musical Director,
Clay Fullum; Associate Choreographer, Dan Siretta; Musical
Supervision, Vocal and Dance and Incidental Music by Mel
Marvin; Production Associate, Mark Siegel; Production As-
sistant, Josh Dietrich

CAST

Rev. Jonathan Beacon/Jonathan .... Russ Thacker
Kalialani/Kalia .... Yolande Bavan
Mano'Ula/Mano .... Edward Rambeau
Muggers .... Dennis Dennehy, Justis Skae, Sal Pernice
Rev. Hiram Burnham .... Dan Merriman
Hepsibah Burnham .... Ann Hodges
Church Elders .... Christopher Barrett, Mary Walling,
Michael Serrecchia
Kaha Kai/The Chanter .... Dennis Dennehy
Alika .... Mokihana
Tourists ....Ann Hodges, Dan Merriman
Hawaiian Boy .... Charles Goeddertz
Policeman.................................. Christopher Barrett
Pueo .... Honey Sanders
Momona-Nui .... Tina Santiago
Boys in jail............. Charles Goeddertz, Michael Serrecchia,
Quitman Fludd

GIRLS AND BOYS: Nancy Dafgek, Jaclynn Villamil, Mary
Walling, Karen Kristin, Dennis Dennehy, Randy DiGrazio,
Quitman Fludd, Charles Goeddertz, Sal Pernice, Michael Ser-
recchia, Justis Skae

UNDERSTUDIES: Jonathan/Kahuna, Christopher Barrett;
Mano/Policeman, Dennis Dennehy; Kalia, Karen Kristin;
Alika, Honey Sanders

MUSICAL NUMBERS: "Paradise," "The Word of the
Lord," "My Sweet Tomorrow," "A Man among Men,"
"Aloha," "Kalialani," "No Way to Hell," "Battle Cry," "This
Is Someone I Could Love," "House of Grass," "Kava Cere-
mony," "For You Brother," "Spear Games," "Christianity,"
"Heathen," "More Better Go Easy," "Eighth Day"

A musical in 2 acts and 20 scenes. The action takes place
in Hawaii in 1819 and 1972.

General Manager: Sherman Gross
Press: Max Eisen, Milly Schoenbaum
Stage Managers: Alan Hall, Jack B. Craig, Karen Kristin
* Closed May 21, 1972 after 1 performance and 6 previews.

Edward Rambeau, Mokihana Above: Yolande Bavan
Mokihana

BROADWAY PRODUCTIONS FROM OTHER SEASONS THAT RAN THROUGH THIS SEASON

IMPERIAL THEATRE

Opened Tuesday, September 22, 1964*
(Moved Feb. 27, 1967 to Majestic; Dec. 14, 1970 to Broadway Theatre)
Harold Prince presents:

FIDDLER ON THE ROOF

Book, Joseph Stein; Based on Sholom Aleichem's stories; Music, Jerry Bock; Lyrics, Sheldon Harnick; Director-Choreographer, Jerome Robbins; Settings, Boris Aronson; Costumes, Patricia Zipprodt; Lighting, Jean Rosenthal; Orchestrations, Don Walker; Musical Direction-Vocal Arrangements, Milton Greene; Dance Music Arrangements, Betty Walberg; Hairstylist, D. Rusty Bonacoorso; Original Cast Album, RCA Victor Records

CAST

Tevye	Paul Lipson†1
Golde	Peg Murray†2
Their daughters:	
Tzeitel	Mimi Turque
Hodel	Susan Hufford
Chava	Peggy Atkinson
Shprintze	Leslie Silvia†3
Bielke	Pamela Greene
Yente	Florence Stanley†4
Motel	Peter Marklin
Perchik	Michael Zaslow
Mordcha	Zvee Scooler
Lazar Wolf	Boris Aplon
Rabbi	Sol Frieder
Mendel	James McDonald
Avram	Jerry Jarrett†5
Nachum	Reuben Schafer
Grandma Tzeitel	Faye Menken
Fruma-Sarah	Harriet Slaughter
Constable	Joseph Sullivan
Fyedka	Don Lawrence†6
Shandel	Laura Stuart
The Fiddler	Marc Scott

VILLAGERS: Bagel Man, Dan Tylor; Streetsweeper, Glen McClaskey; Fishmonger, Bill Bugh; Seltzer Man, Ben Gillespie; Surcha, Maralyn Nell; Woodsman, Tony Gardell; Potseller, Victor Pieran; Grocer, Ross Gifford; Baker, Carlos Gorbea; Knifeseller, Ed Linderman; Fredel, Gretchen Evans; Bluma, Lee Arthur; Berille, Christine Jacobs; Mirala, Charlet Oberley; Rivka, Ann Tell' Cobbler, Roger Brown; Anya, Faye Menken; Hatmaker, Kenneth Henley; Vladimir, Barry Ball; Sasha, Wallace Munro

UNDERSTUDIES: Tevye, Jerry Jarrett; Golde, Yente, Laura Stuart; Tzeitel, Gretchen Evans; Hodel, Christine Jacobs; Chava, Jill Harmon; Shprintze, Bielke, Faye Menken; Perchik, Ed Linderman; Motel, James McDonald; Fyedka, Bill Bugh; Rabbi, Reuben Schafer; Nachum, Dan Tylor; Constable, Ross Gilford; Mendel, Glen McClaskey; Lazar, Jerry Jarrett; Avram, Reuben Schafer; Grandma, Lee Arthur; Fruma, Gretchen Evans; Shandel, Charlet Oberley; Fiddler, Carlos Gorbea; Mordcha, Tony Gardell

MUSICAL NUMBERS: "Tradition," "Matchmaker," "If I Were a Rich Man," "Sabbath Prayer," "To Life," "Miracle of Miracles," "The Tailor," "Sunrise, Sunset," "Bottle Dance," "Wedding Dance," "Now I Have Everything," "Do You Love Me?," "I Just Heard," "Far from the Home I Love," "Anetevka," Epilogue

A musical in two acts. The action takes place in Anatevka, a village in Russia, in 1905 on the eve of the revolutionary period.

Friedman-Abeles Photos

Right Center: Peg Murray, Peggy Atkinson, Paul Lipson, Susan Hufford, Mimi Turque

General Manager: Carl Fisher
Company Manager: Warren O'Hara
Press: Sol Jacobson, Lewis Harmon, Ruth Smuckler
Stage Managers: Ruth Mitchell, Jay Jacobson, David Wolf, Steve Bohm

* On June 17, 1972 "Fiddler" became the longest running production in Broadway history, and closed on July 2, 1972 after 3242 performances. For original production, see THEATRE WORLD, Vol. 21.
† Succeeded by: 1. Jan Peerce, Paul Lipson, 2. Mimi Randolph, Peg Murray, 3. Jill Harmon, 4. Ruth Jaroslow, 5. Donald C. Moore, Jerry Jarrett, 6. Michael Petro

Jan Peerce, Mimi Randolph

BOOTH THEATRE

Opened Tuesday, October 21, 1969*
Arthur Whitelaw, Max J. Brown, Byron Goldman present:

BUTTERFLIES ARE FREE

By Leonard Gershe; Director, Milton Katselas; Set, Richard Seger; Costumes, Robert Mackintosh; Lighting, Jules Fisher; Associate Producer, Ruth Bailey; Hairstylist, Joe Tubens; Title Song, Steve Schwartz

CAST

Don Baker	Kipp Osborne†1
Jill Tanner	Kathleen Miller†2
Mrs. Baker	Rosemary Murphy†3
Ralph Austin	Michael Glaser†4

STANDBYS: Don, Ralph, Richard Backus, Brian Marshall; Jill, Kristina Callahan, Karen Grassle; Mrs. Baker, Patricia Wheel

A comedy in 2 acts and 3 scenes. The action takes place at the present time in Don Baker's apartment on East 11th Street in New York.

General Manager: Marvin A. Krauss
Company Manager: David Wyler
Press: Max Eisen, Milly Schoenbaum
Stage Managers: Elizabeth Caldwell, Preston Fisher

* Closed July 2, 1972 after 1128 performances and 13 previews. For original production, see THEATRE WORLD, Vol. 26.
† Succeeded by: 1. David Huffman, Dirk Benedict, 2. Pamela Bellwood, 3. Gloria Swanson, 4. Michael Shannon, Robert Anthony

David Huffman, Gloria Swanson, Michael Shannon, Pamela Bellwood Top: Swanson, Huffman, Bellwood (R) Swanson, Dirk Benedict

Opened Sunday, April 4, 1971*
Harold Prince in association with Ruth Mitchell presents:

FOLLIES

Book, James Goldman; Music and Lyrics, Stephen Sondheim; Directors, Harold Prince, Michael Bennett; Choreographer, Michael Bennett; Scenic Production, Boris Aronson; Costumes, Florence Klotz; Lighting, Tharon Musser; Musical Direction, Harold Hastings; Orchestrations, Jonathan Tunick; Dance Music Arrangements, John Berkman; Production Supervisor, Ruth Mitchell; Associate Choreographer, Bob Avian; Production Assistant, Ted Chapin; Hairstylist, Joe Tubens; Make-up, Ted Azar; Original Cast Album, Capitol Records

General Manager: Carl Fisher
Press: Mary Bryant, Stanley F. Kaminsky
Stage Managers: Fritz Holt, George Martin, John Grigas, Donald Weissmuller

* Closed July 1, 1972 after 522 performances and 12 previews. For original production, see THEATRE WORLD, Vol. 27. "Follies" received 1971 Drama Critics Circle Award as Best Musical, and 1972 "Tonys" for Best Musical Score, Best Musical Actress (Alexis Smith), Best Musical Director, Best Choreography, Best Sets, Best Costumes, and Best Lighting.
† Succeeded by: 1. Joseph Nelson, 2. Jan Clayton, 3. Marion Marlowe, 4. Jacqueline Payne, 5. Camila Ashland, 6. Dick Latessa, Ted Lawrie, 7. Margot Travers, 8. Alexandra Borrie, 9. John Johann, 10. Christopher Nelson, Roy Barry

Martha Swope Photos

CAST

Major-Domo	Dick Latessa†1
Sally Durant Plummer	Dorothy Collins
Young Sally	Marti Rolph
Christine Crane	Ethel Barrymore Colt†2
Willy Wheeler	Fred Kelly
Stella Deems	Mary McCarty
Max Deems	John J. Martin
Heidi Schiller	Justine Johnston
Chauffeur	John Grigas
Meredith Lane	Sheila Smith†3
Chet Richards	Peter Walker
Roscoe	Michael Bartlett
Deedee West	Helen Blount
Sandra Donovan	Sonja Levkova
Hattie Walker	Ethel Shutta
Young Hattie	Mary Jane Houdina†4
Emily Whitman	Marcie Stringer†5
Theodore Whitman	Charles Welch†6
Vincent	Victor Griffin
Vanessa	Jayne Turner
Young Vincent	Michael Misita
Young Vanessa	Graciela Daniele†7
Solange LaFitte	Fifi D'Orsay
Carlotta Campion	Yvonne De Carlo
Phyllis Rogers Stone	Alexis Smith
Benjamin Stone	John McMartin
Young Phyllis	Virginia Sandifur†8
Young Benjamin	Kurt Peterson†9
Buddy Plummer	Gene Nelson
Young Buddy	Harvey Evans
Dimitri Weismann	Arnold Moss
Kevin	Ralph Nelson†10
Young Heidi	Victoria Mallory

PARTY MUSICIANS: Taft Jordan, Aaron Bell, John Blowers, Robert Curtis

SHOWGIRLS: Suzanne Briggs, Trudy Carson, Jennifer Nairn-Smith, Ursula Maschmeyer, Susanna Clemm, Margot Travers, Kathie Dalton, Linda Perkins

SINGERS AND DANCERS: Denise Pence, Rita Rudner, Jacqueline Payne, Joel Craig, Patricia Garland, Julie Pars, Suzanne Rogers, Roy Barry, Steve Boockvor, Michael Misita, Joseph Nelson, David Roman, Ken Urmston, Graciela Daniele, Donald Weissmuller

STANDBYS AND UNDERSTUDIES: Phyllis, Carlotta, Solange, Marion Marlowe; Sally, Jan Clayton; Buddy, Ted Lawrie; Dimitri, Edwin Steffe; Stone, Peter Walker; Young Sally, Victoria Mallory; Young Phyllis, Suzanne Rogers; Young Ben, Ken Urmston; Vincent, Donald Weissmuller; Solange, Sonja Levkova

MUSICAL NUMBERS: "Beautiful Girls," "Don't Look at Me," "Waiting for the Girls Upstairs," "Listen to the Rain on the Roof," "Ah, Paris!," "Broadway Baby," "The Road You Didn't Take," "Bolero d'Amour," "In Buddy's Eyes," "Who's That Woman," "I'm Still Here," "Too Many Mornings," "The Right Girl," "One More Kiss," "Could I Leave You?," "Loveland," "You're Gonna Love Tomorrow," "Love Will See Us Through," "The God-Why-Don't-You-Love-Me Blues," "Losing My Mind," "The Story of Lucy and Jessie," "Live, Laugh, Love"

A Balding; presented without intermission. The action takes place at the present time on the stage of the Weimann Theatre in New York.

Top Right: Kurt Peterson, Virginia Sandifur, Harvey Evans, Marti Rolph

Alexis Smith, John McMartin, Dorothy Collins, Gene Nelson Above: Michael Bartlett and cast

BILTMORE THEATRE

Opened Monday, April 19, 1968*
Michael Butler presents:

HAIR

Book and Lyrics, Gerome Ragni, James Rado; Music, Galt McDermot; Executive Producer, Bertrand Castelli; Director, Tom O'Horgan; Assistant Director, Dan Sullivan; Dance Director, Julie Arenal; Musical Director, Galt McDermot; Conductor, Margaret Harris; Costumes, Nancy Potts; Scenery, Robin Wagner; Lighting, Jules Fisher; Sound Abe Jacob; Original Cast Album by RCA Victor Records

CAST

Claude ....Robin McNamara†1
Berger...Steven Curry†2
Woof...Alan Braunstein†3
Hud ....Larry Marshall†4
Sheila ....Marta Heflin†5
Jeanie ....Kay Cole†6
Dionne ....•.. Delores Hall†7
Crissy ....Debbie Andrews†8
Mother .... Kay Cole†6, Bryan Spencer, Bobby C. Ferguson
Father...............Clifford Lipson†9, Valerie Williams, Fluffer Hirsch†10
Principal................. George Garcia, Valerie Williams, Gloria Goldman
Tourist Couple.................Bryan Spencer, Jonathan Johnson
Waitress ....Valerie Williams
Young Recruit ....George Garcia†11
General Grant .... Charles O. Lynch†12
Abraham Lincoln .... Valerie Williams
Sergeant .... Larry Marshall†4
Parents ....Kathrynann Wright, Clifford Lipson†13

THE TRIBE: Billy Alessi, Marjorie Barnes, Zenobia Conkerite, Candice Earley, Stephen Fenning, Bobby C. Ferguson, Robert Golden, Gloria Goldman, Ula Hedwig, Jonathan Johnson, Stephanie Parker, Carl Scott, Mary Seymour, Bryan Spencer, George Turner, Valerie Williams, Kathrynann Wright

UNDERSTUDIES: Berger, Peppy Castro, Robert Golden; Hud, George Turner, Bobby C. Ferguson; Claude, Jonathan Johnson; Woof, Jonathan Johnson, Stephen Fenning; Jeanie, Valerie Williams, Zenobia Conkerite; Crissy, Candice Earley; Sheila, Gloria Goldman, Kathrynann Wright

MUSICAL NUMBERS: "Aquarius," "Donna," "Hashish," "Sodomy," "Colored Spade," "Manchester," "Ain't Got No," "Dead End," "I Believe in Love," "Air," "Initials," "I Got Life," "Going Down," "Hair," "My Conviction," "Easy to Be Hard," "Don't Put It Down," "Frank Mills," "Be-In," "Where Do I Go," "Electric Blues," "Black Boys," "White Boys," "Walking in Space," "Abie Baby," "Three-Five-Zero-Zero," "What a Piece of Work Is Man," "Good Morning Starshine," "The Bed," "The Flesh Failures," "Let the Sun Shine in"

The American tribal-love rock musical in two acts.
Company Manager: William Orton
Press: Gifford/Wallace, Michael Gifford, Tom Trenkle
Stage Managers: Fred Reinglas, Ronald Schaeffer, Kenneth Cox

* Closed July 2, 1972 after 1742 performances. For original production, see THEATRE WORLD, Vol. 24.
† Succeeded by: 1. Willie Windsor, 2. Roger Cruz, Gregory V. Karliss, 3. Peppy Castro, 4. Michael Rhone, 5. Beverly Bremers, 6. Dale Soules, 7. Zenobia Conkerite, 8. Debbie Andrews, Shelley Plimpton, 9. Gloria Goldman, 10. Michael Rhone, 11. Bobby C. Ferguson, 12. Cliff Lipson, Stephen Fenning, 13. Robert Golden.

Martha Swope Photos

Top Right: Gregory V. Karliss (C), Willie Windsor, Peppy Castro

Dale Soules, Willie Windsor

BROOKS ATKINSON THEATRE
Opened Wednesday, May 26, 1971*
Jules Fisher, Marvin Worth, Michael Butler present:

LENNY

By Julian Barry; Based on life and words of Lenny Bruce; Music and Direction, Tom O'Horgan; Scenery, Robin Wagner; Costumes, Randy Barcelo; Lighting, Jules Fisher; Executive Producer, Ivor David Balding; Production Assistants, Robyn Watson, Richard Pinter; Produced by the L. B. Co.; Production Supervisor, Richard Scanga; Original Cast Album, Blue Thumb Records

CAST

Lenny Bruce	Cliff Gorman†1
Judges/Sherman Hart/General/Vampire Priest/Plainclothesman/Wollenstein/Photographer	Joe Silver
Lenny's Mother Sadie Kitchenberg alias Sally Marr	Erica Yohn†2
Rusty	Jane House†3
Clubowner/Lenny's Father/Ike/Blah Blah Judge/D.A./Photographer	Robert Weil
Chinese Waiter/Bishop/Cop/Witch Doctor	James Wigfall†4
Trumpet/Nod Out	Vaughn De Forest
Stripper/Aunt Mema/Lucille/Catholic Lady/Matron/Southern Lady/Nurse	Jeannette Ertelt
Bass/Life Reporter/Cop	Ernie Furtado
Trombone/Nod Out	John Gordon
Sax/Bass Clarinet/Flute/Nod Out	Ron Odrich†5
Arty/Igor/Hitler/Radio Announcer/Photographer	Johnny Arment†6
Juan/Primitive Drummer/Cop	Marker Bloomst†7
Stripper/Singer/Mrs. Hart/Secretary/Girl with I.D. Card	Melody Santangelo†8
Piano/Lenny's Lawyer/Eichmann	Warren Meyers
Girl in Wheelchair	Jody Oliver†9
Ernie/Interviewer	Paul Lieber†10
Drums/Cop	Adam Smith

UNDERSTUDIES: Lenny, Ted Schwartz; Mr. Silver, Robert Weil; Miss Yohn, Jeannette Ertelt; Misses House, Milford, Mary Mendum; Misses Ertelt, Mendum, Penelope Milford; Mr. Weil, Warren Meyers; Messrs. Lieber, Schwartz, Gordon, Smith, Victor Lipari; Messrs. Meyers, Silver, Weil, Wigfall, Ernie Furtado; Mr. Weil, James Wigfall; Mr. Lipari, Marker Bloomst; Messrs. DeForest, Keller, John Gordon

A drama in two acts. The action takes place between 1951 and 1966.

General Manager: James Walsh
Press: Gifford/Wallace
Stage Managers: James Bernardi, Marker Bloomst, Victor Lipari

* Closed June 24, 1972 after 453 performances and 16 previews, For original production, see THEATRE WORLD, Vol. 27. Cliff Gorman received 1972 "Tony" for Best Actor in a play.
† Succeeded by: 1. Sandy Baron, 2. Marilyn Chris for vacation, 3. Mary Mendum for vacation, 4. Bob Molock, 5. Bob Keller, 6. Don Calfa, Paul Lieber, 7. Victor Lipari, 8. Mary Mendum, 9. Penelope Milford, Judith Evans, 10. Ted Schwartz

Martha Swope Photos

Top Right: Paul Lieber, Warren Meyers, Robert Weil, Joe Silver, Jane House, James Wigfall
Below: Cliff Gorman

Cliff Gorman, Jane House

EDEN THEATRE

Opened Tuesday, June 17, 1969*
Hillard Elkins in association with Michael White, Gordon Crowe and George Platt presents:

OH! CALCUTTA!

Devised by Kenneth Tynan; Contributors, Samuel Beckett, Jules Feiffer, Dan Greenburg, John Lennon, Jacques Levy, Leonard Melfi, David Newman and Robert Benton, Sam Shepard, Cloris Trouille, Kenneth Tynan, Sherman Yellen; Music and Lyrics, The Open Window (Robert Dennis, Peter Schickele, Stanley Walden); Choreography, Margo Sappington; Scenery, James Tilton; Lighting, David F. Segal; Costumes, Fred Voelpel; Projections, Gardner Compton, Emile Ardolino; Still Photography, Michael Childers; Musical Director, Norman Bergen; Production Supervisor, Michael Thoma; Production Associate, Bill Liberman; Entire Production Conceived and Directed by Jacques Levy; An E.P.I.C. Production

CAST

Mel Auston†	William Knight
Raina Barrett	Mitchell McGuire
Ray Edelstein	Pamela Pilkenton
Samantha Harper	Gary Rethmeier
Patricia Hawkins	Nancy Tribush

Standby: Maureen Byrnes

PROGRAM

ACT I: Prologue, "Taking off the Robe," "Dick & Jane," "Suite for Five Letters," "Will Answer All Sincere Replies," "Paintings of Clovis Trouille," "Delicious Indignities," "Was It Good for You Too?," "Who: Whom," "Much Too Soon," "One on One," "Rock Garden," "Four in Hand," "Coming Together, Going Together"

A musical entertainment in two acts.

General Manager: Bill Liberman
Press: Samuel J. Friedman, Louise Weiner Ment, Shirley Herz
Stage Managers: John Actman, Ray Edelstein

* Closed Aug. 12, 1972 after 1316 performances. For original production, see THEATRE WORLD, Vol. 26.
† During the year, the following appeared in the cast: Cindy Howard, Ed Phillips, Jack Shearer, Evamarii Johnson, Steven Keats, Ron Osborne, Patricia Post, Richard Quarry, David Rosenbaum, Ellie Smith, Patricia Hawkins, Rusty Blitz, Boni Enten, Onni Johnson, Marcia Greene, Mary-Jenifer Mitchell, Richard Ryder, Angelyn Forbes, Marian Ellis, B. J. DeSimone.

Henry Grossman Photos

Jack Shearer, Pamela Pilkenton
Above: Gary Rethmeier, Samantha Harper

FORTY-SIXTH STREET THEATRE
Opened Tuesday, January 19, 1971*
Pyxidium Ltd. presents:

NO, NO, NANETTE

Book, Otto Harbach, Frank Mandel; Music, Vincent Youmans; Lyrics, Irving Caesar, Otto Harbach; Adapted and Directed by Burt Shevelove; Dances and Musical Numbers Staged by Donald Saddler; Designed by Raoul Pene du Bois; Lighting, Jules Fisher; Musical Direction-Vocal Arrangements, Buster Davis; Orchestrations, Ralph Burns; Dance Music Arranged, Incidental Music Composed by Luther Henderson; Colston and Clements at pianos; Production Manager, May Muth; Tap Supervisors, Mary Ann Niles, Ted Cappy; Sound, Jack Shearing; Coiffures, Vidal Sassoon; Bruce Steier, Assistant Choreographer, Mary Ann Niles; Assistant to Producers, Steve Beckler; Beach Ball Instructor, Ernestine Mercer; Entire Production Supervised by Busby Berkeley; Original Cast Album, Columbia Records

CAST

Pauline	Patsy Kelly[†1]
Lucille Early	Helen Gallagher
Sue Smith	Ruby Keeler[†2]
Jimmy Smith	Jack Gilford[†3]
Billy Early	Bobby Van[†4]
Tom	Roger Rathburn
Nanette	Susan Watson[†5]
Flora Latham	Sandra O'Neill[†6]
Betty Brown	Loni Zoe Ackerman[†7]
Winnie Winslow	Pat Lysinger[†8]

NANETTE'S FRIENDS: Douglas Allen, Bob Becker, John Beecher, Marcia Brushingham, Cindi Bulak, Kenneth Carr, Jennie Chandler, Kathy Conry, Andrea Duda, Ellen Elias, Mercedes Ellington, Jon Engstrom, Lynne Gannaway, Marian Haraldson, Gregg Harlan, Sayra Hummel, Scott Hunter, Reggie Israel, Frances Ruth Lea, Christopher Nelson, Frank Newell, Sally O'Donnell, Jill Owens, Shelly Rann, James Robinson, Linda Rose, Bobbie Rhine, Stefan J. Ross, Kathie Savage, Ron Schwinn, Denny Shearer, Monica Tiller, Pat Trott, Phyllis Wallach

STANDBYS AND UNDERSTUDIES: Sue, Ruth Maitland; Jimmy, Ted Tiller; Pauline, Ruth Donnelly; Billy, Denny Shearer; Lucille, Judith Knaiz; Nanette, Kathy Conry; Tom, Kenneth Carr; Betty, Linda Rose; Flora, Cindi Bulak; Winnie, Sayra Hummel

MUSICAL NUMBERS: "Too Many Rings around Rosie," "I've Confessed to the Breeze," "Call of the Sea," "I Want to Be Happy," "No, No, Nanette," "Finaletto," "Peach on the Beach," "Tea for Two," "You Can Dance with Any Girl," "Telephone Girlie," "Where-Has-My-Hubby-Gone Blues," "Waiting for You," "Take a Little One-Step," Finale

A musical comedy in 3 acts. The action takes place on a weekend in early summer of 1925 in Jimmy's New York home, and Chickadee Cottage in Atlantic City.

General Management: Gatchell & Neufeld
Company Manager: James Mennen
Press: Merle Debuskey, Faith Geer, Robert W. Larkin
Stage Managers: Marnel Sumner, Michael Turque, Mary Ann Niles

* Still playing May 31, 1972. Original production opened Sept. 16, 1925 and ran for 321 performances with Eleanor Dawn, Louise Groody, Charles Winninger, and Wellington Cross.

† Succeeded by: 1. Ruth Donnelly during illness, 2. Penny Singleton for 2 weeks vacation, 3. Benny Baker, 4. Larry Ellis, Anthony Teague, 5. Barbara Heuman, 6. Sally Cooke, 7. Jilly Jaress, 8. Gwen Miller, Judith Knaiz.

Friedman-Abeles Photos

Top Right: Barbara Heuman, Roger Rathburn
Below: Ruby Keeler

Anthony Teague, Helen Gallagher
Above: Ruby Keeler, Bobby Van

Patsy Kelly

63

PALACE THEATRE

Opened Monday, March 30, 1970*
Joseph Kipness and Lawrence Kasha in association with Nederlander Productions and George M. Steinbrenner III present:

APPLAUSE

Book, Betty Comden, Adolph Green; Based on film "All about Eve" and original short story by Mary Orr; Music Charles Strouse; Lyrics, Lee Adams; Director-Choreographer, Ron Field; Scenery, Robert Randolph; Costumes, Ray Aghanyan; Lighting, Tharon Musser; Musical Direction-Vocal Arrangements, Donald Pippin; Orchestrations, Philip J. Lang; Dance and Incidental Music Arrangements, Mel Marvin; Production Associate, Phyllis Dukore; Directorial Assistant, Otto Pirchner; Choreographic Assistant, Tom Rolla; Hairstylist, Joe Tubens; Original Cast Album, ABC Records

CAST

Tony Announcer	John Anania
Tony Host	Alan King
Margo Channing	Lauren Bacall[1]
Eve Harrington	Penny Fuller[2]
Howard Benedict	Robert Mandan[3]
Bert	Tom Urich
Buzz Richards	Brandon Maggart
Bill Sampson	Len Cariou[4]
Duane Fox	Lee Roy Reams[5]
Karen Richards	Gwyda DonHowe[6]
Bartender	Jerry Wyatt
Peter	John Anania
Dancer in bar	Sammy Williams[7]
Bob	John Herbert
Piano Player	Orrin Reiley[8]
Stan Harding	Ray Becker
Danny	Bill Allsbrook[9]
Bonnie	Bonnie Franklin[10]
Carol	Carol Petri[11]
Joey	Christopher Chadman[12]
TV Director	Orrin Reiley[8]
Autograph Seeker	Carol Petri[13]
Musicians	Gene Kelton, Nat Horne, David Anderson

SINGERS: Peggy Hagan, Patti Davis, Gail Nelson, Jeannette Seibert, Merrill Leighton, John Herbert, Orrin Reiley, Jerry Wyatt, Judy McCauley, Jozella Reed, Joseph Neal

DANCERS: Renee Baughman, Joan Bell, Debi Carpenter, Patti D'Beck, Bonnie Walker, Marybeth Kurdock, Carol Petri, Bill Allsbrook, David Anderson, Wayne Boyd, John Cashman, Nicholas Dante, Gene Foote, Gene Kelton, Nat Horne, Christopher Chadman, Ed Nolfi, Sammy Williams, Marilyn D'Honou, Kathleen Robey, Larry Merritt, John Medeiros, Gene Aguirre, Paul Charles, Jay Fox, Richard Dodd

UNDERSTUDIES: Eve, Patti Davis; Bill, Tom Urich; Howard, John Anania; Buzz, Ray Becker; Karen, Peggy Hagan; Duane, Gene Foote; Bonnie, Carol Petri, Patti D'Beck; Bert, Stan, Jerry Wyatt; Peter, Lanier Davis, John Herbert

MUSICAL NUMBERS: "Backstage Babble," "Think How It's Gonna Be," "But Alive," "The Best Night of My Life," "Who's That Girl?," "Applause," "Hurry Back," "Fasten Your Seat Belts," "Welcome to the Theatre," "Inner Thoughts," "Good Friends," "She's No Longer a Gypsy," "One of a Kind," "One Halloween," "Something Greater," Finale

A musical in 2 acts and 16 scenes. The action takes place at the present time in and around New York City.

General Manager: Philip Adler
Company Manager: S. M. Handelsman, Milton Pollack
Press: Bill Doll & Co., Dick Williams, Cindy Reagan, Virginia Holden
Stage Managers: Terence Little, Donald Christy, Lanier Davis, John Herbert

* Closed May 27, 1972 after 900 performances. Winner of "Tony" for Best Musical. For original production, see THEATRE WORLD, Vol. 26.
† Succeeded by: 1. Anne Baxter, Arlene Dahl, 2. Janice Lynde, 3. Lawrence Weber, Franklin Cover, 4. Keith Charles, John Gabriel, 5. Tom Rolla, Larry Merritt, 6. Peggy Hagan, Phebe Hagen, 7. Gene Aguirre, 8. Joseph Neal, 9. Larry Merritt, Gene Aguirre, 10. Carol Petri, 11. Kathleen Robey, 12. John Medeiros, 13. Kathleen Robey

Top Right: Bonnie Franklin

Below: Keith Charles, Anne Baxter

Brandon Maggart, Arlene Dahl, Phebe Hagan

MUSIC BOX

Opened Thursday, November 12, 1970*
Helen Bonfils, Morton Gottlieb, Michael White present:

SLEUTH

By Anthony Shaffer; Director, Clifford Williams; Designed by Carl Toms; Lighting, William Ritman; Production Assistant, E. J. Oshins

CAST

Andrew Wyke	Anthony Quayle†1
Milo Tindle	Keith Baxter†2
Inspector Doppler	Philip Farrar†3
Detective Sgt. Tarrant	Harold Newman†4
Police Constable Higgs	Roger Purnell†5

STANDBYS AND UNDERSTUDIES: Andrew, Michael Allinson; Milo, Michael Lipton; Doppler, Henry Raymond; Tarrant, Higgs, John Stephen.

A mystery drama in two acts. The action takes place at the present time in Andrew Ayke's country home in Wiltshire, Eng.

General Manager: Ben Rosenberg
Company Manager: Martin Cohen
Press: Dorothy Ross, Herb Striesfield
Stage Managers: Warren Crane, Clint Jakeman, Henry Raymond

* Still playing May 31, 1972. For original production, see THEATRE WORLD, Vol. 27. Winner of 1971 "Tony" for Best Play.
† Succeeded by: 1. Paul Rogers, Patrick Mcnee, 2. Donal Donnelly, Brian Murray, 3. Stanley Rushton, 4. Robin Mayfield, 5. Liam McNulty

Right: Brian Murray, Paul Rogers
Top: Keith Baxter, Anthony Quayle

BROADWAY PRODUCTIONS FROM OTHER SEASONS THAT CLOSED DURING THIS SEASON

Title	Opened	Closed	Performances
Man of La Mancha	11/22/65	6/26/71	2329
Promises, Promises	12/1/68	1/1/72	1281
1776	3/16/69	2/13/72	1217
Applause	3/30/70	5/27/72	900
Last of the Red Hot Lovers	12/28/69	9/4/71	706
Company	4/26/70	1/1/72	690
Purlie	3/15/70	11/7/71	689
The Me Nobody Knows	5/18/70	11/28/71	587
The Rothschilds	10/19/70	1/2/72	505
Two by Two	11/10/70	9/11/71	343
Paul Sills' Story Theatre	10/26/70	7/3/71	270
How the Other Half Loves	3/29/71	6/26/71	104

PRODUCTIONS AT NEW YORK CITY CENTER

CITY CENTER

Opened Monday, September 27, 1971.*
Pacific World Artists in association with City Center of
Music and Drama presents:

BLACK LIGHT THEATRE OF PRAGUE

Direction and Music, Jiri Srnec; Libretto, Jiri Srnec, Fran-
tisek Kratochvil; Assistant Director, Frantisek Kratochvil;
Scenery, Jiri Srnec, Frantisek Kratochvil; Manager, Ing. P.
Postrehovsky.

CAST

F. Kratochvil	J. Rybova
V. Kubicek	M. Cechova
J. Lutovsky	E. Srncova
M. Matejcek	J. Kozeluhova
F. Spergr	M. Rychlikova
J. Matejckova	

PROGRAM (Presented in two parts): Introduction, Wash-
woman, Horse, Dialogue, Ghosts, Fair of Hands
General Manager: Joel Benjamin
Press: Bill Doll & Co., Dick Williams, Cindy Reagan

* Closed Sunday, Oct. 3, 1971 after limited engagement of 9
performances.

Right: Scenes from Black Light Theatre

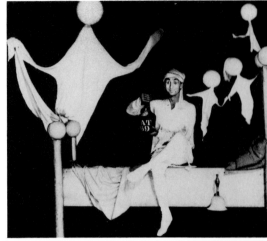

Walterine Ross, Samaki Zuri, David Gardner, Pamela
Sweden, Raymond Wade, Danny Duncan

CITY CENTER DOWNSTAIRS

Opened Monday, March 20, 1972*
Franklin Fried and Bert Wainer in association with City
Center of Music and Drama present the Duncan Com-
pany in:

UHURUH

Book, Music, Lyrics, Direction, and Choreography by
Danny Duncan; Production Coordinator, Alice Alexander;
Assistant Choreographers, Pasy Cain, Raymond Wade; Tech-
nical Director-Lighting, Kueleza Furaha; Musical Director-
Pianist, Rick Appling

CAST
Danny Duncan

Blondell Breed	Pamela Sweden
Gregory Burrell	Raymond Wade
Pasy Cain	Victor Willis
David Gardner	Ebony Wright
Cyril Tyrone Hanna II	Earl Young
Walterine Ross	Samaki Zuri

A revue in two acts.

General Management: Dorothy Olim Associates
Press: Howard Atlee, David Roggensack, Clarence Allsopp

* **Closed March 25, 1972 after 8 performances.**

Bert Andrews Photo

CITY CENTER

Opened Tuesday, December 21, 1971.*
City Center of Music and Drama (Norman Singer, Executive Director) in association with the Charlottetown Festival (Prince Edward Island, Canada) present the Canadian National Musical Theatre production of:

ANNE OF GREEN GABLES

Adapted by Donald Harron from the novel by L. M. Montgomery; Music, Norman Campbell; Lyrics, Donald Harron, Norman Campbell; Direction and Choreography, Alan Lund; Designer, Murray Laufer; Costumes, Marie Day; Lighting, Ronald Montgomery; Musical Director and Orchestrations, John Fenwick; Associate Music Director, Fen Watkin; Additional Lyrics, Mavor Moore, Elaine Campbell; Associate Lighting Designer, Gary Craswell.

CAST

Mrs. Rachel Lynde	Maud Whitmore
Mrs. MacPherson	Cleone Duncan
Mrs. Barry	Nancy Kerr
Mrs. Sloane	Flora MacKenzie
Mrs. Pye	Kathryn Watt
Minister	Lloyd Malenfant
Rev. Smythe Hankinson	Jack Northmore
Earl	Bill Hosie
Cecil	George Merner
Marilla Cuthbert	Elizabeth Mawson
Matthew Cuthbert	Peter Mews
Anne Shirley	Gracie Finley
Mrs. Spencer	Flora MacKenzie
Mrs. Blewett	Roma Hearn
Diana Barry	Glenda Landry
Prissy Andrews	Sharlene McLean
Josie Pye	Barbara Barsky
Ruby Gillis	Patti Toms
Tillie Boulter	Lynn Marsh
Gertie Pye	Deborah Millar
Gilbert Blythe	Jeff Hyslop
Charlie Sloane	George Juriga
Moody MacPherson	Dan Costain
Gerry Buote	Andre Denis
Tommy Sloane	John Powell
Malcolm Andrews	Calvin McRae
Mr. Phillips	Jack Northmore
Lucilla	Cleone Duncan
Miss Stacy	Roma Hearn
Stationmaster	Bill Hosie

MUSICAL NUMBERS: "Great Workers for the Cause," "Where Is Matthew Going?," "Gee I'm Glad I'm No One Else but Me," "We Clearly Requested," "The Facts," "Where'd Marilla Come From?," "Humble Pie," "Oh, Mrs. Lynde!," "Back to School Ballet," "Avonlea We Love Thee," "Wondrin'," "Did You Hear?," "Ice Cream," "The Picnic," "Where Did the Summer Go To?" "Kindred Spirits," "Open the Window!," "The Words," "Nature Hunt Ballet," "I'll Show Him," "General Store," "Pageant Song," "If It Hadn't Been for Me," "Anne of Green Gables."

A Musical in two acts. The action takes place at the turn of the century in Avonlea, a tiny village in Prince Edward Island, Canada's smallest province.

Company Manager: Catherine Parsons
Press: Meg Gordean, Ellen Levene, Jack McAndrew
Stage Managers: David Loynd, J. P. Regan, Ernie Abugov

* Closed Jan. 2, 1972 after limited engagement of 16 performances.

George Wotton Photos

Top Right: Jeff Hyslop, Gracie Finley
Below: Gracie Finley

Gracie Finley (C)

REPERTORY THEATER OF LINCOLN CENTER
Jules Irving, Director
Robert Symonds, Associate Director

FORUM THEATER
Opened Wednesday, September 29, 1971.*
The Repertory Theater of Lincoln Center presents:

PLAY STRINDBERG

By Friedrich Durrenmatt; Translated by James Kirkup;
Director, Dan Sullivan; Setting, Douglas W. Schmidt; Costumes, James Berton Harris; Lighting, John Gleason; Musical
Direction, Roland Gagnon; Hairstylist, Jim Sullivan; Production Assistants, Fay Kasmer, Jo Sennet

CAST

Alice	Priscilla Pointer
Edgar	Robert Symonds
Kurt	Ray Fry
Stage Manager	Richard Greene
Trumpet	Robert Harley
Tuba	Roger Ricci

UNDERSTUDIES: Rhoda Gemignani, Richard Greene

A Play performed in twelve rounds with one intermission.
Press: Susan Bloch, William Schelble

* Closed Oct. 24, 1971 after 29 performances to tour. It had
previously played 42 performances from May 28 through
July 3, 1971.

Martha Swope Photos

Robert Symonds, Priscilla Pointer
Above: Ray Fry, Priscilla Pointer, Robert Symonds

FORUM THEATER

Opened Wednesday, November 3, 1971.*
The Repertory Theater of Lincoln Center (Jules Irving, Director) presents:

KOOL AID

By Merle Molofsky; Director, Jack Gelber; Assistant to the Director, Jack Temchin; Production Assistant, Saraleigh Carney

CAST

"Grail Green"
Douglas One .... Robert DeNiro
Douglas Two .... Kevin O'Connor
The Girl .... Barbara eda-Young
The Master .... Richard Bright
The Counselor .... Jerry Whelan
The Guard .... Luis Avalos
Freddie .... Robert Burgos

A correctional institution five years ago.

"Three Street Koans"
Douglas .... Kevin O'Connor
Doreen .... Barbara eda-Young
Mona .... Verna Bloom
Freddie .... Robert Burgos
Shogen .... Jerry Whelan
Mumon .... Richard Bright
Karen .... Megan Sullivan
Fatboy .... Robert DeNiro
Carlos .... Luis Avalos

The Action takes place on the West side of New York City close to the river at the present time.

Press: Susan Bloch, William Shelble
Stage Managers: Paul Bengston, Janis Checkanow

* Closed Nov. 6, 1971 after limited engagement of 5 perfor-

Martha Swope Photos

Top Right: Barbara eda-Young, Kevin O'Connor Below: Robert Burgos, Verna Bloom, Luis Avalos

Kevin O'Connor

Robert Burgos, Megan Sullivan, Verna Bloom

VIVIAN BEAUMONT THEATER

Opened Thursday, November 1, 1971.*
The Repertory Theater of Lincoln Center (Jules Irving, Director) presents:

MARY STUART

By Friedrich Schiller; Freely Translated and Adapted by Stephen Spender; Director, Jules Irving; Settings, Douglas W. Schmidt; Lighting, John Gleason; Costumes, Malcolm McCormick; Music, Stanley Silverman; Assistant Director, Kent Paul; Hairstylist, Jim Sullivan

CAST

Hannah Kennedy	Aline MacMahon
Sir Amias Paulet	Robert Symonds
Sir Drue Drury	Seth Allen
Mary Stuart	Salome Jens
Sir Edward Mortimer	Robert Phalen
Lord Burleigh	Stephen Elliott
Sir William Davison	Andy Robinson
Talbot, Earl of Shrewsbury	Sydney Walker
Queen Elizabeth	Nancy Marchand
Robert Dudley	Philip Bosco
Earl of Kent	Ray Stewart
Page	Mark Woods
Count Aubespine	Ray Fry
Bellievre	Adolph Caesar†1
Officer of the Queen's Guard	James Tolkan
O'Kelly	Richard Greene
Serving Girl	Crickett Coan
Sir Andrew Melvil	Joseph Maher†2
Sheriff of Northampton	Stuart Pankin
Guards, Courtiers, Gentlewomen	Robert Christian†3, Crickett Coan, Kathleen Doyle, Richard Kline, Marilyn Meyers, Ronald Roston, Peter Weil

UNDERSTUDIES: Mary, Elizabeth, Frances Sternhagen; Leicester, Richard Greene; Burleigh, Ray Fry; Mortimer, Page, Richard Kline; Talbot, Melvil, Ray Stewart; Hannah, Priscilla Pointer; Paulet, James Tolkan; Davison, Officer, Robert Christian; Aubespine, Seth Allen; Bellievre, O'Kelly, Peter Weil; Kent, Ronald Roston; Serving Girl, Kathleen Doyle; Drury, Stuart Pankin; Sheriff, Mark Woods

A Drama in two acts and seven scenes. The action takes place in England in the year 1587.

Press: Susan Bloch, William Schelble
Stage Managers: Barbara-Mae Phillips, Craig Anderson

* Closed Dec. 18, 1971 after 44 performances and 13 previews.
† Succeeded by: 1. Robert Christian, 2. Jack Gwillim, 3. Harold Miller

Martha Swope Photos

Top: (L) Aline MacMahon, Salome Jens (R) Sydney Walker, Philip Bosco, Stephen Elliott

Nancy Marchand, Philip Bosco, Salome Jens
Above: Bosco, Marchand

FORUM THEATER

Opened Thursday, November 18, 1971.*
The Repertory Theatre of Lincoln Center (Jules Irving, Director) presents:

PEOPLE ARE LIVING THERE

By Athol Fugard; Director; John Berry; Setting, Douglas W. Schmidt; Lighting, John Gleason; Costumes, Jeanne Button; Hairstylist, Jim Sullivan

CAST

Milly...Estelle Parsons
Don...Leonard Frey
Shorty...Peter Rogan
Sissy..Diana Davila†

UNDERSTUDIES: Milly, Lois DeBanzie; Don, Peter Weil; Shorty, Mark Woods; Sissy, Kathleen Doyle

A Play in two acts. The action takes place at the present time in the kitchen of an old, two-storied house in Braamfontein, Johannesburg, South Africa.

Press: Susan Bloch, William Schelble
Stage Manager: Patrick Horrigan, Brian Meister

* Closed Dec. 4, 1971 after 20 performances and 6 previews.
† Succeeded by Susan Sharkey

Martha Swope Photos

Peter Rogan, Leonard Frey, Estelle Parsons
Top Right: Leonard Frey, Estelle Parsons

THE FORUM

Opened Wednesday, December 29, 1971.*
The Repertory Theater of Lincoln Center and its Explorations in The Forum present:

DELICATE CHAMPIONS

Written and Directed by Stephen Varble; Production Stage Manager, Craig Anderson; Assistant Stage Manager, Kevin Constant.

CAST

Avis Honor	Sally Kirkland
Stephanie	Patricia Gaul
Natural Clemens	Jude Jade
Roger Reynolds	Tom Parrish
Princess Frefreara	Ruby Lynn Reyner
Eugenia Morse Reynolds	Sharon Gans
Tungsten Deed	Charles Berendt
Brave Trimtriptraum	Martin Kove
The King	J. K. Quinn

"A Series of words and movements concerning love and happiness."
* Closed Jan. 1, 1972 after limited engagement of 6 performances. (No photos available)

VIVIAN BEAUMONT THEATER

Opened Thursday, January 6, 1972.*
The Repertory Theater of Lincoln Center (Jules Irving, Director) presents:

NARROW ROAD TO THE DEEP NORTH

By Edward Bond; Director, Dan Sullivan; Settings, Douglas W. Schmidt; Lighting, John Gleason; Costumes, Carrie Fishbein Robbins; Music, Stanley Silverman; Movement Consultant, Margaret Newman; Production Assistants, Wesley Fata, Paul Zalon, Byrna Wasserman, Shogo Kato, Bruce Brown; Hairstylist, Jim Sullivan

CAST

Basho	Robert Symonds
Kiro	Andy Robinson
Argi	James Cahill
Tola	James Tolkan
Heigoo	Robert Christian
Breebree	Lawrence Wolf
Shogo	Cleavon Little
Prime Minister	Philip Bosco
Commodore	Sydney Walker
Georgina	Martha Henry
First Peasant	Harold Miller
Peasant Woman	Marilyn Meyers
Man in the Sack	Ray Fry
Nun	Susan Sharkey†
Gunner Tar	Richard Greene
Gunner Tar's Mate	Robert Phalen
Second Peasant	Stuart Pankin
Peasant Wife	Susan Sharkey†
Man from the River	Richard Kline
Stage Managers	Luis Avalos, Crickett Coan, James Cook

PEASANTS, SOLDIERS, ETC.: Richard Greene, Richard Kline, Marilyn Meyers, Harold Miller, Stuart Pankin, Ronald Roston, Susan Sharkey, Ray Stewart, Peter Weil, Mark Woods

A Play in two parts and ten scenes with an introduction. The action takes place in Japan about the seventeenth, eighteenth, or nineteenth centuries.

Press: Susan Bloch, William Schelble
Stage Managers: Patrick Horrigan, Barbara-Mae Phillips

* Closed Feb. 12, 1972 after 44 performances and 12 previews.
† Succeeded by Marilyn Meyers

Martha Swope Photos

Cleavon Little Above: Richard Greene, Robert Phalen, Martha Henry

Robert Symonds, Andy Robinson

THE FORUM
Opened Thursday, January 13, 1972*
The Repertory Theater of Lincoln Center presents the
American premiere of:

THE RIDE ACROSS LAKE CONSTANCE

By Peter Handke; Translated by Michael Roloff; Director,
Carl Weber; Settings and Costumes, Dahl Delu; Lighting,
John Gleason; Hairstylist, Jim Sullivan; Musical Direction,
Roland Gagnon; Movement, Don Redlich.

CAST

Kathleen Doyle ....Kathleen Doyle
Stephen Elliott .... Stephen Elliott
Paul Hecht..Paul Hecht
Salome Jens ....Salome Jens
Priscilla Pointer ....Priscilla Pointer
Keene Curtis ....Keene Curtis
Margaret Howell .... Margaret Howell
Kathryn Howell .... Kathryn Howell

STANDBYS AND UNDERSTUDIES: Misses Jens and
Pointer, Lois De Banzie; Messrs Curtis and Elliott, Robert
Stattel; Mr. Hecht, Ray Stewart; Miss Doyle, Susan Sharkey;
Howell Twins, Kathleen Doyle.

A Play presented without intermission.

Press: Susan Bloch, William Schelble

* Closed Jan. 29, 1972 after 20 performances and 6 previews.

Martha Swope Photos

**Top: Salome Jens, Stephen Elliott, Paul Hecht,
Keene Curtis, Priscilla Pointer**

Priscilla Pointer, Keene Curtis

THE FORUM

Opened Wednesday, February 23, 1972*
The Repertory Theater of Lincoln Center presents:

ANNA SOKOLOW'S PLAYERS PROJECT

Directed and Choreographed by Anna Sokolow; General Manager, Judith Hankins; Stage Manager, Penny Peters; Press, Susan Bloch, William Schelble

PROGRAM

"Act without Words" by Samuel Beckett; Music, Joel Thome; Performed by Henry Smith "A Short Lecture and Demonstration on the Evolution of Ragtime as presented by Jelly Roll Morton" narrated by Antonio Azito; Pianist, Henry Smith; Danced by Lorry May and Jim May "Magritte-Magritte": 1. "The Lovers" with music by Alexander Scriabin; danced by Margaret Fargnoli and Henry Smith, 2. "The Great War" with poem by John White and performed by Antonio Azito, 3. "Discovery" with music by Maurice Ravel; danced by Tonia Shimlin, 4. "The Troubled Sleeper" with music by Franz Liszt and Maurice Ravel, danced by Jim May, 5. "The Ideas of the Acrobat" with music by Eric Satie, poem by Paul Eluard, narrated by Antonio Azito, and danced by Lorry May, 6. "The Month of Harvest" with poem by Edgar Allen Poe, performed by Antonio Azito, Jim May, and Henry Smith, 7. "The Threatened Assassin" with music by Bal Musette, text by John White, performed by Margaret Fargnoli, Antonio Azito, Jim May, Henry Smith, 8. "The Red Model" with poem by John White.

* Presented for 6 performances only through Feb. 26, 1972.

Photo by Bil

Antonio Azito, Margaret Fargnoli, Jim May, Henry Smith in "Magritte-Magritte: The Threatened Assassin"

THE FORUM

Opened Thursday, March 9, 1972*
The Repertory Theater of Lincoln Center presents:

THE DUPLEX

By Ed Bullins; Director, Gilbert Moses; Settings, Kert Lundell; Lighting, John Gleason; Costumes, Bernard Johnson; Music, Gilbert Moses; Lyrics, Ed Bullins; Music arranged and directed by Coleridge-Taylor Perkinson; Technical Director, Barnett Epstein; Hairstyles, Jim Sullivan; Production Assistant, Gary Robertson

CAST

Velma Best	Mary Alice
Montgomery Henderson	Johnny Hartman
Tootsie Franklin	Albert Hall†1
Marco Polo Henderson	Carl Mikal Franklin†2
Steve Benson	Les Roberts
Mamma	Clarice Taylor
Sister Sukie	Phylicia Ayers-Allen
Pops	Joseph Attles
O. D. Best	Frank Adu†3
Crook	Kirk Kirksey
Marie Horton	Norma Donaldson
Wanda	Marie Thomas

UNDERSTUDIES: Velma, / Sukie/ Wanda/ Carolyn Byrd; Montgomery/Marco/Crook, J. Herbert Kerr, Jr.; Marie/-Mamma, Yvonne Warden; Pops, Kirk Kirksey

"A Black love fable in four movements." The action takes place in the early 1960's in a duplex in Southern California.

Press: Susan Bloch, William Schelble
Stage Managers: Patrick Horrigan, Brian Meister

* Closed Apr. 1, 1972 after limited run of 28 regular performances and 6 previews.
† Succeeded by: 1. Charles Weldon, 2. J. Herbert Kerr, Jr., 3. James Hainesworth

Martha Swope Photos

Carl Mikal Franklin, Marie Thomas, Norma Donaldson Les Roberts Above: Les Roberts, Mary Alice

VIVIAN BEAUMONT THEATER

Opened Thursday, March 2, 1972*
The Repertory Theater of Lincoln Center presents:

TWELFTH NIGHT

By William Shakespeare; Director, Ellis Rabb; Settings, Douglas W. Schmidt; Lighting, John Gleason; Costumes, Ann Roth; Music, Cathy MacDonaid; Vocal Director, Ronald Gagnon; Production Assistant, Kevin Constant; Hairstyles, Jim Sullivan

CAST

Orsino	Moses Gunn
Curio	Crickett Coan
Valentine	Robert Christian†1
Viola	Blythe Danner
Sea Captain	Richard Greene
Sir Toby Belch	Sydney Walker
Maria	Cynthia Belgrave
Sir Andrew Aguecheek	Leonard Frey
Feste	George Pentecost
Olivia	Martha Henry
Malvolio	Rene Auberjonois
Antonio	Philip Bosco
Sebastian	Stephen McHattie
Fabian	Harold Miller
Soldiers	Charles Turner†2, Richard Kline
Priest	Ray Fry†3
Sailor	Richard Kline
Attendants	Kathleen Doyle, Marilyn Meyers, Stuart Pankin, Robert Phalen, Peter Weil, Mark Woods

A comedy performed in two acts. The action takes place in Illyria.

Press: Susan Bloch, William Schelble
Stage Managers: Barbara-Mae Phillips, Craig Anderson, Robert Lowe

* Closed April 8, 1972 after limited engagement of 44 performances and 12 previews.
† Succeeded by: 1. Charles Turner, 2. Mark Woods, 3. Stuart Pankin

Martha Swope Photos

Blythe Danner, Martha Henry
Top Right: entire cast

George Pentecost, Rene Auberjonois Above: Blythe Danner, Stephen McHattie

VIVIAN BEAUMONT THEATER

Opened Thursday, April 27, 1972*
The Repertory Theater of Lincoln Center presents:

THE CRUCIBLE

By Arthur Miller; Director, John Berry; Lighting and Settings, Jo Mielziner; Costumes, Carrie Fishbein Robbins; Vocal Director, Roland Gagnon; Hairstyles, Jim Sullivan; Production Assistants, Nancy Barron, Douglas Kennedy

CAST

Reverend Parris	Jerome Dempsey
Betty Parris	Alexandra Stoddart
Tituba	Theresa Merritt
Abigail Williams	Pamela Payton-Wright
Susanna Walcott	Crickett Coan
Mrs. Ann Putnam	Pauline Flanagan
Thomas Putnam	Ben Hammer
Mercy Lewis	Kathleen Doyle
Mary Warren	Nora Heflin
John Proctor	Robert Foxworth
Rebecca Nurse	Aline MacMahon
Giles Corey	Sydney Walker
Reverend John Hale	Philip Bosco
Elizabeth Proctor	Martha Henry
Francis Nurse	Wendell Phillips
Ezekiel Cheever	Richard Greene†
Marshal Herrick	Richard Kline
Judge Hathorne	Robert Phalen
Deputy Governor Danforth	Stephen Elliott
Sarah Good	Doris Rich
Hopkins	Stuart Pankin
Deputy	Mark Woods

UNDERSTUDIES: Proctor, Richard Greene; Elizabeth/Ann/Sarah, Barbara Tarbuck; Abigail, Crickett Coan; Tituba, Louise Stubbs; Mary, Kathleen Doyle; Danforth/Giles/Francis, John Newton; Hale, Robert Phalen; Parris/Putnam, Stuart Panken; Hathorne/Cheever, Richard Kline; Rebecca, Doris Rich; Herrick/Hopkins, Mark Woods; Betty/Susanna/Mercy, Nomi Mitty.

A drama in 4 acts performed with one intermission. The action takes place in 1692 in Salem, Mass.

Press: Susan Bloch, William Schelble
Stage Managers: Patrick Horrigan, Barbara-Mae Phillips

* Closed June 3, 1972 after limited run of 44 performances and 13 previews.
† Succeeded by John Newton

Martha Swope Photos

Top Left: Theresa Merritt, Philip Bosco

Philip Bosco, Robert Foxworth Above:
Martha Henry, Robert Foxworth

Martha Henry, Robert Foxworth, Stephen Elliott

THE FORUM
Opened Thursday, May 4, 1972*
The Repertory Theater of Lincoln Center presents:

SUGGS

By David Wiltse; Director, Dan Sullivan; Setting, Douglas W. Schmidt; Lighting, John Gleason; Costumes, Jeanne Button; Hairstyles, Jim Sullivan; Production Assistant, Douglas Kennedy

CAST

Bum .... Charles Turner
Talker.. Robert Levine
Crone .... Joan Pape
Suggs .... William Atherton
Goff ....Ralph Bell
Jo Ann ....Lee Lawson

UNDERSTUDIES: Suggs, Richard Kline; Jo Ann, Nomi Mitty; Goff, John Newton; Bum/Talker, Fred Morsell; Crone, Barbara Tarbuck

A comedy in two acts. The action takes place at the present time in New York City.

Press: Susan Bloch, William Schelble
Stage Managers: Craig Anderson, Robert Lowe

* Closed May 20, 1972 after limited engagement of 20 performances and 6 previews.

Martha Swope Photos

REPERTORY THEATER-IN-THE-SCHOOLS
Opened Wednesday, February 2, 1972*
The Repertory Theater of Lincoln Center presents:

NATURAL

Conceived and Directed by Tim Ward; Music, Arthur Miller; Stage Managers, William Cunningham, Jonathan Penzner; Press, Susan Bloch, William Schelble

CAST

Buddy Butler
Jessie Hill
Mel Johnson, Jr.
Michael Lewis
William Thomas

* Played 42 performances in city and state high schools. (No photos available)

Robert Levine, Lee Lawson, Joan Pape
Top Right: Lee Lawson, William Atherton

Ralph Bell, William Atherton
Above: William Atherton

77

OFF-BROADWAY PRODUCTIONS

THEATRE DE LYS
Opened Wednesday, June 2, 1971.*
C. K. Alexander presents:

THE JUSTICE BOX

By Michael Robert David; Director, Arthur Alan Seidelman; Music, Basheer Qadar; Designed by John Doepp; Costumes, Patrice Alexander; Presented by special arrangement with Lucille Lortel Productions; Technical Director, Jack Magnifico; Production Assistant, Micky Tekoah; Sound, Gary and Timmy Harris

CAST

Le Dix	Michael Lipton
Frechette	C. K. Alexander
Mammalou	Tally Brown
Jules	Michael Procaccino
Oscar	Richard Alfieri
Francoise	Gretchen Corbett
Waiter	Jayme Daniel
Delphine	Sally Kirkland
Bleyer	Jerome Dempsey

Performed without intermission. The action takes place at the present time in Paris.

General Manager: Paul B. Berkowsky
Press: Saul Richman
Stage Managers: Larry Spiegel, Jayme Daniel

* Closed June 5, 1971 after 7 performances.

Sally Kirkland, Tally Brown (above)

EASTSIDE PLAYHOUSE
Opened Sunday, June 6, 1971.*
Art James, Carl Sawyer, Ted Rado present:

CHARLIE WAS HERE AND NOW HE'S GONE

By Dennis Turner; Director, Jerry Adler, Gilbert Moses; Settings, David Chapman; Costumes, Jeanne Button; Lighting, Martin Aronstein; Associate Manager, Bob MacDonald; Production Assistant, Anthony Neely

CAST

Young Charlie	Philip Williamson
Allan	Robert Guillaume
Carla	Rosalind Cash
Charlie	Joe Morton†
First Mover	Jerome Anello
Second Mover	Norman T. Marshall
Scott	David Friedman
Sailor	Robert LuPone

A Drama in 2 acts and 5 scenes. The action takes place in the street, and in Charlie's apartment.

General Managers: Norman E. Rothstein, Patricia Carney
Company Manager: Barry Hoffman
Press: Gifford/Wallace, Carl Sawyer
Stage Managers: Nate Barnett, Norman T. Marshall

* Closed June 20, 1971 after 17 performances.
† Played in previews by Donny Burks

Donny Burks, Rosalind Cash

Martha Swope Photo

THEATRE DE LYS

Opened Thursday, June 17, 1971.*
Henry Street Settlement's New Federal Theatre (Woodie King/Dick Williams) presents:

BLACK GIRL

By J. E. Franklin; Director, Shauneille Perry; Setting, Charles Mills, Lighting, Buddy Butler; Costumes, Femi; Bertram Beck, Executive Director; Production Assistant, Ben Frazier; Technical Director, Jack Magnifico; Presented by special arrangement with Lucille Lortel Productions

CAST

Billie Jean	Kishasha
Little Earl	Arthur W. French III
Sheryl	Lorraine Ryder
Norma	Gloria Edwards
Ruth Ann	Loretta Greene
Mama Rosie	Louise Stubbs
Mu'dear	Minnie Gentry
Mr. Herbert	Jimmy Hayeson
Earl	Arthur French
Netta	Saundra Sharp

A Play presented without intermission. The action takes place at the present time in a small town in Texas.

General Manager: Paul B. Berkowsky
Press: Howard Atlee, David Roggensack, Irene Gandy
Stage Manager: Buddy Butler

* Closed Jan. 16, 1972 after 247 performances.

Bert Andrews Photos

Louise Stubbs, Arthur French, Kishasha, Gloria Edwards
Top: Louise Stubbs, Minnie Gentry (standing)

CIRCLE IN THE SQUARE

Opened Wednesday, June 23, 1971.*
Theodore Mann, Paul Libin, Paul Jacobson present:

THE LAST ANALYSIS

By Saul Bell; Director, Theodore Mann; Scenery, Marsha L. Eck; Costumes, Joseph G. Aulisi; Lighting, Roger Morgan; Presented in association with Howard A. Schwartz and Jack T. Schwartz; Production Manager, Charles Hamilton; Production Assistant, Jonathan Sand

CAST

Bummidge	Joseph Wiseman
Imogen	Diana Davila
Winkleman	David Brooks
Louie Mott	Martin Garner
TV Technician	Joseph Stern
Madge	Grayson Hall
Max	Edward Zang
Bertram	David Margulies
Pamela	Lucille Patton
Aufschnitt	Shimen Ruskin
Bella	Louise Troy
Gallupo	Hansford Rowe
Tante Frumkah	Jane Hoffman
Western Union Messenger	Daniel Kreitzberg
Fiddleman	Humphrey Davis
Kalbfuss	Marvin Silbersher

A Comedy in two acts. The action takes place in a two-story loft in a warehouse on the West side of New York at the present time.

Press: Merle Debuskey, Bob Ullman
Stage Manager: Jane Neufeld

* Closed Aug. 1, 1971 after 46 performances.

Joseph Wiseman (C) and cast

PUERTO RICAN TRAVELING THEATRE

Opened Tuesday, August 10, 1971.*
The Department of Cultural Affairs, and the Mayor's Urban Action Task Force presents:

A DRAMATIZED ANTHOLOGY OF PUERTO RICAN SHORT STORIES

Produced and Adapted by Miriam Colon; Director, Pablo Cabrera; Scenery, Peter Harvey; Costumes, Christina Giannini; Lighting, Roger Morgan; Administrator, Allen Davis III; Community Coordinator, Larry Ramos; Technical Directors, Don Hinde, Robert Ellowitz; Production Assistant, Peter Morales

CAST

Felix Antelo	Iris Martinez
Reinaldo Arana	Betty Miller
Emil Belasco	Linda Monteiro
Don Blakely	Peter Morales
Bob Bowyer	Gilda Orlandi
C. D. Creasap	Iraida Polanco
Shelly Desai	Nelson Ramos
Hector Elias	Susan Ramos
Robert Ellowitz	Marlo Timmons
Edwin Enrique	Manu Tupou
Phillip Filiato	Tomy Vargas
Frances Garcia	Jose Vega
Jose Garcia	Nancy Vega
Don Hinde	James Victor
Ricardo Matamoros	

STORIES: "Black Sun," "Patchouli," "The Innocent," "Compadre Baltasar's Feast," "Kipling and I," "El Josco," "Interlude," "The Ladies' Man," "The Lead Box that Couldn't Be Opened," "The Protest"

Company Manager: C. George Willard
Press: Alan Eichler
Stage Manager: C. D. Creasap
* Closed Sept. 11, 1971 after 39 performances in the City parks and streets.

Iris Martinez, Reinaldo Arana, Betty Miller

Friedman-Abeles Photos

JONES BEACH THEATRE

Opened Thursday, July 8, 1971.*
Guy Lombardo presents:

THE SOUND OF MUSIC

Music, Richard Rodgers; Lyrics, Oscar Hammerstein 2nd; Book, Howard Lindsay, Russel Crouse; Suggested by "The Trapp Family Singers" by Maria Augusta Trapp; Director, John Fearnley; Scenery, Peter Wolf; Costumes, Winn Morton; Lighting, Peggy Clark; Orchestrations, Robert Russell Bennett; Choral Arrangements, Trudi Rittman; Choreography, Vincent Alexander; Musical Direction, Oscar Kosarin; Entire Production under the supervision of Arnold Spector; Assistant Conductor, Fred Manzella; Choral Director, Robert Monteil

CAST

Maria Rainer	Constance Towers
Sister Berthe	Gloria Hodes
Sister Margaretta	Leonore Lanzillotti
Mother Abbess	Maggie Task
Sister Sophia	Jeanne Shea
Captain Georg von Trapp	John Michael King
Franz	John LeGrand
Frau Schmidt	Helen Noyes
Liesl	Karen Jablons
Friedrich	Charles Beattie
Louisa	Doreen Miller
Brigitta	Janina Mathews
Kurt	Richard Arnold Beattie
Marta	Maureen McGrath
Gertl	Barbara Ann Beattie
Rolf Gruber	Vincent Alexander
Elsa Schraeder	Nancy Eaton
Ursula	Sherry Lambert
Max Detweiler	Christopher Hewett
Herr Zeller	Larry Swansen
Frau Zeller	Marilyn Murphy
Baron Elberfeld	Lee Cass
Baroness Elberfeld	Jessica Quinn
A Postulant	Sandi Sanders
Admiral von Schreiber	Jay Velie

NEIGHBORS, NUNS, NOVICES, POSTULANTS, VILLAGERS, GARDENERS, NAZIS, GUESTS, CHILDREN: Jeanette Branin, Lynn East, Cindy Ek, Doris Galiber, Fran Hice, Sherry Lambert, Bobbi Lange, Joan Lindstrom, Lione J. Jodis, Marilyn Murphy, Jessica Quinn, Carol Raymont, Mary Ann Rydzeski, Sandi Sanders, Phyllis Sposta, Dixie Stewart, Rex Bennetts, Jeff Cahn, Peter Clark, Mark East, Paul Flores, Lloyd Harris, Brian McClean, Robert Monteil

STANDBYS AND UNDERSTUDIES: Maria, Jeanne Shea; Captain, Lee Cass; Max, John LeGrand; Mother Abbess, Elsa, Gloria Hodes; Berthe, Jessica Quinn; Sophia, Dixie Stewart; Margaretta, Jeanette Branin; Liesl, Sherry Lambert; Rolf, Rex Bennetts; Frau Schmidt, Marilyn Murphy; Franz, Paul Sposta; Marta, Gretl, Cindy Elk; Friedrich, Kurt, Brian McClean

MUSICAL NUMBERS: Grand Opening, "Praeludium," "The Sound of Music," "Maria," "My Favorite Things," "Do, Re, Mi," "You Are Sixteen," "The Lonely Goatherd," "How Can Love Survive?," "The Laendler Waltz," "So Long, Farewell," "Climb Every Mountain," "No Way to Stop It," "Something Good," "Processional," "Edelweiss."

A Musical in two acts. The action takes place in Austria early in 1938 in and near Nonnberg Abbey and the von Trapp villa.

Managing Director: Arnold Spector
Company Manager: Sam Pagliaro
Press: Saul Richman
Stage Managers: Mortimer Halpern, William Krot, Lloyd Harris, Edward Julien

* Closed Sept. 5, 1971

Barry Kramer Photos

Christopher Hewett, Nancy Eaton
Top: Constance Towers, John Michael King

81

ACTORS PLAYHOUSE

Opened Thursday, September 9, 1971.*
Marlow Ferguson presents:

OUT OF CONTROL

With "The Marriage of the Telephone Company Man," both by Martin Craft; Director, Frank Bara; Set, Alfred Carrier; Costumes, Danny Morgan

CAST

"Out of Control"

Sid Barsh	J. C. Barrett
Maisy Lake	Dianne Trulock
Joe Rice	Kricker James
Jeff Rice	Glenn Peters
Howie	Alexander Duncan
Terri Doolan	Blainie Logan
Mrs. Doolan	Mary Carr Taylor
Cameron Frosch	Duane Morris
Julie Coleman	Mary Magone

In three scenes, the action takes place in 1947 in a small Pennsylvania town.

"The Marriage of the Telephone Company Man"

Lauri's Brother	Alexander Duncan
Irvin	Duane Morris
Lauri	Blainie Logan

Presented in two scenes.

Press: Max Eisen, Milly Schoenbaum
Stage Manager: Blainie Logan

* Closed Sept, 12, 1971 after 5 performances.

Carl Samrock Photo

Dianne Trulock, J. C. Barrett

**Joe Masiell, Lynn Gerb, Yolande Bavan,
Scott Jarvis**

THEATRE FOUR

Opened Sunday, September 12, 1971.*
New Era Productions Inc. presents:

LEAVES OF GRASS

"A Musical Celebration" based on the writings of Walt Whitman; Adaptation and Music by Stan Harte, Jr.; Direction, Stan Harte, Jr., Bert Michaels; Musical Staging, Bert Michaels; Designed by David Chapman; Score Arranged by Bill Brohn; Musical Director, Karen Gustafson; Technical Director, Michael Wheeler; Sound, Gary and Timmy Harris

CAST

Joe Masiell†
Lynn Gerb
Scott Jarvis
Yolande Bavan

MUSICAL NUMBERS: "Come Said My Soul," "There Is That in Me," "Give Me," "Song of the Open Road," "Who Makes Much of a Miracle?," "28 Men," "A Woman Waits for Me," "As Adam," "Do You Suppose," "Enough," "Dirge for Two Veterans," "How Solemn," "Oh Captain! My Captain!," "Pioneers," "Song of Myself," "Excelsior," "Twenty Years," "Unseen Buds," "Goodbye, My Fancy," "Thanks in Old Age," "I Hear America Singing"

Presented in two acts.

General Managers: Norman E. Rothstein,
Patricia Carney
Company Manager: Bob MacDonald
Press: Seymour Krawitz, Patricia Krawitz, Vicki Stein
Stage Manager: Jan Moerel

* Closed Oct. 24, 1971 after 49 performances.
† Succeeded by Ed Evanko

Friedman-Abeles Photo

EASTSIDE PLAYHOUSE

Opened Thursday, October 7, 1971.*
Richard Scanga and Adela Holzer present:

WHERE HAS TOMMY FLOWERS GONE?

By Terrence McNally; Director, Jacques Levy; Sets, David Chapman; Lighting, Marc B. Weiss; Costumes, James Berton Harris; Visuals, Ed Bowes, Bernadette Mayer

CAST

Tommy Flowers	Robert Drivas
Ben Delight	Wallace Rooney
Nedda Lemon	Kathleen Dabney †
The Girls	Barbara Worthington
The Men	F. Murray Abraham
The Women	Marion Paone

A Play in two acts.

General Manager: Michael Brandman
Press: Alan Eichler, James J. O'Rourke
Stage Managers: Nicholas Russiyan, Kate M. Pollock

* Closed Dec. 12, 1971 after 78 performances.
† Succeeded by Sally Kirkland

Martha Swope Photo

Right: F. Murray Abraham, Marion Paone, Robert Drivas

Mary Lynn Kolas, Geoffrey Webb, Zan Charisse, Virginia Seidel

PLAZA 9 MUSIC HALL

Opened Thursday, October 7, 1971.*
Costas Omero in association with "Rio Plaza Productions Ltd." by special arrangement with Cafe Chantant Corp. presents:

LOOK ME UP

Conception and Book, Laurence Taylor; Produced and Directed by Costas Omero; Choreography, Bob Tucker; Musical Arrangements, Horace Diaz; Vocal and Dance Arrangments, Gene Casey; Musical Director, Ozzie Ray; Sets, James Steward Morcum; Costumes, Rosemary Heyer; Lighting, Augusto Martinez; Assistant to the Producer, George Nocera

CAST

Ted Agress	Mary Lynn Kolas
Zan Charisse	Linda Kurtz
Kevin Christopher	Don Liberto
Connie Day†	Jeff Richards
Robin Field	Virginia Seidel
Linda Gerard	Geofrey Webb

MUSICAL NUMBERS: "The Forerunners," "Those Songs and Those Singers," "Hallelujah Get Happy," "Happy Feet," "Someone to Watch over Me," "Making Whoopee," "Button Up Your Overcoat," "In the Park," "Bidin' My Time," "Can't Help Lovin' That Man," "Strike Up the Band," "Drums in My Heart," "It Had to Be You," "If You Knew Susie," "Thinking of You," "Best Things in Life Are Free," "Glad Rag Doll," "Yes, Sir, That's My Baby," "Baby Face," "Aba Daba," "Manhattan," "How Long Has This Been Going On?," "Great Day"

A "Musical Revue of Nostalgia of the years of sophisticated innocence" in two parts.

General Manager: Harry Zweibel
Press: Harvey Sabinson, Lee Solters, Sandra Manley
Stage Manager: Robert Tucker

* Closed May 21, 1972 after 394 performances.
† Succeeded by Marilyn Cooper

GRACE RAINEY ROGERS AUDITORIUM

Opened Saturday, October 9, 1971*
The Metropolitan Museum of Art presents:

A KING FOR ALL AGES

Written and Directed by Carella Alden; Technical Director, Douglas Wallace; Tapes, George Mittag; Projectionist, Louis J. Cardamone; Lighting, Sy Wong; Costumes, Brooks-Van Horn; Art Consultant, Roberta Paine

CAST

King Arthur	Marshall Borden
Warriors	David Kerman, William Kiehl
Merlin	Claude Marks
Sir Hector	Tom McDermott
Sir Kay	George Gitto
Arthur as a boy	Dean Crane, Jr.
Sir Agravaine	Richard Kuss
Sir Gawaine	Igors Gavon
Sir Gaheris	Raymond Lynch
Sir Bedivere	David Kerman
Sir Lucan	William Kiehl
Archbishop	Stanley Bakis
Lady of the Lake	Anne Countryman
Queen Guenevere	Christine Lienard
Sir Lancelot	John H. Fields
Ladies of the court	Susan Tabor, Betty George, Dorothy Leeds, Jean Baur
Chaperone	Lori Shepard
Pages	Michael Colleary, David Bloch
Sir Mordred	Joseph Francis
Sir Gareth	Michael Arle
Lynette	Michelle Bayard
Lady Lyonors	April Gilmore
Unicorn	Lori Shepard
Sir Tristan	Jo Ann Williams
Wizard	Jack Adams
Jousters	Raymond Lynch, Joseph Francis
An Ancient	Stanley Bakis
Sir Galahad	Gregory Long
Narrators	Elsa Raven, William Kiehl

Presented in 6 scenes with prologue and epilogue. The action takes place in Saxon Britain in the early sixth century, and in the Middle Ages.

Stage Managers: Chester Chorney, Vito Luongo, Lori Shepard, Nancy Cole

* Presented for 3 performances only, closing Oct. 11, 1971.

Tom McDermott, Igors Gavin, George Gitto, Dean Crane, Jr.

GUGGENHEIM MUSEUM

Opened Monday, October 11, 1971.*
Brooke Lappin and Bruce Bassman in association with Michael Edlin, presents:

THE JAMES JOYCE MEMORIAL LIQUID THEATRE

Conceived and Directed by Steven Kent in conjunction with the Company Theatre Ensemble; Music, Jack Rowe, Robert Walter, Lance Larsen; Musical Director, Jack Rowe; Scenic and Lighting Designs, Donald Harris; Projections, William Dannevik, Steven Kent; Maze created by Company Theatre; Associate Director, Jean E. McFaddin; Hairstylist, James McLernon; Administrative Director, Barry Opper; Technical Director, Russell Pyle; Production Managers, Bruce Bassman, Donald Harris

CAST

THE COMPANY THEATRE ENSEMBLE: Arthur Allen, Gar Campbell, Gladys Carmichael, William Dannevik, Donald Harris, Nancy Hickey, Larry Hoffman, William Hunt, Steven Kent, Lance Larsen, Candace Laughlin, Polita Marks, Sandra Morgan, Marcina Motter, Michael Carlin Pierce, Dennis Redfield, Wiley Rinaldi, Jack Rowe, Richard Serpe, Trish Soodik, Michael Stefani

THE LIQUID THEATRE COMPANY: Tony Barbato, Bruce Bouchard, Joseph Capone, Carrotte, Doug Carfrae, Richard Cassese, Bob Cohen, Tony Giambrone, Virginia Glynn, Jenny Gooch, Margaret Goodenow, Scott Gruher, Oleta Hale, Nancy Hart, Amy Hass, Michael Haynes, Sandy Helberg, Nancy Heikin, Jonathan Hunter, Janis Jablecki, Kathleen Joyce, Leigh Lanzet, John Livosi, Constance Mellors, Vincent J. Millard, Roger Nelson, Steve Nisbet, Ellen Parker, Cara Robin, John Roddick, Eileen Roehm, Susan Saltz, Ervin Stiggs, Michael Thayer, Gary White, Fritzi Winnick

Press: Gifford/Wallace, Tom Trenkle
Stage Manager: Richard Serpe

* Closed March 15, 1972 after 189 performances.

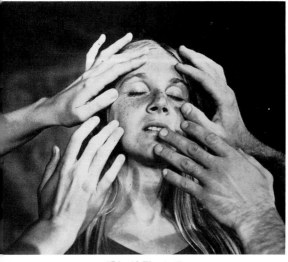

"Liquid Theatre"

BLACKFRIARS' THEATRE

Opened Thursday, October 14, 1971.*
The Blackfriars Guild presents:

LIB COMES HIGH

By Joan Thellusson Nourse; Director, Jerry N. Evans; Settings and Lighting, T. Fabian; Costumes, Susan Spector

CAST

Cora Grady Linton .... Marilyn J. Hudgins or Nita Ramsay
Dr. Stephen Linton .... John Cain or Doc Slevin
Father Thomas Grady ...... John M. Feeney or Jim Murphy

A Comedy in three acts. The action takes place in 1970 in the Lintons' livingroom in a small Westchester community.
Press: Emily Cowan
Stage Managers: Maureen Martin, Richard Dunham

* Closed Nov. 21, 1971 after a limited engagement of 40 performances.

PROVINCETOWN PLAYHOUSE

Opened Thursday, October 14, 1971.*
Tom Millott presents:

FRIENDS AND RELATIONS

By Eugene Yanni; Director, Tom Millott; Designed by Steven Askinazy; Assistant Directors, Marilyn Fried, Elizabeth Stearns; Production Assistant, Dick Shoberg

CAST

"Friends."
Melba .... Grayson Hall
Treesa .... Madeleine Sherwood

The action takes place late afternoon in a Pelham Bay apartment

"Relations"
Nita Moon .... Madeleine Sherwood
Stephanie de Milo .... Grayson Hall

Standby: Pat Lavalle
The action takes place mid-afternoon in a basement in the Bronx

Business Manager: David Chase
Press: Samuel Lurie
Stage Manager: Blair McFadden

* Closed Oct. 17, 1971 after 6 performances and 17 previews.

Bert Andrews Photos

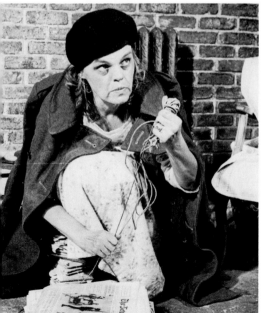

**Madeleine Sherwood, and above with
Grayson Hall**

McALPIN ROOFTOP THEATRE

Opened Monday, October 18, 1971.*
Theatre 1972 (Richard Barr-Charles Woodward) presents:

DRAT!

Book and Lyrics, Fred Bluth; Music, Steven Metcalf; Conceived and Directed by Fred Bluth; Design Supervision, Christian Thee; Lighting, Richard Nelson; Costume Supervision, Tomianne Wiley; Musical Director, Steven Metcalf; Musical Arrangements, Don Pippin; Assistant to Producers, David Zimmerman; Production Supervisor, Peter Forward

CAST

Sally Merryweather	Bonnie Franklin
Widow Merryweather	Jane Connell
Professor Souse	Gary Gage
Eddy Applebee	Walter Bobbie
Elmer Applebee	James "Red" Wilcher
Lotta Lovejoy	Carol Swarbrick
Poppy Applebee	Donna Sands
General Arden Clobber	Jane Connell

STANDBYS AND UNDERSTUDIES: Sally, Widow, Cherry Davis; Eddy Elmer, Charles Repole; Souse, Joseph Palmieri

MUSICAL NUMBERS: "Little Fairies," "Early Bird Eddy," "Walkin' in the Rain," "Friday, Friday," "My Geranium," "Kick It Around," "You and I," "Where Is the Man for Me?," "Frightened of the Dark," "Desperation Quintet," "Drat!," "Has Anyone Here Seen My Daddy?," "Lean on Me," "Sally," "Bye and Bye," "The Chase"

A Musical in 2 acts and 13 scenes. The action takes place in Plasterville, Iowa, and in New York City.

General Manager: Michael Kasdan
Press: Betty Lee Hunt, Ellen Levene, Henry Luhrman, Harriett Trachtenberg, Maria Pucci
Stage Managers: Murray Gitlin, Richard Foltz

* Closed Oct. 18, 1971 after 1 performance and 8 previews.

Martha Swope Photo

Gary Gage, Bonnie Franklin, Carol Swarbrick, Jane Connell

Jean Bruno, Max Gulack

ACTORS PLAYHOUSE

Opened Friday, October 22, 1971*
James J. Thesing and Fredric V. Ralston present:

A SONG FOR THE FIRST OF MAY

By Ted Pezzulo; Director, Anthony Wiles; Scenery, Hal Tine; Costumes, Fran Brassard; Lighting, John Urban; Production Assistant, Rossie Graziano

CAST

Norman	Max Gulack
Momo	William Robertson
Gracie	Jean Bruno
Orchid	Sheila Coonan
Cecil	Colin Hamilton

A play in three acts. The action takes place on the first of May in an upper West Side Irish bar in New York City.

General Manager: Thesing/Ralston Enterprises
Press: Betty Lee Hunt, Michael Alpert, Ellen Levene, Henry Luhrman, Don Parker, Maria Pucci, Harriett Trachtenberg
Stage Manager: Doug Ellis

* Closed Oct. 24, 1971 after 5 performances.

Carl Samrock Photo

CHERRY LANE THEATRE

Opened Sunday, October 24, 1971.*
Ken Gaston, Leonard Goldberg and A. I. Baron in association with Steven Beckler and Jon Delon present:

A GUN PLAY

By Yale M. Udoff; Director, Gene Frankel; Costumes, Sara
Brook; Scenery, Ralph Funicello, Marjorie Kellogg; Lighting,
Paul Sullivan; Associate Producer, William Gumperz; Hairstylist, Joe Tubens; Dance Music, Galt McDermott; Movement, Julie Arenal; Sound, Gary And Timmy Harris

CAST

Stan	Eugene Troobnick
Orlando	Arny Freeman
Wallace	Tony Musante
Lita	Lara Parker
Linden	William Bogert
Norma	M'el Dowd
Jack	Jim Weston
First Motorcycle Officer	John Doherty
George	Robert Moberly
Melinda	Kelly Wood
Fashion Model	Pat Evans
Second Motorcycle Officer	Ralph Maurer
Young Girl	Cheryl Houser
Johnni	Shane Ousey

The action takes place in a small club in a large American
city.

General Manager Fred Walker
Press: Betty Lee Hunt, Ellen Levene, Henry Luhrman,
Harriett Trachtenberg, Maria Pucci, Don Parker
Stage Managers: Peter B. Mumford, John Doherty

* Closed Nov. 13, 1971 after 23 performances.

Ted Yaple Photo

Eugene Troobnick, Tony Musante, Arny Freeman

PLAYERS THEATRE

Opened Monday, October 25, 1971.*
Harrass Productions, Inc. presents:

IN THE TIME OF HARRY HARASS

By Carolyn Rossi; Director, Janet Bruders; Set and Design,
Andy Dobrovich, Bill Balint; Lighting, Edward Goetz; Costumes, Annie Borys

CAST

Harry Harass	Warren Pincus
Charley the White and others	Bernard Erhard
The Wife and others	Heather Haven
The Son and others	Les Shenkel
The Daughter and others	Alice Elliott

Understudy: Don Dolan

A Comedy in two acts. The action takes place within one
day in the life of Harry Harass.

General Manager: Roy Franklyn
Press: Sol Jacobson, Lewis Harmon
Stage Managers: Regina Lynn, Don Dolan

* Closed Oct. 25, 1971 after one performance

Friedman-Abeles Photo

**Heather Haven, Warren Pincus (seated), Bernard
Erhard, Les Shenkel, Alice Elliott**

CIRCLE IN THE SQUARE

Opened Wednesday, October 27, 1971.*
Circle in the Square (Theodore Mann/Paul Libin) and
David J. Seltzer present:

F. JASMINE ADDAMS

Book, Carson McCullers, G Wood, Theodore Mann; Based
on "The Member of the Wedding" by Carson McCullers;
Music and Lyrics, G Wood; Director, Theodore Mann; Musi-
cal Director, Liza Redfield; Musical Arrangements, Luther
Henderson; Scenery, Marsha Louis Eck; Lighting, Roger
Morgan; Costumes, Joseph G. Aulisi; Musical Numbers
Staged by Patricia Birch; Production Manager, Kathleen
McGill; Production Assistant, Jonathan Sand

Johnny Doran, William LeMassena, Theresa Merritt,
Bill Biskup, Neva Small, Ericka Petersen

Friedman-Abeles Photo

CAST

Berenice Sadie Brown	Theresa Merritt
Frankie Addams	Neva Small
John Henry West	Johnny Doran
Honey Camden	Northern J. Calloway
T. T. Williams	Robert Kya-Hill
Mr. Addams	William LeMassena
Sis Laura	Alicia Marcelo
Jarvis	Bill Biskup
Janice	Erika Petersen
Barney MacKean	Edmund Gaynes
Mary Littlejohn	Carol Anne Ziske
Helen Fletcher	Page Miller
Doris Mackey	Merry Flershem

Understudy: Merry Flershem

MUSICAL NUMBERS: "How about You and Me," "If I had
A . . . ," "Miss Pinhead," "Baby, That's Love," "Did I Make
a Good Impression?," "Good as Anybody," "The We of Me,"
"Travellin' On," "Sunshine Tomorrow," "F. Jasmine Ad-
dams," "How Sweet Is Peach Ice Cream," "Do Me A Favor,"
"Another Day," "Quite Suddenly"

A Musical in five scenes without intermission. The action
takes place in the kitchen and backyard of the Addams'
household in a small Southern town from August to November of 1945.

Press: Merle Debuskey, M. J. Boyer
Stage Managers: Suzanne Egan, Bill Biskup

* Closed Oct. 31, 1971 after 6 performances.

SHERIDAN SQUARE PLAYHOUSE

Opened Tuesday, November 2, 1971.*
Edgar Lansbury, Stuart Duncan, Joseph Beruh in association with Nan Pearlman present:

LOUIS AND THE ELEPHANT

By Eddie Lawrence; Director, John Marley; Settings and
Lighting, William Pitkin; Costumes, Stanley Simmons; Sound,
Gigi Cascio; Technical Director, Don Hinds

CAST

"The Beautiful Mariposa"

Juan Ribera	Jaime Sanchez
Maria Rios	Liz Torres
Manuelo	Harvey Solin
Maid	Hope Cameron
Policemen	Josip Elic, Art Vasil

A hotel room in a small Kansas town

"Louis and the Elephant"

The Elephant	Lee Richardson
Thaddeus Armstrong	Josip Elic
Louis Bengal	Dan Frazer
Lulu Hopper	Louise Troy
Press Agent	Harvey Solin

A cellar nightclub in San Francisco

"The Adventure of Eddie Greshaw"

Eddie Greshaw	Lee Richardson
Harriet	Marge Redmond
Hester	Hope Cameron
Hedda Webb-Winters	Louise Troy

A large kitchen in an apartment on Manhattan's West Side

General Manager: Al Isaac
Press: Max Eisen, Milly Shoenbaum
Stage Manager: Gail Bell

* Closed Nov. 7, 1971 after 8 previews only.

Liz Torres, Harvey Solin, Jaime Sanchez

BARBIZON PLAZA THEATRE

Opened Tuesday, November 2, 1971.*
The Gert von Gontard Foundation presents Szene 1971 in:

KABALE UND LIEBE
(Cabals and Loves)

By Friedrich Schiller; Staged by Oscar Fritz Schuh; Scenery and Costumes, Ursula Schuh; Assistant Director, Axel Klingenberg; Technical Director/Lighting, Heinz Kraile, Friedrich Schoberth; Stage Manager, Gunther Seufert

CAST

Miller, Town Musician .... Wolfgang Dorich
His Wife.. Ilse Laux
Wurm, Secretary to the President .... Klaus Munster
Luise, Miller's daughter .... Esther Carola Regnier
Ferdinand, the President's Son................. Albert Rueprecht
President von Walter............................Kaspar Bruninghaus
Court Marshal von Kalb .... Hans von Borsody
Sophie.. Alwy Becker
Lady Milford ....Renate Volkner
Valet .... Gerhard Soor
Servant .... Axel Klingenberg

A Middle-class Tragedy in five acts, presented in two parts

* Closed Nov. 7, 1971 after limited engagement of 8 performances in German.

Opened Tuesday, November 9, 1971.*

DER PROZESS
(The Trial)

By Franz Kafka; Dramatized by Jan Grossman; Staged by Oscar Fritz Schuh; Scenery and Costumes, Ursula Schuh; Music, Eckart Ihlenfield; Assistant Director, Axel Klingenberg; Technical Direction/Lighting, Heinz Kraile, Friedrich Schoberth; Stage Manager, Gunther Seufert; Sound, Gunter Hubner

CAST

Josef K .... Hans von Borsody
First Guard .... Klaus Munster
Second Guard .... Gerhard Soor
Supervisor ....Kaspar Bruninghaus
Frau Grubach.. Ilse Laux
Fraulein Burstner .... Renate Volkner
Judge .... Klaus Munster
Laundress.. Esther Carola Regnier
Student... Axel Klingenberg
Court Attendant .... Gerhard Soor
Thrasher...Kaspar Bruninghaus
Assistant Director .... Axel Klingenberg
Uncle .... Gerhard Soor
Leni .... Alwy Becker
Head Clerk .... Klaus Munster
Lawyer .... Wolfgang Dorich
Manufacturer...Kaspar Bruninghaus
Titorelli .... Albert Rueprecht
Priest .... Kaspar Bruninghaus

* Closed Nov. 14, 1971 after limited engagement of 8 performances in German.

(no photos available)

Entire cast of "Love Me, Love My Children"

Patrick Owens Photo

MERCER-O'CASEY THEATRE

Opened Wednesday, November 3, 1971.*
Joel W. Schenker and Edward F. Kook present:

LOVE ME, LOVE MY CHILDREN

Book, Lyrics, Music, Robert Swerdlow; Dances and Musical Numbers Staged by Elizabeth Swerdlow; Director, Paul Aaron; Vocal Arrangements, Robert DeCormier; Stage form design, Jo Mielziner; Lighting, Dahl Delu; Costumes, Patricia Quinn Stuart; Musical Direction and Arrangements, Michael Alterman; Original Cast Album by United Artists Records

CAST

Don Atkinson
Mark Baker
Salome Bey
Jacqueline Britt
Matthew Diamond
Ed Evanko†1
Sharron Miller

Michon Peacock
Patsy Rahn†2
Chapman Roberts
Myrna Strom
Rose Mary Taylor
Suzanne Walker

MUSICAL NUMBERS: "Don't Twist My Mind," "Reflections," "Don't Twist Her Mind," "See," "Fat City," "Deca Dance," "Leave the World Behind," "Don't Be a Miracle," "Face to Face," "Journey Home," "Critics," "Let Me Down," "Walking in the World," "North American Shmear," "Gingerbread Girl," "Plot and Counterplot," "Do the Least You Can," "You're Dreaming," "Running Down the Sun," "Love Me, Love My Children"

A Rock Musical presented without intermission.

General Managers: Robert S. Fishko, John A. Prescott, Laurel Ann Wilson
Press: Sol Jacobson, Lewis Harmon, Ruth D. Smuckler
Stage Managers: David Taylor, Alisa Jill Adler

* Closed April 23, 1972 after 187 performances.
† Succeeded by: 1. Mike Perrier, 2. Margaret Castleman

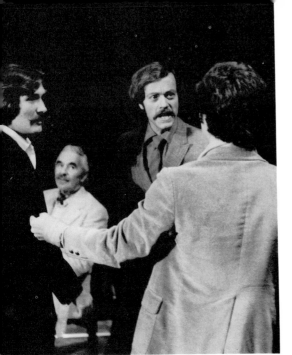

William Snickowski, Luke Wymes, Don
Wakefield, Mark Boli

Katherine Beal Photo

PARK AVENUE COMMUNITY THEATRE

Opened Thursday, November 11, 1971.*
Central Arts Programs (Albert L. DuBose, Producer)
presents the American premiere of:

A NIGHT OUT

By Harold Pinter; Director, Ed Danus; Designer, Clyde
Spooner; Lighting, Gary Marec, Bill Bence; Lighting Consultant, Jennifer Tipton

CAST

Albert Stokes	William Snickowski
Mrs. Stokes	Eve Dmytryk
Seeley	Don Wakefield
Barman	Bernie Friedman
Mr. King	Eric Hanson
Gidney	Mark Boli
Eileen	Norrine Elaine
Horne	Dave Dalan
The Girl	Elice Higgenbotham
Kedge	John Sotak
Mr. Ryan	Luke Wymes
Old Man	Gerry McLaughlin
Joyce	Virgil Katherine Doyle
Betty	Linda Lodge
Barrow	Bill Silver

A Drama in 3 acts and 10 scenes, presented with one intermission. The action takes place in the Stokes' house in the
South of London, a coffee shop, Mr. King's house, and the
girl's room.

General Manager: Al DuBose
Press: Susan Ann Weeks
Stage Managers: Bill Silver, Candy Johnson

* Closed Nov. 27, 1971 after limited engagement of 9 performances on weekends only.

VILLAGE GATE THEATRE

Opened Monday, November 15, 1971.*
Cosmo Richard Falcon and Wayland Flowers in association with Art and Burt D'Lugoff present:

KUMQUATS

Book and Lyrics, Cosmo Richard Falcon; Created and Designed by Wayland Flowers; Music, Gustavo Motta; Arrangements and Musical Direction, Michael Leonard; Lighting,
Ken Moses; Director, Nicolas Coppola; Production Consultant, Pady Blackwood; Scenery, Bob Olson.

CAST

Wayland Flowers
Michael Alogna
Gregory Smith
James Racioppi

ACT I: "In the Name of Love," "Kumquats," "At the Li-
brary," "Old Hat Joke," "American Dream Girl," "Legs!,"
"The Evil Fairy and the Hippie," "The Wee Scotsman,"
"Hello, Dolly!," "The Dirty Word Waltz"

ACT II: "Irma's Candy Heaven," "Old Hat Joke," "Adam
and Eve," "This is Paradise," "The Fairy and the Hard Hat,"
"Madame Meets a Midget," "Legs!," "Mao Tse Tongue,"
"The Sensuous Woman," "The Wee Scotsman," "The Story
of Ooooh!," Finale.

"The World's First Erotic Puppet Show" in two acts.

General Manager: Bob MacDonald
Press: Harvey Sabinson, Lee Solters, Cheryl Sue Dolby
Stage Managers: Margaret Peckham, J. Pat Rogers

* Closed Jan. 2, 1972 after 53 performances.

Gregory Smith, Wayland Flowers

FORTUNE THEATRE

Opened Wednesday, November 17, 1971.*
Free Flow Productions and Jay K. Hoffman present:

RICHARD FARIÑA: LONG TIME COMING AND A LONG TIME GONE

Adapted from the works of Richard Fariña by Nancy Greenwald; Music arranged and directed by Arthur Miller; Sets and Collage, Richard Hammer, Patrick Sullivan; Lighting, John Dodd; Costumes, Joyce and Jerry Marcel; Director, Robert Greenwald; Originally presented by Lenox Arts Center, Mass.; Production Assistant, Michelle Krell.

CAST

Richard	Richard Gere
Richard's Lady	Vicki Sue Robinson
Judith	Penelope Milford
Thomas	Charles Weldon
Ann	Jessica Harper
Harold	Brendan Hanlon
Orchestra	Michael Lewis

PROGRAM: "Comments," "Pack up Your Sorrows," "Celebration for a Gray Day," "Reflections on a Crystal Wind," "The Field near the Cathedral at Chartres," "Nothing Poem," "Joy 'Round My Brain," "An End to a Young Man," "Another Country," "Passing of Various Lives," "House Un-American Activities Blues Dream," "Breaking the Travel Ban," "Morgan the Pirate," "Juan Carlose Rosenbloom," "The Falcon," "November Elegy," "All the World Has Gone By," "Hard Loving Loser," "One Way Ticket," "Monterey Fair," "Birmingham Sunday," "The Dream Song of J. Alfred Kerouac," "St. Vincent's Isle," "Somber Wind," "Kings Die Easy," "Raven Girl," "Children of Darkness"

A Collage of works by Richard Fariña presented without intermission.

Production Manager: Frank Wicks
Stage Manager: Daniel Adams

* Closed Nov. 21, 1971 after 7 performances. (No photos available)

SAINT CLEMENT'S CHURCH

Opened Thursday, November 18, 1971*
Mushroom under the auspices of St. Clement's Church presents:

DON'T WALK ON THE CLOUDS

Book, Terry Miller-Marvin Gordon; Music and Lyrics, John Aman; Conceived and staged by Marvin Gordon; Sets and Costumes, Sue Drobbin; Lighting, George Vaughn Lawther; Sound, Gary Harris; Production Coordinator, Jim Dwyer.

CAST

Death	John Aman
Charlie	Mark Robinson
Faith	Ruth Brisbane
Hope	Wenda Lee
Charity	Nancy Archer
Matthew	Hank McGonigal
Mark	Jim Turner
Luke	Robert Lantz
Lucifer	Gregory Sutter
God	Irving Harmon

Understudies: Holly Gruher, Ric Lake

MUSICAL NUMBERS: "Processional," "Love It or Leave It," "Swinger Boogie," "Love and the World Will Be Yours," "Dante and DaVinci Rag," "Make Music and Love," "What Am I Bid?," "Be My Brother," "Who Am I Now?," "Ultimate Trip," "Blood Bath," "Summer of Love," "Let's Get Our Heads Together," "Don't Walk on the Clouds"

Presented without intermission.

Company Manager: Pat Rogers
Press: Nancy Archer
Stage Managers: Doug Laidlaw, Holly Gruher

* Closed Dec. 11, 1971 after 21 performances and 7 previews. (No photos available)

CIRCLE IN THE SQUARE

Opened Sunday, November 21, 1971*
Walt DeFaria presents:

JFK

Written and adapted by Mark Williams and Jeremiah Collins; Scenery and Lighting, David F. Segal; Staged by Mark Williams and Walt DeFaria; Photography, Ken Howard; Associate Producer, Phil McLaughlin; Production Assistant, Jeri Hansen

CAST

John F. Kennedy	Jeremiah Collins
First Reporter	Frank Baginski
Second Reporter	John Cain
Third Reporter	Jane Loeb

Presented in two parts. The subject matter is adapted or taken directly from the public record of John F. Kennedy, the thirty-fifth President of the United States.

General Managers: Wolsk & Azenberg
Company Manager: Jose Vega
Press: Frank Goodman, Les Schecter
Stage Manager: Patrika Brown

* Closed Nov. 28, 1971 after 10 performances.

Ken Howard Photo

Jeremiah Collins

EDISON THEATRE

Opened Monday, November 22, 1971.*
Yaacov Agmon under the patronage of the Prime Minister of Israel, Mrs. Golda Meir, presents:

ONLY FOOLS ARE SAD

By Dan Almagor; Based on old Hassidic stories and parables; Music derived from Hassidic songs arranged by Yohanan Zarai and Gil Aldema; Director, Yossi Yzraely; Scenery, Dani Karavan; Supervised by Herbert Senn; Lighting, Yehiel Orgal; Supervised by Robert Brand; Costumes Supervised by Helen Pond; Lyrics translated by Robert Friend; Musical Instructor and Adviser, Hanna Hakohen; Translated by Shimon Wincelberg and Valerie Arnon; English Speech Consultant, Nora Dunfee; Production Manager, Naomi Schilo; Assistant Director, Esther Izbicki.

CAST

Galia Ishay	Shlomo Nitzen
Danny Litanny	Michal Noy
Don Maseng	Aviva Schwarz

Understudies: Yael Yaacov, David Zakai

MUSICAL NUMBERS: Part I: "Once There Was a Melody," "Isaac, The Baker (The Treasure)," "A Merry Melody," "Berl, The Tailor (Opening a New Account)," "The Promise That Was Kept," "Don't Suck the Bones," "Eat, Lord, and Enjoy," "Tell Me What the Rain Is Saying," "Don't Sell It Cheap," "A Drinking Song," "The Ten Ruble Note," "Kol Rinah Vishu'ah," "Gedaliah, The Tar Maker"

Part II: "The Goat," "Forest, Forest," "Smoking on the Sabbeth," "Bim-Bam-Bom," "Waiting for the Messiah," "Haim, The Gooseherder," "Getzl, The Shoemaker (Aleph ... Beth)," "The Rabbi Who Promised to Wait," "A Letter to the Rabbi," "Angel, Angel ...," "Only Fools Are Sad," "Avreymele Melamed," "A Sabbath Song," "And God Said Unto Jacob"

A Prize-Winning Musical from Israel in two parts.

General Manager: Lily Turner
Company Manager: Bill Levine
Press: David Lipsky, Joel Dein
Stage Managers: Marko Bechar, Boaz Ben-Zion, David Zakai

* Closed March 26, 1972 after 144 performances and 8 previews.

Danny Massing, Galia Yishay, Shlomo Nitzan, Danny Litani, Aviva Schwarz, Michal Noy

Kay Williams, Barry Corbin

THEATRE FOUR

Opened Sunday, November 28, 1971.*
Masquerade Company presents:

MASQUERADE

By Gertrude Gayle; Director, Don Toner; Sets and Lighting, James Singelis; Costumes, Domingo A. Rodriguez; Assistant to Producer, Loy Moncrief; Management Associate, Derek Mali; Fencing Duel Staged by Barry Corbin; Originally Produced by Theatre Center of Mississippi

CAST

Herald to the Queen/Secretary to Oxford	John Svar
Robert Dudley, Earl of Leicester	Carl Strano
Queen Elizabeth Tudor	Kay Williams
Sir William Cecil/Lord Burghley/Sir Robert Cecil	Barry Corbin
Edward de Vere, Earl of Oxford	C. David Colson
Anne Vavasor, Maid of Honor	Kathleen Moore
Thomas Knyvet, Vavasor's Uncle	Rex Brown
Elizabeth Trentham, Maid of Honor	Jean Toner
Henry Wroseley as a child	Adam Kimmelman
Henry Wroseley, Earl of Southampton	McCoy Baugham
Barmaid/Court Lady	Susan Berger
Commoner/Jailer	Don Chafey
Commoner/Lord of Court	Fred Stone
Commoner/Lady of Court	Becki Davis
Sir Walter Raleigh	Brian Farrell

A Drama in 2 acts and 13 scenes with epilogue. The action takes place between 1580 and 1603.

General Management: Grayson & Olim
Press: Alan Eichler, James J. O'Rourke
Stage Managers: David Godbold, Susan Berger

* Closed Nov. 28, 1971 after one performance.

Bert Andrews Photo

MARTINIQUE THEATRE

Opened Monday, November 29, 1971.*
Afro-American Studio presents:

EL HAJJ MALIK

By N. R. Davidson, Jr.; Director, Ernie McClintock; Associate Producer, Marc Primus; Designed by Ron Walker; Music, William Salter; Choreography, Milo Timmons; Costumes, Augustus Keith; Associate Director, Marc Primus; Technical Director, Ron Walker; Management Associate, Derek Mali; Management Assistants, Thelma Kuperberg, Alfred Roberg.

CAST

Joan Bailey	Deborah Howard
Cindy Burroughs	Augustus Keith
Norman Butler	James Lee
Woody Carter	Jim Mallette
Lee Cooper	Joan Seale
James Harris	

MUSICIANS: George (Duke) Cleamons, Linda Miller, Bob Ralston, George Wheeler

A Drama in two acts, presenting the dramatic life and death of Malcolm X.

General Management: Grayson & Olim
Press: Bill Doll & Company
Stage Manager: John Hines

* Closed Jan. 9, 1972 after 40 performances.

Vernon Smith Photo

James Harris, Norman Butler, Jim Mallette

STAGE 73

Opened Thursday, December 9, 1971*
Jeff Britton in association with the Manhattan Theatre Club presents:

22 YEARS

Written and Directed by Robert Sickinger; Designer, Robert King; Lighting, Gary Marec; Literary Consultant, Jon Surgal.

CAST

Prosecuting Attorney	King Morton
Linda Kasabian	Joan Grove
Charles Manson	Frank Girardeau
Digger	Marc Handier
Flower Child	Diane Jayne
Lynn	Barbara Marchant
Guitarist	Marc Handier
Katie	Julie Burgher
Gypsy	Gail Hayden
Sadie Mae Glutz	Kristin Marie
Leslie Sankster	Louise Garone
Holy Acid Head	Robert Corwin
Cops	Emanuel Kaufman, David Walker
Hitchhiker	Molly Larson
Dennis	Curly Hurley
Missy	Nikki Ana Dominguez
Bobbie	Dennis Kear
Terry	Ron Osborne
Tex Watson	O. B. Lewis
Randy	Chaz Palminteri
Family Guitar Singer	Loree Gold
Defense Attorneys	Dennis Kear, Emanuel Kaufman, David Walker
Other Family Members	Jeanette Arnone, Rita Ballard, Tony Bruni, Iris Landsberg

A "rockumentary" play in two acts.
Press: Bill Bence, M. J. Boyer

* Closed Jan. 29, 1972 after 40 performances.

William E. Miller Photo

Frank Girardeau, Kristen Marie

VANDAM THEATRE

Opened Thursday, December 9, 1971.*
Bill Shirley presents:

NIGHTRIDE

By Lee Barton; Director, Milton Lyon; Scenery, Alan Kimmel; Lighting, Ken Billington; Costumes, Katrin; Sound, Gary and Timmy Harris.

CAST

Erik Fenstrom .... Philip Larson
Marcus Sternberg .... Don Draper
Jon Bristow .... Lester Rawlins
Jab Humble .... Chandler Hill Harben
Peter Duchos .... Jeremy Stockwell

A Play in two acts. The action takes place at the present time in a beach house in Puerto Rico.

General Manager: Jordan Hott
Press: Betty Lee Hunt, Henry Luhrman,
Harriett Trachtenberg
Stage Manager: Charles Roden

* Closed Feb. 27, 1972 after 94 performances.

Patrick Owens Photo

Chandler Hill Harben, Philip Larson, Lester Rawlins

Lou Gossett, Barbara Colby Above: Humbert Allen Astredo, Jean-Pierre Aumont, Donald Symington, Richard Easton

PLAYHOUSE THEATRE

Opened Monday, December 20, 1971.*
Phoenix Theatre (T. Edward Hambleton, Managing Director) by arrangement with Elliot Martin and George W. George presents:

MURDEROUS ANGELS

By Conor Cruise O'Brien; Director, Gordon Davidson; Settings, Peter Wexler; Costumes, Frank Thompson; Lighting, Gilbert Hemsley, Jr.; Sound Score, Pia Gilbert; Film Sequences, Sterling Johnson, Jack Coddington

CAST

Baron Dauge .... Richard Venture
Viscount Tamworth .... Neil Fitzgerald
James Bonham .... Richard Easton
Mr. Ainsworth .... Donald Symington
Mr. Calvin .... Humbert Allen Astredo
Dag Hammarskjold .... Jean-Pierre Aumont
Diallo Diop .... Herbert Jefferson, Jr.
Monsignor Polycarpe .... William Larsen
Father Boniface .... Les Roberts
Patrice Lumumba .... Lou Gossett
Madame Rose Rose .... Barbara Colby
Ambassador of Soviet Union .... Ben Hammer
Ambassador of United States .... John Baragrey
U.N. Sergeant .... Jack Landron
White Settler .... John Clarkson
Congolese Singer .... Ula Walker
Congolese Woman .... Mabel Robinson
Rajat Asdal .... Gilbert Green
Madame Pauline Lumumba .... Ula Walker
U.N. Attendant .... Sharon Laughlin
Col. Alcibiade Zbyre .... Joseph Mascolo
Moise Tshombe .... Leonard Jackson
British Consul .... John Clarkson

SOLDIERS, MEN, WOMEN: Tyrone Browne, Stephen Goff, Gerry Murphy, Lynda Westcott, Elwoodson Williams, Stephen Zulick

UNDERSTUDIES: Hammarskjold, Humbert Allen Astredo; Lumumba, Rajat, J. A. Preston; Bonham, John Clarkson; Rose, Sharon Laughlin; Diallo, Boniface, Jack Landron; Calvin, Polycarpe, Gilbert Green; Ainsworth, Joseph Mascolo; Tamworth, U.S. Ambassador, William Larsen; Pauline, Singer, Mabel Robinson

A Drama in 2 acts and 14 scenes. The action takes place between June 1960 and September 1961.

General Manager: Marilyn S. Miller
Press: Sol Jacobson, Lewis Harmon, Ruth D. Smuckler
Stage Managers: Daniel Freudenberger, David Barber, James S. Lucas, Jr.

* Closed Jan. 9, 1972 after 24 performances and 9 previews.

Van Williams Photos

ORPHEUM THEATRE

Opened Wednesday, December 29, 1971*
D. Brian Wallach presents:

MEMPHIS STORE-BOUGHT TEETH

Book, E. Don Alldredge; Music, William Fisher; Lyrics, D. Brian Wallach; Directed and Staged by Marvin Gordon; Scenery, Robert O'Hearn; Lighting, George Vaughn Lowther; Costumes, William Pitkin; Musical Supervision-Arrangements, Ted Simons; Conductor, Rene Weigert.

CAST

Traveller	Jerry Lanning
William	J. J. Jepson
Jennifer	Alice Cannon
Fanny Crabtree	Travis Hudson
Ora Lee MacNew	Evelyn Brooks
Greely MacNew	Lloyd Harris
Elmira Boone	Sherill Price
Preacher Potter	Hal Robinson
Judge Garmony	Lloyd Harris

MUSICAL NUMBERS: "Quiet Place," "It's Been a Hard Life," "Where Have I Been," "The Lord Bless and Keep You," "Fanny Dear," "My Final Fling," "When I Leave," "That's What a Friend Is For," "Nothing Seems the Same," "Something You Really Want," "Nicest Part of Me," "Something to Hold on to"

A musical performed without intermission. The action takes place during July Present and Memory Past in Sunflower, Alabama.

General Manager: Sherman Gross
Company Manager: Virginia Snow
Press: Frank Goodman, Les Schecter, Margaret Wade
Stage Managers: Doug Laidlaw, Don Honeycutt

* Closed Dec. 29, 1971 after one performance.

Friedman-Abeles Photo

Jerry Lanning, J. J. Jepson, Alice Cannon

Regina Baff, Harold Gary, Sylvia Miles, Ron Rifkin

EASTSIDE PLAYHOUSE

Opened Wednesday, January 5, 1972.*
Harlan Kleiman and Peter Goldfarb present:

ROSEBLOOM

By Harvey Perr; Director, Jered Barclay; Scenery, Merrill Sindler; Lighting, Thomas Skelton; Costumes, Ann Roth; Management Associate, Derek Mali; Assistants to Producers, Todd Myers, Ken Fink; Management Assistants, Thelma Kuperberg, Alfred Roberge.

CAST

Sylvie	Sylvia Miles
Enola Gay	Regina Baff
Mark	Ron Rifkin
Harry Rosebloom	Harold Gary

A Play in two acts. The action takes place at the present time in the living room of Mark and Enola Gay Rosebloom.

General Management: Grayson & Olim
Press: David Powers
Stage Manager: Murray Gitlin

* Closed Jan. 23, 1972 after 23 performances.

Bert Andrews Photo

June Gable, Frank Coppola

CHERRY LANE THEATRE
Opened Wednesday, January 19, 1972*
Arthur D. Zinberg presents:

WANTED

Book, David Epstein; Music and Lyrics, Al Carmines; Director, Lawrence Kornfeld; Scenery, Paul Zalon; Costumes, Linda Giese; Lighting, Roger Morgan; Musical Direction, Susan Romann.

CAST

Starr Faithful Brown	Andra Akers
Billy the Kid	Reathel Bean
Babycakes	Jerry Clark
Opal	Cecelia Cooper
John Dillinger	Frank Coppola
Shorty	June Gable
Jacob Hooper	Merwin Goldsmith
Ma Barker	Lee Guilliatt
Deafy	John Kuhner
Jesse James	Peter Lombard
Sheriff Sweet	Stuart Silver
Miss Susannah Figgit	Gretchen Van Aken
Doc Barker	Stuart Silver
Jelly Barker	John Kuhner
Sister Powhatan Lace	Gretchen Van Aken

MUSICAL NUMBER: "I Am the Man," "Where Have You Been Up to Now?," "Outlaw Man," "Who's on Our Side?," "Parasol Lady," "Jailhouse Blues," "I Want to Ride with You," "You Do This," "Guns Are Fun," "I Do the Best I Can," "Wahoo!," "Whispering to You," "I Want to Blow up the World," "The Indian Benefit Ball," "The Lord Is My Light," "It's Love," "As I'm Growing Older"

A musical in two acts.

General Manager: Bob Skerry
Press: M. J. Boyer
Stage Manager: Jimmy Cuomo

* Closed March 26, 1972 after 79 performances and 6 previews.

Friedman-Abeles Photo

CIRCLE IN THE SQUARE
Opened Sunday, February 6, 1972*
The Tea Party Company presents:

TWO IF BY SEA

Book, Priscilla B. Dewey with Charles Werner Moore; Music, Tony Hutchins; Lyrics, Priscilla B. Dewey; Director, Charles Werner Moore; Musical Direction, Jeff Lass; Musical Numbers staged by Edward Roll; Scenery, John Doepp; Lighting, Roger Morgan; Costumes, Julie Weiss; Orchestrations and Additional Music, Jeff Lass, John Nagy.

CAST

Rachel (Rachel Revere)	Kay Cole
John (John Hancock)	Jack Gardner
Lydia (Lydia Hancock)	Judy Gibson
Hugh (Lord Percy)	Rod Loomis
Sam (Samuel Adams)	Joe Morton
John (John Singleton Copley)	Rick Podell
Dolly (Dolly Quincy)	Jan Ross
Thomas Richardson	John Stratton
Paul (Paul Revere)	John Witham

UNDERSTUDIES: Paul, Hugh, Hancock, Richardson, Rick Gardner; Copley, Mory Houghton
MUSICAL NUMBERS: "The American Revolution," "Paul Revere," "Wouldn't It Be Fine," "Daddy's Footsteps," "There'll Be a Tomorrow," "Stamp out the Tea Tax," "Melt It Down," "Tea Dance," "We're a Young Country," "Lawbreakers," "You Can't Turn off the Stars," "Be More Aggressive," "Throw the Egg," "People Who Live on Islands," "Two if by Sea, I Think," "Lanterns," Finale

A musical in two acts. The action takes place at the present time.

General Manager: Paul B. Berkowsky
Press: Saul Richman, Sara Altshul
Stage Managers: Alan Fox, Rick Gardner

* Closed Feb. 6, 1972 after one performance.

Barry Kramer Photo

Entire cast of "Two if by Sea"

Rue McClanahan, Will Hare

MERCER-O'CASEY THEATRE
Opened Sunday, February 6, 1972*
Joseph Rhodes, Marty Richards, Martin Edelman present:

DYLAN

By Sidney Michaels; Director, Lee D. Sankowich; Set, John Scheffler; Costumes and Lighting, Andrew Greenhut; Associate Producer, Nina Goodman.

CAST

Caitlin	Rue McClanahan
Dylan	Will Hare
Reporters	Karen Gorney, Ed Crowley, Michael Wieben, Jeff Eagle
Brinnin	Carleton Carpenter
Angus	John Coe
Clubwoman	Delphi Lawrence
Meg	Joanna Miles
Annabelle	Karen Gorney
Mattock	Kurt Garfield
Bartender	Jeff Eagle
Miss Wonderland	Karen Gorney
Stagehand	Jeff Eagle
Minister	Ed Crowley
Elena	Delphi Lawrence
Jay Henry	Ed Crowley
Deck Officer	Jeff Eagle

UNDERSTUDIES: Dylan, Kurt Garfield; Caitlin, Delphi Lawrence

A drama in two acts. The action takes place in the early 1950's in America and Wales.

General Manager: Steven Sinn
Press: Betty Lee Hunt, Henry Luhrman, Abner B. Klipstein, Harriett Trachtenberg
Stage Managers: Dan Hild, Michael Wieben

* Closed March 19, 1972 after 48 performances. For original Broadway production, see THEATRE WORLD, Vol. 20.

Martha Swope Photo

BROOKLYN ACADEMY OF MUSIC
Opened Saturday, February 12, 1972*
The Brooklyn Academy of Music presents:

PAPER BAG PLAYERS
in
HOT FEET

Conceived, Designed, and Directed by Judith Martin; Assistant Director, Irving Burton; Music by Donald Ashwander; Administrator, Judith Liss; Technical Supervisor, John Armstrong.

CAST

Irving Burton
Judith Martin
Donald Ashwander
Pilar Garcia
Douglas Richardson

A musical revue preformed without intermission.

* Closed to tour on April 29, 1972 after 12 performances on Saturdays only.

Douglas Richardson, Pilar Garcia, Irving Burton, Judith Martin

THEATRE FOUR

Opened Sunday, February 13, 1972*
Whitecaps Productions presents:

BROTHERS

By Stephen White; Director, David Williams; Setting and Lighting, C. Murawski; Costumes, Jeanne Button; Assistant to Producer, Michelle Cousin.

CAST

Sandy Lewis.. Everett McGill
Ronnie Lewis.. Brian Farrell
Vietnamese Woman.. Tisa Chang
Lawyer... Jim Mallette
Florence Lewis .... Evelyn Page
Frank Lewis... Brendan Fay
Father O'Neill ....Paul Barry
Linda .... Diane Gardner
Marylou .... Elaine Sulka
Soldiers...... Rodney Cleghorne, James J. Mapes, Tim Moses

A play for peace in two acts. The action takes place on a children's beach on a summer resort island in the summer of 1971.

General Management: Dorothy Olim Associates
Press: David Lipsky, Lisa Lipsky, Joel Dein
Stage Managers: Robert J. Bruyr, James J. Mapes

* Closed Feb. 13, 1972 after 1 performance and 5 previews.

Friedman-Abeles Photo

Brian Farrell, Diane Gardner, Everett McGill, Elaine Sulka

JoAnne Belanger, Erle Bjornstad

BLACKFRIARS THEATRE

Opened Wednesday, February 23, 1972*
The Blackfriars Guild presents:

THE RED HAT

By Maureen A. Martin; Director, Jerry N. Evans; Settings and Lighting, Walter Crawford; Costumes, Jacqueline Karch.

CAST

Headsman .... Eric Poppick
Bishop John Fisher ....Ronn Mullen
King Henry VIII.. Paul Meacham
Anne Boleyn ....JoAnne Belanger
Tom More ....Allan Montaine
Catherine of Aragon ....Erle Bjornstad

Press: Rev. T. F. Carey
Stage Manager: Walter Crawford

* Closed March 26, 1972 after 38 performances.

EDEN THEATRE

Opened Monday, February 14, 1972*
Kenneth Waissman and Maxine Fox in association with
Anthony D'Amato present:

GREASE

Book-Music-Lyrics, Jim Jacobs and Warren Casey; Director, Tom Moore; Musical numbers and dances staged by Patricia Birch; Musical Supervision and Orchestrations, Michael Leonard; Musical Direction-Vocal and Dance Arrangements, Louis St. Louis; Scenery, Douglas W. Schmidt; Costumes, Carrie F. Robbins; Lighting, Karl Eigsti; Sound, Bill Merrill; Hairstyles, Jim Sullivan; Assistant to Producers, Barbara Jean Block; Production Assistants, Pinocchio Madrid, Carolyn Ciplet.

CAST

Miss Lynch	Dorothy Leon†1
Patty Simcox	Ilene Kristen
Eugene Florczyk	Tom Harris
Jan	Garn Stephens
Marty	Katie Hanley†2
Betty Rizzo	Adrienne Barbeau
Doody	James Canning
Roger	Walter Bobbie
Kenickie	Timothy Meyers
Sonny LaTierri	Jim Borrelli
Frenchy	Marya Small
Sandy Dumbrowski	Carole Demas
Danny Zuko	Barry Bostwick
Vince Fontaine	Don Billett
Johnny Casino	Alan Paul
Cha-Cha Di Gregorio	Kathi Moss
Teen Angel	Alan Paul

UNDERSTUDIES: Joy Rinaldi, Daniel Deitch

MUSICAL NUMBERS: "Alma Mater," "Summer Nights," "Those Magic Changes," "Freddy, My Love," "Greased Lightnin'," "Mooning," "Look at Me, I'm Sandra Dee," "We Go Together," "Shakin' at the High School Hop," "It's Raining on Prom Night," "Born to Hand-Jive," "Beauty School Dropout," "Alone at a Drive-in Movie," "Rock 'n' Roll Party Queen," "There Are Worse Things I Could Do," "All Choked Up," Finale

A rock musical in 2 acts and 12 scenes. The action takes place in the late 1950's.

General Manager: Edward H. Davis
Press: Betty Lee Hunt Associates, Harriett Trachtenberg, Henry Luhrman
Stage Managers: Joe Calvan, A. Robert Altshuler, Tom Harris

* Moved June 7, 1972 to the Broadhurst Theatre on Broadway after 128 performances Off Broadway.
† Succeeded by: 1. Sudie Bond, 2. Meg Bennett.

Timothy Meyers, Adrienne Barbeau, Garn Stephens, Jim Borrelli, Katie Hanley, Marya Small, Barry Bostwick, James Canning, Walter Bobbie

Carole Demas, Barry Bostwick Above: Timothy Meyers, Adrienne Barbeau, Tom Harris

99

ACTORS STUDIO

Opened Thursday, February 24, 1972*
The Actors Studio Production Unit Presents:

FELIX

By Claude McNeal; Director, Arthur Sherman; Set, Donald Crawford; Music and Sound, Ed Summerlin; Lighting, Edward I. Byers; Technical Director, John Branon; Executive Producer, Arthur Penn; Artistic Director, Lee Strasberg.

CAST

Felix	Clifton James
Davis	David Garfield
Mickey Mouse	Robert Burgos
Hank	Joseph Hardy
Shivver	John Perkins
May	Doris Roberts
Marcia	Sally Kirkland
Disc Jockey	Lee Allen
Fred	Donald Buka
Office Girl	Shelley Hainer
Boyson	Richard Ward
Clerk	Ramon Gordon
Dispatcher	Pat Corley
First Loader	Burt Young
Second Loader	Chad Burton
Companion	Walter Cotton
Teddy	DeWayne Oliver
Bum	Wendell Phillips
Dog	Alan Slepp
Minister	Joseph Wilson
Soapbox Speaker	Lyle Kessler
Cop	Tony Mazzadra
Wrink	Margaret Ladd

IN UNEMPLOYMENT OFFICE: Rod Clavery, Walter Cotton, Lynne Hardy, James Miller, Alfred Newbell, DeWayne Oliver, Michael Shapiro

IN MTA SUBWAY: Judith Carroll, Rod Clavery, Lynne Hardy, Barbara Karro, James Miller, Alfred Newbell, Robert Smith, Laurel Weber

IN BOSTON COMMON: Judith Carroll, Rod Clavery, Eric Cowley, Harold Ellis, Michael Goodman, Lynne Hardy, Barbara Karro, Michael Shapiro, Laurel Weber

A play in 2 acts and 10 scenes. The action occurs at the present time in Boston, Mass.

Press: Alan Eichler
Stage Managers: Elizabeth Stearns, Lee Marsh

* Closed March 5, 1972 after limited engagement of 12 performances.

Cliff James, Richard Ward

SHERIDAN SQUARE PLAYHOUSE

Opened Tuesday, February 29, 1972*
Norman Kean and John Heffernan present:

THE SHADOW OF A GUNMAN

By Sean O'Casey; Director, Philip Minor; Set, Lloyd Burlingame; Lighting, Fred Allison; Costume Supervisor, Margaret M. Mohr

CAST

Donal Davoren	Leon Russum†1
Seumas Shields	John Heffernan
Mr. Maguire	Joseph Daly
Mr. Mulligan	James Carruthers
Minnie Powell	Jacqueline Coslow
Tommy Owens	Bruce French†2
Mrs. Henderson	Paddy Croft
Mr. Gallogher	Bernard Frawley†3
Mrs. Grigson	Estelle Omens
Adolphus Grigson	James Gallery
An Auxiliary	Joseph Daly

A drama in two acts. The action takes place in May 1920 in a room in a Dublin tenement.

Press: Robert Ganshaw
Stage Managers: Dean Compton, Bruce French, James Carruthers

* Closed April 30, 1972 after 70 performances and 4 previews.
† Succeeded by 1. Bruce French, 2. Robert Moberly, 3. Kermit Brown

Bruce French, John Heffernan

Gene Ward Photo

HENRY STREET PLAYHOUSE

Opened Thursday, March 16, 1972*
The New Federal Theatre presents:

JAMIMMA

By Martie Evans-Charles; Director, Shauneille Perry; Setting, C. Richard Mills; Lighting, Shirley Prindergast; Costumes, Edna Waston; Production Coordinator, Mayme Mitcham

CAST

Jameena Caine	Marcella Lowery
Omar Butler I	Dick Williams
Vivian Williams	Lucretia R. Collins
Viola Caine Robinson	Roxie Roker
Crazy Man Johnson	Arnold Johnson
Tyrone Jackson	Charles Weldon
Gil Washington	Aston S. Young
Hussein	Lester Forte
Radio Lady	Vi Higgins

A play about life in a Harlem apartment house.

General Manager: Beldon Raspberry
Press: Howard Atlee, David Roggensack
Stage Manager: Fred Seagraves

* Closed March 26, 1972 after a limited engagement of 8 performances; re-opened May 15, 1972 at the New Federal Theatre, and closed June 25, 1972 after 49 performances.

Patrick Owens Photo

Marcella Lowery, Arnold Johnson, Roxie Roker

Vinie Burrows

MERCER-BRECHT THEATRE

Opened Thursday, March 16, 1972*
Ananse Productions present:

WALK TOGETHER CHILDREN

Arranged and Adapted by Vinie Burrows; Taped Music under the direction of Brother Ahh (Robert Northern); Gowns designed by Arthur McGee; Technical Assistant, Njomo Talley; Sound, Gary Burnett; Recorded by Spoken Arts Records.

CAST

Vinie Burrows

in a one-woman performance depicting the Black journey from auction block to new nation time. Presented in two acts.

Company Manager: Gilberto Zaldivar
Press: Bill Doll & Co.
Stage Manager: Ken Starrett

* Closed July 2, 1972 after 89 performances.

THEATRE DE LYS

Opened Sunday, March 19, 1972*
Cheryl Crawford and Jean Dalrymple in association with
Robert S. Mankin and Jim Wise present:

THE WEB AND THE ROCK

By Dolores Sutton; Adapted from novel by Thomas Wolfe;
Director, Jose Ferrer; Settings, Peter Wexler; Lighting, Roger
Morgan; Costumes, Edith Lutyens Bel Geddes; Sound, Gary
Harris; Technical Director, Jack Magnifico; Presented by spe-
cial arrangement with Lucille Lortel Productions.

CAST

Usher	Sal Carollo
Esther Jack	Dolores Sutton
Julia Webber	Elsa Raven
George Webber	James Naughton
Jim Plemmons	Peter Jason
Lily Farrell	Carolyn Groves
Mary Morgan	Darlene Parks
Max	David Kerman
Fritz Jack	Eugene Stuckman
Joe	Sal Carollo
Policeman	David Kerman

UNDERSTUDIES: George, Peter Jason; Fritz, David Ker-
man; Max, Policeman, Sal Carollo; Jim, Joe, Usher, Brandwell
S. Teuscher; Lily, Mary, Anita Frazier

A "memory play" in two acts, which begins in 1938, and
recalls events between the years 1924 and 1931.

General Manager: Paul B. Berkowsky
Company Manager: Peter A. Berkowsky
Press: Jean Dalrymple, Homer Poupart
Stage Managers: Maxine S. Taylor, Brandwell S. Teuscher

* Closed March 26, 1972 after 13 performances and 3 previews.

Friedman-Abeles Photo

Dolores Sutton, Elsa Raven, James Naughton

James Cahill, Madeleine le Roux, Beeson Carroll

ASTOR PLACE THEATRE

Opened Thursday, March 23, 1972*
Bruce Mailman presents:

RAIN

By John Colton; Based on story by W. Somerset Maugham;
Director, Michael Flanagan; Costumes, Raoul Pene Du Bois;
Setting, Stuart Wurtzel; Lighting, Barry Arnold; Production
Assistants, Peter Schneider, Karen Toffler; Technical Direc-
tor, Ron Carrier.

CAST

Mrs. Horn	Antonia Rey
Private Griggs	John Travolta
Corporal Hodgson	Richard Ryder
Sergeant O'Hara	Beeson Carroll
Joe Horn	Ben Slack
Mrs. Davidson	Patricia O'Connell
Dr. MacPhail	Paul Milikin
Mrs. MacPhail	Elizabeth Farley
Quartermaster Bates	Bernie Passeltiner
Sadie Thompson	Madeleine le Roux
Rev. Alfred Davidson	James Cahill
Native Policeman	Bob Parlan
Natives	Valcour Lavizzo, Vincent Michael Galici, Vincenetta Gunn, Richard Camargo

UNDERSTUDIES: Sadie, Elizabeth Farley; Davidson, Beeson Carroll; O'Hara/Bates, Richard Ryder; Horn/MacPhail,
Bernie Passeltiner

A drama in three acts. The action takes place in Joe Horn's
hotel-store on the Island of Pago Pago in the South Seas
during the rainy season in 1922.

General Manager: Albert Polan
Press: Saul Richman, Sara Altshul
Stage Managers: Robert Vandergriff, Richard Ryder

* Closed March 28 after 7 performances.

Kenn Duncan Photo

EASTSIDE PLAYHOUSE

Opened Monday, March 27, 1972*
William Craver presents:

IN CASE OF ACCIDENT

By Peter Simon; Director, Ted Cornell; Set, John Scheffler; Lighting, Marc B. Weiss; Costumes, David James; Production Assistant, Steve DePue.

CAST

Jack	Michael Shannon
Betts	Fay Sappington
Styles	Joseph Boley
Frances	Patricia Elliott
Eugene	Terry Kiser
Edward	Henderson Forsythe

A play in 2 acts and 6 scenes. The action takes place at the present time in an old country house in upstate New York.

General Manager: Harry Chittenden
Press: Gifford/Wallace
Stage Managers: Kate M. Pollock, Stanton Coffin

* Closed April 1, 1972 after 8 performances.

Martha Swope Photo

Michael Shannon, Joseph Boley, Fay Sappington, Henderson Forsythe, Patricia Elliott, Terry Kiser

MARTINIQUE THEATRE

Opened Sunday, March 26, 1972*
Bert Steinberg and Howard Crampton-Smith present:

WHITSUNTIDE

By Tom LaBar; Director, Russell Treyz; Lighting, Johnny Dodd; Costumes, A. E. Kohout; Vocal Arrangements and Direction, Peter Schlosser; Production Assistant, Mark Donnenfeld.

CAST

Matthew Thornton	Michael Miller
Mary Thornton	Joyce Elliott
Frank Eaton	George DiCenzo
Sue Eaton	Susanne Wasson
Flo Betton	Grace Carney
Gilbert Gordon	Dallas Alinder
Edna Thorpe	Celia Howard
Cora Campbell	Elizabeth George
Ernest Campbell	Robert Molnar
Bobby Campbell	Alan Howard
Bishop Pomeroy	Dallas Alinder
Canon Mudd	Robert Molnar

A play performed without intermission. The action takes place at the present time among the congregation of St. Thomas-on-the-Green Episcopal Church in Westwood, an old Connecticut town within commuting distance of New York City.

General Manager: NR Productions
Press: Seymour Krawitz, Martin Shwartz
Stage Managers: Jeff Hamlin, Alan Howard

* Closed March 26, 1972 after one performance.

Richard Stone Photo

Elizabeth George, Dallas Alinder, Robert Molnar, Grace Carney, Celia Howard (kneeling)

STAGE 73

Opened Tuesday, April 11, 1972*
Ivan Mars presents:

THE SOFT CORE PORNOGRAPHER

By Martin Stone and John Heller; Director, Word Baker; Scenery, Ed Wittstein; Lighting, David F. Segal; Costumes, Caley Summers; Music, Michael Tschudin.

CAST

Grace Comfort	Dorrie Kavanaugh
Trenton Corbett	Frank Raiter
Arthur Comfort	Richard Latessa

A comedy in two acts. The action takes place at the present time on a New Jersey cliff overlooking Manhattan.

General Manager: Steven Sinn
Press: Dorothy Ross, Herb Striesfield

* Closed April 11, 1972 after one performance.

Bert Andrews Photo

Richard Latessa, Dorrie Kavanaugh, Frank Raiter

TRUCK & WAREHOUSE THEATRE

Opened Sunday, April 2, 1972*
(Moved June 6, 1972 to the New Theatre)
Ecco Productions, Robert Currie, Mario DeMaria, William Orton Present:

SMALL CRAFT WARNINGS

By Tennessee Williams; Director, Richard Altman; Designed by Fred Voelpel; Lighting, John Gleason; Assistant to the Producers, Terence Erkkila.

CAST

Violet	Cherry Davis[1]
Doc	David Hooks[2]
Monk	Gene Fanning
Bill McCorkle	Brad Sullivan
Leona Dawson	Helena Carroll
Steve	William Hickey
Quentin	Alan Mixon[3]
Bobby	David Huffman[4]
Tony the cop	John David Kees

A play in two acts. The action takes place at the present time in a bar along the Southern California coast.

Company Managers: Ronald Lee, James Herald
Press: Gifford/Wallace
Stage Managers: Robert Currie, John David Kees

* Still playing May 31, 1972
† Succeeded by: 1. Candy Darling, 2. Tennessee Williams during Mr. Hooks' absence, 3. Patrick Bedford, 4. Ron Martin

Right: Brad Sullivan, Gene Fanning, William Hickey, Helena Carroll, David Hooks
Above: Alan Mixon, Helena Carroll, David Huffman

McALPIN ROOFTOP THEATRE

Opened Monday, April 17, 1972*
Square Root Productions presents:

GOD SAYS THERE IS NO PETER OTT

By Bill Hare; Director, Leland Ball; Settings, David Chapman; Lighting, Judy Rasmuson; Costumes, Pamela Scofield; Incidental Music Composed by Arthur B. Rubinstein.

CAST

Avis	Rue McClanahan
Mary	Ann Sweeny
Peter Ott	Tom Ligon
Marcia	Alice Drummond
Harry	Hansford Rowe

A comedy in 2 acts and 6 scenes. The action takes place at the present time in Avis' living room on Cape Cod.

General Managers: Norman E. Rothstein, Patricia Carney, Bob MacDonald
Press: Seymour Krawitz, Martin Shwartz
Stage Manager: Bud Coffey

* Closed April 23, 1972 after 8 performances.

Bert Andrews Photo

Rue McClanahan, Hansford Rowe, Ann Sweeny, Alice Drummond, Tom Ligon

EDISON THEATRE

Opened Friday, April 14, 1972*
Gordon Crowe in association with J. Robert Breton presents:

THAT'S ENTERTAINMENT

Lyrics and Music, Howard Dietz and Arthur Schwartz; Director, Paul Aaron; Choreography, Larry Fuller; Orchestrations-Arrangements-Musical Direction, Luther Henderson; Scenery-Lighting, David F. Segal; Costumes, Jane Greenwood; Sound, Anthony Alloy; Assistant Choreographer Merry Lynn Katis; Hairstyles, Henri Chevrier.

CAST

Greg	David Chaney
Richard	Jered Holmes
Carol	Judith Knaiz
Adele	Michon Peacock
Lena	Vivian Reed
Jack	Scott Salmon
Lucille	Bonnie Schon
Donald	Michael Vita
Sam	Alan Weeks

STANDBYS: Sharron Miller, Ken Ploss

MUSICAL NUMBERS: "Dance Medley," "Triplets," "High and Low," "How Low Can a Little Worm Go," "Absent Minded," "High Is Better Than Low," "We Won't Take It Back," "Hammacher Schlemmer, I Love You," "Come, Oh, Come," "I'm Glad I'm Single," "You're Not the Type," "Miserable with You," "Something to Remember You By," "Hottentot Potentate," "Day after Day," "Fly by Night," "Everything," "Blue Grass," "Fatal Fascination," "White Heat," "Right at the Start of It," "Confession," "Smoking Reefers," "How High Can a Little Bird Fly?," "Keep off the Grass," "I See Your Face Before Me," "Experience," "Two Faced Woman," "Foolish Face," "By Myself," "That's Entertainment," "If There Is Someone Lovlier than You," "I've Made a Habit of You," "I Guess I'll Have to Change My Plan," "New Sun in the Sky," "Farewell My Lovely," "Alone Together," "Shine on Your Shoes"

A musical in two acts.

General Managers: Norman Maibaum, John J. Miller
Press: Samuel J. Friedman, Louise Ment
Stage Managers: May Muth, Herman Magidson, Ken Ploss

* Closed April 16, 1972 after 4 performances.

Henry Grossman Photo

Michon Peacock, Michael Vita, David Charney, Alan Weeks

PLAYHOUSE THEATRE

Opened Wednesday, April 19, 1972*
(Moved June 13, 1972 to Edison Theatre)
Edward Padula and Arch Lustberg present Vinnette Carroll's Urban Arts Corps production of:

DON'T BOTHER ME, I CAN'T COPE

Conceived and Directed by Vinnette Carroll; Written by Micki Grant; Scenery, Richard A. Miller; Costumes, Edna Watson; Lighting, B. J. Sammler; Musical Direction and Arrangements, Danny Holgate; Associate Producer, Gordon Gray, Jr.; Production Supervisor, Sam Ellis; Assistant to the Producers, Robert Moeser; Presented in association with Ford's Theatre Society.

CAST

Alex Bradford
Hope Clarke†
Micki Grant
Bobby Hill
Arnold Wilkerson

SINGERS: Alberta Bradford, Charles Campbell, Marie Thomas

DANCERS: Thommie Bush, Gerald G. Francis, Ben Harney, Leona Johnson

MUSICAL NUMBERS: "I Gotta Keep Movin'," "Harlem Streets," "Lookin' over from Your Side," "Don't Bother Me, I Can't Cope," "When I Feel Like Moving," "Help," "Fighting for Pharoah," "Good Vibrations," "Love Power," "You Think I Got Rhythm?," "They Keep Coming," "My Name Is Man," "Questions," "It Takes a Whole Lot of Human Feeling," "Time Brings about a Change," "So Little Time," "Thank Heaven for You," "So Long Sammy," "All I Need"

A musical entertainment in two acts.

General Management: Gatchell & Neufeld
Company Manager: Donald Tirabassi
Press: Robert Ganshaw, Betty Lee Hunt Associates
Stage Managers: Robert Moeser, Marie Thomas

* Still playing May 31, 1972
† Arlene Rolant for 2 weeks

Micki Grant (C) and cast

Opened Friday, April 21, 1972*
All Souls Players presents:

GYPSY

Book, Arthur Laurents; Music, Jule Styne; Lyrics, Stephen Sondheim; Director-Choreographer, Jeffery K. Neill; Designed by Robert Edmonds; Costumes, Charles Roeder; Lighting, R. S. Winkler; Technical Direction, Arthur Martinsen; Musical Direction-Special Arrangements, Wendell Kindberg; Producer, Howard Van Der Meulen.

CAST

Uncle Jocko/Cigar	Richard Pohlers
Georgie/Stage Hand/Yonkers/Farm Boy	Richard Sabellico
Frederick/Urchin/Newsboy	Virgil Ferdinand
Balloon Girl	Gaye Hall
Mothers	Mary Hall, Helen Jennings, Dorothy Smith, Marlene Williamson
Contestants	Kathrine Avildsen, Helen Jennings, Dana Langhofer, Sarah McNeill, Christina Padgett, Willa Padgett, John Ryan
Baby Louise	Jennifer McCray
Baby June	Tracey Eman
Rose	Doris Balin Bianchi
Pop/Goldstone	Max Brandt
Rich Man/L.A./Farm Boy/Bougeron-Cochon	Michael Palmer
Rich Man's Son	John Ryan
Newsboys/Boy Scouts	Danny Langhofer, Duncan McNeill, Barry Ryan, Lauckie Walton
Weber/Sonny/Farm Boy/Phil	Walter Walker
Stagehand/Angie/Farm Boy	Neil Howard
Herbie	Walter Landa
Louise	Sofia Andoniadis
June	Jacqueline Clark
Tulsa	Douglas Clark
Bubsy/Cow/Pastey	Ronald Talbert
Kringelein	Edwin Folts
Gladys/Ruby	Barbara Price
Nellie/Electra/Showgirl	Trudy Smith
Miss Cratchitt/Thelma	Martina Presson
Agnes/Showgirl	Corie Sims
Geraldine/Showgirl/Renee	Ruthann Trenary
Dolores/Showgirl	Ginny Biagini
Mazeppa/Showgirl	Mary McCartney
Tessie/Showgirl	Nancy Beth Falloon
Pinky Chiffon/Showgirl	Marlene Williamson

MUSICAL NUMBERS: "May We Entertain You," "Some People," "Small World," "Mama's Talkin' Soft," "Mr. Goldstone, I Love You," "Little Lamb," "You'll Never Get Away from Me," "If Momma Was Married," "All I Need Is the Girl," "Everything's Comin' Up Roses," "Together Wherever We Go," "You Gotta Have a Gimmick," "Let Me Entertain You," "Rose's Turn"

A musical in two acts. The action takes place in various places during the 1920's and 1930's.
Stage Managers: Robert Charles, Joanie Martin

* Closed April 30, 1972 after limited engagement of 6 performances.

Opened Friday, April 21, 1972*
Ted Menten presents:

AND THEY PUT HANDCUFFS ON THE FLOWERS

By Arrabal; Translation by Charles Marowitz; Revised by Lois Messerman; Director, Arrabal; Designed by Arrabal, Duane Mazey; Assistants to Arrabal, James Denton, Claudine Lagrive; Lighting, Barbara Kopit; Tapes, James Denton, Arrabal.

CAST

Amiel	George Shannon
Katar	Peter Maloney
Pronos	Ron Faber
Tosan	Baruk Levi
Drima	Muriel Miguel
Lelia	Patricia Gaul
Falidia	Ellen Schindler
Apparition	Riley Kellogg

A drama performed without intermission.

General Manager: Albert Poland
Press: Alan Eichler, James J. O'Rourke
Stage Manager: Lawrence Sellars

* Still playing May 31, 1972.

Top Left: Walter Landa, Doris Balin Bianchi, Sofia Andoniadis in "Gypsy" Below: Peter Maloney, Ron Faber, George Shannon in "And They Put Handcuffs on the Flowers"

THEATRE FOUR

Opened Sunday, April 23, 1972*
Susan Richardson, Lawrence Goossen and Seth Schapiro present:

THE REAL INSEPCTOR HOUND
and
AFTER MAGRITTE

By Tom Stoppard; Director, Joseph Hardy; Scenery, William Ritman; Lighting, Richard Nelson; Costumes, Joseph G. Aulisi; Hairstyles, Joe Tubens; Choreography, Patricia Birch; Technical Assistant, Archie Gresham.

CAST

"After Magritte"
In a room during early evening

Harris	Konrad Matthaei
Thelma	Carrie Nye†
Mother	Jane Connell
Foot	Remak Ramsay
Holmes	Edmond Genest

"The Real Inspector Hound"
Opening night in a theatre

Moon	David Rounds
Birdboot	Tom Lacy
Mrs. Drudge	Jane Connell
Simon	Konrad Matthaei
Felicity	Boni Enten
Cynthia	Carrie Nye†
Magnus	Remak Ramsay
Inspector Hound	Edmond Genest
BBC Voice	Brian Murray
Body	Abe de la Houssaye

Standbys: Lynn Milgrim, George Backman

Company Managers: Dorothy Olim, Phyllis Restaino
Press: Max Eisen, James J. O'Rourke
Stage Manager: Suzanne Egan

* Still playing May 31, 1972 (43 performances)
† Succeeded by Lynn Milgrim

Martha Swope Photos

Boni Enten, Edmond Genest, Carrie Nye, Jane Connell, Remak Ramsay in "The Real Inspector Hound" Above: Remak Ramsay, Jane Connell, Carrie Nye, Konrad Matthaei in "After Magritte"

Frank Vohs, Jeri Archer

PLAYERS THEATRE

Opened Monday, April 24, 1972*
D. Frederick Baker, Stuart Goodman, Frank M. Celecia and FM Productions present:

COLD FEET

By Marvin Pletzke; Director, Stuart Goodman; Set and Lighting, Kay L. Coughenour; Costumes, Kathleen Sacchi.

CAST

Stanford Flud	Frank Vohs
Winthrop Figg	Joe Kottler
Rosemarie Figg, Jr	Catherine Bacon
Rosemarie Figg, Sr	Jeri Archer
Janice Mog	Aurelia De Felice
Angel Flud	Sally De May

A comedy in two acts. The action takes place at the present time in Stanford's apartment in New York City, on a Saturday afternoon.

General Manager: Roy Franklyn
Press: Saul Richman, Sara Altshul
Stage Manager: John Bernabei

* Closed April 24, 1972 after 1 performance and 8 previews.

Ronald Sterkx Photo

BIJOU THEATRE

Opened Wednesday, April 26, 1972*
Dudley Field Malone and Van Rapoport present:

THE DIVORCE OF JUDY AND JANE

By Arthur Whitney; Director, Roderick Cook; Set, Helen Pond, Herbert Senn; Lighting, Gilbert Hemsley; Costumes, Edith Lutyens Bel Geddes; Hairstyles, Ronald DeMann; Production Assistant, Steve DePue.

CAST

Elaine	Louise Troy
Jackie	Parker McCormick
Greta	Delphi Lawrence
Maxine	Estelle Gettleman
Elinore	Lois de Banzie
Baby	Constance Forslund
Pat	Ruth Manning

A play in two acts. The action takes place at the present time, several days before Christmas, in an Eastside Manhattan duplex.

General Managers: William Craver, Harry Chittenden
Press: Sol Jacobson, Lewis Harmon, Ruth D. Smuckler
Stage Managers: Mark Healy, Lad Brown

* Closed April 30, 1972 after 7 performances.

Constance Forslund, Ruth Manning, Louise Troy, Parker McCormick, Delphi Lawrence

Friedman-Abeles Photo

ACTORS PLAYHOUSE

Opened Sunday, May 7, 1972*
Rick Hobard presents:

ANNA K.

Variations on Tolstoy's "Anna Karenina" Conceived and Directed by Eugenie Leontovich; Lighting, Richard Nelson; Movement, Elizabeth Keen; Sound, Port-o-vox; Production Associate, Michele Bejarano; Music, George Bamford.

CAST

Anna	Catherine Ellis
Dolly/Betsy/Hostess	Ann Mitchell
Princess Scherbatsky/Princess Maykoff/Masha/ Ambassador's Wife/Seriozha	Cam Kornman
Kitty/Sapho	Lanna Saunders
Countess Lydia/Annushka/Countess Vronsky	Eugenie Leontovich
Karenin	Arthur Roberts†1
Stiva/Vladimir/Kritsky	Rudolph Willrich
Serpuhovsky/Nikolai Scherbatsky/Footman/Valet/Waiter/ Trainman	Richard Ooms
Levin/Ambassador/Trainman	George Bamford
Vronsky	Mark MacCauley
Tuskevich/Landau/Kuzma/Matvey/Footman/Valet/Tartar Waiter	Dick Fuchs†2

Presented in 2 acts and 43 scenes. The action takes place in a New York City rehearsal studio.

Company Manager: Allan Sobek
Press: Max Eisen, Milly Schoenbaum
Stage Managers: Michael J. Frank, Richard Ooms

* Still playing May 31, 1972
† Succeeded by: 1. Liam Sullivan, 2. Stephen McHattie, Don Hamilton

Ann Mitchell, Rudolph Willrich, Lanna Saunders
Above: Eugenie Leontovich

ORPHEUM THEATRE

Opened Wednesday, May 3, 1972*
Paul B. Reynolds presents:

GOD BLESS CONEY

By John Glines; Director, Bob Schwartz; Musical Direction-Orchestrations-Arrangements, Robert Rogers; Scenery, Don Tirrell; Lighting, William Mintzer; Costumes, Margaretta Maganini; Technical Director, Glenn Hill.

CAST

Homer	Bill Hinnant
Christine	Ann Hodapp
Toula	Marcia Lewis
Father William	William Francis
Bertie	Liz Sheridan
Maxie	Johnny LaMotta

MUSICAL NUMBERS: "Subway to Coney," "Seagulls," "Throw out the Lifeline," "Love Life," "Eight-horse Parlay," "Man and Wife," "Goodbye Hives," "He Looked at Me," "The Coney Island," "Intermission Rag," "Here We Are," "God Bless All the Misfits," "Music Hall Medley," "Here Comes the Rabbi," "God Bless Coney"

A musical in two acts. The action takes place on July 14, 1964 on the beach at Coney Island.

Press: M. J. Boyer
Stage Managers: Brooks Fountain, Johnny LaMotta

* Closed May 5, 1972 after 3 performances and 13 previews.

Friedman-Abeles Photo

Jacqueline Brookes, Estelle Parsons, Clinton Allmon in "The Silent Partner"

ACTORS STUDIO

Opened Thursday, May 11, 1972*
The Actors Studio Production Unit presents the World Premiere of:

THE SILENT PARTNER

By Clifford Odets; Directed by Ed Setrakian; Artistic Director, Lee Strasberg; Executive Producer, Arthur Penn; Associate Producer, Dorothy Fowler; Design Consultant and Projections, Wolfgang Roth; Costume Consultant, Ruth Morley; Lighting Consultant, Ed Greenberg; Technical Director, John Branon.

CAST

Narrator	David Yanowitz
Schimmel	Sully Boyar
Barney	Pat Corley
Christy	Chad Burton
Crane	Howard Green
Pearl	Joyce Roth
Anthony	Vincent Duke Milana
Lovelace	Sam Schacht
Sheriff Bush	Don Fellows
Gracie	William Prince
Cutler	Peter Masterson
Miss Stone	Marcia Haufrecht
Pope	James Tolkan
Jelke	Jack Waltzer
Bruno	Simon Deckard
Zip	Clinton Allmon
Sweet Notes	Chris Allport
Nick Carter	Dimo Condos
Mayor	Tom Newman
Mr. Dove	Hy Anzel
Mr. Drumm	John Ryan
Mr. Lord	Jack Hollander
Mr. Fink	Bill Macy
Mr. Schwanda	Maury Cooper
Corelli	Constantine Katsanos
Clara	Irene Robinson
Carrie	Jacqueline Brookes
Marnie	Susan Peretz
Mrs. Finch	Lenka Peterson
Roxie	Bryarly Lee
Sam Eaton	David Patch
Ross	Rudy Bond
Thug	Henry Stanley
Peters	John Perkins
Telegram Boy	Philip Bond
Mr. Simpson	Mathew Anden
Phillip Bliss	Joseph Hardy
Mrs. Lovelace	Estelle Parsons
Eddie	Lazaro Perez
Women in Bake Shop	Mary Anisi, Cheryl Bronstein, Francesca deSapio, Rosemary Foley, Shelley Hainer, Marcia Haufrecht, Jennifer Main, Ashley Simmons, Frances Trotta

A play in 2 acts and 8 scenes. The action takes place in the industrial city of Appollo in the early 1930's.

Press: Alan Eichler
Stage Managers: Alan Coleridge, Lowell Fink, Michael Shapiro

* Closed May 21, 1972 after limited engagement of 12 performances.

Syeus Mottel Photo

Left Center: Ann Hodapp, William Francis, Marcia Lewis in "God Bless Coney"

EDISON THEATRE

Opened Monday, May 15, 1972*
Bob Yde in association with Andy Wiswell presents:

HARD JOB BEING GOD

Lyrics and Music, Tom Martel; Director, Bob Yde; Musical Staging, Lee Theodore; Designed by Ray Wilke; Costumes, Mary Whitehead; Lighting, Patrika Brown; Audio, Bill Sandreuter; Musical Director, Roy Bittan; Technical Director, Ray Wilke; Musical Arrangements, Roy Bittan, Tom Martel.

CAST

Sarah/Jacob's Wife/Slave/Pharoah's Soldier/
Moabite/Judean/Susanna .... Gini Eastwood
Jacob's Son/Moses/Moabite/David .... Stu Freeman
God .... Tom Martel
Slave/Pharoah's Soldier/Ruth/Judean/
Shepherd .... Anne Sarofeen
Abraham/Jacob/Pharoah/Moabite/Judean/
Amos .... John Twomey

MUSICAL NUMBERS: "Hard Job Being God," "Wherever You Go," "Famine," "Buy a Slave," "Prayer," "Moses' Song," "The Ten Plagues," "Passover," "The Eleven Commandments," "Tribes," "Ruth," "Festival," "Hail, David," "A Very Lonely King," "Battle," "You're on Your Own," "A Psalm of Peace," "I'm Countin' on You," "Shalom L'chaim!," "Amos Gonna Give You Hell," "What Do I Have to Do?"

A rock musical in 14 scenes.

General Manager: Ted Thompson
Press: Sol Jacobson, Lewis Harmon, Ruth D. Smuckler
Stage Manager: Ray Wilke

* Closed May 20, 1972 after 7 performances and 7 previews.

Friedman-Abeles Photo

Stu Freeman, Gini Eastwood, John Twomey,
Anne Sarofeen, Tom Martel

Miriam Colon, Manu Tupou

CATHEDRAL CHURCH

Opened Thursday, May 18, 1972*
The Puerto Rican Traveling Theatre presents:

THE PASSION OF ANTIGONA PEREZ

By Luis Rafael Sanchez; Translated by Charles Pilditch; Director, Pablo Cabrera; Set and Lighting, Karl Eigsti; Costumes, A. Christina Giannini; Community Coordinator, Jerry Benjamin; Technical Directors, Joe Gluerkert. John Ryerson.

CAST

Antigona Perez .... Miriam Colon
The Press .... Tomy Vargas, Luis Cadiz, Jose Rodriquez,
Eddie Velez, Jose Ocasio
Aurora .... Mary Bell
Creon Molina.. Manu Tupou
Pilar .... June Adams
Monsignor Bernardo Escudero...................... Peter Blaxill
Irene... Irene De Bari
Waiter .... George Burgenon

TOWNSPEOPLE: Marcos Abril, Freddie Aponte, Ana Bonilla, Pura Cintrol, Phyllis Collins, Lillian Cortez, Lourdes Ferre, Raphael Henriguez, Gloria Lake, Soraida Lara, Marie McFarlane, Ramon L. Ortiz, Anna Maria Otero, Ralph Oxios, Jo-Anne Robinson
STANDBYS: Antigona, Irene DeBari; Aurora, Pilar, Irene, Iris Martinez

The action takes place at the present time in the Republic of Molina, somewhere in the Americas.

Company Manager: C. George Willard
Press: Alan Eichler, James J. O'Rourke
Stage Manager: C. D. Creasap

* Toured the city for a limited run of 18 performances.

Friedman-Abeles Photo

MERCER-O'CASEY THEATRE
Opened Monday, May 22, 1972*
Robert Lissauer presents:

HARK!

Lyrics, Robert Lorick; Music, Dan Goggin, Marvin Solley; Staged by Darwin Knight; Scenery and Lighting, Chenault Spence; Costumes, Danny Morgan; Musical Arrangements-Orchestrations, John Lissauer; Vocal Arrangements-Musical Direction, Sande Campbell; Sound, Bill Merrill; Production Assistant, Janis Powell.

CAST
Dan Goggin
Marvin Solley
Elaine Petricoff
Danny Guerrero
Sharron Miller
Jack Blackton

MUSICAL NUMBERS: "Hark," "Take a Look," "George," "Hip Hooray for America," "Smart People," "What D'ya Wanna Be?," "Six Little Kids," "Icarus," "Sun Down," "Conversation Piece," "The Outstanding Member," "How Am I Doin', Dad?," "All Good Things," "Molly," "In a Hundred Years," "It's Funny about Love," "Coffee Morning," "Suburbia Square Dance," "I See the People," "Pretty Jack," "Big Day Tomorrow," "Lullaby," "Here's to You, Mrs. Rodriguez," "Early Sunday," "What's Your Sun Sign, Mr. Simpson?," "A Dying Business," "Waltz with Me, Lady"

A musical in two acts with prologue and epilogue.

General Manager; Steven Sinn
Company Manager: Norman Kean
Press: Betty Lee Hunt Associates, Henry Luhrman, Harriett Trachtenberg, Maria C. Pucci
Stage Managers: John Toland, Ron Vaad

* Still playing May 31, 1972.

Dan Goggin, Elaine Petricoff, Danny Guerrero, Marvin Solley, foreground, Jack Blackton, Sharron Miller

Nancy Hamilton (C), Pat Lysinger, Liz Otto, Georgia Engel, Joy Garrett, Pamela Adams, Douglas Houston, Geoff Leon, Charles Murphy, Edward Penn, Jess Richards

EASTSIDE PLAYHOUSE
Opened Wednesday, May 24, 1972*
Charles Forsythe presents:

ONE FOR THE MONEY, ETC.

Sketches and Lyrics, Nancy Hamilton; Music, Morgan Lewis; Musical Direction and Arrangements, Peter Howard; Costumes and Scenery, Fred Voelpel; Lighting, Judy Rasmuson; Production Assistant, Ted Bouton; Directed and Choreographed by Tom Panko; At twin pianos, Peter Howard, John Williams.

CAST

Pamela Adams	Pat Lysinger
Georgia Engel†	Charles Murphy
Joy Garrett	Liz Otto
Douglas Houston	Edward Penn
Geoff Leon	Jess Richards

SKITS AND MUSICAL NUMBERS: "An Ordinary Family," "Post-Mortem," "Teeter Totter Tessie," "I Only Know," "The Guess It Hour," "Born for Better Things," "Wisconsin or Kenosha Canoe," "If It's Love," "The Russian Lesson," "The Old Soft Shoe," "The Christmas Tree Bauble," "A House with a Little Red Barn," "How High the Moon," "The Story of the Opera," "Goodnight Mrs. Astor"

A revue presented in two acts.

General Manager: Norman E. Rothstein
Press: Sol Jacobson, Lewis Harmon, Ruth D. Smuckler
Stage Manager: Bud Coffey, Peter vonMayrhauser

* Closed June 11, 1972 after 23 performances.

Friedman-Abeles Photo

111

Florence Lacey

THE NEW THEATRE

Opened Thursday, May 25, 1972*
Proscenium Productions presents:

SWEET FEET

Music and Lyrics, Don Brockett; Book, Dan Graham; Director, Don Brockett; Scenery and Lighting, James French; Costumes, Tom Fallon; Production Supervisor, Norman Roth; Production Assistants, Leslie Mulvilhill, Richard Pinter.

CAST

The Piano Player	Marty Goetz
Rennie DuPont	Lenora Nemetz
C. B. Seatenbourgh	Dan Graham
Prop Boy	Scott Burns
Rubulous Diamond	John Dorish
Jack Ruffus	Bert Lloyd
Florence Carter (Sweet Feet)	Florence Lacey
Sweet Feet's Friend	Barney McKenna

MUSICAL NUMBERS: "Opening," "Sweet Feet," "Falling in Love Again Boogie," "Your Eyes Danced," "Prop-Room Ballet," "Everybody Dance," "Is This Love?," "Making a Star," "The Show Must Go On," "The Kind of a Woman," "Boompies," Finale

A musical in two acts. The action takes place during the Forgotten Forties in a Hollywood studio.

Press: Gifford/Wallace, Ellen Chenoweth
Stage Managers: Kate Pollock, Barney McKenna

* Closed May 27, 1972 after 6 performances.

Stanley L. Franzos Photo

OFF-BROADWAY PRODUCTIONS FROM OTHER SEASONS
THAT CLOSED DURING THIS SEASON

Title	Opened	Closed	Performances
The Effect of Gamma Rays on Man-in-the-moon Marigolds	4/7/70	5/14/72	819
The Dirtiest Show in Town	6/26/70	9/17/71	516
The Basic Training of Pavlo Hummel	5/19/71	4/2/72	365
The House of Blue Leaves	2/10/71	12/3/71	337
A Doll's House	1/13/71	6/26/71	111
Long Day's Journey into Night	4/21/71	8/22/71	109
Life in Bed	4/1/71	6/6/71	79
Hedda Gabler	2/17/71	6/26/71	26
(in repertory with "A Doll's House")			

OFF-BROADWAY PRODUCTIONS FROM OTHER SEASONS
THAT RAN THROUGH THIS SEASON

SULLIVAN STREET PLAYHOUSE
Opened Tuesday, May 3, 1960*
Lore Noto presents:

THE FANTASTICKS

Book and Lyrics, Tom Jones; Suggested by Edmond Rostand's play "Les Romantiques"; Music, Harvey Schmidt; Director, Word Baker; Musical Direction-Arrangements, Julian Stein; Designed by Ed Wittstein; Associate Producers, Sheldon Baron, Dorothy Olim, Robert Alan Gold; Origianl Cast Album by MGM Records

CAST

The Narrator .... Michael Tartel†1
The Girl .... Virginia Gregory†2
The Boy .... Geoffrey Taylor†3
The Boy's Father .... Donald Babcock†4
The Girl's Father .... David Vaughan†5
The Actor .... Justin Gray†6
The Man Who Dies .... Bill McIntyre
The Mute .... Les Shenkel†7
At the piano .... William F. McDaniel
At the harp .... Sally Foster

MUSICAL NUMBERS: Overture, "Try to Remember," "Much More," "Metaphor," "Never Say No," "It Depends on What You Pay," "Soon It's Gonna Rain," "Rape Ballet," "Happy Ending," "This Plum Is Too Ripe," "I Can See It," "Plant a Radish," "Round and Round," "They Were You"

A musical in two acts.

General Manager: Bob MacDonald
Press: Harvey B. Sabinson, Cheryl Sue Dolby
Stage Managers: Geoffrey Brown, Donald Babcock

* Still playing May 31, 1972. For original production, see THEATRE WORLD, Vol. 16.
† Succeeded by: 1. Joe Bellomo, David Cryer, Martin Vidnovic, 2. Leta Anderson, Marty Morris, 3. Erik Howell, Michael Glenn-Smith, Phil Killian, 4. Lore Noto, 5. Ray Stewart, Gonzalo Madurga, 6. Ron Prather, 7. Robert Schrock

Bill McIntyre, Eric Howell, Marty Morris, Robert Shrock, Justin Gray   *Van Williams Photos*
Above: Joe Bellomo, Marty Morris

Joe Masiell

Elinor Ellsworth

Betty Rhodes

J. T. Cromwell

Jack Blackton

Chevi Colton

Rita Gardner

Joseph Neal

Stan Porter

Barbara Gutterman

VILLAGE GATE

Opened Monday, January 22, 1968*
3W Productions Inc. presents:

JACQUES BREL IS ALIVE AND WELL AND LIVING IN PARIS

Production conception, English Lyrics, additional material by Eric Blau and Mort Shuman; Based on Brel's lyrics and commentary; Music, Jacques Brel; Director, Moni Yakim; Musical Director, Mort Shuman; Music arranged and conducted by Wolfgang Knittel; Scenery, Henry E. Scott III; Vocal Direction, Lillian Strongin; Lighting, James Nisbet Clark; Production supervised by Eric Blau; Original Cast Album by Columbia Records

CAST

Elly Stone†	Shawn Elliot
Mort Shuman	Alice Whitefield

MUSICAL NUMBERS: "Marathon," "Alone," "Madeleine," "I Loved," "Mathilde," "Bachelor's Dance," "Timid Frieda," "My Death," "Girls and Dogs," "Jackie," "The Statue," "Desperate Ones," "Sons of," "Amsterdam," "The Bulls," "Old Folks," "Marieka," "Brussels," "Fannette," "Funeral Tango," "Middle Class," "You're Not Alone," "Next," "Carousel," "If We Only Have, Love"

A musical entertainment in two acts.

General Manager: Lily Turner
Press: Ivan Black
Stage Managers: Phillip Price, Steve Helliker

* Closed July 2, 1972 after 1847 performances. A gala performance to celebrate its fifth year was given in Carnegie Hall on Tuesday, January 25, 1972. For original production, see THEATRE WORLD, Vol. 24.
† During the season the following appeared in the cast: Amanda Bruce, Howard Ross, Stan North, Betty Rhodes, Henrietta Valor, Elinor Ellsworth, Aileen Fitzpatrick, Joe Masiell, Barbara Gutterman, George Lee Andrews, John C. Attle, Chevi Colton, Joseph Neal, Janet McCall, George Ball, J. T. Cromwell, Jack Blackton, Margery Cohen, Rita Gardner, Fran Uditsky.

Elly Stone, Mort Shuman

MERCER-O'CASEY THEATRE

Opened Tuesday, April 7, 1970*
(Moved Aug. 11, 1970 to the New Theatre)
Orin Lehman presents:

THE EFFECT OF GAMMA RAYS ON MAN-IN-THE-MOON MARIGOLDS

By Paul Zindel; Director, Melvin Bernhardt; Music and Sound, James Reichert; Setting, Fred Voelpel; Lighting, Martin Aronstein; Costumes, Sara Brook; Associate Producer, Julie Hughes; Production Assistant, Peggy Cohen

CAST

Tillie	Swoosie Kurtz
Beatrice	Carolyn Coates†1
Ruth	Jennifer Harmon
Nanny	Judith Lowry†2
Janice Vickery	Marlena Lustik

STANDBYS: Tillie, Marlena Lustik; Ruth, Janice, Katherine Bruce

A drama in two acts. The action takes place at the present time in the home of Beatrice.

General Manager: Norman E. Rothstein
Company Managers: Patricia Carney, Bob MacDonald
Press: Seymour Krawitz
Stage Managers: Bud Coffey, Nyla Lyon

* Closed May 14, 1972 after 819 performances. Winner of 1971 Pulitzer Prize, and 1970 Drama Critics Circle Citation. For original production, see THEATRE WORLD, Vol. 26.
† Succeeded by: 1. Joan Blondell, 2. Ann Ives during vacation.

Bert Andrews Photos

Top: Joan Blondell, Judith Lowry

Joan Blondell, Swoosie Kurtz
Above: Jennifer Harmon, Carolyn Coates 115

MERCER-HANSBERRY THEATRE

Opened Tuesday, March 23, 1971*
Sankowich/Golyn Productions presents:

ONE FLEW OVER THE CUCKOO'S NEST

By Dale Wasserman; From novel by Ken Kesey; Director, Lee D. Sankowich; Producer, Rudi Golyn; Designed by Neil Peter Jampolis; Production Supervisor, Harvey Medlinsky; Music, James Barnett, John Blakeley; Costumes, Carolyn Klay; Sound, Gary and Timmy Harris

CAST

Chief Bromden	William Burns
Aide Williams	William Paterson, Jr.†1
Aide Washington	John Henry Redwood†2
Nurse Ratched	Janet Ward
Nurse Flinn	Eve Packer†3
Dale Harding	James J. Sloyan†4
Billy Bibbitt	Lawrie Driscoll†5
Charles Atkins Cheswick III	William Duff-Griffin†6
Frank Scanlon	Jon Richards†7
Anthony Martini	Danny DeVito†8
Ruckly	Joseph Napoli
Randle Patrick McMurphy	William Devane†9
Dr. Spivey	Jack Aaron†10
Aide Turkle	Jeffrey Miller†11
Candy	Louie Piday
Technician	Kelly Monaghan†12
Sandy	Sydney Adreani

VOICES: John Garber, Doug Armand, Joseph Napoli, Danny Rich, Mark Nelsen, Teddi Kern, James Barnett, John Blakeley, Lee D. Sankowich
UNDERSTUDIES: Bromden/McMurphy/Washington, Reno Mascarino; Harding/Cheswick/Scanlon, James Himelsback; Spivey, Scott Bruno; Candy/Sandy/Nurse Flinn, Ruth Saada

A drama in two acts. The action takes place at the present time in a ward in a state mental hospital.

General Manager: William Carver
Company Manager: Harry Chittenden
Press: Gifford/Wallace
Stage Manager: Philip Cusack

* Still playing May 31, 1972
† Succeeded by: 1. James Dickson, 2. Earl Ferguson, 3. Carolyn Cunningham, Wenda Lee, 4. Arthur Berwick, 5. Jerry Dodge, Kelly Monaghan, 6. John D. Gowans, 7. Sherman Lloyd, 8. Larry Spinelli, 9. Lane Smith, 10. Lou Bullock, 11. Charles Kashi, 12. Thomas Barrett, James Himelsback.

Yapa, Friedman-Abeles Photos

Lane Smith, Arthur Berwick Top Right: Janet Ward, John Redwood, William Devane

Arthur Berwick, Louie Piday, Lane Smith, Sydney Andreani

GRAMERCY ARTS THEATRE

Opened Wednesday, March 24, 1971.*
(Moved to Mercer-Shaw Arena April 28, 1971)
Manon Enterprises Ltd. and Propositions, Inc. present:

THE PROPOSITION

Conceived and Directed by Allan Albert; Designed by Allan Albert, Ron Ginsberg, Clint Helvey; Musical Director and Pianist, Danny Troob; Costumes, Arthur McGee

CAST

Paul Kreppel	Jane Curtin
Josh Mostel†	Munson Hicks
Karen Welles	Judy Kahan

An Improvisational Musical Revue in two parts.

General Manager: Cynthia Parker
Press: Harvey B. Sabinson, Lee Solters, Sandra Manley, Alan Eichler

* Still playing May 31, 1972.
† Succeeded by Sam Jory.

Friedman-Abeles Photo

Paul Kreppel, Jane Curtin, Munson Hicks, Sam Jory

CHERRY LANE THEATRE

Opened Monday, May 17, 1971*
(Moved Aug. 10, 1971 to Promenade Theatre)
Edgar Lansbury, Stuart Duncan, Joseph Beruh present:

GODSPELL

Music and Lyrics, Stephen Schwartz; Conceived and Directed by John-Michael Tebelak; Based on "The Gospel According to St. Matthew;" Lighting, Lowell B. Achziger; Costumes, Susan Tsu; Production Supervisor, Nina Faso; Musical Director, David Lewis; Associate Producer, Charles Haid; Musical Arrangement and Direction, Stephen Schwartz; Assistant to the Producers, Darrell Jonas

CAST

Lamar Alford	Sonia Manzano
Peggy Gordon	Gilmer McCormick
David Haskell	Jeffrey Mylett
Joanne Jonas	Stephen Nathan
Robin Lamont	Herb Simon†

MUSICAL NUMBERS: "Tower of Babble," "Prepare Ye the Way of the Lord," "Save the People," "Day by Day," "Learn Your Lessons Well," "Bless the Lord," "All for the Best," "All Good Gifts," "Light of the World," "Turn Back, O Man," "Alas for You," "By My Side," "We Beseech Thee," "On the Willows," Finale.

A musical in 2 acts and 16 scenes.

General Manager: Al Isaac
Company Manager: Gary Gunas
Press: Gifford/Wallace, Ellen Chenoweth
Stage Manager: Peter Kean

* Still playing May 31, 1972
† Succeeded by Herb Braha

Robin Lamont, Stephen Nathan, Jeffrey Mylett
Above: Entire cast with John-Michael Tebelak (C)

NEW YORK SHAKESPEARE FESTIVAL PUBLIC THEATER

Joseph Papp, Producer Bernard Gersten, Associate Producer

PUBLIC/ANSPACHER THEATER

Opened Thursday, June 10, 1971.*
The New York Shakespeare Festival Public Theater presents:

DANCE WI' ME
or "The Fatal Twitch"

By Greg Antonacci; Director, Joel Zwick; Lighting, Laura Rambaldi; Production Manager, Andrew Mihok; Music Coordinator, Herbert Harris; Administrative Assistant, Duane Wolfe; Associate Producer, Bernard Gersten

CAST

Honey Boy	Greg Antonacci
Jimmy Dick	Johnny Bottoms
Judy Jeanine	Judy Allen
Professor Alan	Alan Wynroth
Venerable Zwish	Joel Zwick
Pepper Pot	Sarah Venable
Sailor Avocado	Peter Alzado
Dr. Sincere	Tommie St. Cyr
Jane Trinculo	June Margaret Whitehill
The Band	Tumbs Bumpin', Peter Frumkin

A Play with music presented without intermission. The action takes place at the present time, and in Honey Boy's mind during the "good old days" of the 1950's.

General Manager: David Black
Press: Merle Debuskey, Faith Geer, M. J. Boyer

* Closed July 18, 1971 after 53 performances.

Right: Greg Antonacci, Judy Allen, Peter Alzado

PUBLIC/ANSPACHER THEATER

Opened Sunday, November 7, 1971.*
The New York Shakespeare Festival Public Theater presents:

STICKS AND BONES

By David Rabe; Director, Jeff Bleckner; Setting, Santo Loquasto; Costumes, Theoni V. Aldredge; Lighting, Ian Calderon; Associate Producer, Bernard Gersten; Production Manager, Andrew Mihok; Assistant to the Producer, Gail Merrifield; Technical Director, Mervyn Haines; Song, Lyrics, David Rabe; Music, Galt MacDermot

CAST

Ozzie	Tom Aldredge
Harriet	Elizabeth Wilson
David	David Selby
Rick	Cliff DeYoung
Sergeant Major	Hector Elias
The Priest	Charles Siebert
The Girl	Asa Gim

The action takes place in the autumn of 1968 in the family home.

General Manager: David Black
Press: Merle Debuskey, Faith Geer, Robert Ullman
Stage Managers: David Eidenberg, Tom Gardner

* Closed Feb. 20, 1972 after 129 performances. Re-opened Wednesday, March 1, 1972 in Broadway's Golden Theatre for an indefinite run. (see Broadway Calendar)

Friedman-Abeles Photos

PUBLIC/OTHER STAGE

Opened Thursday, June 24, 1971*
The New York Shakespeare Festival Public Theater, and the Cornbread Players present;

NIGGER NIGHTMARE

By Walter Jones; Directed by Novella Nelson; Choreography by George Faison

CAST

Hope Clark
Noorma Darden
Judi Dearing
Tommy Jonsen
Garret Morris
Freda Vanterpool
Lennal Wainwright
Dick Williams

* Closed June 27, 1972 after limited run of 4 performances.

(no photos available)

Cliff DeYoung, Hector Elias, Elizabeth Wilson, Tom Aldredge, David Selby

PUBLIC/OTHER STAGE
Opened Wednesday, November 10, 1971.*
The New York Shakespeare Festival Public Theater
presents:

THE BLACK TERROR

By Richard Wesley; Director, Nathan George; Setting,
Marjorie Kellogg; Lighting, Buddy; Costumes, Edna Watson;
Kuumba Dance, Bob Johnson; Associate Producer, Bernard
Gersten

CAST

Ahmed	Kirk Young
Keusi	Kain
M'Bahlia	Susan Batson
Antar	Paul Benjamin
Geronimo	Don Blakely
Radcliffe	Earl Sydnor
Brothers	Niger O. Akoni, Preston Bradley, Kim Sullivan, James Buckley III, Dudley Lloyd
Sisters	Sylvia Soares, Dolores Vanison, Freda Vanterpool
Drummers	Babafemi Akinlana, Ladji Camara, Ralph Dorsey
Radio Voices	Ron Dozier, William Mooney, Dolores Vanison, Ed VanNuys

A Drama in 2 acts and 7 scenes. The action takes place in
the very near future, given the nature of American Society.

Press: Merle Debuskey, Faith Geer
Stage Managers: Ron Dozier, James Buckley III

* Closed March 26, 1972 after 180 performances.

Friedman-Abeles Photos

**Top Right: Preston Bradley, Paul Benjamin, Don
Blakely, Dolores Vanison, Freda Vanterpool, Kirk Young
Below: Kain, Paul Benjamin, Susan Batson**

PUBLIC/MARTINSON HALL
Opened Thursday, December 16, 1971.*
The New York Shakespeare Festival (Joseph Papp, Pro-
ducer) presents:

THE WEDDING OF IPHIGENIA and IPHIGENIA IN CONCERT

Adapted from Euripides by Doug Dyer, Peter Link,
Gretchen Cryer; Music, Peter Link; Lyrics, Euripides; Director, Gerald Freedman; Music Arranged by Peter Link and
Goatleg; Setting, Douglas Schmidt; Costumes, Theoni V. Aldredge; Lighting, Laura Rambaldi; Associate Producer, Bernard Gersten

CAST

Agamemnon	Manu Tupou
Clytemnestra	Madge Sinclair
Iphigenia	Nell Carter, Margaret Dorn, Leata Galloway, Bonnie Guidry, Patricia Hawkins, Marta Heflin, Lynda Lee Lawley, Andrea Marcovicci, Julienne Marshall, Pamela Pentony, Marion Ramsey, Sharon Redd

MUSICIANS: Henry "Bootsie" Normand, Chip McDonald,
Leon Medica, Robert Patriquin, Fred Sherry, Peter Link

A Rock Musical in two parts.

Press: Merle Debuskey, Robert Ullman
Stage Manager: Michael Turque

* Closed April 16, 1972 after 139 performances.

Manu Tupou (C) Above (C): Madge Sinclair

PUBLIC THEATER ANNEX

Opened Tuesday, February 29, 1972*
The New York Shakespeare Festival Public Theater presents:

BLACK VISIONS

Four one-act plays directed by Kris Keiser and Novella Nelson; Setting, Ademola Olugebefola; Costumes, Grasanne Driskell; Lighting, Ernest Baxter; Choreography, Hope Clarke; Producer, Joseph Papp, Associate Producer, Bernard Gersten

CASTS

"Sister Son/ji"
by Sonia Sanchez; Director, Novella Nelson
Sister Son/ji .... Gloria Foster

"Players Inn"
by Neil Harris; Director, Kris Keiser
Barmaid .... Juanita Clark
Customer .... Bill Cobbs
Tittylip .... Berk Costello
Johnny .... Walter Cotton
Spabby .... Tommy Lane
Deadeye .... Hank Frazier
Numberman .... Sylvester Vonner
First Junkie .... Jeffrey Miller
Second Junkie .... JoJo Koyaki
White Detective... Norman Beim
Black Detective .... Tucker Smallwood
Drop Man .... Lou Rogers III
At the present time in Harlem.

"Cop and Blow"
by Neil Harris; Director, Kris Keiser
Tex .... Bill Cobbs
Nosegut .... Robert Judd
Barmaid .... Barbara Montgomery
Frank .... J. A. Preston
Knowledge.. JoJo Kokayi
Tittylip .... Berk Costello
Zulu .... Tommy Lane
Hitman .... Tucker Smallwood
Policeman.. Sylvester Vonner
First White Detective .... Frank Bara
Second White Detective .... Rick Petrucelli
Black Detective .... John Henry Redwood
At the present time in Harlem.

"Gettin' It Together"
by Richard Wesley; Director, Kris Keiser
Nate .... Morgan Freeman
Coretta .... Beverly Todd
Radio Disc Jockey.. Lou Rogers III
At the present time in Newark, N.J.

Press: Merle Debuskey, Bob Ullman
Stage Managers: Garland Lee Thompson, Lou Rogers III

* Closed April 30, 1972 after 64 performances.

Friedman-Abeles Photos

**Top Right: Morgan Freeman, Beverly Todd
in "Gettin' It Together"**

Gloria Foster, J. A. Preston

PUBLIC/NEWMAN THEATER

Opened Tuesday, May 2, 1972*
The New York Shakespeare Festival Public Theater
presents:

THAT CHAMPIONSHIP SEASON

By Jason Miller; Director, A. J. Antoon; Setting, Santo
Loquasto; Costumes, Theoni V. Aldredge; Lighting, Ian Calderon

CAST

Tom Daley.. Walter McGinn
George Sikowski .... Charles Durning
James Daley... Michael McGuire
Phil Romano .... Paul Sorvino
Coach .... Richard A. Dysart

Understudy: Jason Miller

The action takes place at the present time in the coach's
house, somewhere in the Lackawanna Valley of Pennsylvania.

Press: Merle Debuskey, Bob Ullman
Stage Managers: Ron Abbott, Joseph Kavanagh

* Still playing May 31, 1972. Winner of Drama Critics Circle
Award for Best Play of the season.

Friedman-Abeles Photos

Michael McGuire, Richard A. Dysart, Paul Sorvino, Charles Durning, Walter McGinn
Top Right: Michael McGuire, Paul Sorvino, Charles Durning

PUBLIC/ANSPACHER THEATER

Opened Sunday, May 14, 1972*
The New York Shakespeare Festival Theater presents:

OLDER PEOPLE

By John Ford Noonan; Director, Mel Shapiro; Setting, Ming Cho Lee; Costumes, Theoni V. Aldredge; Lighting, Roger Morgan; Music, Peter Link; Lyrics, John Ford Noonan

CAST

Roger/Dubufay/Man/Felix Devine .... Will Hare
Clarice/Wendy/Fay/Woman .... Bette Henritze
Sam   Beckman/Dubufay/Gastoni/Francis/Hooch/Harry/-
Stanley .... Barnard Hughes†
Stella Beckman/Kay/Zelda .... Polly Rowles
Dubufay/Dunbar/Bubber/Sidney/Howardina's
Brother .... Stefan Schnabel
May/Maggie/Geraldine/Howardina .. Madeleine Sherwood
    Musicians: Margaret Dorn, Henry "Bootsie" Normand,
                    Peter Link

A comedy in two acts.
Press: Merle Debuskey, Bob Ullman
Stage Managers: John Margulis, Dan Sedgwick

* Closed June 25, 1972 after 70 performances.
† Succeeded by Philip Sterling

Friedman-Abeles Photo

**Will Hare, Bette Henritze, Stefan Schnabel,
Polly Rowles, Barnard Hughes, Madeleine Sherwood**

PUBLIC THEATER ANNEX

Opened Tuesday, May 23, 1972*
New York Shakespeare Festival Public Theater presents:

THE HUNTER

By Murray Mednick; Director, Kent Paul; Setting, Ralph Funicello; Costumes, Theoni V. Aldredge; Lighting, Spencer Mosse; Music, Peter Link; Associate Producer, Bernard Gersten; Military Sequences, Richard Morse; Production Assistant, Zoe Myers

CAST

Lee .... Michael Hadge
Harry .... Robert Glaudini
Hunter .... Douglass Watson
Marianne .... Kathleen Cramer

A play in three acts.
Press: Merle Debuskey, Bob Ullman
Stage Manager: Jeff Hamlin

*Closed July 16, 1972 after 96 performances.

Friedman-Abeles Photo

**Robert Glaudini, Kathleen Cramer, Michael
Hadge, Douglass Watson (back)**

122

EQUITY LIBRARY THEATRE PRODUCTIONS
George Wojtasik, Managing Director
Twenty-ninth Season

MASTER THEATRE

Opened Thursday, October 21, 1971.*
Equity Library Theatre presents:

JUNE MOON

By Ring Lardner and George S. Kaufman; Director, Gordon Hunt; Musical Director, Ed Linderman; Scenery and Costumes, Danny Morgan; Lighting, R. S. Winkler

CAST

Maxie Schwartz	Herb Aronson
Miss Rixey	Anne Ashcraft
Brainard	Glover Buck
Eileen Fletcher	Dianne Deckard
Lucille Sears	Aurelia De Felice
Edna Baker	Suellen Estey
Hart	Joe Kottler
Goldie	Laura May Lewis
Benny	Stuart Michaels
Window Cleaner	Harvey Siegel
Fred Stevens	Michael Sklar
Paul Sears	Arlen Dean Snyder

A Comedy in three acts. The action takes place in the 1930's in a Parlor Car, in the Sears' livingroom, and at Goebel's publishing house.

Production Director: Lyn Montgomery
Press: Sol Jacobson, Lewis Harmon
Stage Managers: Julia Fremon, Rob Ellowitz

* Closed Oct. 31, 1971 after limited engagement of 14 performances.

Gene R. Coleman Photos

**Right: Aurelia DeFelice, Michael Sklar,
Herb Aronson, Arlen Dean Snyder
in "June Moon"**

MASTER THEATRE

Opened Thursday, November 11, 1971.*
Equity Library Theatre presents:

PARK

Book and Lyrics, Paul Cherry; Music, Lance Mulcahy; Director, Bick Goss; Musical Director and Arranger, John L. DeMain; Scenery, Billy Puzo; Costumes, Paulette Olson; Lighting, Art Grand; Pianist, John R. Williams; Production Assistants, Steve Rich, Ira S. Stoller

CAST

Jamie	Don Amendolia
Elizabeth	Lynn Archer
Austin	John High
Sara	Louise Shaffer

MUSICAL NUMBERS: "A Park Is for People," "Hello Is the Way Things Begin," "Bein' a Kid," "Elizabeth," "He Talks to Me," "Tomorrow Will Be the Same," "All the Little Things in the World Are Waiting," "I Want It to Just Happen," "One Man," "We Live for Another Day," "Jamie," "I'd Marry You Again"

A Musical in two acts. The action takes place at the present time in a park during spring.

Production Director: Lynn Montgomery
Press: Lewis Harmon, Sol Jacobson
Stage Managers: Joe Lane, Larry Rothenberg

* Closed Nov. 28, 1971 after limited engagement of 22 performances.

LIBRARY & MUSEUM OF THE PERFORMING ARTS

Opened Monday, October 18, 1971.*
Equity Library Theatre Informals presents:

A WARM-BLOODED DAME

Scattered Sketch Material by Doris Adler; Music and Lyrics, Shirley Grossman

CAST

Sally	Jane Heit

* Closed Oct. 20, 1971 after limited engagement of 3 performances. (No photos available)

**Louise Shaffer, John High, Don Amendolia
in "Park"**

123

MASTER THEATRE

Open Thursday, December 9, 1971.*
Equity Library Theatre presents:

MIDDLE OF THE NIGHT

By Paddy Chayefsky; Director, Nick Havinga; Scenery, Boyd Dumrose; Costumes, Evelyn Thompson; Lighting, John Nathan; Music Composed and Performed by J. Raul Bernardo; Technical Director, George Turski

CAST

Betty Preiss	Margo Ann Berdeshevsky
Mrs. Nieman	Shirl Bernheim
Mrs. Carroll	Mary Boylan
George Preiss	Edward Easton
Alice Mueller	Illa Cameron Howe
Jack Englander	Charles Isen
Jerry Kingsley	Joe Kottler
Marilyn	Avis McCarther
Mrs. Mueller	Stacy Palmer
Evelyn Kingsley	Natalie Priest
Lillian Englander	Dalen L. Sciarra

A Comedy-Drama in 3 acts and 8 scenes. The action takes place in Mrs. Mueller's apartment, and in Jerry Kingsley's apartment.

Managing Director George Wojtasik
Press: Sol Jacobson, Lewis Harmon
Stage Manager: Curtiss W. Sayblack

* Closed Dec. 19, 1971 after limited engagement of 14 performances.

Margo Ann Berdeshevsky, Joe Kottler

LIBRARY & MUSEUM OF THE PERFORMING ARTS

Opened Monday, December 20, 1971.*
Equity Library Theatre Informals presents:

THE WEB
and
THREE'S A CROWD

Director, Jeff Hamlin; Stage Manager, Robert Thomas

CAST

"The Web" by Albert Bermel

Fardl	Bill LaVallee
Banna	Philip Mackenzie
Dondi	Alice Elliott

"Three's a Crowd" by Donald Kvares

Jan	Edie Cowan
Jed	Paul Tully

* Closed Dec. 22, 1971 after limited engagement of 3 performances. (No photos available)

MASTER THEATRE

Opened Thursday, January 13, 1972.*
Equity Library Theatre presents:

ONE FOR THE MONEY
TWO FOR THE SHOW
THREE TO MAKE READY

Sketches and Lyrics, Nancy Hamilton; Music, Morgan Lewis; Direction and Choreography, Jeffery K. Neill; Musical Direction, Arrangements, Musical Continuity, Frederick S. Roffman; Settings, Jimmy Cuomo; Costumes, Lin; Lighting, Dennis R. Haber; Technical Director, George Turski; Pianist, John R. Williams

CAST

Barbara Coggin	Robert Hendersen
Beth Fortenberry	Douglas Houston
Mary Jo Gillis	Geoff Leon
Geraldine Hanning	Michael Makman
Pam Martin	Edward Penn
Liz Otto	John Remme
Carol Ann Ziske	Marshall Thomas

Understudies: Pauline Frechette, Neil Howard

ACT I: "Ordinary Family," "Post-Mortem," "The Old Soft Shoe," "The Guess It Hour," "If It's Love," "The Story of the Opera," "How High the Moon," "Wisconsin, or Kenosha Canoe"

ACT II: "ELT Blues," "Teeter Totter Tessie," "Born for Better Things," "The Shoe on the Other Foot," "The Yoo-Hoo Blues," "The Russian Lesson," "I Only Know," "At the Drop of a Hat," "The Christmas Tree Bauble," "A House with a Little Red Barn," "Cold Water Flat," "Goodnight, Mrs. Astor"

Selections from the three revues presented on Broadway in 1939, 1940, and 1946, in two acts.

Press: Sol Jacobson, Lewis Harmon
Stage Managers: Michael Newton, John Urban

* Closed Jan. 30, 1972 after limited engagement of 21 performances. Re-opened at Eastside Playhouse on Wednesday, May 24, 1972.

Gene Coleman Photos

Marshall Thomas, Barbara Coggin, Geoff Leon, Pam Martin, Carol Ann Ziske, Edward Penn, Geraldine Hanning, Douglas Houston, Mary Jo Gillis, Michael Makman, Beth Fortenberry, Robert Hendersen

MASTER THEATRE

Opened Thursday, February 10, 1972*
Equity Library Theatre presents:

OEDIPUS AT COLONUS

By Sophocles; Translated by Theodore Howard Banks; Conceived and Directed by David Bamberger; Music Composed, Recorded, Directed by William E. Boswell; Sets, Ernie Smith; Costumes, Dina Harris; Lighting, David Bamberger; Makeup, Dianne Hulburt; Sound, Tom Flynn; Choreographic Staging, Dianne Hulburt; Production Director, Lynn Montgomery; Technical Director, George Turski

CAST

Oedipus	James Harkey
Antigone	Hillary Wyler
Alto	Joan Maniscalco
Bass	Peter Platten
Baritone	Gale McNeeley
Tenor	Samuel Bruce
Soprano	Jacqueline Johnson
Ismene	Gloria Zaglool
Theseus	Gregory Abels
Creon	Benjamin H. Slack
Guards	Don McGrath, Martin Brandfon
Citizen-Soldier	Jerry Glover
Another Athenian Soldier	Chris King
Polyneices	David Beckman

Understudies: Don McGrath, Judy Metskas
A tragedy performed in two acts.
Press: Lewis Harmon, Sol Jacobson, Ruth D. Smuckler
Stage Managers: Eve Sorel, Robert Charles

* Closed Feb. 20 after limited engagement of 14 performances.

er Platten, Hillary Wyler in "Oedipus at Colonus"

Mary Louise, Robert Tananis in "No Strings"

LIBRARY & MUSEUM OF THE PERFORMING ARTS

Open Monday, February 14, 1972.*
Equity Library Theatre Informals presents:

THREE ONE ACT PLAYS

Director, Frank Errante; Stage Manager, Bob Perricone

CAST

"Mrs. Minter" by Donald Kvares
Mrs. Minter .... Annette Krasko

The action takes place at the present time in a New York City building.

"Blind Guy" by Michael Mathias
Blind Guy .... Stacy McAdams
Worm .... Tracey Walter

The action takes place in a park in the 1960's.

"I used to See My Sister" by Norman Dietz
Young Man .... Gary Sandy

The action takes place in a room at the present time.

* Closed Feb. 16, 1972 after limited engagement of 3 performances. (No photos available)

MASTER THEATRE

Opened Thursday, March 9, 1972*
Equity Library Theatre presents:

NO STRINGS

Book, Samuel Taylor; Music and Lyrics, Richard Rodgers; Director, Richard Michaels; Designed by Billy Puzo; Costumes, Sally Krell; Lighting, Cammie Caroline Lavine; Choreography, Lynne Gannaway; Musical Direction-Vocal Arrangements, Don Sturrock; Technical Director, George Turski; Pianist, Don Sturrock

CAST

Barbara Woodruff	Mary Louise
David Jordan	Robert Tananis
Jeanette Volmy	Patti Haine
Luc Delbert	Ronn Hansen
Mollie Plummer	Martha Greenhouse
Mike Robinson	Richard Stack
Louis de Pourtal	Michael Amber
Comfort O'Connell	Ann Hodges
Racing Fan	Pat Sciortino
Countessa de Blevard	Susan Cartt
Jack Mone	Paul Gilbert
Maria Mone	Pat Garland
Spanish Lady	Lynda Goodfriend
Show Girl	Pat Garland
Croupiers	Jim Frank, Derek Wolshonak
Marcello Agnolotti	Paul Gilbert
Pit Singers	Dinah Day, Fran Dorsey, Leah Horen, Jane Scheckter

MUSICAL NUMBERS: "The Sweetest Sounds," "La, La, La," "Loads of Love," "The Man Who Has Everything," "Be My Host," "You Don't Tell Me," "Love Makes the World Go," "Nobody Told Me," "Look No Further," "Maine," "An Orthodox Fool," "Eager Beaver," "No Strings," Finale

A musical in two acts.

Press: Sol Jacobson, Lewis Harmon, Ruth D. Smuckler
Stage Managers: Patrick Reaves, John Craig, Bonnie Sue Schloss
* Closed March 26, 1972 after limited engagement of 22 performances.

Gene Coleman Photos

LIBRARY & MUSEUM OF THE
PERFORMING ARTS
Monday, March 13, 1972*
Equity Library Theatre Informals presents:

IN NEED OF CARE

By David E. Rowley; Director, Jerry Grant; Lighting,
Carolyn Richter.

CAST

Shirley	Sandy Martin
Rita	Eileen Brady
Nobby	Rory Kelly
Jeff	Tom Patrick Dineen

The action of the play passes in the interior of a semi-
derelict farm outbuilding on a Saturday morning in spring.

* Repeated on March 14, 15, 1972. (No photos available)

MASTER THEATRE
Opened Thursday, April 6, 1972*
Equity Library Theatre presents:

THE SERVANT OF TWO MASTERS

By Carlo Goldoni; Translation, Edward J. Dent; Director,
Clinton J. Atkinson; Sets and Costumes, Charles Otis
Sweezey; Lighting, Atlee Stephan, III; Properties, Ara Soner;
Sound, Sanda Kayden; Sound, Michael Paulle; Duel Staged by
Eric Uhler; Technical Director, George Turski

CAST

Silvio	Jay Jammer
Pantalone	Randy Kim
Clarice	Carolyn Mignini
Dr. Lombardi	Robert Machray
Smeraldina	Regina Ress
Brighelia	Barry Michlin
Truffaldino	James Sutorius
Beatrice	Nancy Weems
Waitress	Cleve Roller
First Porter	W. C. Reilly
Florindo	Robert Sevra
Second Porter	Jack Hallett
Waiter	Winston May

A comedy in three acts. The action takes place within a
single day in Venice.

Press: Lewis Harmon, Sol Jacobson, Ruth D. Smuckler
Stage Managers: Susan K. Robison, Michael Paulle,
Bernard Uhfelder

* Closed April 16, 1972 after limited engagement of 14 performances.

Gene Coleman Photos

MASTER THEATRE
Opened Thursday, May 4, 1972*
Equity Library Theatre presents:

DU BARRY WAS A LADY

Music and Lyrics, Cole Porter; Book, Herbert Fields, B.
DeSylva; Direction and Musical Staging, Marvin Gord⬛
Music Arranged and Directed by William Boswell; Settin⬛
Donald Padgett; Costumes, Danny Morgan; Lighting, Che⬛
Thacker; Tap Choreography, Jack Dyville; Hairstyles, To⬛
Marrero; Pianist, Victor Byrd, Randy Barnett

CAST

Reporter/Actress	Jane Roberts
Jones/Zamore	Peter Plat⬛
Kelly/Le Duc de Choiseul	Elliott Ma⬛
Harry/Capt. of the Guard	Bruce I⬛
Alice/Marquise Alisande	Pat Stev⬛
Vi/Duchesse de Vi	Katie And⬛
Louis Blore/King of France	William Lin⬛
May Daly/Comtesse DuBarry	Diane Find⬛
Alex/Alexandre	Paul Eic⬛
Charley/Dauphin of France	Danny De V⬛
Doctors	Jane Robertson, Ike Feat⬛
Reporters	James Adrian, Jerry Bell, Ike Feath⬛
	Ronald Simon⬛
Starlets	Noreen Bartolomeo, Lois Ann Hall, Est⬛
	Koslow, Mary June Will, Madonna Young, Ja⬛
	Robertson, Linda Gol⬛
Duchesse du Coeur Flottant	Noreen Bartolon⬛
Marquise du Pont l'Eveque	Lois Ann H⬛
Comptesse de Cammembert	Esther Kosl⬛
Princesse Gruyere	Mary Jane W⬛
Baronne de Brie	Madonna You⬛
Les Messieurs	James Adrian, Ike Feather, Jerry B⬛
	Ronald Simon⬛
Gatekeeper	Ike Feat⬛

MUSICAL NUMBERS: "Ev'ry Day's a Holiday," "It A⬛
Etiquette," "When Love Beckoned," "Come on In," "Dre⬛
Song," "Mesdames et Messieurs," "What Have I," "But in ⬛
Morning, No," "Do I Love You," "DuBarry Was a Lad⬛
"Give Him the Oooh-La-La," "Well, Did You Evah," "⬛
Just Yours," "Katie Went to Haiti," "Friendship," Final⬛

A musical in 2 acts and 9 scenes. The action takes place⬛
the Club Petite in New York, and at Versailles outside Pa⬛

Press: Sol Jacobson, Lewis Harmon, Ruth D. Smuckle⬛
Stage Managers: Curtiss W. Sayblack, Rob Ellowitz,
Ellen Couch, Phyllis Sidersky

* Closed May 21, 1972 after limited engagement of 22 perf⬛
mances.

**James Sutorius, Randy Kim, Robert Machray
in "Servant of Two Masters"**

**Bruce Lea, Diane Findlay, Pat Stevens
in "DuBarry Was a Lady"**

LIBRARY & MUSEUM OF THE PERFORMING ARTS
Monday, May 22, 1972*
Equity Library Theatre Informals presents:

PLAGUESHIP—NINE DAYS OUT OF BARBADOS!

By Alex Panas; Director, Janet McCall; Designed by Bill Stabile; Costumes, Penny Davis and Bill Stabile; Lighting, Jonell Polansky; Sound, Jeff Peters; Theme Music, Bob Drumm; Stage Manager, Te R. D'Emilio.

CAST

Chief of Police	Paul Geier
His Son	Edmund Gaynes
The Mayor	Harry Carlson
Herringbone	John Tarrant
Hermione	Karlene Wiese
Christina	Lois De Banzie
The Imperialissimo	Chris Manor
Voovoo	Neville Richen
Populace	Chris Anastasio

The action takes place NOW! on an island in the waters of . . .

* Repeated May 23, 24, 1972. (No photos available)

Tom Ligon

ANTA MATINEE SERIES
Lucille Lortel, Artistic Director
Sixteenth Season

THEATRE DE LYS
Monday, December 6, 1971
and Tuesday Matinee, December 7, 1971.
The ANTA Matinee Series presents:

A BIO IN SONG

An evening of songs by and with lyrics by Irving Caesar; Robert Croll at the piano; Lighting, Guy J. Smith

PROGRAM

"And Still I Love You," "At My Time of Life," "Crazy Rhythm," "I Want to Be Happy," "Just a Gigolo," "Ladies, Ladies," "Love Is Such a Cheat," "Let the Ball Roll," "Remember Your Name and Address," "How to Spell Friendship," "Thomas Jefferski," "Let's Make the World of Tomorrow Today," "Sometimes I'm Happy," "Song to End All War," "The Good Good Lord Never Made a Bad Bad Day," "Tea for Two," "Umbriago."

Presented without intermission.

General Manager: Paul B. Berkowsky
Company Manager: Terry Grossman
Press: Jean Dalrymple

THEATRE DE LYS
Monday, December 20, 1971 and Tuesday Matinee, December 21, 1971.
The ANTA Matinee Series presents:

SALLY, GEORGE AND MARTHA

By Sam Dann; Director, David Brooks; Lighting, Guy J. Smith

CAST

Mrs. Sally Cary Fairfax	Kathryn Walker
Colonel George Washington	Michael Higgins
Mrs. Martha Dandridge Washington	Gloria Maddox

A Play in two acts. The action takes place in 1755 on the Fairfax estate in Virginia, and in 1758 in the Chamberlayne House in Virginia.

General Manager: Paul B. Berkowsky
Company Manager: Terry Grossman
Press: Jean Dalrymple

THEATRE DE LYS
Monday, January 10, 1972 and Tuesday Matinee, January 11, 1972.
The ANTA Matinee Series presents:

A PLACE WITHOUT MORNINGS

By Robert Koesis; Director, Josef Warik; Music, John Lines; Assistant to Mr. Koesis, Barbara Benziger; Lighting, Guy J. Smith

CAST

Meg	Leora Dana
Ted	Tom Ligon
Liz	Linda DeCoff
Matt	Brian Freiland
John	Staats Cotsworth
Sister Agatha	Martha Miller

A Play in two acts. The action takes place during a long night, in and around the house of Meg and John, and in places of their memories

General Manager: Paul B. Berkowsky
Press: Jean Dalrymple
Stage Manager: Jane E. Neufeld

(No photos available)

Wynn Handman, Director; Julia Miles, Associate Director
Paul Bernard, Director of Development
Eighth Season

AMERICAN PLACE THEATRE

Opened Wednesday, December 22, 1971.*
The American Place Theatre presents:

FINGERNAILS BLUE AS FLOWERS
and
LAKE OF THE WOODS

"Fingernails Blue as Flowers" by Ronald Ribman; Director, Martin Fried; Scenery, Kert Lundell; Lighting, Roger Morgan; Costumes, Patricia McGourty; Production Assistant, Steven W. Bergquist

CAST

Eugene Naville .... Albert Paulsen
Waiter .... Zakes Mokae
Estelle Singer .... Pamela Shaw
Jesse .... Larry Block
Rosemary .... Karli Dwyer
Understudies: Martin Shakar, Peri Dwyer

The action takes place during 1971 in a resort hotel in Jamaica

"Lake of the Woods" by Steve Tesich; Director, Frederick Rolf; Scenery and Costumes, Kert Lundell; Lighting, Roger Morgan; Music and Lyrics, Ron Panvini; Technical Director, James Ascareggi

CAST

Winnebago .... Hal Holbrook
Christo .... Armand Assante
Juanita .... Esther Benson
Forest Ranger .... Will Hussung
Musician .... Ron Panvini
Understudy: Martin Shakar

The action takes place at the present time in two scenes in the Great Outdoors.

Press: Howard Atlee, David Roggensack
Stage Managers: Franklin Keysar, Grania M. Hoskins

* Closed Jan. 8, 1972 after limited engagement of 33 performances.

Martha Holmes Photos

**Hal Holbrook, Esther Benson, Armand Assante
in "Lake of the Woods"**

AMERICAN PLACE THEATRE

Opened Tuesday, February 22, 1972*
The American Place Theatre presents:

SLEEP

By Jack Gelber; Director, Jacques Levy; Scenery, Kert Lundell; Lighting, Roger Morgan; Costumes, Willa Kim; Technical Director, Steve Crowley; Production Assistant, Rock Townsend

CAST

The Subject:
Gil .... David Spielberg
Sleep Scientists:
Dr. Morphy .... Don Fellows
Dr. Merck .... Conard Fowkes
Dream Figures:
Black Actress .... Verona Barnes
Black Actor .... Norman Bush
White Actor .... Barton Heyman
White Actress .... Dorrie Kavanaugh

A play in two acts. The action takes place at the present time in an experimental sleep lab.

Press: Howard Atlee, David Roggensack
Stage Managers: Franklin Keysar, Grania M. Hoskins

* Closed March 1, 1972 after limited engagement of 35 performances.

**Don Fellows, Verona Barnes, Dorrie Kavanaugh,
David Spielberg, Barton Heyman, Norman
Bush, Conard Fowkes in "Sleep"**

AMERICAN PLACE THEATRE

Opened Saturday, April 8, 1972*
American Place Theatre presents:

METAMORPHOSIS

By Charles Dizenzo; Dramatized from the stories of Franz
Kafka; Director, Jacques Cartier; Scenery and Costumes,
John Conklin; Lighting, Roger Morgan; Make-up, Joe Cranzano; Technical Director, Steve Crowley; Production Assistant, Deborah Packard

CAST

"The Judgment"
Georg .... Christopher Walken
Father... Sy Travers

"The Metamorphosis"
Gregor Samsa .... Oliver Clark
Mrs. Samsa .... Sylvia Gassell
Anna .... Jennifer Merin
Mr. Snize .... Bill Moor
Mr. Samsa .... Leonardo Cimino
Grete Samsa... Catherine Burns
Alta .... Avril Gentles
First Boarder .... Sy Travers
Second Boarder .... Al Corbin

UNDERSTUDIES: Mr. Samsa, Bill Moor; Grete, Alta, Jennifer Merin; First Boarder, Al Corbin

Press: Howard Atlee, David Roggensack
Stage Managers: Franklin Keysar, Grania M. Hoskins

* Closed May 6, 1972 after limited engagement of 34 performances.

Martha Holmes Photos

**Sylvia Gassell, Leonardo Cimino, Catherine Burns
in "Metamorphosis"**

Sab Shimono, Randy Kim, Leonard Jackson

AMERICAN PLACE THEATRE

Opened Saturday, May 27, 1972*
The American Place Theatre presents:

THE CHICKENCOOP CHINAMAN

By Frank Chin; Director, Jack Gelber; Scenery, John Wulp;
Costumes, Willa Kim; Lighting, Roger Morgan; Technical
Director, Steve Crowley; Production Assistants, Deborah
Packard, Liz Stein

CAST

Tam Lum..Randy Kim
Hong King Dream Girl .... Joanna Pang
Kenji .... Sab Shimono
Lee .... Sally Kirkland
Robbie .... Anthony Marciona
Tonto ....Calvin Jung
Lone Ranger .... Merwin Goldsmith
Charley Popcorn ....Leonard Jackson
Tom ....Calvin Jung
Standby for Charley, John McCurry

A play in 2 acts and 6 scenes. The action takes place at the
present time in Pittsburgh, Pa.

Press: Howard Atlee, David Roggensack, Clarence Allsopp

* Closed June 24, 1972 after limited engagement of 33 performances.

THE NEGRO ENSEMBLE COMPANY

Douglas Turner Ward, Artistic Director; Frederick Garrett, Administrative Direct

ST. MARKS PLAYHOUSE
Opened Tuesday, November 23, 1971.*
The Negro Ensemble Company presents:

THE STY OF THE BLIND PIG

By Phillip Hayes Dean; Director, Shauneille Perry; Setting, Edward Burbridge; Lighting, Ernest Baxter; Sound, Chuck Vincent; Technical Director, Michael Farrell; Costume Supervision, Steve Carter

CAST
Weedy ....Clarice Taylor
Doc... Adolph Caesar
Alberta Warren .... Frances Foster
Blind Jordan .... Moses Gunn

A Drama in three acts and nine scenes. The action takes place in the Warren apartment on the south side of Chicago in the 1950's, just before the beginning of the civil rights movement.

Company Manager: Gerald S. Krone
Press: Howard Atlee, David Roggensack, Clarence Allsopp
Stage Manager: Horacena J. Taylor

* Closed Jan. 9, 1972 after limited engagement of 64 performances.

Bert Andrews Photos

ST. MARKS PLAYHOUSE
Opened Wednesday, January 12, 1972.*
The Negro Ensemble Company presents:

WORKS IN PROGRESS

Cast, credits, and photos not available.

* Closed Feb. 7, 1972 after 22 performances.

(no photos available)

Frances Foster, Moses Gunn

Clarice Taylor, Adolph Caesar Above:
Frances Foster, Moses Gunn

130

ST. MARKS PLAYHOUSE
Opened Tuesday, March 15, 1972*
The Negro Ensemble Company presents:

A BALLET BEHIND THE BRIDGE

By Lennox Brown; Director, Douglas Turner Ward; Setting, Edward Burbridge; Lighting, Jennifer Tipton; Choreography, Louis Johnson; Costumes, Bernard Johnson; Arrangements, Sonny Morgan; Sound, Chuck Vincent; Technical Director, Michael Farrell; Assistant Production Manager, Coral Hawthorne; Technical Assistant, Dick Krider

CAST

Joseph Drayton	David Downing
Vain Women	Michle Shay
Commander of National Guard	Duane Jones
Maraval	Neville Richen
Borbon	David Connell
Lalsigh	Adolph Caesar
Achong	Stephen Cheng
Alcoholic	Jack Landron
Mrs. Drayton	Frances Foster
Mano Drayton/King	Gilbert Lewis
European King/Mahon	C. David Colson
European Queen	Carolen Ross
Priest	Howland Chamberlain
Mahal	Larry Desmond
Shouter Woman	Esther Rolle
African Queen/Prostitute	Lauren Jones
Jesus Monkey	Norman L. Jacob
Head Teacher	Robert Stocking
Soldiers	Tom Jenkins, Cary Barnes, Ron Hines, Bernard Wyatt
Off Stage Four	Sonny Morgan, Nathaniel Bettis, Eliebank Crichlow, Richard Pablo Landrum

A drama in two acts. The action takes place in East Dry River, popularly called Behind the Bridge, a ghetto in Port-of-Spain, Trinidad. Scenes alternate between Bridge locale, the home of the Draytons, and flashbacks to 15th Century European and African palaces.

Company Manager: Gerald S. Krone
Press: Howard Atlee, David Roggensack, Clarence Allsopp
Stage Manager: Horacena J. Taylor

* Closed April 16, 1972 after 39 performances.

**Gilbert Lewis, Lauren Jones
in "A Ballet behind the Bridge"**

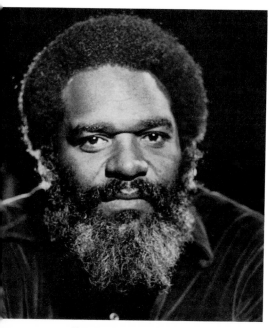

Douglas Turner Ward

ST. MARKS PLAYHOUSE
Opened Tuesday, May 9, 1972*
The Negro Ensemble Company presents:

FREDERICK DOUGLASS ... THROUGH HIS OWN WORDS

A program based on the play by Arthur Burghardt and Michael Egan; Scenery, Edward Burbridge; Technical Director, Michael Farrell; Technical Assistant, Dick Krider; Costume Coordinator, S. Carter; Sound, Collin Allan

CAST

Adolph Caesar
Duane Jones
Douglas Turner Ward

Selections from the words of Frederick Douglass presented in two acts.

Press: Howard Atlee, David Roggensack, Clarence Allsopp

* Closed June 4, 1972 after 32 performances.

Bert Andrews Photos

131

ROUNDABOUT THEATRE
Gene Feist, Producing Director

ROUNDABOUT THEATRE
Opened Sunday, October 17, 1971*
The Roundabout Repertory Company presents:

THE MASTER BUILDER

By Henrik Ibsen; Translated by Michael Meyer; Director, Gene Feist; Score, Philip Campanella; Designed by Holmes Easley; Costumes, Mimi Maxmen; Lighting, Robert Murphy; Assistant Director, Nancy Rhodes; Technical Director, Roger Cunningham

CAST

Halvard Solness	Paul Sparer
Aline Solness	Elizabeth Owens
Dr. Herdal	Sterling Jensen
Knut Brovik	Fred Stuthman
Ragnar Brovik	Gene Galusha
Kaja Fosli	Eren Oxker†1
Hilde Wagnel	Jill O'Hara†2

A drama in three acts presented with one intermission. The action takes place in Solness' studio in September.

Press: Michael Fried
Stage Manager: William Stiegel

* Closed Dec. 19, 1972 after 88 performances.
† Succeeded by: 1. Diane Elliot, 2. Eren Ozker

Martha Swope Photos

**Top Right: Paul Sparer, Jill O'Hara
in "The Master Builder"**

ROUNDABOUT THEATRE
Opened Sunday, January 23, 1972*
The Roundabout Repertory Company presents:

THE TAMING OF THE SHREW

By William Shakespeare; Directed by Gene Feist and Gui Andrisano; Original Score, Philip Campanella; Scenic Design, Holmes Easley; Costumes, Mimi Maxman; Masks, Jean Held; Lighting, Robert Murphy; Properties, Pat Reich; Production Assistant, Linda Lewis

CAST

Baptista	Sterling Jensen
Katherina	Joan Bassie
Bianca	Judith Sullivan
Hortensio	Philip Campanella
Gremio	Fred Stuthman
Vicentio	Lyle J. Lorentz
Lucentio	David Hendricks
Tranio	Louis G. Trapani
Biondello	Robert Zay
Petruchio	Michael Wager
Grumio	Gui Andrisano
Curtis	Lyle J. Lorentz
A Pedant	Philip Campanella
Widow	Nancy Sondag
Tailor	Louis G. Trapani

A comedy presented in two acts. The action takes place in Padua, and Petruchio's country house.

Press: Michael Fried
Stage Manager: Lauren Weiner

* Closed Feb. 20, 1972 after limited engagement of 45 performances.

ROUNDABOUT THEATRE
Opened Monday, December 20, 1971*
The Roundabout Repertory Company presents:

AN EVENING OF RUSSIAN THEATRE

Set and Light Designer, Roger Cunningham; Costume Designer, Ellen Ryba; Music Coordinator, Philip Campanella; Sound, Robert Murphy; Technical Assistants, David Petersen, Linda Lewis, Claudia Borrell, Rachel Brody

PROGRAM

"Tales of Odessa" by Isaac Babel
Isaac Babel .... John Guerrasio
"On the Harmfulness of Tobacco" by Anton Chekhov
Ivan Ivanovich Nyukhin .... Fred Stuthman
Both Directed by Nancy Rhodes

"The Proposal" by Anton Chekhov
Choobukov .... Fred Stuthman
Natalia Stepahova .... Melinda Peterson
Lomov .... John Guerrasio
Directed by Sterling Jensen

* Closed Dec. 26, 1971 after limited run of 9 performances.

**Michael Wager, Joan Bassie
in "The Taming of the Shrew"**

ROUNDABOUT THEATRE
Opened Tuesday, March 28, 1972*
The Roundabout Repertory Company presents:

MISALLIANCE

By George Bernard Shaw; Director, Gene Feist; Scenic Design, Holmes Easley; Costumes, Mimi Maxmen; Lighting, Robert Murphy; Musical Supervision, Philip Campanella; Assistant Director, Nancy Rhodes; Technical Director, Roger Cunningham; Technical Assistants, Claudia Borrell, John Quitt

CAST

Johnny Tarleton	Ian Stuart
Bentley Summerhays	Lou Trapani
Mrs. John Tarleton	Ruth Warrick
Hypatia Tarleton	Christine Sumerfield
Lord Summerhays	Fred Stuthman
John Tarleton	Hugh Franklin
Joey Percival	Tom V. V. Tammi
Lina Szczepanowska	Elizabeth Owens
Gunner	Philip Campanella

A comedy performed in two acts. The action takes place in the home of John Tarleton, Surrey, England, early spring in the late 1920's.

Press: Michael Fried
Stage Manager: Lauren Weiner

* Closed Apr. 30, 1972 after 46 performances and 14 previews.

Right: Tom V. V. Tammi, Philip Campanella, Christine Sumerfield Above: Hugh Franklin, Ruth Warrick in "Misalliance"

ROUNDABOUT THEATRE
Opened May 29, 1972*
The Roundabout Repertory Company presents:

CONDITIONS OF AGREEMENT

By John Whiting; Director, Gene Feist; Scene Design, Holmes Easley; Costumes, Mimi Maxmen; Original Score, Philip Campanella; Lighting, Robert Murphy; Assistant Director, Nancy Rhodes; Technical Director, Roger Cunningham; Technical Assistants, Mark Arnold, John Quitt

CAST

Emily Doon	Ruth Warrick
Peter Bembo	Fred Stuthman
A. G.	Humphrey Davis
Nicholas Doon	Tom V. V. Tammi
Patience Doon	Christine Sumerfield

A drama in two acts and four scenes. The action takes place in September 1948 in the living room of Emily Doon's house in a small town near Oxford, England.

Press: Michael Fried
Stage Manager: Lauren Weiner

* Closed May 29, 1972 after 1 performance and 23 previews.

Amnon Nomis Photo

Tom V. V. Tammi, Fred Stuthman in "Conditions of Agreement"

133

GREENWICH MEWS
SPANISH THEATRE
Gilberto Zaldivar, Producer

RIVERSIDE PARK
Opened Friday, August 13, 1971*
The Greenwich Mews Spanish theatre, with the cooperation of the Department of Cultural Affairs of the Parks, and the Urban Action Task Force, presents:

FUN IN THE STREETS
ALEGRIA EN LAS CALLES

Producer, Gilberto Zaldivar; Director, Luz Castanos; Musical Director, Juan Viccini; Choreographer, Gloria Irizarry; Costumes, Harlan Villegas, Robert Federico; Guitarists, Hector Doel Rios, Fernando Arizmendi; Press, Marian Graham

COMPANY
Miriam Cruz, Jean Rosado, Juan Carlos Sawage, Nino Roger, Maria Dolores, Alice Kaplan, Carmen Iris, Maria Luisa Martel, Marta Ygarte, William Rabanal, Gabrielle Gazon, Lina Centeno, Jenisa, Idalia Diaz, Feliz Enrique Fernandez

PROGRAM
"El Mazo Que Caso con Mujer Brava"
"Los Mangos"

* Closed Aug. 31, 1971 after 20 performances in the city parks.

GREENWICH MEWS
Opened Wednesday, August 25, 1972*
The Greenwich Mews Spanish Theatre presents the English and Spanish productions of:

EL SI DE LAS NINAS
WHEN A LADY SAYS YES

By Moratin; English translation, William M. Davis; Director, Norberto Kerner; Designed by Robert Federico; Lighting, Tony Quintavalla; Hairstyles, Lee Rios; Sound, Isabel Segovia

CAST
Don Diego .... Alberto Beraldo, Alfonso Manosalvas
Simon .... Jean Paul Delgado, Jean Cacharel
Dona Francisca .... Ilka Tanya Payan, Magaly Raffo
Dona Irene .... Lolina Gutierrez, Florencia Moncada
Rita .... Conchita Vargas, Irma Soledad
Calamocha ...... Emilio Rodriguez, Felix Enrique Fernandez
Don Carlos .... Jose Rodriguez, Jean Paul Delgado

Press: Marian Graham
Stage Manager: Susan Seltzer

* Closed Oct. 30, 1971 after 47 performances.

GREENWICH MEWS
Opened Wednesday, November 3, 1971*
Greenwich Mews Spanish Theatre presents:

DEBORAH

By Federico S. Inclan; a solo performance, and New York debut of Mexico's stage, film, and television star:

CARMEN MONTEJO

* Closed Nov. 7, 1971 after limited engagement of 4 performances.

Bert Andrews Photos

134

Carmen Montejo Above: Lolina Gutierrez, Alberto Beraldo

GREENWICH MEWS THEATRE

Opened Thursday, December 23, 1971*
The Greenwich Mews Spanish Theatre presents in English and Spanish:

LIFE IS A DREAM
"La Vida Es Sueno"

By Pedro Calderon de la Barca; English version by Kathleen Raine, R. M. Nadal; Director, Rene Buch; Designed by Bob Troie; Musical Director, Juan Viccini

CAST

Rosaura ....Miriam Cruz
Clarin ....Esteban Chalbaud
Segismundo .... Jose Redriguez
Clotaldo .... Ernesto Gonzalez
Astolfo .... Jean-Paul Delgado
Estrella .... Isabel Segovia
Basilio ....George Dal Lago or James H. Poulliott
Soldier .... Felix Enrique Fernandez
and Marco Abril, Jean Cacharel, Leo Centeno,
Idalia Diaz, Maria Dolores

A play in 3 acts. The action takes place in Poland.

Press: Marian Graham

* Closed Feb. 27, 1972 after 60 performances.

Right: Jose Rodriguez, Isabel Segovia
Top: Miriam Cruz, Ernesto Gonzalez
in "Life Is a Dream"

GREENWICH MEWS THEATRE

Opened Sunday, March 19, 1972*
Greenwich Mews Spanish Theatre (Gilberto Zaldivar, Producer) and the Institute for Advanced Studies in the Theatre Arts present in Spanish and English:

THE HOUSE OF FOOLS

By Master Joseph De Valdivielso; English translation, Aida Alvarez and John D. Mitchell; Director, Miguel Narros; Associate Director, Rene Buch; Production Supervisor, Aida Alverez; Music Composed and Conducted by Carmelo Bernaola; Set and Lighting, Robert Troie; Costumes, Andrea D'Odorico; Production Assistant, Lina Centeno

CAST

Guilt..............................Tamara Daniel/Elisavietta
Madness .... Elektrah Lobel/Marco Santiago
Lust .... Sadel Alamo/Charles Lara
Deceit....................................... Harold Cherry/Jose Ocasio
Lucifer .... Shelly Desai/Jose Rodriguez
Mankind........................... Antonio Flores/Con Roche
Gluttony...................... Davida Manning/Conchita Vargas
Envy...................................... Ketti Melonas/Isabel Segovia
World .... Peter Blaxill/Estaban Chalbaud
Flesh........................... Maria Dolores/Connie Keyse
Reason .... Miriam Mitchell/Irma Soledad
Soul .... Irene De Bari/Judy Greenaway
Inspiration .... Reinaldo Arana
St. Peter .... Tyrus Cheney/Julio Weber
Christ .... Richard Abel/Pedro Vega
Acolytes .... Jean Cacharel/Danny Metelitz

A morality play performed without intermission.

Press: Marian Graham
Stage Managers: Robert Main, Santos Ramos, Lina Centeno

* Closed May 21, 1972 after 42 performances.

Lina Centeno Photos

Sadel Alamo, Irene DeBari
in "House of Fools"

135

THE CHELSEA THEATER CENTER
Robert Kalfin, Artistic Director
Michael David, Executive Director

BROOKLYN ACADEMY OF MUSIC
Opened Tuesday, October 19, 1971*
The Chelsea Theater Center Brown Bag Series presents:

FOUR AMERICANS

Designed by John Scheffler; Lighting, Bennet Averyt; Production Manager, Burl Hash.

CASTS

"Now There's Just the Three of Us"
by Michael Weller; Director, Roger Hendricks Simon

Perry .... Tobias Haller
Deke ....Stephen McHattie
Frank .... Tony Travis
Nancy .... Linda Rubinoff
Agent ....Michael Vale

"The Reliquary of Mr. & Mrs. Potterfield"
by Stephen H. Foreman; Director, Dennis Rosa

Simon .... Edward Zang
Chloe ....Jeanne Hepple

Opened Wednesday, October 20, 1971*

"Tall and Rex"
By David Wiltse; Directed by Roger Hendricks Simon

Lorna .... Margaret Winn
Homer ....Michael Vale
Richard .... Drout Miller

"Things"
by David Kranes; Directed by Dennis Rosa

Sheila .... Ruth Baker
Mrs. Fibbs...Alice Beardsley
Arthur Harris .... Kermit Brown

* Closed Nov. 6, 1971 after limited engagement of 12 performances (6 for each duo on alternating nights)

Alan B. Tepper Photos

Top Right: Stephen McHattie, Tobias Haller
Below: Margaret Winn, Michael Vale

BROOKLYN ACADEMY OF MUSIC
Opened Wednesday, December 29, 1971.*
Chelsea Theater Center of Brooklyn presents:

THE INTERROGATION OF HAVANA

By Hans Magnus Enzensberger; Translated by Peter Mayer; Director, Louis Criss; Designed by John Scheffler; Lighting, Bennet Averyt; Assistant to the Director, Julie Taymor; Sound, Stanley Silberman; Technical Director, Neil Bleifeld

CAST

Guards .... Rocko Cinelli, Andre Pavon, Roland F. Sanchez
Interrogators:
Louis Gomes Wanguemert .... Robert Baines
Carlos Franqui...Martin Shakar
Carlos Rafael Rodriguez...................................... Ben Slack
Raul Valdes .... Brad Sullivan
Prisoners:
Carlos Manuel de Varona.......................... Donald Warfield
Manuel Perez Garcia .... Roger Robinson
Angel Fernandez Urdanivia .... Joseph Leon
Fabio Freyre Aguilera .... Jeff David
Pablo Organvides Parada .... Joseph Ragno
Jose Andreu Santos.................................... Dwight Schultz
Fermin Asla Polo alias Ismael de Lugo .... David Margulies
Felipe Rivero Diaz .... Nicholas Kepros
Ramon Calvino Insua .... Andrew Jarkowsky
Witnesses:
Octavio Louit Cabara .... Rocko Cinelli
Maria Elena .... Koula Antoniadou

Presented in two parts, the interrogation takes place at a press conference in Havana, Cuba four days after the Bay of Pigs invasion.

Production Manager: Burl Hash
Press: Ron Christopher, Monica Frakes
Stage Managers: Virginia Friedman, Harriett Wahrsager

* Closed Jan. 15, 1972 after limited engagement of 21 performances.

"Interrogation of Havana"

BROOKLYN ACADEMY OF MUSIC

Opened Tuesday, December 7, 1971.*
The Chelsea Theater Center of Brooklyn presents:

THE SCREENS

By Jean Genet; Director, Minos Volanakis; Scenery, Robert Mitchell; Costumes, Willa Kim; Lighting, Bennet Averyt; Translation, Minos Volanakis; Technical Director, Neil Bleifeld; Production Assistants, Karen John, Jeremy Unger, Jeff Sisco, Stanley Silberman.

CAST

Said	Robert Jackson
Mother	Julie Bovasso
Mustapha/Judge	John Capodice
Brahim	Henry Smith
Ahmed/Condemned Man	David Pendleton
Warda	Grayson Hall
Maid/Srira	Reah Smith
Malika	Joan Harris
Legionnaire	Greg Macosko
Leila	Janet League
Sir Harold	Charles Bartlett
Habib/Guard/Old Man	Joseph della Sorte
Taleb	John Coe
Kadidja	Despo
Nedjima	Marilyn Diane
Chigha/Mmme. Bonneuil	Marilyn Chris
Habiba	Linda Rubinoff
Policeman/M. Bonneuil	Robert Einenkel
Flute Player/Academician	Jerrold Ziman
Man who pissed/Banker	Gene Elman
Woman/Aicha	Vira Colorado
Scribe/Photographer	Gerald Finnegan
Cadi	Martin Garner
Madoni(The Mouth)	James Cahill
Gendarme/Si Slimane	Kurt Garfield
Mr. Blankensee/General	Richard Ramos
Malik/Salem	Jeff Druce
Abdil/Kaddur	Matt Greene
Sergeant	Barry Bostwick
Mrs. Blankensee/Aziza	Dorothy Chace
Arab Dignitary	Greg Etchison
Lassen (Old Chief)	Thomas Barrett
Vamp	Sasha von Scherler
Soldier	Dwight Schultz
Little Girl	Diana Bero
Old Woman/Djemila	Marilyn Sokol
Sir Harold's Son	Tobias Haller
M'Barek/Abdesselem/Grocer	Roland Sanchez
Kuider	Andre Pavon
Azuz	Henry Smith
Ommu	Osceola Archer

ARABS: Tom Barrett, Stephen Billias, John Capodice, Gerald Finnigan, Dwight Schultz, Henry Smith
Legionnaires: Greg Macosko, Dwight Schultz, Henry Smith, Robert Einenkel, John FitzGibbon
COMBATANTS: John Capodice, Joseph Della Sorte, Wayne Mitchell, David Pendleton
UNDERSTUDIES: Sergeant, Charles Bartlett; Warda, Vamp, Marilyn Chris; Mother Ommu, Dorothy Chace; Cadi, John Coe; Said, Joseph Della Sorte; Blankensee, Robert Einenkel; Leila, Linda Rubinoff; Lt., Medani, Sir Harold, Dwight Schultz; Kadidja, Chigha, Reah Smith

A Drama in 17 scenes with one intermission

Production Manager: Burl Hash
Press: Ron Christopher, Monica Frakes
Stage Manager: Stephen McCorkle

* Closed Dec. 26, 1971 after limited engagement of 25 performances. Received Drama Critics Circle Award as Best Foreign Play of the season.

Alan B. Tepper Photos

Top Right: The Revolutionaries

The Europeans, Above: Grayson Hall

BROOKLYN ACADEMY OF MUSIC

Opened Thursday, February 10, 1972*
The Chelsea Theater Center of Brooklyn presents:

KADDISH

Based on poem by Allen Ginsberg; Director, Robert Kalfin; Video by Arthur Ginsberg and Video Free America; Set and Costumes, John Scheffler; Lighting, Bennet Averyt; Production Manager, Burl Hash; Technical Director, Neil Bleifeld

CAST

Allen	Michael Hardstark
Naomi	Marilyn Chris
Young Allen	Glenn Weitzman
School Boy	Valcour Lavizzo
Bus Driver/Attendant/Policeman	Gregory Etchison
Attendant/Voice/Dr. Mabuse/Evangelist/Crapp/Dr. Luria/Policeman	Bernie Passeltiner
Football Hero	John Nichols
Louis	Michael Vale
Nurse/Bus Clerk/Woman/Greystone Nurse/Art Teacher/-Pilgrim State Nurse	Jani Brenn
Attendant/Pharmacist	David Elyah
Eugene	Jerrold Ziman
Man	Tim Wernet
Eleanor	Nina Hansen

UNDERSTUDIES: Naomi, Jani Brenn; Louis, Bernie Passeltiner; Allen, Young Allen, Eugene, Chip Zien

A drama in 6 parts with one intermission. The action covers a period from the late 1930's to the mid 1950's.

Press: Ron Christopher, Monica Frakes
Stage Managers: Virginia Friedman, David Elyah

* Closed Feb. 20, 1972 after limited engagement of 21 performances; re-opened Tuesday, March 7, 1972 at the Circle in the Square where it closed May 14, 1972 after 80 performances. Chip Zien was Allen; Ronica Stern, Mrs. Fields and Eleanor.

Alan B. Tepper Photos

**Marilyn Chris, Michael Hardstark
in "Kaddish"**

**Stephen D. Newman (C), Kathleen Widdoes (R)
in "The Beggar's Opera"**

BROOKLYN ACADEMY OF MUSIC

Opened Tuesday, March 21, 1972*
The Chelsea Theater Center of Brooklyn presents:

THE BEGGAR'S OPERA

By John Gay; Musical score newly realized by Ryan Edwards; Director, Gene Lesser; Set, Robert U. Taylor; Costumes, Carrie F. Robbins; Lighting, William Mintzer; Dances, Elizabeth Keen; Musical Director, Roland Gagnon; Production Manager, Burl Hash; Technical Director, Neil Bleifeld; Production Assistant, Phillip Himberg

CAST

Beggar (Jimmy Twitcher)	Joseph Palmieri
Mr. Peachum	Gordon Connell
Filch	John Long
Mrs. Peachum	Jeanne Arnold†1
Polly Peachum	Kathleen Widdoes†2
Macheath	Stephen D. Newman
Ben Budge	Roy Brocksmith
Matt of the Mint	William Newman
Crook-Fingered Jack	Neil Hunt
Diana Trapes	Connie Van Ess
Dolly Trull	Joan Nelson
Mrs. Coaxer	Lynn Ann Leveridge
Jenny Diver	Tanny McDonald†3
Suky Tawdry	Irene Frances Kling†4
Lockit	Reid Shelton
Lucy Lockit	Marilyn Sokol

UNDERSTUDIES: Polly, Joan Nelson; Macheath, Neil Hunt; Lucy, Lynn Ann Leveridge; Lockit, Joseph Palmieri; Peachum, William Newman; Mrs. Peachum, Connie Van Ess; Jenny, Irene Frances Kling; Matt, Roy Brocksmith

A play with music in two acts. The action takes place in the early 18th Century in and around the Peachums' house, a tavern near Newgate, and in and around Newgate Prison.

Press: Monica Frakes, Mark S. Andrews
Stage Managers: James Doolan, David Elyah

* Closed Apr. 16, 1972 after limited engagement of 28 performances. Re-opened Tuesday, May 30, 1972 in the McAlpin Rooftop Theatre. Cast changes were Timothy Jerome (Macheath), Ralston Hill (Lockit), Jill Eikenberry (Dolly)
† Succeeded at the McAlpin by: 1. Mary Louise Wilson, 2. Leila Martin, 3. Irene Frances Kling, 4. Deborah Deeble

BROOKLYN ACADEMY OF MUSIC

Opened Tuesday, April 25, 1972*
The Chelsea Theater Center presents:

EROS AND PSYCHE

Written and Directed by John Argue; Designed by Jeremy Unger; Composer, James Fulkerson; Technical Director, Neil Bleifeld

CAST

Story-Teller/Chorus	Anna Brennen
Aphrodite	Diane Salinger
Eros	Andrew Potter
Psyche	Cassandra Case
Sisters	Sheila Kotkin, Billie Jo Williams
Pan	John Guerrasio
Echo	Susan Brickell
The Graces	Gillian Gordon, Charlotte Linzer, Angelita Reyes
The Uroborus	Donald Larkin, Kenneth Weiss, Anthony White

Understudies: Tibor Feldman, Louise Williams

A dance-drama performed without intermission
Press: Monika Frakes
Stage Managers: Margaret Peckham, Philip Himberg

* Closed May 16, 1972 after limited engagement of 19 performances.

Alan B. Tepper Photos

**Cassandra Case (R)
in "Eros and Psyche"**

**Joey Fitter, Wil Albert, James Cahill
Above: Paul Sparer, Garn Stephens**

BROOKLYN ACADEMY OF MUSIC

Opened Tuesday, May 9, 1972*
The Chelsea Theater Center of Brooklyn present:

THE WATER HEN

By Stanislaw Ignacy Witkiewicz; Translation, Daniel C. Gerould; Director, Carl Weber; Set, Fred Kolouch; Costumes, Theodora Skipitares; Lighting, Richard M. Devin; Music, William Bolcom; Production Manager, Burl Hash; Technical Director, Neil Bleifeld

CAST

Elizabeth Gutzie-Virgeling (Water Hen)	Garn Stephens
Edgar Valpor	James Cahill
Tadeuz Gutzie-Virgeling (Tadzio)	Mickey Finn
Lamplighter	Vincent Schiavelli
Albert Valpor	Paul Sparer
Footmen	James Banick, Hank Borwinik, James Donnellan, Anthony Werner
Alice, Duchess of Nevermore	Patricia Elliott
Richard de Korbowa-Korbowski	Joseph della Sorte
Ephermer Typowicz	Joseph Leon
Isaak Specter	Joey Fitter
Alfred Evader	Martin Meyers
Jan Parblichenko	Ronnie Newman
Afrosia Yupupova (Nanny)	Elaine Grollman
Adolph Orsin	Wil Albert
Detectives	James Himelsbach, John Stravinsky

UNDERSTUDIES: Water Hen, Alice, Veronica Castang; Edgar, John Stravinsky; Albert, Wil Albert; Korbowski, Ronnie Newman

A tragicomedy in three acts. The action takes place in an open field, a barracks courtyard, and in Nevermore Castle.

Press: Monika Frakes, Mark S. Andrews
Stage Managers: Stephen McCorkle, Dan Hild

* Closed May 28, 1972 after limited engagement of 21 performances.

THE CUBICULO

Philip Meister, Artistic Director
Elaine Sulka, Managing Director
Maurice Edwards, Program Director

THE CUBICULO

June 9–12, 1971
(4 performances)

REQUIEM/A CELEBRATION directed by John Sillings, and performed by a theatre collective "The Intense Family": Xavier Arenas, Michael Brennen, Richard Crook, Richard Dill, Joanne Dunaway, Bolen High, Linn Malkin, Gordon Metcalfe, Jim Robiscoe, John Sillings, David Smith, Clint Spencer, Clyde Spencer

June 10–19, 1971
(6 performances)

MONKEY MAN'S PICK-UP by William Schlottmann; Director, Dick Garfield; Choreography, Elizabeth Keen; Performed by Lawrence Stern

NO-LUGGAGE PEOPLE by William Schlottmann; Director, Dick Garfield; Performed by Ingrid Lothigius (Hotel Maid), Kay Williams (Ruth Felton), Davidson Lloyd (Alexander)

July 21–24, 1971
(5 performances)

THE EVERLASTING SORROW by Richard Helfer; Director, Howard Vichinsky; performed by Angelynn Bruno, Ben Gotlieb, Michelle Jacobs, Martin Luther Kelly, Gordon O. King, Paula Maliandi, Ann McCormack, Leslie Ornstein, Neil Piper, Matthew Posnick, Elliott Raines, Jason Shulman

THE RED BRASSIERS: MASS TO THE SENTOSZA directed by Ted Feder; Composed by Gershon Freidlin; Performed by Gershon Freidlin, Jan Fleder, Joel Sorkin, Mary Handorff, Kilgore Trout, Spencer Aarons

June 25–26, 1971
(3 performances)

THE KAAKA-MAKAAKOO by Tone Brulin, with Graham Paul (Ego #1), Roger Babb (Lukie), David Daukins (Flipper), Cynthia Moore (Charity), Nelson Camp (Forsythe), Stephe Stern (Uncle), Diane Brown (Hannah)

July 7–10, 1971
(5 performances)

TWENTIETH CENTURY TAR written and directed by Tom Sydorick with Stanley Brock (Tony), Ed Kuczewski (Tim), Shelby Leverington (Rebecca), Parker McCormick (Tessie), John Merensky (California), Theodore Sorel (Dan), Ann Whiteside (Barbara)
Repeated Oct. 7–16, 1971 (9 performances)

July 28—August 7, 1971
(7 performances)

HORSESHOES by Paul Dexter, directed by Michel Corbeil, and performed by Mary Fogarty (Mother), Bob Horen (Father), Terriann Howard (Sister), Dan Lutzky (Husband), Robert Shea (Insurance Man), James Richardson (Son), Stephen Ommerle (Son)

July 30—August 7, 1972
(4 performances)

THE DARK MAIDEN FROM THE NINTH HEAVEN performed by Julia Callahan (Subito), F. William Parker (Husband), Beverly Oxley (Demon)

HOW THUNDER AND LIGHTNING BEGAN with Beverly Oxley (Boy), Lynn MacGregor (Girl)

EURYDICE with Kathy Chalfant (Eurydice), Robert Burgos (Orpheus), Julia Callahan (Fatima), Garet Church (Hermes)

All three plays by Holly Beye; directed and choreographed by Beverly Oxley

October 20–30, 1971
(10 performances)

KINGDOM BY THE SEA by Helen Duberstein with Leona Chamberlin (Joanna), Isabel Wolfe (Joanna as a young girl), Louise Shaffer (Joanna as a woman), Mark Suben (Richard)

SAMPLINGS OF PERCEPTION with Leona Chamberlin, Elaine Sulka, Joanne Joseph, Isabel Wolfe

DUET by Joanne Joseph with Mark Suben (He) and Louise Shaffer (She)

Conrad Ward Photos

Ed Kuczewski, Parker McCormick, Stanley Brock
in "20th Century Tar"

Katrin Tralongo
in "The Whores of Broadway"

Antony Ponzini, Edward Cohen, Attilio Barbato
in "Rome, Rome"

October 21–30, 1971
(10 performances)

THE WHORES OF BROADWAY by Gregory Rozakis; Director, Ron Link; Performed by Barry Bostwick (Chris), Katrin Tralongo (Colette), Moti Baharav (David), Michaele Lawton (Iris), Chez Smith (Katherine), Sheila Byrd (Cecelia)

November 5–13, 1971
(10 performances)

ROME, ROME by Louis Guss; Director, Al Lewis; With Joanne March (Virgilio), Anthony Caldarella (Carlo), Jeanne Kaplan (Domenica), Michael Enserro (Primo), Atillio Barbato (Ciro), Elaine Sulka (Brighella), Bill Da Prato (Pindar), Aldo Bonura (Scrupoli), Jo Ann Tedesco (Ascension), Antony Ponzini (Pasca), Edward Cohen (Angelo), Maurice Moston (Waiter), Joe Jamrog (Boss), Geraldine Hanning (Mme. Tutti), Bill Da Prato (Cogliosto), Alicia Kaplan (Whore), Jo Ann Tedesco (Whore), Alicia Kaplan (Maid), Maurice Moston (Brugieri), Jo Ann Tedesco (Cassandra), Joe Jamrog (Inspector), Maurice Moston (Butcher)

November 18—December 4, 1971
(16 performances)

In repertory: DRACULA, EXILES, REQUIEM directed by John Sillings, and performed by The Intense Family: Greg Abels, Tom Alaimo, Xavier Arenas, Frederic Blankfein, John Beltrane, Edward Crescimanni, Mary Dierson, Richard Dill, Susan Dill, Reily Hendrickson, Bolen High, Jan Kapral, Mitchell Kreindel, George Lindquist, James Rider, Mary Rockhill, Anne Silver, David Smith, Giulio Sorrentino, Clyde Spooner, Rod Suter, Midge Tenney, John Sillings

November 23–27, 1971
(5 performances)

TEAMS by Drew Kalter; Director, Barbara Rosoff; with Scott Mansfield (Jed), Phil Alton (Fred), Geoffrey R. Smith (Frank), Thomas C. McKown (Rick), Drew Katzman (Bill), Ted Kubiak (Quarterback), Fred Pierce (Albert), Peter Burnell (Kenneth), John Erdman (Carl), Jenny Charnay Maybruck (Stacy), John Thomas Waite (Julius), Ann Sweeny (Celia)

December 1–11, 1971
(10 performances)

SMUDGE by Myron Levoy; Director, Kent Wood; with Don Dolan (Richard), Carl Don (Eli), Lee Golden (Rudolph), Sarah Harris (Cyn), Adelle Reel (Marcia), Stefen Peters (Mark), Paul Knowles (Greg)

December 8–19, 1971
(10 performances)

THE DEATH OF J. K. by W. Nicholas Knight; Staged by Maria Piscator; with Dolph Sweet (Narrator), Wendell Phillips (Actor), Elia Braca (Actress), Ray Atherton (Historian), Albert Verdesca (Preacher), Cindy Ames (Librarian), Judy Jenkins (Librarian)

December 27–31, 1971
(7 performances)

RICHARD MORSE MIME THEATRE with Richard Morse and Wendy Young in "Flirtations," "Sports," "Meetings and Partings," "Recollection Piece," "Gargoyles of Notre Dame," "Lawyers of Daumier," "Death of a Poet," "Joseph and Mary," "The Tender-hearted Christmas Tree Feller"

Janurary 3–4, 1972
(2 performances)

PERIMETERS by Frank Parman with Terry Moore

ATEM by Mauricio Kagel performed by James Fulkerson

Janurary 15–29, 1972
(10 performances)

CONFESSIONS OF A SPENT YOUTH by Vance Bourjaily; Director, John Pearson; Associate Director, Dale Olson; performed by Vance Bourjaily (Himself), Elinor Ellsworth (Francine), Stefan Peters (Hal), Ron Martin (Quincy), John Milligan (Mort), Rhonda Saunders (Cynthia), Mike Wickerheiser (Eddie)

Janurary 20–22, 1972
(4 performances)

PROCESS: THE KADENSHO by Ze-Ami with Harry White and Mike Miller

REPORT TO AN ACADEMY by Franz Kafka with Mike Miller both directed by Manfred Bormann

Conrad Ward Photos

Peter Burnell, Geoffrey Smith, Phil Alton, Scott Mansfield in "Teams" (Meryl Joseph Photo)

Elaine Sulka, Dina Paisner in "Medea"
Above: Raymond Cole, Eileen Dietz in
"Ontological Proof . . ."

141

THE CUBICULO

February 3–19, 1972
(12 performances)
ONTOLOGICAL PROOF OF MY EXISTENCE by Joyce
Carol Oates; Music, George Prideaux; Director, Maurice Edwards; with Eileen Dietz (Shelley), Ray Cole (Peter), Jess
Adkins (Shelley's Father), Dan Lutzky (Martin)

February 3–12, 1972
(9 performances)
TELEPHONE POLE by Jean Reavey; Director, Jane Odin;
with Tom Davis (Harry), Peter Craig (Jasper), Marlene Fisher
(Pearl), Harry White (Dead Man)

February 16—March 5, 1972
(12 performances)
MOTHERLOVE by Strindberg; Director, Philip Meister;
with Gwendolyn Galsworth (Helene), Connie Van Ess (Amelie), Elia Braca (Augusta), Jane Hallaren (Lisen)
THE STRONGER by Strindberg; Director, Philip Meister;
Music, Norman Berman; with Elaine Sulka (Mrs. X), Kathryn Loder (Miss Y)

March 8–25, 1972
(12 performances)
ECHOES FROM GIBRAN adapted and performed by Kathryn Loder
SOMEWHERE IN BETWEEN by Katherine Rao; Director,
Lynn Michaels; with Suzanne Anderson (Stella), Bryan Dunlap (Eugene), Larry Hassman (George), Claire Ann Maguire
(Christine), Marcia Mohr (Martha), George Patelis (Sam)

April 6–22, 1972
(12 performances)
MEDEA by Jean Anouilh; Director, Paul Bengston; with
Elaine Sulka (Medea), Dina Paisner (Nurse), Christopher Cox
(Messenger), Mel Weinstein (Creon), David Tress (Jason),
Jessica Tress and Sam Schoemann (Children)

April 19–23, 1972
(5 performances)
GUNSIGHT by Theodore Weiss; Director, Nancy Rubin;
with Laurence Nadell (Ghost), David Leopold (Patient), Joel
Simon (Soldier), Anne Schedeen (Susie), Joseph Adorante
(Frank), Blainie Logan (Laura), John Kelly (Soldier), Irene
Roseen (Mother), Bob Gabriel (Father)

April 24—May 6, 1972
(9 performances)
VENICE: THE AGONY OF A CITY by Franco Zardo;
Director, Renato Padoan; with Maurice Edwards (Voice of
priest), Michael Enserro (Visitor), Robert Giarratano (Citizen), Mitchell Carrey (Policeman), Aldo Bonura (Citizen),
Floyd Levine (Workman), Gary Swartz (Professor), Robert
Shockley (Technician), James Kierman (Waiter), Sal Carollo
(Mayor), Frank Biancamano (Court Leader), Maryann
Fahey, Robert Shockley, Derek Steeley (Councilors of the
Left), Charmian Sorbello (Leader of Right Wing), Cynthia
Frost, Nick Discenza, James Kleeman (Right Wing Councilors), Mitchell Carrey, Gary Swartz (Councilors of the Center), Aldo Bonura (Alderman), Derek Steeley, James
Kleeman, Gary Swartz (Architects), Frank Biancamano
(President of New Town Committee), Robert Shockley, Nick
Discenza (members of committee), Harriet All (Caterina),
Tom Kubiak (Head of Delegation), Deborah Ashira (member
of delegation), Cynthia Frost (Director of Museums)

April 26—May 6, 1972
(8 performances)
SHALL WE GATHER AT THE RIVER: (3 plays by Maurice Noel; Directed by John Merensky) SCARLET SISTER
MARY with Jane Cronin (Rosemary), Molly Adams
(Momma), George Loros (Kevin) IONA STRAKER with
George Loros (Mike), Jane Cronin (Pagan Fury), Jane Lowry
(Bonnie) THE WITCH OF PURGITSVILLE with Jane
Lowry (Irene), Roy London (Simon) Jane Cronin (Opal)

Conrad Ward Photos

Top Right: Kathryn Loder in "Echoes from Gibran"
Below: David Tress, Elaine Sulka in "Medea"

**Aldo Bonura, Michael Enserro, Mitchell
Carey, Robert Giarratano in "Venice"**

THEATRE AT NOON
Miriam Fond, Artistic Director

ST. PETER'S GATE
November 8–12, 1971
(10 performances)

TWO BY LARDNER: "Haircut" adapted and performed by Herbert DuVal; "Golden Honeymoon" adapted and performed by Chet Carlin.

November 15–22, 1971
(16 performances)

THE BREAD TREE by Kit Jones; performed by Chet Carlin and Lucy Lee Flippin

December 6–22, 1971
(26 performances)

A LADY NAMED JO by Ben Finn; Musical adaptation of Louisa May Alcott's "Little Women"; Musical Director, Elise Bretton; Costumes, Virginia Lim. CAST: Joanne Dalsass (Jo), Sheryl Simms (Meg), Anne O'Donnell (Beth), Becki Davis (Amy), Peter Bartlett (Laurie), Leila Holiday (Marmee), Betty O'Rear (Aunt March), Barry Ford (Prof. Bhaer)

January 17–21, 1972
(10 performances)

LET'S HEAR IT FOR MISS AMERICA by Gloria Gonzalez, performed by Patricia Bryant, (Mrs. Gledhill), and Valerie Ogden (Vicky)

January 24—February 4, 1972
(20 performances)

RED EYE OF LOVE by Arnold Weinstein, with Tony Lang (Wilmer), Frank A. Ammirati (O. O. Martinas), Carol Nadell (Selma)

February 7—March 3, 1972
(40 performances)

THE MARRIAGE BROKER by Robert Hold-Theo Carus (Music and Lyrics), and Tom Tippett (Book); Musical Direction, William Foster McDaniel; performed by Susan Lehman (Jenny), Joe Vaccarella (Paul), Jay Bonnell (Nussbaum)

April 17—28, 1972
(20 performances)

TELEMACHUS, FRIEND by Sally Dixon Wiener (music, lyrics, book) performed by Richard Marr (Pop), Tom Roberts (Salesman), Bill LaVallee (Paisley), Arne Gunderson (Telemachus), Suzanne Oberjat (Widow)

All productions directed and staged by Miriam Fond; Stage Manager, Tom Roberts

Arnold Weinstein, Sally Wiener, Robert Hold Photos

Right: Suzanne Oberjat, Arne Gunderson, Bill LaVallee, also above with Richard Marr, Tom Roberts in "Telemachus, Friend"

Susan Lehman, Jay Bonnell in "The Marriage Broker"

Tony Lang, Carol Nadell in "Red Eye of Love"

AND MISS REARDON DRINKS A LITTLE

By Paul Zindel; Director, Melvin Bernhardt; Scenery, Fred Voelpel; Costumes, Sara Brook; Lighting, Martin Aronstein; Wardrobe Mistress, Berta M. Rogers; Presented by James B. McKenzie, Spofford Beadle, Seth L. Schapiro, Kenneth Waissman, Maxine Fox; Produced in association with Gordon Crowe; Opened Sept. 6, 1971 in the Mechanic Theatre, Baltimore, and closed March 12, 1972 at the Civic in Chicago.

CAST

Catherine Reardon	Kim Hunter[1]
Mrs. Pentrano	Virginia Payne
Delivery Boy	David Friedman
Ceil Adams	DeAnn Mears
Anna Reardon	Julie Harris[2]
Fleur Stein	Jo Flores Chase
Bob Stein	Bill Macy[3]

STANDBYS: Natalie Norwick, Alan Coleridge

A drama in three acts. The action takes place at the present time in the apartment of Catherine and Anna Reardon.

General Manager: Ralph Roseman
Company Manager: Robert W. Hulter
Press: Harvey B. Sabinson, Lee Solters, Fred Weterick
Stage Managers: Heinz Hohenwald, Frank Savino, Alan Coleridge

[†] Succeeded by 1. Betty Garrett, 2. Sandy Dennis, 3. Frank Savino

Irv Antler Photos

Right: Kim Hunter, Bill Macy, Julie Harris, Jo Flores Chase, DeAnn Mears Above: Sandy Dennis, Jo Flores Chase, Betty Garrett, Frank Savino, DeAnn Mears

Julie Harris, DeAnn Mears

Kim Hunter

APPLAUSE

Book, Betty Comden, Adolph Green; Music, Charles Strouse; Lyrics, Lee Adams; Director-Choreographer, Ron Field; Scenery, Robert Randolph; Costumes, Ray Aghayan; Lighting, Tharon Musser; Musical Direction-Vocal Arrangements, Donald Pippin; Musical Conductor, Jack Lee; Orchestrations, Philip J. Lang; Dance and Incidental Music Arrangements, Mel Marvin; Production Associate, Phyllis Dukore; Directorial Assistant, Otto Pirchner; Original Choreography re-staged by Ed Nolfi; Original Cast Album, ABC Records; Hairstylist, Michael Wasula, Maserone; Presented by Joseph Kipness and Lawrence Kasha in association with Nederlander Productions and George M. Steinbrenner III; Opened Monday, Nov. 29, 1971 in Royal Alexandra Theatre, Toronto, and still touring May 31, 1972.

CAST

Tony Announcer	Ray Thorne
Margo Channing	Lauren Bacall†
Eve Harrington	Virginia Sandifur
Howard Benedict	Norwood Smith
Bert	George McDaniel
Buzz Richards	Ted Pritchard
Bill Sampson	Don Chastain
Duane Fox	Lee Roy Reams
Karen Richards	Beverly Dixon
Bartender	David Steele
Dancer in bar	Sammy Williams
Peter	Burt Bier
Piano Player	Stan Page
Stan Harding	Ray Thorne
Danny	Steve Bauman
Leland	Leland Palmer
Carol	Lesley Rogers
Joey	Christopher Chadman
Musicians	Ed Nolfi, Stan Page, Ed Pfeiffer
TV Director	David Steele
Autograph Seeker	Peggy Haug

SINGERS: Margaret Cowie, Jeanne Lehman, Meg Scanlan, Bonnie Snyder, David Steele

DANCERS: Melanie Denis, Christa Fridinger, Dorothy Wyn Gehgan, Peggy Haug, Lesley Rogers, Jeannette Williamson, Steve Bauman, Christopher Chadman, Bryan Nicholas, Ed Nolfi, Ed Pfeiffer, Brennan Roberts, Albert Stephenson, Gary Wales, Thomas J. Walsh, Sammy Williams

UNDERSTUDIES: Margo, Beverly Dixon; Eve, Jeanne Lehman; Bill, George McDaniel; Howard, Burt Bier; Buzz, Ray Thorne; Karen, Bonnie Snyder; Duane, Christopher Chadman; Leland, Melanie Denis; Bert, David Steele; Stan, Peter, Stan Page

MUSICAL NUMBERS: (see Broadway calendar)

General Manager: Philip Adler
Company Manager: Joseph M. Grossman
Press: Bill Doll & Co., Bev Kelley
Stage Managers: Edward Preston, Mark S. Krause,
Barry-Robert Molitch, Stan Page

† Succeeded by Eleanor Parker
For original New York Production, see THEATRE WORLD, Vol. 26.

Top Right: Lauren Bacall, Lee Roy Reams, Sammy Williams Below: Norwood Smith, Lauren Bacall

Lauren Bacall

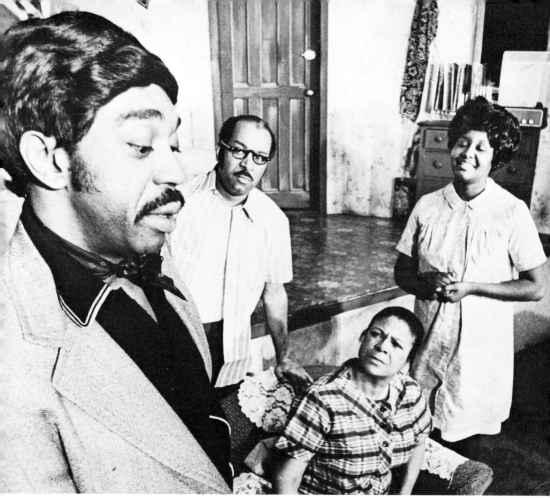

BLACK GIRL

By J. E. Franklin; Director, Shauneille Perry; Costumes, Femi; Set, C. Richard Mills; Wigs, Charles Reuben; Presented by Nederlander Productions; Opened Tuesday, January 4, 1972 in Mechanic Theatre, Baltimore, and closed there Jan. 23, 1972.

CAST

Billie Jean	Peggy Pettitt
Little Earl	Troy Warren
Sheryl	Stacey Durant
Norma	Charliese Drakeford
Ruth Ann	Judith Richardson
Mama Rosie	Juanita Clerk
MuDear	Gertrude Jeannette
Mr. Herbert	Kent Martin
Earl	Bill Cobbs
Netta	Vickie Thomas

UNDERSTUDIES: Herbert, Harrison Avery; Earl, Kent Martin; Norma, Ruth, Netta, Rosalyn Gibson; Mama, Mu'-Dear, Lil Henderson; Billie Jean, Judith Richardson

A drama performed without intermission. The action takes place at the present time in a small town in Texas.

Press: Sol Jacobson, Lewis Harmon, Robert Gibson
Stage Managers: Fred Seagraves, Harrison Avery

Friedman-Abeles Photos

Top: Bill Cobbs, Kent Martin, Gertrude Jeannette, Juanita Clark

Charliese Drakeford, Judith Richardson, Peggy Pettitt, Vickie Thomas

CANDIDE

Music, Leonard Bernstein; Lyrics, Richard Wilbur, John LaTouche; Based on play by Lillian Hellman; This version conceived and directed by Sheldon Patinkin; Producer, Edwin Lester; Scenery, Oliver Smith; Costumes, Freddy Wittop; Lighting, Peggy Clark; Music Director, Maurice Peress; Conductor, Ross Reimueller; Orchestrations, Leonard Bernstein, Hersy Kay; Additional Orchestrations, Dance Adaptations, Maurice Peress; Dances and Musical Numbers staged by Michael Smuin; Opened Tuesday, July 6, 1971 in Curran Theatre, San Francisco, and closed Nov. 13, 1971 at the Kennedy Center, Washington, D. C.

CAST

Narrator/Pangloss/Martin	Douglas Campbell
Candide	Frank Porretta
Cunegonde	Mary Costa, Barbara Meister
Baron/Inquisitor/Marquis/Ship Captain/Governor/ Ferone	William Lewis
Baroness/Princess/Lady of Paris/Pilgrim Mother/Governor's Mistress/Lady Frilly	Annette Cardona
Body Guard/Herald/Major Domo/First Mate/Page/Keeper of Masks	Robert Ito
King of Hesse/Inquisitor/Sultan/Pilgrim Father/Maximillian/Chief of Police	Joshua Hecht
Hessian General/Conjurer/Gentleman of Paris/Pilgrim/ Senores/Croupier	Harold Brown
Herman/Inquisitor/Guest/Pilgrim/Senores/ Gambler	Eugene Green
Barker	Howard Chitjian
Soldiers of Lisbon	Juleste Salve, Garold Gardner
Assistant to Second Inquisitor	Danny Villa
Old Lady	Rae Allen
Beggars	Lucy Andonian, Marvin Samuels, James L. Cutlip
Lady Silly	Cecile Wilson
Lady Willy Nilly	Tina Blandy
Lady Lightly	Maris O'Neill
Lady Brightly	Damita Freeman
Lady Fly-by-Nightly	Marie Patrice
Venetian Gentleman	Georgelton McClain
Lisbonian Gentleman	Juleste Salve
Buenos Airian Gentleman	Danny Villa
Parisian Gentleman	Robert Bakanic

CITIZENS, SOLDIERS, BEGGARS: Dana Alexis, Lucy Andonian, Lonna Arklin, Tina Blandy, Catherine Drew, Susan Gayle, Damita Freeman, De Maris Gordon, Anne Kaye, Brenda Lynn, Daphne Payne, Maris O'Neill, Marie Patrice, Kelly Maxwell, Anne Turner, Cecile Wilson, Karen Yarmat, Robert Bakanic, David Bender, Chward Chitjian, James L. Cutlip, Clifford Fearl, Garold Gardner, Georgelton McClain, Autris Paige, Casper Roos, Marvin Samuels, Juleste Salve, Paul Veglia, Danny Villa

STANDBYS AND UNDERSTUDIES: Alternate for Messrs. Porretta and Lewis, David Bender; Mr. Campbell, Joshua Hecht; Mr. Hecht, Eugene Green; Misses Costa and Meister, Anne Kay, Daphne Payne; Miss Allen, Dana Alexis; Mr. Green, Casper Roos; Mr. Brown, Paul Veglia; Miss Cardona, Brenda Lynn; Mr. Ito, Danny Villa

MUSICAL NUMBERS: "The Best of All Possible Worlds," "Marriage," "Oh, Happy We," "War and Peace," "Wedding Procession," "Candide's Lament," "It Must Be So," "The Paris Waltz," "Glitter and Be Gay," "You Were Dead, You Know," "Pilgrim's Procession," "My Love," "I Am Easily Assimilated," "Quintet," "Words, Words, Words," "Ballad of Eldorado," "Quiet," "It Must Be Me," "Barcarolle: The Simple Life," "Pickpocket Ballet," "What's the Use?," "Venice Gavotte," "No More Than This," "Make Our Garden Grow"

A musical in 2 acts and 8 scenes.

Rothschild Photos

**Top Right: Harold Brown, Annette Cardona
Below: Harold Brown, Rae Allen, William
Lewis, Mary Costa,**

Frank Porretta, Mary Costa

147

COMPANY

Music and Lyrics, Stephen Sondheim; Book, George Furth; Sets and Projections, Boris Aronson; Costumes, D. D. Ryan; Lighting, William H. Batchelder; Musical Direction, Jonathan Anderson, Richard Kaufman; Orchestrations, Jonathan Tunick; Dance Arrangements, Wally Harper; Musical Numbers Staged by Michael Bennett; Original Cast Album, Columbia Records; Director, Harold Prince; Presented by Harold Prince in association with Ruth Mitchell; Opened Thursday, May 20, 1971 in Ahmanson Theatre, Los Angeles, and closed May 20, 1972 at National Theatre, Washington, D. C.

CAST

Robert	George Chakiris†1
Sarah	Marti Stevens†2
Harry	Charles Braswell†3
Susan	Milly Ericson†4
Peter	Gary Krawford†5
Jenny	Teri Ralston†6
David	Lee Goodman†7
Amy	Beth Howland†8
Paul	Del Hinkley
Joanne	Elaine Stritch†9
Larry	Robert Goss†10
Marta	Pamela Myers†11
Kathy	Donna McKechnie†12
April	Bobbi Jordan†13

The Vocal Minority: Barbara Broughton, Carolyn Kirsch, Mary Roche, Marilyn Saunders†14

UNDERSTUDIES: Robert, Johnny Stewart; Joanne, Barbara Broughton; Peter, Larry, Randall Robins; Harry, David, Paul, Alan Sanderson; Jenny, April, Marta, Leilani Johnson; Amy, Susan, Kathy, Sindy Hawke

MUSICAL NUMBERS: "Company," "The Little Things You Do Together," "Sorry-Grateful," "You Could Drive a Person Crazy," "Have I Got a Girl for You," "Someone Is Waiting," "Another Hundred People," "Getting Married Today," "Side by Side by Side," "What Would We Do without You," "Poor Baby," "Tick Tock," "Barcelona," "The Ladies Who Lunch," "Being Alive"

A musical in 2 acts and 15 scenes. The action takes place at the present time in New York City.

General Manager: Carl Fisher
Company Manager: Donald Antonelli
Press: Robert W. Jennings
NY Promotion Manager: Bernard Simon
Stage Managers: Moose Peting, Kathleen A. Sullivan

† Succeeded by: 1. Allen Case, Gary Krawford, 2. Barbara Broughton, 3. Bernie McInerney, 4. Ann Johnson, 5. Johnny Stewart, 6. Jane A. Johnston, 7. George Wallace, 8. Tandy Cronyn, 9. Julie Wilson, 10. Nolan Van Way, 11. Louise Flaningam, 12. Carolyn Kirsch, Susan Plantt, 13. Rolly Fanton, 14. Sindy Hawke, Leilani Johnson, Mary Roche

For original NY production, see THEATRE WORLD, Vol. 26.

Top Left: Lee Goodman, George Chakiris, Teri Ralston

George Chakiris, Robert Goss, Elaine Stritch

Allen Case, Nolan Van Way, Julie Wilson

A DOLL'S HOUSE

By Henrik Ibsen; New adaptation, Christopher Hampton; Director, Hillard Elkins; Sets, Costumes, Lighting, John Bury; Production Supervisor, F. Mitchell Dana; Dance Consultant, Patrick Cummings; Presented by Hillard Elkins; Opened Monday, Sept. 13, 1971 in Royal Alexandra Theatre, Toronto; Opened the Eisenhower Theatre in John F. Kennedy Center for Performing Arts, Washington, D. C. on Monday, Oct. 18, 1971, and closed there on Nov. 7, 1971.

CAST

Nora Helmer ....Claire Bloom
Torvald Helmer .... Ed Zimmermann
Helene .... Camila Ashland
Mrs. Kristine Linde .... Patricia Elliott
Nils Krogstad .... Robert Gerringer
Dr. Rank ....James Ray
Anne-Marie ....Kate Wilkinson

STANDBYS AND UNDERSTUDIES: Nora, Patricia Elliott; Torvald, Haig Shepherd; Kristine, Helene, Jane Singer; Anne-Marie, Camila Ashland; Rank, Krogstad, Haig Shepherd

A drama in 3 acts. The action takes place at Christmas in the Helmers' flat.

General Managers: Bill Liberman, Edmonstone F. Thompson, Jr.
Press: Samuel J. Friedman, Shirley E. Herz
Stage Manager: Haig Shepherd

Martha Swope Photos

Claire Bloom, James Ray Above: Robert Gerringer, Claire Bloom (L)Gerringer, Patricia Elliott

Top: (L) Claire Bloom, Ed Zimmermann (R) Claire Bloom, Patricia Elliott

THE EFFECT OF GAMMA RAYS ON MAN-IN-THE-MOON MARIGOLDS

By Paul Zindel; Director, Melvin Bernhardt; Music and Sound, James Reichert; Setting, Fred Voelpel; Lighting, Martin Aronstein; Costumes, Sara Brook; Associate Producer, Julie Hughes; Production Manager, Bud Coffey; Production Supervisor, Ben Janney; Wardrobe, Billie White; Presented by Orin Lehman and Nederlander Productions; Opened Monday, Oct. 26, 1971 in Fisher Theatre, Detroit, and closed Dec. 11, 1971 at the Mechanic in Baltimore.

CAST

Tillie	Kathryn Baumann
Beatrice	Dorothy Loudon
Ruth	Adrienne Kent
Nanny	Anne Ives
Janice Vickery	Faith Catlin

Standby: Elaine Kussack

A drama in two acts. The action takes place at the present time in Beatrice's home.

General Manager: Norman E. Rothstein
Press: Sol Jacobson, Lewis Harmon
Stage Manager: Gisela Caldwell

For original NY production of this Pulitzer Prize play, see THEATRE WORLD, Vol. 26.

Friedman-Abeles Photos

Adrienne Kent, Dorothy Loudon

Kathryn Baumann, Anne Ives
Top: Dorothy Loudon

THE GINGERBREAD LADY

By Neil Simon; Director, Jeremiah Morris; Setting, David Hays, Costumes, Frank Thompson; Lighting, Martin Aronstein; Wardrobe, Viola Martin; Presented by Arthur Whitelaw in association with Seth Harrison; Opened Friday, Oct. 22, 1971 in Huntington Hartford Theatre, Los Angeles, and closed at the Playhouse in Wilmington on May 6, 1972.

CAST

Jimmy Perry .... Michael Lombard
Manuel .... Manuel Sebastian
Toby Landau .... Betsy von Furstenberg
Evy Meara .... Nancy Kelly
Polly Meara .... Maureen Silliman
Lou Tanner .... Michael Fairman

STANDBYS: Evy, Fayne Blackburn; Toby, Polly, Billie McBride; Jimmy, Lou, K. Lype O'Dell; Manuel, J. Victor Lopez

A drama in 3 acts. The action takes place at the present time in a brownstone apartment in the West 70's in New York City.

General Manager: Marvin A. Krauss
Company Manager: James O'Neill
Press: Max Eisen, Reginald Tonry
Stage Managers: Herbert Vogler, J. Victor Lopez

For original NY Production, see THEATRE WORLD, Vol. 27.

Left: Maureen Silliman, Nancy Kelly

Michael Lombard, Nancy Kelly

Nancy Kelly

151

HAIR

Book and Lyrics, Gerome Ragni, James Rado; Music, Galt McDermott; Executive Producer, Bertrand Castelli; Re-Staged by Robert Farley; Choreography, Julie Arenal; Costumes, Nancy Potts; Scenery, Robin Wagner; Lighting, Jules Fisher; Musical Direction, Fred Waring, Jr.; Conductor, Peter Malick; Sound, Abe Jacob; Original Cast Album, RCA-Victor Records; Presented by Michael Butler; Tour Manager, R. Robert Lussier; Production Assistant, Timothy Harbert; Sound Supervisor, Rich Mowdy; Opened in the University Auditorium Jan. 7, 1971 in Kalamazoo, Mich. and still touring May 31, 1972.

CAST

Claude	Claude Carlsen
Berger	Richard Siegel
Sheila	Candi Earley
Hud	Michael Rhone
Woof	Bob Herrmann
Jeanie	Linda Milburn
Crissy	Lynn Conner
Shirley	Caroline Cunningham
Jimi	Carlos Milton
Mother	Lynn Conner, Doug Lee, Michael Greenblatt
Father	Freda Walker, Ken Ortega, Lynn Connor
James Brown	Bruce Taylor
Jewish Mom	Michael Greenblatt
Principal	Merria Ross, Bruce Taylor, Robin Turrill
Tourist Couple	Jeffrey Hillock, Rick Pfleeger
Policeman	Skip Bowe
Young Recruit	Michael Greenblatt
General Grant	Ken Ortega
Abe Lincoln	Caroline Cunningham
War Parents	Jeffrey Hillock, Robin Turrill

UNDERSTUDIES: Claude, Skip Bowe, Pat Eimon; Berger, Ken Ortega, Jeffrey Hillock; Woof, Jeffrey Hillock, Greg Nagasawa; Hud, Doug Lee, Bruce Taylor; Sheila, Alice Lilly, Robin Turrill; Jeanie, Joyce Macek, Robin Turrill; Crissy, Tish Diskin, Freda Walker

MUSICAL NUMBERS: (see Broadway productions)

General Manager: Maurice Schaded
Company Managers: Donald Tirabassi, Susan V. Sedgwick
Press: Gifford/Wallace, George Deber
Stage Managers: Dan B. Sedgwick, Jr., Gary D. Anderson, Robert Ossenfort

For original NY production, see THEATRE WORLD, Vol. 24.

Top Left: Cast of "Hair"

KEEP OFF THE GRASS

By Ronald Alexander; Director, Shepard Traube; Scenery, Peter Harvey; Costumes, Zoe Brown; Presented by Shepard Traube and Edwin S. Lowe; Opened Monday, Apr. 3, 1972 at Mechanic Theatre, Baltimore, and closed at the Hanna in Cleveland on Apr. 22, 1972.

CAST

Billie Malone	Rita Gardner
Dan Shaw	Richard Morse
Poon	Kim Chan
Consuela Manning	Julie Newmar
Mike Balter	Steven Gilborn
A Visitor	Charles Silona
Gladys Wagner	Margaret Phillips
Detective	Jess Osuna

UNDERSTUDIES: Dan, Poon, Detective, Charles Cilona; Billie, Consuela, Gladys, Barbara Logan

A comedy in 2 acts and 4 scenes. The action takes place at the present time in the studio apartment of Billie Malone in a high-rise building in New York City.

General Manager: Monty Shaff
Press: Lenny Traube
Stage Managers: Perry Bruskin, Barbara Logan

(no photographs available)

Rita Gardner

HARVEY

By Mary Chase; Director, Stephen Porter; Scenery and
Lighting, James Tilton; Costumes, Nancy Potts; Presented by
Phoenix Theatre (T. Edward Hambleton, Managing Director); Opened Saturday, July 31, 1971 in Central City, Colo.,
and closed Nov. 20, 1971 at the Studebaker in Chicago.

CAST

Myrtle Mae Simmons	Tandy Cronyn
Veta Louise Simmons	Shirley Booth
Elwood P. Dowd	Gig Young
Ethel Chauvinet	Dorothy Blackburn
Ruth Kelly	Jennifer Warren
Duane Wilson	Jesse White†
Dr. Lyman Sanderson	Phillip R. Allen
Dr. William R. Chumley	Richard Woods
Betty Chumley	Michaele Myers
Judge Omar Gaffney	Edgar Meyer
E. J. Lofgren	Dort Clark

UNDERSTUDIES: Veta, Dorothy Blackburn; Myrtle, Ruth,
Pamela Fenwick; Wilson, Sanderson, Lofgren, Don Fenwick;
Elwood, Edgar Meyer; Ethel, Betty, June Renfrow; Chumley,
Gaffney, John Cecil Holm

A comedy in 3 acts and 5 scenes. The action takes place in
the Far West in the library of the old Dowd family mansion,
and the reception room of Chumley's Rest.

General Manager: Marilyn S. Miller
Company Manager: Gintaire Sileika
Press: F. B. Kelley
Stage Managers: Paul H. Waigner, Don Fenwick

† Succeeded by Dana Elcar, Judd Hirsch
For original NY production, see THEATRE WORLD, Vol.
1.

Van Williams Photos

Shirley Booth, Dorothy Blackburn, Gig Young
Top Right: Shirley Booth, Tandy Cronyn

LIGHT UP THE SKY

By Moss Hart; Director, Harold J. Kennedy; Production Supervisor, Ben Janney; Presented by Nederlander Productions; Opened Tuesday, Aug. 17, 1971 in the Fisher Theatre, Detroit, and closed Dec. 11, 1971 at the O'Keefe Center, Toronto, Canada.

CAST

Miss Lowell	Peggy Winslow
Carleton Fitzgerald	Harold J. Kennedy
Frances Black	Vivian Blaine†1
Owen Turner	Hayden Rorke
Stella Livingston	Ruth McDevitt†2
Peter Sloan	Michael Goodwin
Sidney Black	Sam Levene
Irene Livingston	Kitty Carlisle
Tyler Rayburn	Russell Nype†3
William H. Gallagher	Paul Ford†4
Plainclothesman	Bruce Blaine

STANDBYS: Sidney, Jack Collard; Irene, Peggy Winslow; Miss Lowell, Martha Miller

A comedy in 3 acts. The action takes place in the living room of Irene's Ritz-Carlton Hotel suite in Boston.

Press: Jon Essex, Jack Karr
Stage Managers: Henry Garrard, Bruce Blaine

† Succeeded by: 1. Jane Kean, 2. Margaret Hamilton, 3. Peter Adams, 4. Jack Collard
For original NY production, see THEATRE WORLD, Vol. 5.

Friedman-Abeles Photos

Sam Levene, Vivian Blaine, Ruth McDevitt, Hayden Rorke, Michael Goodwin, Kitty Carlisle, Harold J. Kennedy Top: Vivian Blaine, Harold J. Kennedy, Ruth McDevitt, Kitty Carlisle, Hayden Rorke, Sam Lev

MAN OF LA MANCHA

Book, Dale Wasserman; Music, Mitch Leigh; Lyrics, Joe Darion; Staged by Anthony De Vecchi; Settings, Lighting, Howard Bay; Costumes, Howard Bay, Patton Campbell; Dance Arrangements, Neil Warner; Musical Arrangements, Musick Makers; Musical Direction, Joseph Klein; Original Cast Album, Kapp Records; Opened Tuesday, Nov. 9, 1971 at the National Theatre, Washington, D. C., and closed Dec. 18, 1971 at O'Keefe Centre, Toronto, Canada.

CAST

Captain of the Inquisition	Joel Tropper
Don Quixote (Cervantes)	Allan Jones
Sancho	Edmond Varrato
Aldonza	Gerrianne Raphael
Innkeeper	Rowan Tudor
Padre	Taylor Reed†
Dr. Carrasco	Leon Shaw
Antonia	Marcia O'Brien
Barber	John Ferrante
Innkeeper's Wife	Sue Waldman
Pedro, Head Muleteer	Antony De Vecchi
Anselmo, Muleteer	John Ferrante
Housekeeper	Louise Armstrong
Jose, Muleteer	Farid Farah
Juan, Muleteer	Chet D'Elia
Tenorio	Ron Capozzoli
Paco	Andy Hostetler
Horses	Ron Capozzoli, Andy Hostetler
Fermina, Moorish Dancer	Marcia O'Brien
Guitarist	Robin Polsino

UNDERSTUDIES: Aldonza, Marcia O'Brien; Antonia, Fermina, Sue Waldman; Tenorio, Ron Capozzoli; Juan, Chet D'Elia; Pedro, Barber, Antony De Vecchi; Jose, Farid Garah; Innkeeper, Padre, John Ferrante; Paco, Andy Hostetler; Barber, Carrasco, Anselmo, Joel Topper

MUSICAL NUMBERS: "Man of La Mancha," "It's All the Same," "Dulcinea," "I'm Only Thinking of Him," "I Really Like Him," "What Does He Want of Me?," "Little Bird," "Barber's Song," "Golden Helmet," "To Each His Dulcinea," "The Quest," "The Combat," "The Dubbing," "The Abduction," "Moorish Dance," "Aldonza," "Knight of the Mirrors," "The Psalm"

A musical in 2 acts, suggested by the life and works of Miguel de Cervantes. The action takes place in a dungeon in Seville at the end of the 16th Century, and in the imagination of Cervantes.

Company Manager: Irving Cone
Press: Willard Keefe
Stage Managers: Richard Hughes, Keith Zickefoose
† Succeeded by Norman Kelley
For the original NY production, see THEATRE WORLD, Vol. 22.

Governor Morris Photos

Rowan Tudor, Allan Jones
Top: Allan Jones, John Ferrant

Edmond Varrato

THE ME NOBODY KNOWS

Music, Gary William Friedman; Lyrics, Will Holt; Adapted by Robert H. Livingston and Herb Schapiro; Based on book of same title edited by Stephen M. Joseph; Director, Robert H. Livingston; Musical Director, Milton Setzer; Musical Numbers Staged by Patricia Birch; Additional Lyrics, Herb Schapiro; Arrangements-Orchestrations, Gary William Friedman; Scenery-Lighting, Clarke Dunham; Costumes, Patricia Quinn Stuart; Media Design-Photography, Stan Goldberg, Mopsy; Assistant to Producer, Erlinda Zetlin; Original Cast Album, Atlantic Records; Presented by Moe Septee by arrangement with Jeff Britton; Opened Locust St. Theatre, Philadelphia, Tuesday, Oct. 19, 1971, and closed there Nov. 7, 1971.

CAST

Rhoda	Angela Miller
Lillian	Shelley Russek
Carlos	Jon Heron
Lillie Mae	Toni Lund
Benjamin	Michael Malone
Catherine	Jill Streisant
Melba	Judy Gibson
Lloyd	Danny Beard
Donald	Bobby Lee
Clorox	Andre De Shields
William	Darius Smith
Nell	Louise Heath

MUSICAL NUMBERS: "Dream Babies," "Light Sings," "This World," "Numbers," "What Happens to Life," "Take Hold the Crutch," "Flying Milk and Runaway Plates," "I Love What the Girls Have," "How I Feel," "If I Had a Million Dollars," "Fugue for Four Girls," "Rejoice," "Sounds," "The Tree," "Robert, Alvin, Wendell, and Jo Jo," "Jail-Life Walk," "Something Beautiful," "Black," "The Horse," "Let Me Come In," "War Babies"

A musical entertainment in two acts. The action takes place at the present time in New York's ghetto.

General Managers: Malcolm Allen, Marvin A. Krauss
Press: Eugene Palatsky
Stage Managers: Jeanne Fornadel, Andre De Shields

For original NY production, see THEATRE WORLD, Vol. 26.

THE ME NOBODY KNOWS

All credits same as above listing, except Musical Director, David Frank; Presented by Jeff Britton in association with Sagittarius Productions; Opened Monday, Feb. 8, 1971 in Chicago's Civic Theatre, and still playing May 31, 1972.

CAST

Rhoda	Trudy Bordoff
Lillian	Tricia Ann Smith
Carlos	Joe Rifici
Lillie Mae	Kelly Richardson
Benjamin	David Kruger
Catherine	Julienne Ciukowski
Melba	Debra Kelly
Lloyd	Greg Sullivan
Donald	Tony Michael Pann
Clorox	Andre De Shields
William	Marshaund Chandler
Nell	Jo Ann Brown

UNDERSTUDIES: Merrell Jackson, Karen Grannum, Dwight Dean Mahabir, Marshaund Chandler, Charles Marc Weissman

General Manager: Jose Vega
Company Manager: Paul Montague
Press: Herbert M. Kraus
Stage Managers: Robert Keegan, Deirdre Combs, Andre De Shields

(Jack Hoffman Photo)

Top Left: Philadelphia Company

Chicago Company

NATIONAL SHAKESPEARE COMPANY

Artistic Director, Philip Meister; Managing Director, Elaine Sulka; Tour Director, Mildred Torffield; Directors, Louis Criss (12th Night), William Francisco (She Stoops), Philip Meister (Romeo); Sets, Clyde Wachsberger; Costumes, Terry Leong; Lighting, William Lambert; Dueling coach, Rod Colbin; General Manager, Albert Schuemann; Stage Manager, Richard Ronald Beebe; Press, Lloyd Kay; Opened Monday, Sept. 27, 1971 at Queens College(NYC), and closed in Jamestown, Va. on May 13, 1972.

CASTS

ROMEO AND JULIET

Escalus	Jeffrey DeMunn
Paris	Craig LaPlount
Montague	Harlan Schneider
Capulet	Dennis Sook
Lady Capulet	Judith Hink
Romeo	James Lavin
Mercutio	Harlan Schneider
Benvolio	James Klawin
Juliet	Sharyn Martin
Nurse	Janet Gladish
Tybalt	Ernest Gray†
Friar Laurence	Ronald Wendschuh
Friar John	Ernest Gray†
Peter	Craig LaPlount
Apothecary	Jeffrey DeMunn

TWELFTH NIGHT

Feste	James Lavin
Viola	Sharyn Martin
Sea Captain	Dennis Sook
Orsino	Ernest Gray†
Curio	Craig LaPlount
Valentine	James Klawin
Sir Toby Belch	Richard Ronald Beebe
Maria	Janet Gladish
Sir Andrew Aguecheek	Harlan Schneider
Olivia	Judith Hink
Malvolio	Ronald Wendschuh
Antonio	Dennis Sook
Sebastian	Craig LaPlount
Officer, Priest	James Klawin

SHE STOOPS TO CONQUER

Sir Charles Marlow	Ronald Wendschuh
Young Marlow	James Klawin
Squire Hardcastle	Richard Ronald Beebe
George Hastings	Jeffrey DeMunn
Tony Lumpkin	Harlan Schneider
Diggory	Dennis Sook
Mrs. Hardcastle	Janet Gladish
Kate Hardcastle	Judith Hink
Constance Neville	Sharyn Martin
Stingo	Ronald Wendschuh
Jeremy	Craig LaPlount
Pimple	Ernest Gray†
Roger	James Lavin

† Succeeded by Jerry Rogers

Conrad Ward Photos

Harlan Schneider, Janet Gladish, Richard Ronald Beebe in "She Stoops ..." Top Right: James Lavin, Ronald Wendschuh, Sharyn Martin in "Romeo"

Harlan Schneider, James Lavin, John Linton, Richard Ronald Beebe, Janet Gladish in "12th Night"

NO, NO, NANETTE

Book, Otto Harbach, Frank Mandel; Music, Vincent Youmans; Lyrics, Irving Caesar, Otto Harbach; Adapted and Directed by Burt Shevelove; Dances and musical numbers staged by Donald Saddler; Lighting, Jules Fisher; Designed by Raoul Pene du Bois; Musical Direction-Vocal Arrangements, Buster Davis; Orchestrations, Ralph Burns; Dance Music arranged and Incidental Music composed by Luther Henderson; Conductor, Al Cavaliere; Production Manager, Ben D. Kranz; Production Supervised by Busby Berkeley; Presented by Pyxidium Ltd.; Opened Monday, Dec. 27, 1971 in Hanna Theatre, Cleveland, and still playing May 31, 1972.

CAST

Pauline	Judy Canova
Lucille Early	Sandra Deel
Sue Smith	June Allyson
Jimmy Smith	Dennis Day
Billy Early	Jerry Antes
Tom Trainor	Bill Biskup
Nanette	Dana Swenson
Flora Latham	Laura Waterbury
Betty Brown	Connie Danese
Winnie Winslow	Gwen Hillier

NANETTE'S FRIENDS: Rita Abrams, Darlene Anders, Sarah Chattin, Melanie Clements, Karen Crossley, Judy Endacott, Denise Hefner, Jackie Keith, Linda Kinnaman, Dottie Lester, Ellen Manning, Kathy Meloche, Janyce Nyman, Cindy Owens, Terry Rieser, Cheri Ann Schear, Suzie Swanson, Marcia Lynn Watkins, Sandra Zancan, Dennis Attkisson, Dennis Boyle, Jimmy Brennan, Bjarne Buchtrup, Tedd Carrere, Ron Crofoot, Jason Holt, Gary Kean, Michael Kozyra, David McDaniel, Ken Mitchell, Mike Mitchell, Ronald Stafford

UNDERSTUDIES: Pauline, Marye Brent; Lucille, Connie Danese; Sue, Ruth Maitland; Jimmy, Rod MacDonald; Tom, David McDaniel, Mike Mitchell; Billy, Dante D'Paulo, David McDaniel; Nanette, Darlene Anders; Flora, Sarah Chattin; Betty Marcia, Lynn Watkins; Winnie, Dottie Lester

MUSICAL NUMBERS: (see Broadway listings)

General Manager: Victor Samrock
Company Manager: Oscar Berlin
Press: Merle Debuskey, Paul G. Anglim
Stage Managers: Ben D. Kranz, Patricia Drylie, Rod MacDonald

Friedman-Abeles Photos

Top Right: Dennis Day, June Allyson

Judy Canova

Dana Swenson, Bill Biskup
Above: Sandra Deel, Jerry Antes

PROMISES, PROMISES

Book, Neil Simon; Based on film "The Apartment" by Billy Wilder and I. A. L. Diamond; Music, Burt Bacharach; Lyrics, Hal David; Director, Robert Moore; Musical Numbers Staged by Michael Bennett; Sets, Robin Wagner; Costumes, Donald Brooks; Lighting, Martin Aronstein; Musical Direction, Joseph Lewis; Orchestrations, Jonathan Tunick; Dance Arrangements, Harold Wheeler; Associate Producer, Samuel Liff; Original Cast Album, United Artists Records; Tour Direction, Columbia Artists Theatricals; Presented by David Merrick in association with Theatre Now, Inc.; opened Thursday, Sept. 16, 1971 in Mosque Auditorium, Scranton, Pa., and closed May 14, 1972 in Comerford Theatre, Wilkes-Barre, Pa.

CAST

Chuck Baxter	Will Mackenzie
J. D. Sheldrake	Mace Barrett
Fran Kubelik	Sydnee Balaber
Bartender Eddie	William James
Dobitch	J. Michael Bloom
Sylvia Gilhooley	B. J. Hanford
Kirkeby	Thomas Boyd
Eichelberger	Thomas Ruisinger
Vivien Della Hoya	Patricia Cope
Dr. Dreyfuss	Alan North
Jesse Vanderhof	Zale Kessler
Ginger	Trudie Green
Dentist's Nurse	Cheryl Clark
Company Nurse	Trudie Green
Company Doctor	Marius Hanford
Peggy Olson	Kathie Kallaghan
Lum Ding Hostess	Janet Saunders
Waiters	Louis Guzman, Edmond Wesley
Madison Square Attendant	Larry Giroux†
Dining Room Hostess	Cheryl Clark
Miss Polansky	B. J. Hanford
Miss Blackwell	Trudie Green
Bartender Eugene	Brandt Edwards
Marge MacDougall	Channing Chase
Clancy's Employee	Cheryl Clark
Helen Sheldrake	Shelley Rayburn
Karl Kubelik	William James
New Young Executive	Brandt Edwards
Interns and Dates	Josie Haskin, Janet Saunders, Robin Reseen, Richard Schneider

CLANCY'S LOUNGE PATRONS: Patricia Cope, Trudie Green, Louis Buzman, B. J. Hanford, Marius Hanford, Josie Haskin, Kathie Kallaghan, Shelley Rayburn, Janet Saunders, Richard Schneider, Edmond Wesley

UNDERSTUDIES: Chuck, J. D., William James; Fran, Peggy, Patricia Cope; Dreyfuss, Zale Kessler; Marge, Kathie Kallaghan; Dobitch, Eichelberger, Jesse, Thomas Boyd; Kirkeby, Marius Hanford; Sylvia, Vivien, Trudie Green; Ginger, Nurse, Josie Haskin; Dentist's Nurse, Shelley Rayburn; Karl, Brandt Edwards; Helen, Cheryl Clark; New Young Executive, Edmond Wesley

MUSICAL NUMBERS: "Half as Big as Life," "Upstairs," "You'll Think of Someone," "Our Little Secret," "She Likes Basketball," "Knowing When to Leave," "Where Can You Take a Girl?" "Wanting Things," "Turkey Lurkey Time," "A Fact Can Be a Beautiful Thing," "Whoever You Are," "A Young Pretty Girl Like You," "I'll Never Fall in Love Again," "Promises, Promises"

A musical in 2 acts and 14 scenes. The action takes place at the present time in New York City.

General Manager: Jack Schlissel
Company Managers: Horace Wright, Boris Bernardi
Press: Morton J. Langford, Dan Langan
NY Promotion Manager: Bernard Simon
Stage Managers: Pat Tolson, F. R. McCall, William James, Timothy Devitt

† Succeeded by Richard Schneider, Dennis Grimaldi
For original NY production, see THEATRE WORLD, Vol. 25.

**Top Right: Trudie Green, Patricia Cope, B. J. Hanford
Below: Sydnee Balaber, Alan North, Will Mackenzie, Channing Chase**

Will Mackenzie, Mace Barrett

PURLIE

Book, Ossie Davis, Peter Udell, Philip Rose; Based on play "Purlie Victorius" by Ossie Davis; Music, Gary Geld; Lyrics, Peter Udell; Scenery, Ben Edwards; Lighting, Thomas Skelton; Costumes, Ann Roth; Orchestrations-Choral Arrangements, Garry Sherman, Luther Henderson; Musical Supervisor, Garry Sherman; Musical Conductor, Joyce Brown; Dance Music Arrangements, Luther Henderson; Choreography, Louis Johnson; Director, Philip Rose; Original Cast Album, Ampex Records; Presented by Philip Rose; Opened Saturday, Nov. 20, 1971 at Shubert Theatre, Philadelphia, and still playing May 31, 1972.

CAST

Purlie	Robert Guillaume
Church Soloist	Shirley Monroe
Lutiebelle	Patti Jo
Missy	Carol Jean Lewis
Gitlow	Sherman Hemsley
Field Hands	Andy Torres, Lonnie McNeil, Ted Ross
Charlie	Tommy Breslin
Idella	Helen Martin
Ol' Cap'n	Art Wallace

UNDERSTUDIES: Purlie, Ra Joe Darby; Lutiebelle, Demarest Grey, Synthia Jackson; Gitlow, Ted Ross; Cap'n Charlie, James Hall; Swing Dancer, Ted Goodridge; Missy, Barbara Joy; Idella, Frances Salisbury

DANCERS: Zelda Pulliam, Doris deMendez, Linda Griffin, Debbie Palmer, Joan Palmer, Cleo Quitman, Michel Silva, Donald Ray Shannon, Every Hayes, Raphael Gilbert, Ted Goodridge, Lonnie McNeil, Charles Neal, Andy Torres

SINGERS: Laura Cooper, Demarest Grey, Synthia Jackson, Barbara Joy, Shirley Monroe, Frances Salisbury, Vanessa Shaw, Billy Abernathy, D. Morris Brown, Howard Porter, Ted Ross, Joe Williams, Jr.

MUSICAL NUMBERS: "Walk Him up the Stairs," "New Fangled Preacher Man," "Skinnin' a Cat," "Purlie," "The Harder They Fall," "Charlie's Song," "Big Fish, Little Fish," "I Got Love," "Great White Father," "Down Home," "First Thing Monday Mornin'," "He Can Do It," "The World Is Comin' to a Start," Finale.

A musical in 2 acts and 6 scenes, with prologue and epilogue. The action takes place in Georgia not too long ago.

General Manager: Walter Fried
Company Manager: Helen Richards
Press: Merle Debuskey, Maurice Turet, Irene Gandy
Stage Managers: Mortimer Halpern, Jerry Laws, Ra Joe Darby

For original NY production, see THEATRE WORLD, Vol. 26.

Friedman-Abeles Photos

Top Right: Carol Jean Lewis, Patti Jo, Sherman Hemsley, Robert Guillaume

Tommy Breslin, Helen Martin

Sherman Hemsley, Carol Jean Lewis, Patti Jo, Robert Guillaume Above: Guillaume, Patti Jo

THE ROTHSCHILDS

Music, Jerry Bock; Lyrics, Sheldon Harnick; Book, Sherman Yellen; Based on book by Frederic Morton; Directed-Choreographed by Michael Kidd; Settings-Costumes, John Bury; Lighting, F. Mitchell Dana; Orchestrations, Don Walker; Musical Direction-Vocal Arrangements, Milton Greene; Dance Music Arranged by Clay Fullum; Production Supervisor, Jose Vega; Presented by Lester Osterman; Opened Tuesday, May 9, 1972 in the Curran Theatre, San Francisco, and still playing May 31, 1972.

CAST

Prince William of Hess	Reid Shelton
Guard	Ralph Vucci
Mayer Rothschild	Hal Linden
Urchins	David Craig Moskin, Kevin Ellicott, Keith Luckett
Mama Rothschild	Carol Fox Prescott
Vendors	Richard Walker, Robert Hendersen, Joseph Petrullo
Budurus	John Eames
Bankers	Ralph Vucci, Robert Lenn
Young Amshel	Jason Howard
Young Solomon	Kevin Ellicott
Young Nathan	Paris Themmen
Young Jacob	David Craig Moskin
Blum	Joseph Petrullo
Mrs. Kaufman	Jacqueline Penn
Mrs. Segal	Brenda Gardner
Peasant	Dennis Landsman
Amshel Rothschild	Richard Balin
Solomon Rothschild	Mark Lamos
Jacob Rothschild	Joel Parks
Nathan Rothschild	C. David Colson
Kalman Rothschild	Allan Gruet
Joseph Fouche/Herries	Reid Shelton
Skeptic	Robert Lenn
Brokers	Richard Walker, Ray LaManna
Hannah Cohen	Sandra Thornton
Prince Metternich	Reid Shelton
Town Crier	Robert Hendersen

COURTIERS, PEASANTS, BANKERS, ETC.: Kathy Bartosh, Henry Brunjes, Richard Cousins, Clifford Fearl, Vicki Frederick, Brenda Gardner, Susan Gayle, Robert Hendersen, Peter J. Humphrey, Diane Korf, Ray LaManna, Dennis Landsman, Robert Lenn, Melanie Lerner, John Lillard, Donald Mark, John Melof, Jacqueline Penn, Joseph Petrullo, Lani Sundsten, Ralph Vucci, Richard Walker

UNDERSTUDIES: Mayer, Joseph Petrullo; Nathan, Richard Balin; Mama, Brenda Gardner; Prince, Fouche, Herries, Metternich, Robert Lenn; Hannah, Vicki Frederick; Solomon, Henry Brunjes; Amshel, Ray LaManna; Jacob, Richard Walker; Kalman, Robert Hendersen; Young Rothschilds, Keith Luckett; Urchins, Jason Howard

MUSICAL NUMBERS: "Pleasure and Privilege," "One Room," "He Tossed a Coin," "Sons," "Everything," "Rothschilds and Sons," "Allons," "Give England Strength," "This Amazing London Town," "They Say," "I'm in Love!," "In My Own Lifetime," "Have You Ever Seen a Prettier Little Congress?," "Stability," "Bonds"

A musical in 2 acts and 18 scenes. The action takes place in Europe between 1772 and 1818.

General Manager: Emanuel Azenberg
Company Manager: Robert Kamlot
Press: Theresa Loeb Cone
Stage Managers: Martha Knight, Jason Steven Cohen, Patrick Cummings

For original NY production, see THEATRE WORLD, Vol. 27.

Rothschild Photos

op Right: Joel Parks, Richard Balin, Carol Fox Prescott, Allan Gruet, Mark Lamos, C. David Colson Below: Hal Linden, Reid Shelton

Sandra Thornton, C. David Colson

THE SCHOOL FOR WIVES

By Moliere; New English verse translation, Richard Wilbur; Director, Stephen Porter; Scenery-Lighting, James Tilton; Costumes, Nancy Potts; Music, Conrad Susa; Presented by the Phoenix Theatre (T. Edward Hambleton, Managing Director); Opened Monday, Aug. 23, 1971 in the Huntington Hartford Theatre, Los Angeles, and closed Jan. 15, 1972 in O'Keefe Center, Toronto, Can.

CAST

Chrysalde	David Hooks
Arnolphe	Brian Bedford
Alain	James Greene
Georgette	Peggy Cooper
Agnes	Joan Van Ark†1
Horace	David Dukes
Notary	Anthony Manionis
Enrique	Mario Siletti
Oronte	Peter Harris†2

UNDERSTUDIES: Arnolphe, Peter Harris; Agnes, Georgette, Sharon Smith; Horace, Tony Manionis; Chrysalde, Mario Siletti; Enrique, Oronte, Notary, Tony Manci

A comedy presented in two acts. The action takes place on a street in front of Arnolphe's house.

General Manager: Marilyn Miller
Company Manager: James O'Neill
Press: Sol Jacobson, Lewis Harmon, Paul G. Anglim
Stage Managers: Robert Beard, Tony Manzi

† Succeeded by: 1. Sharon Smith, 2. Tom Tarpey

Van Williams Photos

David Dukes, Brian Bedford Above:
David Dukes, Joan Van Ark

Brian Bedford, Joan Van Ark

1776

Book, Peter Stone; Based on cenception by Sherman Edwards; Music and Lyrics, Sherman Edwards; Scenery-Lighting, Jo Mielziner; Costumes, Patricia Zipprodt; Musical Direction, Gordon Lowry Harrell, Glen Clugston; Orchestrations, Eddie Sauter; Hairstylist, Ernest Adler; Musical Numbers Staged by Onna White; Associate Dance Director, Martin Allen; Director, Peter Hunt; Original Cast Album, Columbia Records; presented by Stuart Ostrow; Opened Thursday, April 23, 1970 at the Curran in San Francisco, and still touring May 31, 1972.

CAST

John Hancock	Jack Murdock†1
Dr. Josiah Bartlett	Lee Winston†2
John Adams	Patrick Bedford
Stephen Hopkins	Truman Gage†3
Roger Sherman	Stanley Simmonds†4
Lewis Morris	Ray Lonergan
Robert Livingstone	Larry Devon†5
Rev. John Witherspoon	Robert Gross†6
Benjamin Franklin	Rex Everhart
John Dickinson	George Hearn†7
James Wilson	Ed Preble
Caesar Rodney	Douglas Gordon†8
Col. Thomas McKean	Gordon Dilworth
George Read	Michael Shaw†9
Samuel Chase	Leon Spelman†10
Richard Henry Lee	Gary Oakes†11
Thomas Jefferson	Robert Elston†12
Jospeh Hewes	Walter Charles†13
Edward Rutledge	Jack Blackton†14
Dr. Lyman Hall	Richard Mathews
Charles Thomson	John Eames†15
Andrew McNair	Stuart Germain†16
A Leather Apron	James Ferrier†17
Courier	Michael Glenn-Smith†18
Abigail Adams	Barbara Lang
Martha Jefferson	Kristen Banfield†19

UNDERSTUDIES: Adams, Richard Mathews; Franklin, Dickinson, Gordon Dilworth; Rutledge, Larry Small; McKean, Hancock, Christopher Wynkoop; Jefferson, Hopkins, Thomson, Hall, Lee, Gil Robbins; Abigail, Martha, Victoria Hall; Rodney, Donald Norris; Bartlett, James Todkill; McNair, Kevin O'Leary; Courier, Don Estes; Wilson, Ray Lonergan; Hewes, Livingstone, Witherspoon, Leather Apron, Read, Sherman, Chase, Morris, John Dorrin

MUSICAL NUMBERS: "Sit Down John," "Piddle, Twiddle and Ressolve," "Till Then," "The Lees of Old Virginia," "But, Mr. Adams," "Yours, Yours, Yours," "He Plays the Violin," "Cool, Cool, Considerate Men," "Momma Look Sharp," "The Egg," "Molasses to Rum," "Is Anybody There?"

A musical play in 2 acts and 7 scenes. The action takes place for 2 months before and up to July 4, 1776.

General Managers: Joseph Harris, Ira Bernstein
Company Manager: Harold Kusell
Press: Lee Solters, Harvey B. Sabinson, Harry Davies
Stage Managers: Charles Durand, David Gold, John Dorrin

† Succeeded by 1. Richard Graham, 2. Larry Small, 3. William Griffis, 4. Donald Norris, 5. James Todkill, 6. Gil Robbins, 7. Edmund Lyndeck, 8. Roland Ireland, 9. Kevin O'Leary, 10. Graham Pollock, 11. Virgil Curry, 12. Michael Beirne, 13. Christopher Wynkoop, 14. Michael Davis, 15. William Major, 16. Edwin Cooper, 17. Don Estes, 18. James Ferrier, 19. Chris Callen
For original NY production, see THEATRE WORLD, Vol. 25.

Top Left: Michael Davis (C) Below: "Cool, Cool, Considerate Men"

Edmund Lyndeck, Rex Everhart, Ed Preble
Above: Barbara Lang, Patrick Bedford

SLEUTH

By Anthony Shaffer; Director, Clifford Williams; Designed by Carl Toms; Lighting, William Ritman; Presented by Helen Bonfils, Morton Gottlieb, Michael White; Opened Wednesday, Oct. 6, 1971 in the Royal Alexandra Theatre, Toronto, Canada, and still touring May 31, 1972.

CAST

Andrew Wyke .... Michael Allinson†
Milo Tindle .... Donal Donnelly
Insepctor Doppler ....Philip Farrar
Detective Sgt. Tarrant............................ Harold K. Newman
Police Constable Higgs .... Roger Purnell

UNDERSTUDIES: Wyke, Michael Lewis; Tindle, Ian Thomson; Doppler, Charles Fredrick; Tarrant, Higgs, William Frank

A mystery drama in two acts. The action takes place at the present time in Andrew Wyke's country home in Wiltshire, England.

General Manager: Ben Rosenberg
Company Manager: Sam Pagliaro
Press: Dorothy Ross, John L. Toohey
Stage Managers: Warren Crane, Paul Foley, Ian Thomson

† Succeeded by Anthony Quayle
For original NY production, see THEATRE WORLD, Vol. 27.

Bert Andrews Photos

**Top Right: Donal Donnelly, Michael Allinson
Below: Donal Donnelly, Anthony Quayle**

James Whitmore as Will Rogers

WILL ROGERS' U.S.A.

Adapted and Directed by Paul Shyre; Production Design, Eldon Elder; Associate Producer, Bryan Sterling; Presented by George Spota, in association with Marc Merson; Original Cast Album, Columbia Records; Opened in the Loretto Hilton Center, St. Louis, on Monday, September 13, 1971, and closed Feb. 27, 1972 in John Hancock Hall, Boston, Mass.

CAST

JAMES WHITMORE

in a one-man performance adapted from the words of Will Rogers.

General Manager: Seth Schapiro
Company Manager: Johanna Pool
NY Promotion Manager: Bernard Simon
Stage Manager: James Whitmore III

THE TIME OF YOUR LIFE

The Pulitzer Prize Play by William Saroyan; Director, Edwin Sherin; Settings, Oliver Smith; Costumes, Kate Drain Lawson; Lighting, Paul Sullivan; Production Associate, Carleton Alsop; Production Assistant, Michael Colefax; Presented by the Plumstead Playhouse; Opened Wednesday, January 12, 1972 in the Eisenhower Theatre, Kennedy Center for the Performing Arts, Washington, D.C., and closed Apr. 8, 1972 at Huntington Hartford Theatre, Los Angeles.

CAST

Newsboy	Tony Farella
Drunk	Lee DeBroux
Willie	Ron Thompson
Joe	Henry Fonda
Nick	Victor French
Tom	Pepper Martin
Kitty Duval	Jane Alexander
Dudley	Richard Dreyfuss
Harry	Lewis J. Stadlen
Wesley	Henry Shed
Lorene	Lila Teigh
Blick	Bert Freed
Arab	Lou Gilbert
Mary L	Gloria Grahame
Krupp	Richard X. Slattery
McCarthy	John Crawford
Kit Carson	Strother Martin
Sailor	Richard Kuller
Elsie	Enid Kent
Killer	Eve Marchand
Sidekick	Nancy Jeris
Society Lady	Patricia Walter
Society Gentleman	Edmon Ryan
Cop	Richard Kuller

STANDBYS AND UNDERSTUDIES: Joe, Edmon Ryan; Females, Nancy Jeris; Nick, Blick, Krupp, Carson, Lee DeBroux; Willie, Wesley, Dudley, Harry, Newsboy, Richard Kuller

A comedy in 3 acts and 5 scenes. The action takes place in San Francisco in Nick's Pacific Saloon, and a hotel room.

General Manager: Diana Shumlin
Company Manager: Robert I. Goldberg
Press: John Springer Associates
Stage Managers: Randall Brooks, Carleton Alsop

Enid Kent, Richard Dreyfus, Nancy Jeris, Victor French, Eve Marchand
Top: Henry Fonda, Strother Martin Below: Rehearsal shot with Lewis J. Stadlen dancing

AMERICAN SHAKESPEARE
FESTIVAL
Stratford, Conn.
June 15—September 5, 1971

Executive Producer, Joseph Verner Reed; Managing Producer, Berenice Weiler; Director Educational Projects, Mary Hunter Wolf; Artistic Director, Michael Kahn; Production Manager, Lo Hardin; Musical Director-Conductor, Conrad Susa; Assistant Conductor, Walter Wich; Assistant Directors, Charles Haid, Garland Wright; Stage Managers, Nikos Kafkalis, Walter W. Meyer; Wardrobe Mistress, Dorothy Silvernail; Production Assistants, Craig Anderson, Stephen Nasuta, Patricka Brown; Press, Reginald Denenholz, Morton Langbord; Resident Manager, Donald Bundock

COMPANY

Jane Alexander, Maureen Anderman, Robert Blumenfeld, Tobi Brydon, W. B. Brydon, Morris Carnovsky, Rob Evan Collins, Matt Conley, Maury Cooper, Roy Cooper, Kevin Ellicott, Janice Fuller, D. Jay Higgins, David Hurst, Edwin McDonough, Martha Miller, Jan Miner, Gene Nye, Dan Plucinski, Jess Richards, Lee Richardson, Robert Stattel, Tom Tarpey, Peter Thompson, Sada Thompson, Josef Warik, Dianne Wiest, Mary Wright, Wanda Bimson, Wesley Eure, John Guerrasio, Dan Held, Don Mandigo, Susan Merson, Peter Subers, Mark Winkworth

PRODUCTIONS

"The Tempest" (Director, Edward Payson Call), "The Merry Wives of Windsor" (Director, Michael Kahn), "Mourning Becomes Electra" (Michael Kahn)

Martha Swope Photos

**Top Left: Jess Richards, Morris Carnovsky, David Hurst
in "The Tempest"**

**David Hurst, Morris Carnovsky, Dianne Wiest
in "The Tempest"**

**Tobi Brydon, W. B. Brydon, Jane Alexander
Above: Lee Richardson, Tom Tarpey, Tobi Brydon, Jane
Alexander, Maury Cooper in "Merry Wives ..."**

Jan Miner, W. B. Brydon Above: Sada Thompson, Lee Richardson, Jane Alexander Top: Maureen Anderman, Peter Thompson

Sada Thompson, Jane Alexander Above: Peter Thompson, Jane Alexander in "Mourning Becomes Electra"

NEW YORK SHAKESPEARE FESTIVAL
Delacorte Theater, Central Park
June 30—August 29, 1971
Fifteenth Season

Producer, Joseph Papp; Associate Producer, Bernard Gersten; General Manager, David Black; Press, Merle Debuskey, Faith Geer, M. J. Boyer; Sets, Ming Cho Lee; Costumes, Theoni V. Aldredge; Lighting, Martin Aronstein, Lawrence Metzler; Stage Managers, R. Derek Swire, John Beven, Ken Glickfeld; Technical Coordinator, Michael Hopper; Production Assistants, Paul Schneider, Alan Fox

DELACORTE THEATER
June 30—July 18, 1971

TIMON OF ATHENS

Directed by Gerald Freedman; Music, Jonathan Tunick; Choreography, Joyce Trisler

CAST

Albert Stratton (Lucius), Michael Dunn (Apemantus), Louis Galterio (Lucullus), Louis Turenne (Sempronius), Robert Ronan (Poet), Geoff Garland (Painter), Norman Snow (Merchant), Stuart Pankin (Jeweller), Shepperd Strudwick (Timon), John Nichols (Hortensius), Ron Peer (Old Athenian), Mark Zeray (Lucilius), Marco St. John (Alcibiades), W. K. Stratton (Servilius), Reno Roop (Flavius), Robert Reilly (Ventidius), Sam Tsoutsouvas (Cupid), Nedra Marlin, Peggy Myers, Debbie Zalkind, Christina Zompakos (Ladies of the Masque), Michael Richardson (Servant to Lucius), Nathan Young (Philotus), James Cahill (Senator), Brooks Rogers (Senator), Jeff Eagle (Caphis), Peter Weil (Servant to Varro), Ernest Gray (Servant to Isidore), Sam Tsoutsouvas (Whore's Page), Carl M. Franklin (Flaminius), Charles Randall, Stephen P. Schnetzer (Senators), William Strohmeier (Titus), Jeff Eagle, Peter Weil, Ernest Gray (Bandits), John Nichols (Messenger), Norman Snow (Courier to Alcibiades)

July 27—August 8, 1971*

TWO GENTLEMEN OF VERONA

Adapted by John Guare and Mel Shapiro; Music, Galt MacDermot; Lyrics, John Guare; Director, Mel Shapiro; Choreography, Jean Erdman; Musical Director, Margaret Harris

CAST

Frederic Warriner (Friar Laurence), Carla Pinza (Julia), Alix Elias (Lucetta), Albert Insinnia (Sir Brilliantine), Gale McNeeley (Mercatio), Raul Julia (Proteus), Clifton Davis (Valentine), Frederic Warriner (Antonio), Jerry Stiller (Launce), Jose Perez (Speed), Anthony Cuascut, Ralph Cuascut, Alex Velez (Urchins), Norman Matlock (Duke of Milan), Frank O'Brien (Thurio), Jonelle Allen (Silvia), Frederic Warriner (Tavern Host), Alvin Lum (Eglamour), and Citizens: Christopher Alden, Paul DeJohn, Richard DeRusso, Richard Erickson, Brenda Feliciano, Sheila Gibbs, Jeff Goldblum, Albert Insinnia, Elizabeth Lage, Ken Lowrie, Gale McNeeley, Douglas Riddick, Madeleine Swift

* Re-opened on Broadway in St. James Theatre on Dec. 1, 1971 (see Broadway Calendar)

Friedman-Abeles Photos

Right Center: Clifton Davis, Jonelle Allen in "Two Gentlemen of Verona"

August 17—29, 1971

THE TALE OF CYMBELINE

Director, A. J. Antoon; Music, Galt MacDermot; Arranged by Ken Guilmartin; Animal Battles, Diane Adler

CAST

Tom Aldredge (Cymbeline), Karen Grassle (Imogen), Sam Waterston (Cloten), Jane White (Queen), Christopher Walken (Posthumus Leonatus), Bruce Cobb (Arviragus), Sam Tsoutsouvas (Guiderius), Mark Hammer (Belarius), Don Plumley (Pisanio), Joseph Stern (Second Lord), Stephen P. Schnetzer (First Lord), Diana Kirkwood (Dorothy), William Devane (Iachimo), Norman Snow (Philario), Carl Mikal Franklin (Frenchman), Joseph Ragno (Cornelius), Alexander Panas (Caius Lucius), William Strohmeier (Messenger), and Birds: Carl Mikal Franklin (Hornbill), Ernest Gray (Cockatoo), Dennis Klein (Crowned Crane), W. K. Stratton (Egret), Nathan Young (Hoatzin), Mark Zeray (Crown Pigeon), and Beasts: Stuart Pankin (Elephant), Ronald Peer (Walrus), Michael Richardson (Boar), Robert Reilly (Frog), Norman Snow (Alligator), Peter Weil (Armadillo)

Raul Julia, Carla Pinza, Jerry Stiller in "Two Gentlemen of Verona"

Marco St. John, Shepperd Strudwick (also top)
Above: Michael Dunn, Strudwick in "Timon"

Sam Waterston, Karen Grassle Above: William
Devane, Christopher Walken Top: Jane White,
Sam Waterston in "Cymbeline"

NORTH SHORE SHAKESPEARE
FESTIVAL
Beverly, Mass.
April 24, through May 26, 1972
Tenth Season

Managing Director, Stephan Slane; Directors, William Driver, Pirie MacDonald; Sets, Eve Lyon; Costumes, Betsy Potter; Lighting, Theda Taylor; Press, Peter Downs; Stage Managers, Robert J. Bruyr, Jerry Rice

COMPANY

Andra Akers, Herman O. Arbeit, Eugene Brezany, David Kukes, Paul Gilbert, Michael Goodwin, Ron Hale, William Henning, Michael Holmes, Richard Jenkins, Richard Kavanaugh, Jeremy Lawrence, Philip Littell, Edwin Owens, Wesley Phillips, George Wolf Reily, Carolen Ross, Richard Rossomme, Jeanne Rostaing, Patrick Shea, Donald Warfield
PRODUCTIONS: "Macbeth," "Great Scenes from Shakespeare"

Ulrike Welsch Photos

Richard Cavanaugh Above: (C) Andra Akers, David Dukes in "Macbeth"

Top: (L) Carolen Ross, Michael Holmes, Wesley Phillip (R) Andra Akers, Edwin Owens, Carolen Ross in "Macbe

OREGON SHAKESPEARE FESTIVAL
Ashland, Oregon
June 19, through September 12, 1971
Thirty-first Season

Founder-Producing Director, Dr. Angus L. Bowmer; Producing Director, Dr. Jerry Turner; General Manager, William W. Patton; Directors, Raye Birk, Philip Davidson, Larry Oliver, Pat Patton; Costumes, Jean Schultz Davidson; Designers, Richard L. Hay, Peter Maslan; Lighting, Steven A. Maze, Jerry L. Glenn; Technical Director, Skip Hubbard; Music Directors, W. Bernard Windt, Todd Barton; Choreography, Judith Kennedy; Production Coordinator, Pat Patton; Press, Robert F. Knoll, Anne Batzer; Photographer, Carolyn Mason Jones; Stage Managers, Jerry Gatchell, Gerald R. Phipps, Bruce McLeod; Sound, Andrew Bass.

COMPANY

Christine Abbott, Lynda Lynnea Ainsworth, Peter O. Ashbaugh, Len Auclair, Jim Baker, Glorianne Beard, Keith Beard, Will Beard, Barbara Beebe, Diana Bellamy, Michael Bennett, Marilyn Joy Berry, Candace Birk, Judy Bjorlie, Jerry Brown, Dave Buffam, Jr., Jane Burchell, Barbara Byrne, Keith Cameron, Sally Chaney, Scott Chase, Joel Colodner, Rebecca Colodner, Betsy Allen Cope, Rob Cope, Timothy D'Arcy, Diane Dimeo, Tom Donaldson, Michael Donohue, Georgia Doty, Stephen R. Drewes, Mavourneen Dwyer, Richard Allen Edwards, Rogert Eiffert, Claudia Everett, Steve Frazier, Robert Gage, Jo Goff, Teresa Gregory, Bernard Paul Guenther, Ric Hamilton, Mark Haney, David A. Hart, Cliff Hay, James Barton Hill, Will Huddleston, Byron Jennings, Dan Johnson, Daryl Johnson, Vicki Jones, Nancy Joyce, Sherill Kannasto, Dan Kern, Harry Kinnery, Kim Kovac, Philip Kraus, Gisela Krause, Mary Alice Kurr, Meg Landry, Julian Lopez-Morillas, Larry Martin, Bryn Alison McCornack, William A. McCoy, Ken McGanty, Donald A. McPherson, Susan Gail Min, Garry Moore, Payl Myrvold, Pancho Nahoe, Chuck Olsen, Fredi Olster, Kent Patton, Shirley Patton, Ranny Paulger, Emily Phelps, Kendra S. Phipps, Monica Prendergast, Ray A. Rantapaa, Shari Robinson, David Rodger, James C. Ric, Kenneth Roth, Gregory Ward Schroeder, Mark Schultz, M. David Scott, Suzanne Seiber, Marilyn J. Sheldon, Susan Diane Sheldon, Wardell D. Sheldon, Marsha Skudlarek, Claudia Sommers, Mary Elizabeth Still, Dave Studach, Tony Tait, Gregory Scott Temple, Martha J. Tippin, James Roy Tompkins III, James Verdery, Channing Walker, David Williams, Mary Woolsey, J. Steven White, Michael Winters, Paul Wynne, Richard Yarnell

PRODUCTIONS

"Much Ado about Nothing," "A Midsummer Night's Dream," "Macbeth," "Henry IV, Part I," "A Man for All Seasons," "The Glass Menagerie"

Carolyn Mason Jones Photos

Right: "A Midsummer Night's Dream"
Above: Gregory Schroeder, Richard Edwards,
Tom Donaldson in "Henry IV"

James Tompkins, Jim Baker, Richard Edwards,
gory Temple in "Much Ado ..." Top Right: Raye Birk,
Garry Moore in "Macbeth"

Larry Martin (R) in "A Man for All Seasons"

STRATFORD FESTIVAL OF CANADA
Stratford, Ontario
June 7—October 16, 1971
Nineteenth Season

Artistic Director, Jean Gascon; General Manager, William Wylie; Associate Director, William Hutt; Production Director, John Hayes; Press, Mary Webb, Sandra Fresco, Anne Selby; Assistant Artistic Director, Michael Bawtree; Production Managers, Jack Hutt, Keith Green; Music Administrator, Andree Gingras; Company Manager, Max Helpmann; Stage Managers, Thomas Hooker, Tina Boden, Ron Francis, Elspeth Gaylor, Brian Longstaff, Patrick McEntee, Christopher Root; Technical Director, Robert M. Hall; Stage Directors, Jean Gascon, William Hutt, Peter Gill, David William, Stephen Porter, Michael Bawtree; Designers, Alan Barlow, Desmond Heeley, Deirdre Clancy, Annena Stubbs, Lewis Brown, Art Penson

COMPANY

Tom Alway, Malcolm Armstrong, Christine Bennett, Colin Bernhardt, Mervyn Blake, Pamela Brook, Trudy Cameron, J. Kenneth Campbell, Joyce Campion, Carol Carrington, Jane Casson, Susan Chapple, Dinah Christie, Patrick Christopher, Stanley Coles, Giuseppe Condello, Jack Creley, Richard Curnock, Neil Dainard, Peter Donat, Eric Donkin, Peter Elliott, Bernard Engel, Donald Ewer, Eillean Ferguson, Gary Files, Patrick Gage, Pat Galloway, Robin Gammell, Marilyn Gardner, Lewis Gordon, Mari Gorman, Patricia Grant, Suzanne Grossmann, Sheila Haney, Edward Henry, Martha Henry, Roland Hewgill, Ian Hogg, Ruby Holbrook, Elva Mai Hoover, William Hutt, Marc Jacobs, Jeff Jones, Joel Kenyon, Michael Liscinsky, Karen Ludwig, Barry MacGregor, Iris MacGregor, Stephen Markle, Robin Marshall, Howard Mawson, Robert McKennitt, Elizabeth Milne, William Needles, Bette Oliver, Blaine Parker, Gerard Parkes, Wyman Pendleton, Leon Pownall, Douglas Rain, Jack Roberts, Hamish Robertson, Stewart Robertson, Paul Roland, Joseph Rutten, Mary Savidge, Elsie Sawchuk, David Schurmann, Joseph Shaw, Donna Sherman, Brian Sinclair, Charles Sitler, Edwin Stephenson, Don Sutherland, Powys Thomas, Joseph Totaro, Tony van Bridge, Kenneth Welsh, Tim Whelan, Carolyn Younger

PRODUCTIONS

"Much Ado about Nothing," "The Duchess of Malfi," "Macbeth," "Volpone," "An Italian Straw Hat," "There's One in Every Marriage," "The Red Convertible"

Douglas Spillane Photos

Top Left: Roland Hewgill, Pat Galloway
in "The Duchess of Malfi"

Ian Hogg as Macbeth

Kenneth Walsh, Jane Casson in "Much Ado About Nothing"
Top: (L)Richard Curnock, Marilyn Gardner in "There's One in Every Marriage"
(R) William Hutt, Ruby Holbrook in "Volpone"

NATIONAL SHAKESPEARE FESTIVAL
San Diego, Calif.
June 8 through September 12, 1971
22nd Season

Producing Director, Craig Noel; General Manager, Adrienne Butler; Art Director, Peggy Kellner; Press, William B. Eaton; Technical Director, Gene Reilly; Directors, Craig Noel, Eric Christmas, Nagle Jackson, Ellis Rabb

COMPANY

John Arnone, Larry Carpenter, Herbert Foster, Alan Fudge, Laurence Guittard, Elizabeth Huddle, Michael Keenan, Michael Learned, Tom McCorry, Judy Mueller, Peter Nyberg, Ken Ruta, Paul Shenar, Marc Singer, Jeffrey Tambor, Tom Toner, Wayne Smith, Trina Ciuffo, Stephen C. Bradbury, Dawn Daniel, Cynthia Avila, Marie Ardron-Finlay, Larry Golden, Jean Holloway, Carla Kirkwood, Tom Kopache, David Lawson, Gerald Nawrocki, William Parker, William Parker, William Quiett, Charles Riendeau, Don Sparks, Miki Heller, Kathe Argo, Karen Winder, Ron Heller, Don Jenkins, Dan Lawler, Scott McDonald, Hau Minn, Carl Reggiardo, Scott Sampietro, Joe Teague, Richard Trent

PRODUCTIONS

"Antony and Cleopatra," "A Midsummer Night's Dream," "The Taming of the Shrew," "Play It Again, Sam"

Right: Alan Fudge, Paul Shenar, Tom Toner, Laurence Guittard in "Antony and Cleopatra"
Above: Elizabeth Huddle, Paul Shenar, Tom Kopache in "A Midsummer Night's Dream"

Herbert Foster, Elizabeth Huddle, Laurence Guittard in "Taming of the Shrew"

Michael Biers, Trina Cuiffo in "Play It Again, Sam"

174

PROFESSIONAL RESIDENT COMPANIES THROUGHOUT THE UNITED STATES

lure to meet deadline unfortunately necessitated omission of several companies)

ACTORS THEATRE OF LOUISVILLE
Louisville, Kentucky
August 24, 1971—May 14, 1972

Producing Director, Jon Jory; General Manager, Alexander Speer; Press, Trish Pugh; Company Manager, Vaughn McBride; Business Manager, Janet Levy; Directors, Jon Jory, Victor Jory, Christopher Murney, Ken Jenkins, Patrick Tovatt; Designers, Paul Owen, Geoffrey T. Cunningham, Jim Knox, Kurt Wilhelm, Dusty Reeds, Judy Rasmuson; Costumiere, Mary Lou Owen; Wardrobe Mistress, Jania Szatanski; Photographer, David S. Talbott; Stage Managers, David Semonin, Charles Traeger; Technical Staff, Johnny Walker, Mark Luking, Kim McCallum, John Manning, Steve Woodring, Marty Crawley

COMPANY

Eunice Anderson, Stanley Anderson, George Cavey, David Clennon, Carolyn Connors, Dale Carter Cooper, Peggy Cowles, Donna Curtis, Ronald Durling, Lee Anne Fahey, Clarence Felder, John Glover, Joseph Hindy, Larry Holt, Katharine Houghton, Jean Inness, Ken Jenkins, Victor Jory, Stephen Keep, Karl Kirchner, Charles Kissinger, Judith Long, Helen MacDonald, Leona Maricle, Vaughn McBride, Sandy McCallum, Michael McCarty, Mary Michaels, Lynn Milgrim, Roger Miller, Christopher Murney, Adale O'Brien, Tom Owen, Stuart Paine, Ted Pejovich, Danny Sewell, Arnold Stang, Eric Tavaris, Patrick Tovatt, Charles Traeger, Bruce Weitz, Dianne Wiest, John Wiley, Max Wright

PRODUCTIONS

"Play It Again, Sam," "Prime of Miss Jean Brodie," "Glass Menagerie," "Tricks," "Night Must Fall," "Angel Street," "A Midsummer Night's Dream," "Marat/Sade," "Hedda Gabler," "Dear Liar," "My Three Angels", "Death of a Salesman"

David S. Talbott Photos

**Right: Adale O'Brien, Ken Jenkins
in "A Midsummer Night's Dream"
Top Right: Eric Tavaris, Adale O'Brien,
Christopher Murney in "Tricks"**

Katharine Houghton in "Glass Menagerie"

Victor Jory in "Death of a Salesman"

ALLEY THEATRE
Houston, Texas
October 19, 1971—June 25, 1972
Silver Anniversary

Producing Director, Nina Vance; Managing Director, Iris Siff; Business Manager, Bill Pogue; Press, Bob Feingold; Producing Associate, H. Wilkenfeld; Production Manager, Bettye Fitzpatrick; Company Manager, Bob Leonard; Choreographer, Carolyn Franklin; Technical Directors, John Hagan, Paul Prentiss; Sound, Jonathan Duff; Stage Managers, John Hagan, Henry Westin, Varney Knapp; Designers, Jerry Williams, Rick Cortright, Ferruccio Garavaglia, Jonathan Duff; Directors, Nina Vance, Jack Westin, William Glover, R. Edward Leonard, William Trotman, Robert Leonard, Beth Sanford

COMPANY

David Adamson, Clint Anderson, Lauren Ann Carner, Timothy Casey, Rutherford Cravens, Ron Dortch, Jack Dupuy, Woody Eney, Lillian Evans, Joe Finkelstein, Lauren Frost, William Glover, Michael Hall, William Hardy, I. M. Hobson, Ted Hoerl, Burk Holaday, Ron Hudson, Nancy Leonard, Rick Lieberman, Russ Marin, David Mauro, Amanda Mayo, Donna O'Connor, Charles Robinson, Karen Shallo, Anne Shropshire, Woody Skaggs, Joel Stedman, Ray Stricklyn, Dixie Taylor, William Trotman, Mark Varian, Ann Walker, Justine Wasielewski, Marifran Yoder

PRODUCTIONS

"Camino Real," "A Flea in Her Ear," "Spoon River," "Hadrian VII," "The Taming of the Shrew," "Child's Play"

Dome City, Richard Pipes Photos

Right: Bettye Fitzpatrick and cast in "Spoon River"
Above: Lillian Evans, Woody Eney in "Taming of The Shrew"

George Ebeling, William Trotman, Timothy Casey
in "Child's Play"

Woody Skaggs, Rick Lieberman, I. M Hobson,
Michael Hall in "Camino Real"

AMERICAN CONSERVATORY THEATRE
San Francisco, Calif.

General Director, William Ball; Executive Producer, James B. McKenzie; Executive Director, Edward Hastings; Development Director, Edith Markson; Conservatory Director, Allen Fletcher; General Manager, Charles Dillingham; Production Director, Benjamin Moore; Stage Directors, William Ball, Francis Ford Coppola, Peter Donat, Allen Fletcher, Edward Hastings, Ellis Rabb; Designers: Scenery, Robert Blackman, Paul Staheli, James Tilton; Costumes, Elizabeth Covey, Robert Fletcher, Ann Roth, Julie Staheli, Walter Watson; Lighting, Maurice Beesley; Associate Directors, Eugene Barcone, Robert Bonaventura; Production Stage Manager, James Haire; Staff Writer, Dennis Powers; Press, Cheryle Elliott

COMPANY

Robert Ari, Martin Berman, Joseph Bird, Karie Cannon, Joy Carlin, Larry Carpenter, Lee Cook, Richard Council, Peter Donat, Jay Doyle, Herbert Foster, Patrick Gorman, Dudley Knight, Anne Lawder, Michael Learned, Winifred Mann, Larry Martin, Lee McCain, Nancy McDoniel, Frank Ottiwell, William Paterson, E. Kerrigan Prescott, Ray Reinhardt, Ken Ruta, Paul Shenar, Howard Sherman, R. E. Simpson, Marc Singer, Deborah Sussel, Scott Thomas, Ann Weldon, Mark Wheeler, Rick Winter, G. Wood

PRODUCTIONS

"Caesar and Cleopatra," "Antony and Cleopatra," "The Tavern," "Dandy Dick," "Rosencrantz and Guildenstern Are Dead," "Paradise Lost," "Private Lives," "The Contractor," "Sleuth"

Hank Kranzler Photos

Top Left: Paul Shenar, Winifred Mann in "Paradise Lost" Below: Ken Ruta, Larry Carpenter, Marc Singer in "Rosencrantz and Guildenstern Are Dead"

William Paterson, Martin Berman, Anne Lawder, Joy Carlin in "The Tavern"

Peter Donat, Lee McCain in "Caesar and Cleopatra"

AMERICAN MIME THEATRE
New York, N.Y.
Twentieth Anniversary

Director, Paul Curtis; Stage Manager, Charles Barney; Press, Jean Barbour.

COMPANY

Jean Barbour, Charles Barney, Paul Curtis, Linda Faulhaber, Kender Jones, Marion Knox, Marc Maislen, Nina Petrucelli, Bill Stavers, Rick Wessler, Stan Winston, Arthur Yorinks, Mr. Bones

PRODUCTIONS

"The Lovers," "The Scarecrow," "Dreams," "Evolution," "Hurlyburly," and full repertoire of mime plays

Jim Moore Photos

"Dreams" Above: "The Lovers"

ARENA STAGE
Washington, D.C.
October 22, 1971—July 2, 1972

Producing Director, Zelda Fichandler; Directors, Gene Lesser, Alan Schneider, Jeff Bleckner, Jerry Adler, George Keathley, Richard Pearlman, Norman Gevanthor; Sets, Santo Loquasto, John Conklin, Gwynne Clark, Georgiana Jordan; Lighting, William Mintzer, Vance Sorrells, Hugh Lester, Henry Gorfein; Production Manager, Hugh Lester; Stage Managers, Elizabeth Darr, Nikos Kafkalis; Technical Director, Henry Gorfein; Executive Director, Thomas C. Fichandler; Business Manager, JoAnn M. Overholt; Press, Alton Miller; Photographer, Fletcher Drake.

COMPANY

Richard Bauer, Robert Prosky, Howard Witt, Carl Mikal Franklin, Lou Gilbert, Gary Bayer, Michael Tucker, Bruce Weitz, Linda Geiser, Leslie Cass, Macon McCalman, Richard Sanders, Robert Ronan, Paul Benedict, Traber Burns, Thomas Busch, John Heard, Raynor Johnston, Bruce Kaiden, Don Sutton, Kevin Conway, Maureen Anderman, Edward Herrmann, Christopher Guest, Stephen Collins, Jill Eikenberry, James Woods, Cara Duff-MacCormick, Donegan Smith, Ronald McLarty, Ted Hannan, Ben Kapen, Russel Carr, Mark Robinson, Richard David, Barbara Callander, Nicola Marie Barthen, Mary Anne Dempsey, Alan Fendler, Martin Busler, Richard Levan, Marc Alaimo, Joan Ulmer, Margaret Linn, Paul Giovanni, Zina Jasper, Roy Shuman, Dorothea Hammond, Halo Wines, Grayce Grant, Madelyn Coleman, Bryan Clark, Phyllis Somerville, Dane Clark, Michael Higgins, Morris Engle, Glenn Taylor, Anne Willmarth, Walter Abel, John Devine, Cecelia Ward, Ann Sachs

PRODUCTIONS

"Pantagleize," "Twelfth Night," "The House of Blue Leaves," "Status Quo Vadis," "Tricks"

U.S. PREMIERES: "Moonchildren," "Uptight"

WORLD PREMIERES: "A Conflict of Interest," "The Dream Machine"

Fletcher Drake Photos

Top Right: Kevin Conway, Maureen Anderman, Christopher Guest, Stephen Collins, Edward Hermann in "Moonchildren" Below: Richard Bauer, Leslie Cass in "Pantagleize"

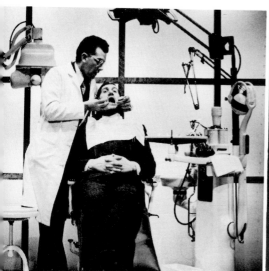

Richard Bauer, Paul Benedict in premier of "Uptight"

Michael Higgins, Dane Clark in "A Conflict of Interest" Above: Margaret Linn, Marc Alaimo in "12th Night"

179

ASOLO, STATE THEATER COMPANY
Sarasota, Fla.
February 18—September 5, 1971
February 17—September 3, 1972

Executive Director, Richard G. Fallon; Managing Director, Howard J. Millman; Artistic Directors, Eberle Thomas, Robert Strane; Costumes, Catherine King; Stage Manager, Marian Wallace; Technical Director, Victor Meyrich; Properties, Bob Naismith; Lighting, James Meade; Press, Edith N. Anson

GUEST ARTISTS: Set Designers, James Tilton, Ray Perry, Henry Swanson, Holmes Easley, William King, John Ezell, Rick Pike; Costumes, Barbara J. Costa; Playwright, Frederick Gaines; Directors, Richard D. Meyer, Bradford Wallace, Robert Lanchester

COMPANY

Bradford Wallace, Polly Holliday, Walter Rhodes, Sharon Spelman, Patrick Egan, Barbara Redmond, William Leach, Robert Lanchester, James L. Sutorius, Kathleen O'Meara Noone, Susan Sandler, Richard Hopkins, Bill E. Noone, Kathleen Kelin, Philip LeStrange, B. G. Ross, Justin T. Deas, Penelope Willis

PRODUCTIONS

"Comedy of Errors," "Born Yesterday," "Candida," "Joe Egg," "Love for Love," "The Subject Was Roses," "Charley's Aunt," "Our Town," "Indians," "Puppet Prince," "Snow Queen," "Front Page," "Best Man," "Hay Fever," "Dracula," "House of Blue Leaves," "Matchmaker," "Devil's Disciple," "War and Peace," "Time of Your Life," "Just So Stories," "Yellow Laugh," "Legend of Sleepy Hollow," "King Stag"

Henry Watt Photos

Right: Bradford Wallace, Walter Rhodes, Polly Holliday, James Sutorius, Barbara Redmond, Patrick Egan in "Candida" Above: B. G. Ross, Philip LeStrange, Kathleen O'Meara, Justin Deas, Penelope Willis in "The Matchmaker"

Barbara Redmond, Polly Holliday, Bradford Wallace in "House of Blue Leaves" Above: Sharon Spelman (C) in "Born Yesterday"

Patrick Egan, Polly Holliday, William Leach in "The Subject Was Roses" Above: Backstage shot during "Charley's Aunt"

BARTER THEATRE
Abingdon, Va.
April 1971—May 1972

Founder-Managing Director, Robert Porterfield†; Business Manager, Pearl Hayter; Resident Director, Owen Phillips; Guest Director, Michael Norell; Costumes, Martha Kelly; Sets, Bennet Averyt, David Murphy; Stage Managers, Rex Partington, James Gillespie, Dale Olson; Technical Director, Frank Moss; Musical Director, Byron Grant; Press, Owen Phillips; Lighting, Bryan H. Ackler, Frank Moss

COMPANY

Jay Bell, Ann Buckles, Ginger Bowen, Marlene Caryl, Roy Clary, Dale Carter Cooper, Jeffrey Dalton, Robert Foley, James Gillespie, Linde Hayen, Liz Ingleson, Virginia Mattis, Ellen March, John Milligan, Thomas D. Moore III, Michael Norell, Jerry Oddo, Rex Partington, James Sargent, William Schilling, Marilee Sennett, Cindy Tarver, Milton Tarver, Owen Phillips, Dorothy Marie, Kristina Callahan, Richard Sanders, Joseph Russo, Dale Olson, Evelyn Lea Moricle

PRODUCTIONS

"Much Ado about Nothing," "I Do! I Do!," "Forty Carats," "Don't Drink the Water," "Glass Menagerie," "Angel Street," "Our Town," "Dracula"

PREMIERES: "A Stand in the Mountains" by Peter Taylor, "Too Young for Spring" by Jasper Oddo

† Mr. Porterfield died Oct. 28, 1971, and was succeeded by Rex Partington.

Top: Milton Tarver, Cynthia Shallat, Robert Foley, Marilee Sennett in "Too Young for Spring" Below: James Sargent, Dale Carter Cooper, Michael Norell in "Glass Menagerie"

Marilee Sennet, Michael Norell in "Angel Street"
: "Much Ado about Nothing" Top: Ann Buckles, Milton Tarver in "Forty Carats"

BUCKS COUNTY THEATRE COMPANY
New Hope, Pa.
June 1, 1971—May 31, 1972

Artistic Director-Managing Director, Lee R. Yopp; Production Manager, Robert Anderson; Musical Director, Arthur Frank; Sets, Robert Walker; Costumes, Betsey Roberts; General Manager, Carol J. Gilbert; Press, Marsha A. Frazier, Nancy W. Bousum; Business Managers, Nancy F. Margerum, Winifred L. Palmer; Photographer, Jack Conover; Technical Director, Don Chafey; Stage Managers, Frank Davis, Robert Anderson, Penny Gebhard; Production Assistants, Gail Abrahamson, Gail Fein, Jim Flint, George Foote, Gail Greenberg

COMPANY
(names not submitted)

GUEST ARTISTS: Gloria DeHaven, George Grizzard, Dana Andrews, Tom Poston, Jerry Dodge, Ed Evanko, Howard Morris, Patrick Crean, Dan Simon

PRODUCTIONS

"Arsenic and Old Lace," "Child's Play," "Plaza Suite," "Prime of Miss Jean Brodie," "Man of La Mancha," "A Funny Thing Happened on the Way to the Forum," "I Do! I Do!," "The Fantasticks," "West Side Story," "Romeo and Juliet," "Our Town," "Once upon a Mattress," "Cyrano de Bergerac," "You're a Good Man, Charlie Brown"

WORLD PREMIERES: "When Do the Words Come True," "The Headhunters," "Only the Shadow Knows," "Zing"

Jack Conover Photos

Top: Robert Coucill, Dana Andrews in "Child's Play"
Below: Bill Gerber, Gloria DeHaven, Paul Keith in "When Do the Words ..."

Tom Poston as Cyrano de Bergerac
Above: George Grizzard in "The Headhunters"

CENTER STAGE
Baltimore, Md.
October 29, 1971—April 30, 1972
Tenth Season

Producing Director, Peter W. Culman; Artistic Director, John Stix; General Manager, David Frank; Directors, Robert Lewis, John Lithgow, Alfred Ryder, Lee D. Sankowich, John Stix; Scenery, Eldon Elder, Marjorie Kellogg, Leo Kerz; Costumes, Eldon Elder, Leo Kerz, Mary Strieff; Lighting, Peter W. Culman, Eldon Elder, Leo Kerz, John Sichina; Music, John Sichina; Technical Directors, Thomas Brady, John Sichina; Stage Managers, Cindy Kite, Carl Schurr, Shana Sullivan; Press, Flo Harbold; Company Manager, Clarke Taylor; Workshop Director, Vivienne Shub.

COMPANY

John Costopoulos, Barbara Frank, Bert Houle, Judith Hordan, Wil Love, John Newton, Louis Plante, Margaret Ramsey, Carl Schurr, Vivienne Shub, Henry Strozier, David Tyrrel, Sophie Wibaux, Woodward Mann, P. H. Murray, John Rothman, Jimmy Seibold, Debora Smith

GUEST ARTISTS: Elaine Aiken, Terry Alexander, Mathew Anden, Fran Brill, Barbara Clarke, Ward Costello, Roger de Koven, Kay Doubleday, Jon L. Feather, Stanley Greene, Earle Hyman, Arthur Malet, Barbara Mealy, Howard Rollins, Alfred Ryder, Richard Sanders, Dennis Tate, Irv Turner, Richard Ward

PRODUCTIONS

"Trial of the Catonsville 9," "The Seagull," "The Beaux' Stratagem," "Andorra," "An Evening of Mime," "Staircase," "Death of a Salesman," "Mimes and Pantomimes," "Under Milkwood," "Children's Story Theatre"

C. B. Nieberding Photos

Right: Dennis Tate, Richard Ward, Terry Alexander, Barbara Clarke in "Death of a Salesman" Above: Kay Doubleday, Earle Hyman in "The Seagull"

Alfred Ryder, Arthur Maler in "Staircase" Above: Ward Costello, John Newton in "Trial of the Catonsville 9"

Wil Love (C) in "Andorra" Above: Fran Brill, Wil Love in "Beaux Stratagem"

183

CENTRE THEATRE GROUP
AHMANSON THEATRE
Music Center of Los Angeles
October 12, 1971—April 15, 1972

Managing Director, Robert Fryer; Manager, Charles Mooney; Assistant Manager, Barbara Stocks; Press, David Bongard, Rupert Allan, Regina Gruss, Farrar Cobb, Brooke Karzen; Technical Supervisor, H. R. Poindexter; Production Associate, Robert Linden; Production Coordinator, Michael Grossman; Stage Managers, Bill Holland, Scott Stevenson, Don Winton, Ron Lewis

PRODUCTIONS AND CASTS

A FUNNY THING HAPPENED ON THE WAY TO THE FORUM (see Broadway Calendar) The following cast members did not join NY production: Nancy Walker, Lew Parker, Marc Breaux, Marc Wilder, Ann Jilliann

THE CAINE MUTINY COURT-MARTIAL directed by Henry Fonda, with Hume Cronyn, John Forsythe, Andrew Prine, Joe Don Baker, Edward Binns, Paul Stewart, Bruce Davison, Whit Bissell, Henry Brandon, George Wyner, Gary Barton, Craig Gardner, Scott Stevenson, Richard Farmer, Ted Hartley, Aron Kincaid, Jarion Monroe, Myron Natwick, Chuck Schneider

SLEUTH directed by Clifford Williams, with Anthony Quayle, Donal Donnelly (see Broadway Calendar)

RICHARD II directed by Jonathan Miller, with Richard Chamberlain, Sorrell Booke, Patrick Hines, Jack Ryland, Priscilla Morrill, Tom Toner, Byron Webster, Vickery Turner, Jonathan Farwell, Philip Taylor, Todd Crespi, Al Alu, Colby Chester, Lee Corrigan, Joseph Culliton, Richard Farmer, Robert Rovin, John Ventantonio, John Wiltshire, Thomas Bellin, Oren Curtis, Stephen Jacques, Fergus Kirkpatrick, Karen Kondan, James McHugh, Susan Merril-Taylor, Ruth Warshawsky

Left: John Forsythe, Hume Cronyn, Above: Bruce Davison, Paul Stewart, Edward Binns in "Caine Mutiny Court Martial" Top: Marc Breaux, Garrett Lewis, Joe Ross, Nancy Walker, Larry Blyden in "A Funny Thing Happened on the Way to the Forum"

184 **Patrick Hines, Richard Chamberlain, Jack Ryland, Sorrell Booke in "Richard II"**

Richard Chamberlain, Vickery Turner in "Richard II"

CENTER THEATRE GROUP
MARK TAPER FORUM
Music Center of Los Angeles
June 1, 1971—May 31, 1972

Artistic Director, Gordon Davidson; General Manager, Francis Von Zerneck; Press, Richard Kitzrow, Brooke Karzen, Susan Cobb, Ronald Warden; Design Consultant, Peter Wexler; Lighting, Tharon Musser; Technical Supervisor, H. R. Poindexter; Production Manager, John DeSantis; Stage Managers, Tom A. Larson, David Barber, Don Winton, Madeline Puzo; Assistant Directors, Wallace Chappell, Robert Greenwald

PRODUCTIONS AND CASTS

THE TRIAL OF THE CATONSVILLE NINE directed by Gordon Davidson, with Gwen Arner, John S. Battersby, Jason Bernard, Anthony Costello, Lou Fant, Ed Flanders, Mary Jackson, Richard Jordan, Nancy Malone, Donald Moffat, Leon Russom, William Schallert, Harv Selsby, David Spielberg, Peter Strauss, Douglass Watson

MAJOR BARBARA directed by Edward Parone, with Ivor Barry, William H. Bassett, David Birney, Eric Christmas, Liza Cole, Doria Cook, Blythe Danner, Robert Doyle, Richard Dreyfuss, John Dullaghan, Pamela Dunlap, William Glover, Barra Grant, Kathryn Grody, Scott Hylands, Edward J. Kelly, Norman Lloyd, Victoria Thompson, Nicolas Ullett, Diana Webster, Helen Winston

GODSPELL directed by John-Michael Tebelak, Stephen Schwartz, Nina Faso, with Lamar Alford, Roberta Baum, Herb Braha, Peggy Gordon, David Haskell, Robin Lamont, Jeanne Lange, Jeffrey Mylett, Andy Rohrer, Lynne Thigpen

HERE ARE LADIES directed by Sean Kenny, with Siobhan McKenna

THE WORKS OF BECKETT adapted and performed by Jack MacGowran

VOLPONE directed by Edward Parone, with Anthony Costello, Richard Doran, Herb Edelman, Ernest Harada, Marian Mercer, Ted Pejovich, Herman Poppe, Jack Rowe, William Schallert, Avery Schreiber, John Schuck, Ezra Stone, Joyce Van Patten, Ronald Warden, Sam Waterston, Adam West

OLD TIMES directed by Jeff Bleckner, with Verna Bloom, W. B. Brydon, Faye Dunaway

Top: Avery Schreiber, Sam Waterston with cast of "Volpone" Below: Ed Flanders and cast of "Catonsville 9"

David Birney, Blythe Danner in "Major Barbara" Above: Andy Rohrer in "Godspell" Top: Verna Bloom, W. B. Brydon, Faye Dunaway in "Old Times"

CENTER THEATRE GROUP
NEW THEATRE FOR NOW
June 1, 1971—May 31, 1972

Director, Edward Parone; Managers, Ellen Tarlow, William P. Wingate; Directors, Michael Monte, Edward Parone, James Bridges; Designers, Jeremy Railton, Donald Harris, Harold Oblong, Michael Devine, William Barbe

PRODUCTIONS AND CASTS

AUBREY BEARDSLEY, THE NEOPHYTE by Jon Renn McDonald, with Catherine Burns, Bill Callaway, David Dukes, Sharon Gans, Harold Oblong, Robert H. Rovin, Leon Russom, Louise Sorel, Clyde Ventura, Paul Winfield

TEN COM. ZIP COM. ZIP by Matthew Silverman, with Mark Bramhall, Barbara Colby, Larry Ferguson, Barra Grant, Michael Pataki, Ayn Ruymen, Helene Winston

A RAP ON RACE adapted from Margaret Mead and James Baldwin's book of the same name by Marian Barnett, with Roscoe Lee Browne, Sarah Cunningham

A MEETING BY THE RIVER by Christopher Isherwood and Don Bachardy, with Jack Bender, Susan Brown, Florida Friebus, Gordon Hoban, Laurence Luckinbill, Sirri Murad, Logan Ramsey, John Ritter, Sam Waterston, Jason Wingreen

IN A FINE CASTLE by Derek Walcott, with Jason Bernard, Georg Stanford Brown, William Clouser, Mitzi Hoag, Kurt Kaznar, Paula Kelly, Davis Roberts, Anthony Sweeting, Marco St. John, Joan Van Ark, Diana Webster

Right: Georg Stanford Brown, Joan Van Ark, Marco St. John, Diana Webster, Davis Roberts, Kurt Kaznar Above: Joan Van Ark, Diana Webster in "In a Fine Castle"

Barra Grant (background), Barbara Colby in "Ten Com. Zip Com. Zip"

Susan Brown, Laurence Luckinbill in "A Meeting by the River"

CLEVELAND PLAY HOUSE
Cleveland, Ohio
September 8, 1971—May 14, 1972
56th Season

Managing Director, Richard Oberlin; Company Manager, Nelson Isekeit; Business Manager, James Sweeney; Press, Dennis Brown, Bruce Bossard; Production Coordinator, Larry Tarrant; Designer, Richard Gould; Costumes, Joe Dale Lunday, Harriet Cone, Estelle Painter, Diane Dalton Smith; Lighting, Jeffrey Dallas; Properties, David Smith; Directors, Jonathan Bolt, Peter Coe, Eric Conger, J. J. Garry, Jr., Andrew Lack, Bob Moak, Douglas Seale, Bertram Tanswell, George Touliatos, Tunc Yalman; Photographers, Joel Warren, James Fry

COMPANY

Robert Allman, Jean Barrett, Brenda Curtis, John Bergstrom, Norm Berman, Jon Beryl, Jonathan Bolt, John Buck, Jr., John DeVenne, Paula Duesing, David O. Frazier, Richard Halverson, Douglas Jones, Allen Leatherman, Ben Letter, Evie McElroy, Bob Moak, Richard Oberlin, Edith Owen, Dorothy Paxton, Bjorn Pernvik, Mary Shelley, Liam Smith, Robert Snook, Larry Tarrant, Robert Thorson, Carolyn Younger

GUEST ARTISTS: Julia Curry, June Gibbons, Myrna Kaye, Philip MacKenzie, Peter Ostrum, Sheila Russell, Vivienne Stotter

PRODUCTIONS

"Plaza Suite," "Dark of the Moon," "Doll's House," "The Birds," "What the Butler Saw," "Child's Play," "Frank Merriewell," "Moby Dick, Rehearsed," "Prime of Miss Jean Brodie," "House of Blue Leaves," "The Price," "The Liar," "Forty Carats," "The Portable Chekhov"

WORLD PREMIERE of "Woman in the Dunes" by Kobo Abe, adapted and directed by Peter Coe

Joel Warren, James Fry Photos

Left: "Dark of the Moon" Top: Evie McElroy, Mary Shelley, Richard Halverson in "House of Blue Leaves"

Julia Curry, Jonathan Bolt in
"Woman in the Dunes"

Jonathan Bolt, Richard Oberlin
in "Moby Dick, Rehearsed"

COMPANY THEATRE
Los Angeles, Calif.
June 1, 1971—May 31, 1972

Administrative Director, Barry Opper; Press, Bill Hunt; Production Manager, Daniel Sonneborn; Directors, Steven Kent, Michael Carlin Pierce, Larry Hoffman, Dennis Redfield; Designers, Russell Pyle, Donald Harris; Costumes, Steven Kent, Marcina Motter; Lighting, Gladys Carmichael, Donald Harris, Russell Pyle; Music, Kerri Gillette, Steven Kent, Michael Monroe, Wiley Rinaldi, Jack Rowe, Daniel Sonneborn, Robert Walter; Lyrics, Bill Hunt, Michael Monroe, Sam Eisenstein, Roxann Pyle

COMPANY

Arthur Allen, Roger Barnes, Stephen Bellon, Gar Campbell, William Dannevik, Barbara Grover, Donald Harris, Nancy Hickey, Larry Hoffman, Bill Hunt, Steven Kent, Lori Landrin, Lance Larsen, Candace Laughlin, Polita Marks, Sandra Morgan, Marcina Motter, Barry Opper, Don Opper, Michael Carlin Pierce, Roxann Pyle, Dennis Redfield, Wiley Rinaldi, Jack Rowe, Richard Serpe, Trish Soodik, Daniel Sonneborn, Michael Stefani, Bob Walter

APPRENTICES: Jerry Hoffman, J. Thomas Hudgins, John Sefick

PRODUCTIONS

"The James Joyce Memorial Liquid Theatre," "The Plague," "The Emergence," "Caliban," "Duet," "The Los Angeles Art Ensemble and Grill," "Intersections 7," "Cherub and Meatball," "Passion Play," "Balls," "Riders to the Sea," "Conquest of Mr. Everest," "Crabs," "Cross-Country"

Left: Dennis Redfield, Trish Soodik in "The Emergence" Top: "James Joyce Memorial Liquid Theatre"

"The Plague" (also above)

Michael Stefani, Jack Rowe in "The Plague"

DALLAS THEATER CENTER
Dallas, Texas
October 12, 1971—August 12, 1972

Director, Paul Baker; Assistant Director, Mary Sue Jones; Administrative Director, Gary Moore; Technical Director, Campbell Thomas; Press, Lynn Trammell; Directors, Reginald Montgomery, Bryant Reynolds, Campbell Thomas, Michael Dendy, Preston Jones, Ken Latimer, Judith Davis; Designers, John Henson, Kathleen Latimer, Jo Stalker, Marian-Smith Martin, Russell Guinn, Yoichi Aoki, Marshall Kaufman, Sam Nance, Randy Moore, Robyn Flatt, Allen Hibbard, Sally Netzel

COMPANY

Judith Davis, Michael Dendy, John Figmiller, Robyn Flatt, Mary Sue Jones, Kathleen Latimer, Ken Latimer, Gene Leggett, John Logan, Steven Mackenroth, Ryland Merkey, Randy Moore, Louise Mosley, Sally Netzel, Synthia Rogers, Randolph Tallman, Campbell Thomas, Jacque Thomas, Lynn Trammell
GUEST ARTISTS: Carole Cook, Tom Troupe, Molly McGreevy, Don Eitner, C. Bernard Jackson, Takis Muzenidis, Lee Theodore, Rallou Manou, Dale Barnhart, Rocco Bufano

PRODUCTIONS

"Apple Tree," "Private Lives," "Lion in Winter," "School for Scandal," "J. B.," "Lysistrata," "Our Town," "Diary of a Madman," "The Price," "Exit the King," "Dear Love," "A Trio of Originals"

Andy Hanson Photos

Top: "Lysistrata" Below: Toni Zbranek, Mike Wray in "Our Town"

Mary Sue Jones, Randy Moore in "School for Scandal" Above: Carole Cook, Tom Troupe in "Lion in Winter"

**Errol Fortin, Jesse Newton
in "Of Mice and Men"**

DETROIT REPERTORY THEATRE
Detroit, Mich.
October 7, 1971—May 6, 1972

Artistic Director-Producer, Bruce E. Millan; Sets, Earl D. Smith, William Seybold, Bruce Millan; Costumes, Dolores Andrus, Katy Trainor; Choreographer, Dolores Andrus; Lighting, Dick Smith, Jon Kaplan; Directors, Bruce E. Millan, Earl D. Smith; Technical Assistants, Donald Jobes, Diane Reiman, Rick Burke; Stage Manager, Venida Evans

COMPANY

Kent Martin, Alma Parks, Dolores Maddox, Council Cargle, Randy Williams, Barbara Busby, Errol Fortin, Jessie Newton, Frank Monico, Hamid Dana, William Boswell, Dolores Andrus, Charles Roseborough, Lee O'Connell, Woody Miller, Mark Murri

PRODUCTIONS

"Behold! Cometh the Vanderkellans," "I Do! I Do!", "Of Mice and Men"

**Alma Parks in "Behold! Cometh the Vanderkellans"
Above: Barbara Busby, Council Cargle in "I Do! I Do!**

FORD'S THEATRE
Washington, D.C.
September 15, 1971—May 31, 1972

Executive Producer, Frankie (Mrs. Don)Hewitt; General and Company Manager, Ed Yoe; Press, Jan Du Plain; Lighting, Tom Berra; Director of Operations and Development, Linda Stern Lachowicz

PRODUCTIONS AND CASTS

DON'T BOTHER ME, I CAN'T COPE with Alex Bradford, Hope Clarke, Micki Grant, Arnold Wilkerson, Carl Bean, Charles E. Campbell, Bobby L. Hill, Willie James McPhatter, Gerald Francis, J. L. Harris, Leona Johnson, Philip A. Stamps

MOTHER EARTH by Ron Thronson and Toni Shearer, with Patti Austin, Christine Avila, Elaine Bankston, Ron deSalvo, Michael Devin, Joel Kimmel, Peter Jason, Tip Kelley, Carol Kristy, Arlene Parness

FESTIVAL AT FORD'S with Bob Hope, Carol Channing, Henry Mancini, Raymond Burr, Jonathan Winters, Charley Pride, Pat Boone Family, Melba Moore

BOB AND RAY THE TWO AND ONLY with Bob Elliott and Ray Goulding

ECHOES OF THE LEFT BANK with Jamie Thomas, Suzanne Oberjat, Harrison Somers, Ed Evanko, Danielle Odderra

MARK TWAIN TONIGHT! a solo performance by Hal Holbrook

MOBY DICK a solo performance by Jack Aranson

AN UNPLEASANT EVENING WITH H. L. MENCKEN a solo performance by David Wayne

GODSPELL with Bart Braverman, Scotch Byerley, Antony Hoty, Irving Lee, Dean Pitchford, Maggie Huatt, Doris Jamin, Patti Mariano, Lynne Thigpen, John-Ann Washington, Joanne Jonas, Mark Planner, Michael Makman, Baillie Gerstein, Belinda Tolbert, Rune Kuptur, Lynn Zidanic

Right: "Echoes of the Left Bank" Above: Cast of "Mother Earth"

Hal Holbrook as Mark Twain

David Wayne as H. L. Mencken

191

GOODMAN THEATRE
Chicago, Ill.
September 21, 1971—May 31, 1972

Producing Director, John Reich; Managing Director. Ken Myers; Press, Mel Kopp, Rhona Schultz; Directors, Patrick Henry, Christopher Hewitt, Brian Murray, Douglas Seale, Stuart Vaughan; Musical Staging and Choreography, Bob Herget; Musical Direction, John Cina; Sets, James Maronek, Sandro LaFerla, Alicia Finkel; Costumes, Alicia Finkel, Virgil Johnson; Lighting, G. E. Naselius, Bengt Nygren, Wayne Tignor, Jerrold Gorrell; Stage Managers, John Hickey, Judith Ann Binus, Patricia Christian, Robert Keil, Lois Nygren

COMPANY

Gwen Arment, Rebecca Balding, Marji Bank, Paul J. Benjamin, Dale Benson, Mary Best, Val J. Bettin, Carol E. Bishop, Suzi Bolen, Jose Borcia, Bill Boss, Marie Brady, Pauline Brailsford, J. Frederick Brown, Lonnie Burr, Allan Carlsen, Danny Carroll, Will Cleary, Connie Cooper, Maurice Copeland, Kenneth Cory, Bob Curry, Dalton Dearborn, Jonathan Farwell, Ralph Foody, Gale Gill, Clark James, Art Kassul, Joel Kazar, Leonard Kelly, Dennis Kennedy, Philip Kerr, Mark Lamos, J. Robert Lange, Jana Lapel, Lu Leonard, Richard Lyle, Connie Mango, Joseph Martinez, Denise Mauthe, Lawrence McCauley, Ann Meacham, Douglas Mellor, Frank Miller, Anthony Mockus, Robert Morgan, Mike Nussbaum, James O'Reilly, Vincent Park, Mark Petrakis, Nick Polus, LuAnn Post, Ray Rayner, Jimmy Roddy, Melody Rogers, Stephen Sodaro, Roy Sorrels, James Stephens, Tom Tammi, Anne Thompson, Matthew Tobin, Paul Tomasello, Rudy Tronto, Susanna Walker, Marrian Walters, Melva Williams, Lee Young

GUEST ARTISTS: Eric Brotherson, Nancy Coleman, Mildred Dunnock, Alvin Epstein, Brenda Forbes, Laurence Guittard, Murray Matheson, Cathleen Nesbitt, Russell Nype, Hiram Sherman, Shepperd Strudwick, Donald Woods

PRODUCTIONS

"A Place without Doors," "Assassinations, 1865," "The Importance of Being Earnest," "The Royal Family," "The Ruling Class," "The Boys from Syracuse"

David Fishman Photos

Left: Cathleen Nesbitt, Philip Kerr, Mike Nussbaum, Rebecca Balding in "The Royal Family" Above: Shepperd Strudwick, Donald Woods in "Assassination 1865"

Brenda Forbes, Philip Kerr in
"The Importance of Being Earnest"

Mildred Dunnock, Alvin Epstein in
"A Place without Doors"

GUTHRIE THEATER COMPANY
Minneapolis, Minn.
July 22, 1971—January 15, 1972

Artistic Director, Michael Langham; Managing Director, Donald Schoebaum; Associate Director, David Wheeler; Production Manager, Dan Bly; Designer, John Jensen; Musical Director, Robert Samarotto; Press, Charlotte Solomon; Company Manager, Denny Spence; Technical Directors, Kerry Lafferty, Robert Jackson; Technical Assistants, Paul Daniels, Robert Bye; Wardrobe Mistress, Georgia Wick; Costume Coordinator, Michael Stauffer

CAST

Paul Hecht, Roberta Maxwell, Mary Savidge, Katherine Ferrand, Sandor Szabo, Bronia Stefan, Penelope Allen, Jon Cranney, Betty Leighton, Joseph Maher, Max Wright, Lance Henriksen, Paul Ballantyne, Diana Barrington, Bernard Behrens, Ross Bickell, James Blendick, Barbara Bryne, Len Cariou, Patricia Conolly, Peggy Cosgrave, Saylor Creswell, David Feldshuh, Warren Frost, Ron Glass, Peter Michael Goetz, Ellin Gorky, Mary Hitch, James J. Lawless, Betty Leighton, Fred R. Miller, Robert Pastene, Briain Petchey, Ken Pogue, Leon Pownall, Gerald J. Quimby, William Rhys, Michele Shay, Evalyn Baron, Ivar Brogger, Lance Davis, Tovah Feldshuh, Steven Ryan

PRODUCTIONS

"Cyrano de Bergerac," "The Taming of the Shrew," "Misalliance," "A Touch of the Poet," "The Diary of a Scoundrel," "Fables Here and Then"

Top: Roberta Maxwell, Len Cariou in "Cyrano"
Below: Len Cariou (C) in "Taming of the Shrew"

Sandor Szabo, Paul Ballantyne in "Misalliance"
bove: "The Diary of a Scoundrel" Top: "A Touch of the Poet"

193

HARTFORD STAGE COMPANY
Hartford, Conn.
October 15, 1971—June 18, 1972

Producing Director, Paul Weidner; Managing Director, William Stewart; Press, Ann Vermel; Stage Managers, Fred Hoskins, Gary Lamagna, Stephen Nasuta; Technical Director, Richard Masur; Costumes, Carola Meleck, June Stearns, Colleen Callahan; Technical Assistants, Craig Watson, Peter Riddle; Production Assistant, David Winslow; Photographer, David Robbins; Director of Creative Theatre, Irene Lewis

COMPANY

Carryl Croxton, Paul Rudd, Rod Perry, Elizabeth Eis, Jessie Saunders, Colostine Boatwright, Harold Pierson, Tana Hicken, Joseph Attles, Frank Biancamano, David O. Petersen, Arthur Stedman, Hillman Jones, Gary Lamagna, Jack Murdock, Harris Yulin, George Taylor, David H. Leary, Henry Thomas, John Dignan, Diana Kirkwood, Darthy Blair, Bernard Frawley, Robert Moberly, Richard Pilcher, Christopher Andrews, Geddeth Smith, Donald Bell, Russell Horton, Barbara Caruso, Veronica Castang, Gary Dontzig, Maureen Hurley, Kathleen Miller, Sandra Thornton, James Valentine, Larry Bryggman, Jordan Christopher, Donald Ewer, Charlotte Moore, Stephen Mendillo, David Clennon

PRODUCTIONS

"No Place to Be Somebody," "Henry V," "Charley's Aunt," "Tiny Alice," "Loot"

U.S. PREMIERE of "Rooted" by Alexander Buzo, directed by Paul Weidner, with David H. Leary, Jack Murdock, Barbara Caruso, David O. Petersen, Veronica Castang

David Robbins Photos

Right: Paul Rudd, Harris Yulin, Bernard Frawley in "Henry V"

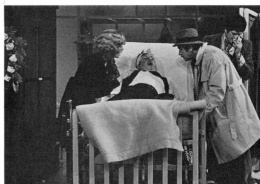

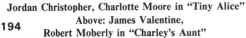

Jordan Christopher, Charlotte Moore in "Tiny Alice"
Above: James Valentine,
Robert Moberly in "Charley's Aunt"

Jack Murdock, Veronica Castang, David Petersen, Barbara Caruso in "Rooted" Above: "Loot"

INNER CITY REPERTORY THEATRE
Los Angeles, Calif.
June 1, 1971—May 31, 1972

Executive Director, C. Bernard Jackson; General Manager, Josie Dotson; Press, Bruce R. Feldman, Dorothy A. Carr; Technical Supervisor, Lupre Autajay; Stage Manager, Annette Ensley; Lighting, William Collins; Sound, Federico Bernache; Production Assistants, Austin Beidleman, Tomas Gomez; Wardrobe Mistress, Janet Allen

COMPANY

Beah Richards, Jack Crowder, Bette Treadville, Gene Simms, Gloria Calomee, Charles M. Kray, Judy Jean Berns, Elizabeth Herron, Beverly A. Johnson, Thurman Scott, Baxter Harris, Bette Howard, Tina Sattin, Clyde Kusatsu, Mako, Nobu McCarthy, Joanne Lee, Serena McCarthy, Jesse Dixon, Richard Kato, Irvin Paik, Elaine Kashiki, John Mamo

PRODUCTIONS

"To Be Young, Gifted and Black," and PREMIERES of "One Is a Crowd," and "Gold Watch," and hosted the ten-day Chicano theatre festival "Fiesta de los Teatros"

Top: (L) Jack Crowder, Beah Richards
in "One Is a Crowd" (R)Cast of "To Be Young,
Gifted and Black"

Nobu McCarthy, Mako in "Gold Watch"

Donald Madden, Eileen Herlie in
premiere of "Out Cry" Right: Anita
Dangler, James Broderick, Irene Dailey
in "House of Blue Leaves"

IVANHOE THEATRE
Chicago, Ill.
July 8, 1971—May 31, 1972

Producer, George Keathley; Associate Producer, Aaron
Gold; Press, Gold/Wilson, Carol Minchin; Sets, Wrick Paul;
Lighting, Thomas M. Guerra; Technical Director, Ivan Carl-
son

PRODUCTIONS AND CASTS

OUT CRY by Tennessee Williams (U.S. Premiere), directed
by George Keathley, with Eileen Herlie and Donald Madden

STATUS QUO VADIS written and directed by Donald
Driver (World Premiere) with David Wilson, Gail Strickland,
Rebecca Taylor, Geraldine Kay, Otto Senz, Otto L. Schle-
singer, Dick Sasso, Judd Reilly, Lee Zara, Don Marston,
Doug Alleman, Max Howard, George Womack, Bob Thomp-
son, William Vines, Kathy Korla, William Vines, Edward
Topel, Steven Rupp, Treofilo Bruno, George Ramos

THE HOUSE OF BLUE LEAVES with James Broderick,
Irene Dailey, Anita Dangler, Jonathan Hogan, Adrienne
Kent, Joe Greco, Pamela Danser, Margaret Christopher,
Judith Bergan, David Whitaker, Barry Bernstein

Dick Klein Photos

World Premiere of "Status Quo"

196

LONG WHARF THEATRE
New Haven, Conn.
October 22, 1971—June 3, 1972

Executive Director, M. Edgar Rosenblum; Artistic Director, Arvin Brown; Directors, Malcolm Black, Morris Carnovsky, Barry Davis, Edward Gilbert; Designers, Whitney Blausen, John Conklin, Virginia Dancy, David Jenkins, Marjorie Kellogg, Kert Lundell, Bill Walker, Elmon Webb; Lighting, Ron Wallace, Judy Rasmuson; Technical Director, David Snyder; Stage Managers, Anne Keefe, Liz Neuman, Nina Seely; Artistic Director Children's Theatre, Isaac Schambelan; Press, Lorraine Osborne

COMPANY

Madeline Adams, Tom Atkins, Emery Battis, Louis Beachner, John Beal, John Braden, Peter Brouwer, Shirley Bryan, Morris Carnovsky, John Cazale, Matt Conley, Jane Connell, Staats Cotsworth, Peter Donat, Joyce Ebert, George Ede, Jim Erickson, Will Fenno, Minnie Gaster, Stefan Gierasch, Gordon Gould, Sarina C. Grant, William Hansen, Christopher Hastings, Linda Hunt, William Jay, Stacey Keach, Laurie Kennedy, Richard Kuss, Sue Lawless, Will Lee, Joseph Leon, Roberta Maxwell, James Naughton, Ruth Nelson, Patricia Pearcy, Austin Pendleton, Joseph Remmes, Jay Romig, Paul Rudd, Leon Russom, David Sabin, Martha Schlamme, Terrence Sherman, Frank Speiser, Caryl Stern, William Swetland, George Taylor, Carol Teitel, John Tillinger, Charles Turner, Stephen Van Benschoten, Cindy Veasey, Helen Verbit, Lee Wallace, Kitty Winn, Teresa Wright

PRODUCTIONS

"You Can't Take It with You," "The Contractor," "A Streetcar Named Desire," "Hamlet," "The Way of the World," "Troika: An Evening of Russian Comedy," "The Iceman Cometh," "Patrick's Day"

Craig Scherfenberg Photos

Right: Kitty Winn, Stefan Gierasch, Leon Russom, Joyce Ebert in "Hamlet"

Tom Atkins, Joyce Ebert in "A Streetcar Named Desire"

Will Lee, Morris Carnovsky in "A Swan Song"

197

MEADOW BROOK THEATRE
Rochester, Mich.
October 14, 1971—May 21, 1972

Artistic Director, Terence Kilburn; Managing Director, Frank F. Bollinger; Business Manager, Tommy Whisman; Press, Rose Marie McClain; Scenery and Lighting, Richard Davis; Costumes, Mary Schakel; Technical Director, Lyalls Phillips; Stage Managers, Roy Martin, Bradlee Shattuck, Michael Tolaydo; Directors, Terence Kilburn, Charles Nolte, John Going, Joseph Shaw, John Ulmer; Photographer, Bayard Lawes

COMPANY

Glynis Bell, Diane Bugas, Robert Englund, David Himes, Elisabeth Orion, Michael Tolaydo, Bradlee Shattuck, Suzanne Toren, J. L. Dahlmann, David Robert Kanter, Christopher Ross-Smith

GUEST ARTISTS: Harry Ellerbe, Naomi Stevens, William Needles, Booth Colman, Bernard Kates, Jack Bell, Angela Wood, Roland Hewgill, David Little, William LeMassena, Page Johnson, Paul Ballantyne, Gloria Maddox, Peter Brandon, Warren Burton, Susan E. Scott, Adam Grammis, Anne Wakefield, Wilfred Schuman, Geoffrey Webb, Laurence Hugo, Maco McCalman, Albert M. Ottenheimer

PRODUCTIONS

"The Matchmaker," "The Andersonville Trial," "Heartbreak House," "Glass Menagerie," "Odd Couple," "A Doll's House," "The Boy Friend," "The Price"

Top Right: Naomi Stevens, Harry Ellerbe in "The Matchmaker" Below: Gloria Maddox, Peter Brandon in "A Doll's House"

Page Johnson, William LeMassena in "The Odd Couple" Above: Albert Ottenheimer, Macon McCalman, 198 Elisabeth Orion, Laurence Hugo in "The Price"

Harry Ellerbe, Booth Colman, Bernard Kates in "The Andersonville Trial"

MILWAUKEE REPERTORY THEATER
Milwaukee, Wisc.
October 8, 1971—June 11, 1972

Artistic Director, Nagle Jackson; Managing Director, Charles R. McCallum; Press, Donald Donne, Michael Keawczyk; Directors, Rod Alexander, Nagle Jackson, Charles Kimbrough, Raye Birk; Sets, Christopher M. Idoine, John Jensen, Kert Lundell; Costumes, James Edmund Brady; Lighting, William Mintzer, Ken Billington; Stage Managers, Merry Tigar, Margie Perkins, Laurence Coleman, Marc Rush; Photographer, Jack Hamilton

COMPANY

Jim Baker, Candace Barrett, Raye Birk, Jerry Brown, Robert Ground, Ric Hamilton, John Hancock, Stephanie J. Harker, Jim Jansen, Charles Kimbrough, Mary Jane Kimbrough, Judith Light, William McKereghan, Josephine Nichols, Fredi Olster, Penelope Reed, Jack Swanson, Jeffrey Tambor, Martha Tippin, Blake Torney

PRODUCTIONS

"Cat among the Pigeons," "The English Mystery Plays," "White House Murder Case," "Measure for Measure," "Delicate Balance," "Easter Cycle of English Mystery Plays," "Journey of the Fifth Horse"

Jack Hamilton Photos

Right: Blake Torney, Martha Tippin, Robert Ground, Judith Light, Raye Birk in "English Mystery Plays"
Below: Josephine Nichols, Jeffrey Tambor, Jim Baker in "Journey of the Fifth Horse"

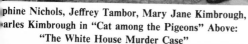

phine Nichols, Jeffrey Tambor, Mary Jane Kimbrough,
arles Kimbrough in "Cat among the Pigeons" Above:
"The White House Murder Case"

Fredi Olster, Penelope Reed
in "A Delicate Balance"

199

MUMMERS THEATRE
Oklahoma City, Okla.
December 4, 1971—May 27, 1972

Producer-Director, Mack Scism; Directors, John Wylie, John Going; Sets, Charles G. Stockton; Costumes, William Schroder, Barbara Ragan; Lighting, Richard Harden; Stage Managers, Peter Hajduk, Judy Schoen; General Manager, George Anderson; Press, Midge Richards

COMPANY

Anne Ault, Gwyllum Evans, George Ede, Tony Aylward, Peter Stuart, Vincent Milana, Garry Phillips, Michael Parrish, Joan Bassie, David Sabin, Tom Kroutil, Scott Porter, Mary Ed Porter, Virginia Seidel, Lee Powell, David Christmas, Tamara Long, Carveth Wells, James Carruthers, George Connoly, Gwenneth Goller, Angela Wood

GUEST ARTISTS: Dody Goodman, Ethel Barrymore Colt

PRODUCTIONS

"The Taming of the Shrew," "Dear Liar," "The Man Who Came to Dinner," "Dames at Sea," "The Odd Couple," "The Matchmaker"

**Left: George Ede, Dody Goodman
in "The Matchmaker" Below: Mack Scism,
Angela Wood in "Dear Liar"**

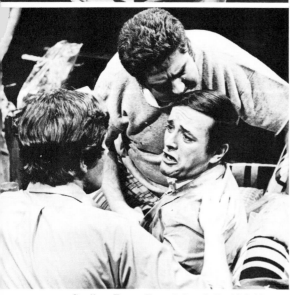

**Gwyllum Evans, Tony Aylward, David Sabin
in "The Odd Couple"**

**John Wylie in "The Man Who Came to Dinner"
Above: Scott Porter, Gwyllum Evans in
"Taming of the Shrew"**

200

Henry Thomas, Vera Lockwood in "The
Physicists" Right: Theodore Sorel, Vera
Lockwood in "Plaza Suite"

PAF PLAYHOUSE
Huntington Station, N.Y.
July 1, 1971—May 27, 1972

Executive Director, Clint Marantz; Resident Director,
Richard Jamieson; Sets, John Shane; Lighting, William Gen-
sel; Photographer, Joan James; Stage Managers, Mary Ann
Carlin, Peggy Bendiner

COMPANY

Clement Fowler, Sean G. Griffin, Jay Hampton, Howard
Honig, Richmond Hoxie, Lauren Levian, Vera Lockwood,
Laurie Kennedy, Heidi Mefford, Beverly Ostroska, Kelley
Patton, William Pardue, Mary Lou Schertz, and Bern W.
Budd, Ronn Kistler, Warren Motley

GUEST ARTISTS: Kahalil Balakrishna, Valerie Beaman, Joe
Bellomo, Jon Burr, Walter Chaskel, Jacqueline Coslow, Carol
Dickey, Flora Elkins, Thomas James, Donald Gantry, Ra-
phael Grinage, Beverly Feite Hanson, William Lawrence, Mi-
chael Mackman, Ilona Murai, Eric Nebbia, Patricia
O'Connell, Lynn Rudner, Theodore Sorel, Carol Thomas,
Henry Thomas

PRODUCTIONS

"A Thurber Carnival," "The Fantasticks," "A Thousand
Clowns," "School for Wives," "The Physicists," "Plaza
Suite," "Miracle Worker," "Arms and the Man," "Birthday
Party," "Song Is a Blue Fish,"
U.S. PREMIERE of "ffinest ffamily in the land" by Henry
Livings

Joan James Photos

Right (C): Sean Griffin, Richmond Hoxie,
Clement Fowler in "The Odd Couple"

Jacqueline Coslow, Richard Jamieson
in "Arms and the Man"

PHILADELPHIA DRAMA GUILD
Philadelphia, Pa.
November 30, 1971—April 29, 1972

Producer, Sidney S. Bloom; Artistic Director, William Ross; Artistic Consultant, John Randolph; Scenery and Lighting, Clarke Dunham; Costumes, Joseph F. Bella; Company Manager, Philip Klein; Stage Managers, Gerald Nobles, Jeanna Belkin; Photographer, Ed Eckstein; Press, Eugene Palatsky; Directors, Stephen Porter, William Ross, William Woodman, Daniel M. Petrie

COMPANY

Andrea Bell, Patrick J. Cronin, JoAnn Cunningham, Alan Manson, Thomas Markus, George Pentecost, William Preston, Valerie von Volz, C. L. Williams, Douglas Wing, Ken Zimmerman, Elowyn Castle, Barbara Colton, Sue Farley, Dan Hogan, Mordecai Lawner, Louis Schaefer, Douglas Wing, David Dukes, Patricia Elliott, James Lambert, Janet League, Anne O'Donnell, Christine Carter, Ed Flanders, Charles Hudson, Hugh Hurd, Don Kersey, Beverlee McKinsey, Arnold Soboloff, Ted Thurston

GUEST ARTISTS: Howard DaSilva, Ken Howard, Louise Sorel, Imogene Coca, King Donovan, John McGiver, Ray Walston, Laurence Guittard, Earle Hyman, John Randolph, Ruby Dee, Tammy Grimes, E. G. Marshall

PRODUCTIONS

"The Imaginary Invalid," "Born Yesterday," "The Rivals," "Volpone"

Jack Hoffman Photos

Ken Howard, Howard DaSilva in "Volpone"
Above: Chita Rivera, John Randolph in "Born Yesterday"

Top: Patricia Elliott, Ray Walston, Imogene Coca in "The Rivals" Below: E. G. Marshall, Tammy Grimes in "Imaginary Invalid"

PITTSBURGH PLAYHOUSE
Pittsburgh, Pa.
Thirty-eighth Season

Executive Producer, S. Joseph Nassif; Artistic Director, Kenneth Costigan; General Manager, Robert L. Mervick; Business Manager, Robert Klimenko; Press, Charlotte Nelson, Molly Cochran; Production Manager, W. Valentine Mayer; Technical Director, Robert Kuiper; Stage Manager, Ned Schmidtke; Designers, Mary Ellen Kennedy, Leonard Feldman; Lighting, Pat Simmons; Costumes, Frank Childs; Wardrobe Mistress, Mary Hersey; Make-up, James Martin; Photographer, Michael Friedlander; Musical Director, James Reed Lawlor; Playwright, Tom Thomas; Directors, S. Joseph Nassif, Ken Costigan, W. Valentine Mayer, John David Lutz, Ned Schmidtke; Choreography, Paul Draper.

COMPANY

Earl Boen, Alan Clarey, Bruce Detrick, Doris Hackney, Eileen Letchworth, Richard Michaels, S. Joseph Nassif, Ned Schmidtke, Pattie Tomc, Charlotte Casciotti, Jane Coleman, Paul Draper, Peggy Ann Hughes, John David Lutz, George MacGuire, Helen Wayne Rauh, Julie Stevens, Jennifer Williams, Richard Casper, Ken Costigan, David Emge, Keith Langsdale, W. Valentine Mayer, Daniel Mooney, Martha Schlamme, Barbara Lynn Block, Betty Gillett, Hal Robinson, George Eisenhauer, Ron Capozzoli, Doug Sortino.

PRODUCTIONS

"Anything Goes," "Boys in the Band," "Blithe Spirit," "Plaza Suite," "Lion in Winter," "Play It Again, Sam," "Cactus Flower," "Never Too Late," "Man of La Mancha,"

Michael Friedlander Photos

**David Emge, Barbara Lynn Block in "Never Too Late"
Above: Ken Costigan, Peggy Ann Hughes in "Play It
Again, Sam" Top: Earl Boen, Martha Schlamme in "Lion
in Winter"**

**Top: (clockwise) David Stuckrath, David Emge,
Daniel Mooney, Ken Costigan, Wayne Cook, Earl
Boen, Ned Schmidtke in "Boys in the Band"** 203

PLAYHOUSE IN THE PARK
Cincinnati, Ohio

Director, Word Baker; General Manager, William Carver; Company Manager, Dan Early; Business Manager, Audrey Teljeur; Press, Patricia Gerhardt, M. J. Boyer; Stage Managers, Sherman F. Warner, Chris Comer; Technical Director, John Saalfeld; Costumes, Caley Summers; Production Assistants, Tom Belleville, DeWitt Stewart; Photographer, Walt Burton; Directors, Word Baker, Michael Flanagan, Dan Early, Neil Flanagan

PRODUCTIONS AND CASTS

THE LAST SWEET DAYS OF ISAAC with Alice Playten and Austin Pendleton

CARAVAGGIO with Cal Bellini, Tom Margolis, Luigi, Dave Holbrook, Tom Burke, Michael Flanagan, John Ventantonio, Jerry Cunliffe, Tom Belleville, Arthur Morey, Tony Gaetano, J. Frederick Jones, Bill Burnett, Max Hager, Paul Forste, Pat King, Dean Builter, Steve Buck, William Duff-Griffin, Steve O'Banion, Prue Warren, Jim O'Connor, Dudley Sauve, R. A. Dow, Gene Wolters, Paul Milikin, Jack Gwillim, William Larsen, Michael Mullins, Roger Kozol, Lieux Dressler

RAIN with Madeleine le Roux, Dorthi Fox, Ike Moxley, Paul Forste, R. A. Dow, William Duff-Griffin, Carol Keefe, Paul Milikin, Katina Commings, David Stanley Lyman, James Cahill

HAMLET with Daniel Davis, Frank Raiter, Ann Kinsolving, Jack Gwillim, John Ventantonio, Gastone Rossilli, Ed Dundon, Max Hager, Tony Gaetano, Garry George, Paul-Mathew Eckhart, Stefan Mark Weyte, Richard Loder, Paul Kindt, Jerry Cunliffe, Tom Belleville, Tom Burke, Dave Holbrook, Walt Weidenbacher, Steve Burdick, Phillip Romito, Ted Deucher, Ric Gerwin, James Hartman, Ira-Kent Hill, Marsha Wishusen, Dorothy Reynolds, Robert Stocking

WHY HANNA'S SKIRT WON'T STAY DOWN with Helen Hanft, Steven Davis, Karole Kaye Stevenson

LIFE WITH FATHER with Laurence Hugo, Ludi Claire, Gary Dontzig, Tom Burke, Riley Miles, Brooks Tomb, Anne Murray, Nancy Foy, Paul Milikin, Max Hager, Dorothy Reynolds, Anita Trotta, Patty Romito, Sarah-Jane Gwillim, Dana Hibbard

Walt Burton Photos

Left: Tom Burke, Laurence Hugo, Nancy Foy, Anne Murray, Riley Mills, Ludi Claire, Brooks Tomb in "Life with Father" Top: Alice Playten, Austin Pendleton in "Last Sweet Days of Isaac"

Helen Hanft, Stephen Davis in "Why Hanna's Skirt Won't Stay Down"

Cal Bellini in "Caravaggio"

THE REPERTORY THEATRE
St. Louis, Mo.
October 21, 1971—April 15, 1972

Managing Director, Walter Perner, Jr.; General Manager, John Economos; Directors, Charles Haid, Walter Perner, Jr., Dennis Rosa, William Woodman; Composer, Mel Marvin; Music Director, David Stein; Sets, Clarke Dunham, Grady Larkins; Costumes, Jeanne Button, Bruce Harrow, Lawrence Miller; Lighting, Clarke Dunham, Gilbert Hemsley, Jr., Peter E. Sargent; Press, Sherry Burns, M. Rose Jonas; Stage Managers, Joseph DePauw, Arnold Aronson, James McDermott; Technical Director, John Conant

COMPANY

Paul Blake, Robert Browning, Brendan Burke, J. Robert Dietz, Mike Genovese, Lilene Mansell, Martin Molson, Arthur A. Rosenberg, James Scott, George Vafiadis

GUEST ARTISTS: Lenny Baker, Laurinda Barrett, Robert Barton, Genevieve Bierman, Tom Brannum, Laurie Brooks-Jefferson, Lynn Cohen, Deborah Deeble, Laura Esterman, Ronny Graham, Joan Hanson, John Harkins, Lloyd Hubbard, Duane Jones, Bruce M. Kornbluth, Martin Kove, Myron Kozman, Gretchen Oehler, Giulia Pagano, James Calvin Paul, Richard Ramos, Richard Reicheg, William Shust, Penelope Windust

PRODUCTIONS

"Room Service," "Marat/Sade," "After the Rain," "Sherlock Holmes"

WORLD PREMIERE of "Horatio"

T. Mike Fletcher, Bill Thielker Photos

Left: William Schust (C) in "After the Rain"
Above: Lilene Mansell, Brendan Burke, Duane Jones, Robert Browning in "Marat/Sade"

Arthur Rosenberg, Richard Reicheg, James Scott in "Room Service"

World Premiere of "Horatio"

SEATTLE REPERTORY THEATRE
Seattle, Wash.
October 20, 1971—February 26, 1972
Ninth Season

Artistic Director, W. Duncan Ross; Producing Director, Peter Donnelly; Stage Directors, W. Duncan Ross, Clayton Corzatte, Robert Loper, Wayne Carson; Sets, Jason Phillips; Costumes, Lewis D. Rampino; Lighting, William Mintzer; Stage Manager, John Page Blakemore; Technical Director, Floyd Hart; Press, Shirley Dennis

COMPANY

John Abajian, John Aylward, Tom Carson, Clayton Corzatte, Don Freeman, Margaret Hilton, Pat Hodges, Jo Leffingwell, Robert Loper, Gun-Marie Nilsson, Eve Roberts, Nancy Zala

GUEST ARTISTS: Gwen Arner, Susan Carr, Thayer David, George Ede, Pauline Flanagan, Ronny Graham, Margaret Hamilton, Michael Keenan, Barbara Kyle, Marian Mercer, Donald Moffat, Priscilla Morrill, Margaret Phillips, Jay H. Sheffield, Josef Sommer, John Tillinger, Gwen Van Dam, George Vogel, Byron Webster, William Young

PRODUCTIONS

"Ring Round the Moon," "House of Blue Leaves," "Hotel Paradiso," "Getting Married," "And Miss Reardon Drinks a Little," "Adaptation" and "Next"

Right: Marian Mercer, Nancy Zala in "And Miss Reardon Drinks a Little"

Jay Sheffield, Margaret Phillips in "Getting Married" Above: Gun-Marie Nilsson, Tom Carson, Michael Keenan, Clayton Corzatte in "Adaptation"

George Ede, Margaret Hilton, Margaret Hamilton in "Ring Round the Moon" Above: Gwen Arner, Donald Moffat, Don Freeman in "Hotel Paradiso"

206

Harold Ramis, Eugenie Ross-Leming, John Belushi, Joe O'Flaherty, Judy Morgan, Joe Fisher

SECOND CITY
Chicago, Ill.
June 1, 1971—May 31, 1972

Producer-Director, Bernard Sahlins; Associate Producer, Joyce Sloan; General Manager, Tom Wing; Stage Manager, Paul Taylor; Press, Gold/Wilson & Associates

COMPANY

John Belushi, Jim Fisher, Harold Ramis, Joseph O'Flaherty, Judy Morgan, Eugenie Ross-Leming

PRODUCTIONS

Improvisational revues, this season's entitled "43rd Parallel"

Dick Klein Photo

STAGE/WEST
West Springfield, Mass.
November 12, 1971—April 23, 1972

Producing Director, Stephen E. Hays; Artistic Director-Stage Manager, William Guild; Press, Samuel Scheckter

COMPANY

Hannah Brandon, Humphrey Davis, Jerry Hardin, Dianne Hill, Richard Larson, Raymond Singer, Eric Tavaris, Hamp Watson, Carole Couche, John Wardwell, Richmond Hoxie

PRODUCTIONS

"The Miracle Worker," "Count Dracula," "This Agony," "This Triumph," "Scapin," "Slow Dance on the Killing Ground," "Plaza Suite," and a children's theatre

Pecum, and Paramount Photos

Top Left: Eric Tavares, Jack Gianino in "This Agony, This Triumph" Below: Eric Tavares in "Count Dracula"

Bob Casals, Philip McKenzie, Linda Harris, Jerry Hardin, Eric Tavares, Glen Lane, Raymond Singer, Hannah Brandon, Richard Larson, Diane Hill, Humphrey Davis in "Scapin" Right Center: Ron Glass, Humphrey Davis, Hannah Brandon in "Slow Dance on the Killing Ground"

STUDIO ARENA THEATRE
Buffalo, N.Y.
October 7, 1971—June 4, 1972

Executive Producer, Neal Du Brock; General Manager, Robert Tolan; Assistant Director, Kathryn Kingdon; Press, Blossom Cohan; Business Manager, William E. Lurie; Associate Director, Warren Enters; Stage Managers, Ingrid von Wellsheim Cantarella, Steve Andersen; Lighting, Peter J. Gill; Technical Directors, Dennis Shenk, Paul R. Lombardo; Design Assistant, Douglas Lebrecht

PRODUCTIONS AND CASTS

THE GINGERBREAD LADY with Jo Van Fleet, Virginia Kiser, Carol Willard, Alex Colon, Kurt Garfield, Dean Dittmann

BUYING OUT by Lawrence Roman (World Premiere), with Irene Dailey, George Voskovec, Harold J. Stone, Harold Gould, Joanna Roos, Charlotte Jones, Sylvia Gassell, Nicolas Surovy, Paul Vincent, Lois Avery

THE ME NOBODY KNOWS with Nancy Lee Baxter, Jonathon Brooks, John Charles, Wanda Covington, Jose Luis Gomez, Cynthia Hamilton, Denise Mack, James Mahady, Stan Shaw, Phillipina Williams, Sandra Wypych, Anthony Young

MAMA by Neal Du Brock and John Clifton (World Premiere), with Celeste Holm, Jill O'Hara, Wesley Addy, Michael Kermoyan, Pamela Saunders, Charlotte Jones, Lois Holmes, Marijane Maricle, Marilynn Scott, Bruce Detrick, Curtis Wheeler, Nelson Welch, Eva Grant, Leslie Barrett, Todd Dorfman, Lee Daniels

THE TRIAL OF THE CATONSVILLE NINE with Jake Dengel, Marion Belcher, Richard Branda, Dori Brenner, Barry Ford, Bill Herndon, Munson Hicks, Jack Landron, Jean Paul Lavin, Tom Mardirosian, Michael Miller, Elsie Robertson, Kenneth E. Sherman

ROMEO AND JULIET with Kristoffer Tabori, David Birney, Susan Sharkey, Armand Assante, Francis Bethencourt, Saylor Creswell, James Dybas, Christian Grant, Ron Hale, Jay Higgins, Charlotte Jones, Phil Killian, Tom Mardirosian, Richard McKenzie, Paul Rosson, Sally Rubin, Steve Andersen, Kathleen Ann Andrews, Virginia Anton, John Fisgus, Kevin Kearney, Gina Paigen, James Perry, Carl John Rosser, Paula A. Stevens, John Stevenson

THE PROPOSITION with Shelley Burns, Ray Baker, Paul Kreppel, Ginny Russell, Diane Bulgarelli

PLAY STRINDBERG with Robert Benson, Ray Fry, Priscilla Pointer, Robert Symonds

MAN OF LA MANCHA with Stephen Arlen, Martin Ross, Gloria Zaglool, Louise Armstrong, Eddie Barnes, Clay Causey, Don Croll, James Dannen, Jon Delon, Carol Gelfand, Ryan Hilliard, David Holland, Rand Mitchell, David Vosburgh

Greenberg-May Photos

Top: Charlotte Jones, Kristoffer Tabori, David Birney in "Romeo and Juliet" (R) Jo Van Fleet in "The Gingerbread Lady" Below: Wesley Addy, Celeste Holm in "Mama"

Harold J. Stone, Harold Gould, Irene Daily, George Voskovec in "Buying Out"

209

SYRACUSE REPERTORY THEATRE
Syracuse, N.Y.
March 3—May 14, 1972

Managing Director, Rex Henriot; Visiting Director, Tom Roland; Press, Kit Sine; Business Manager, Walter Innes; Musical Director, Steve Metcalf; Sets, Leonard Dryansky, Robert Lewis Smith, Robert K. Cloyd; Production Supervisor, Leonard Dryansky; Lights, Robert Alexander; Costumes, Sue Ann Smith; Technical Directors, Robert Lewis Smith, Richard Milster, Donald Wiltshire; Stage Manager, Barbara Rosoff; Properties, Judy Schoen, Ellen Couch; Sound, Dan Wooley; Wardrobe Mistress, Jane Ryack; Photographer, Pat Dohnke

COMPANY

Tom Brennan, Carolyn Porter Beck, Jack Collard, Ellen E. Culver, Patrick Desmond, David Deardorff, Ruth Fenster, Gary Gage, Gail Goldsman, Bob Gunton, Susan Harney, Tiffany Hendry, Zoaunne LeRoy Henriot, Fran Herbert, Jay Higgins, Hal Holden, Charles Morey, Scott Mansfield, Eve Packer, Gerald Richards, James "Red" Wilcher, Roberta Vatske, George Wyner

PRODUCTIONS

"She Loves Me," "One Flew over the Cuckoo's Nest," "Sign in Sidney Brustein's Window," "House of Blue Leaves," "Happy Birthday, Wanda June"

Pat Dohnks Photos

Right: Sam Henriot, Tom Brennan, Tiffany Hendry, Patrick Desmond in "Happy Birthday, Wanda June"

Hal Holden, Patrick Desmond in "She Loves Me"

Fran Herbert, Jack Collard in "House of Blue Leaves"

THEATRE COMPANY OF BOSTON
Boston, Mass.

Artistic Director, David Wheeler; Managing Director, Peggy Forbes; Administrative Assistant, Lisa Tatlock; Sets, John Thornton; Lighting, Eugene Lowery; Stage Manager, Clint Spencer; Costumes, Rebecca Goldman

COMPANY

Al Pacino, Tisa Chang, Carolyn Pickman, Gustave Johnson, James Spruill, Jack Rehoe, Clarence Felder, Jan Egleson, Burr Debenning, Tom Bower, Matthew Chait, Joseph Wilkins, Brent Jennings, Marc Sachs, Ron Hunter, Andrea Petersen, Josephine Lane, Richard Lynch, Steve Evets, Jon Terry, Gary Halcott, Steve Seidel, Walter Lott, Irma Sandrey, Barry Snider, Lance Henriksen

PRODUCTIONS

"Ask Me No Questions," "Exploding the Mother Earth Myth," "Clearance," "On the Rocks of Mandalay," "The Basic Training of Pavlo Hummel"

Rod Fierman, Yendor Namreif Photos

Right: Al Pacino in "Basic Training of Pavlo Hummel"

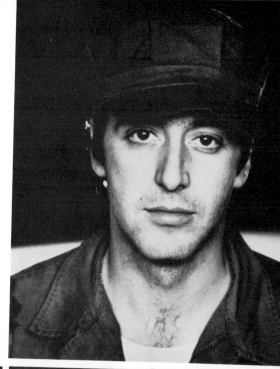

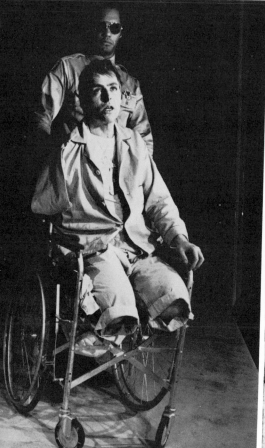

Gustave Johnson, Richard Lynch
in **"Basic Training of Pavlo Hummel"**

Al Pacino, Irma Sandrey

TRINITY SQUARE REPERTORY COMPANY
Providence, R.I.
September 21, 1971—May 11, 1972

Director, Adrian Hall; Assistant, Marion Simon; General Manager, Lamont E. Smith II; Press, David Wynne; Music Director, Richard Cumming; Sets, Eugene Lee, Robért D. Soule, David Jenkins; Lighting, Roger Morgan; Costumes, John Lehmeyer, A. Christina Giannini, Betsey Potter; Stage Managers, William Radka, Bree Cavazos; Stage Directors, Adrian Hall, Larry Arrick; Photographer, William L. Smith

COMPANY

Ruth Benson, William Cain, Robert J. Colonna, Timothey Crowe, Joseph Culliton, William Damkoehler, James Eichelberger, Robert Farber, Michael Gorrin, Richard Jenkins, David C. Jones, Richard Kavanaugh, David Kennett, Jon Kimbell, Richard Kneeland, Howard London, Mina Manente, George Martin, T. Richard Mason, David McKenna, Barbara Orson, Glenn Palmer, Norman Ranone, Donald Somers, Alan Tongret, Cynthia Wells, Jobeth Williams

PRODUCTIONS

"Child's Play," "Troilus and Cressida," "School for Wives," "The Price"
PREMIERE of "Down by the River Where Waterlilies Are Disfigured Every Day" by Julie Bovasso

William L. Smith Photos

Left: Richard Kavanaugh, Donald Somers, Joseph Culliton, Norman Ranone, Jon Kimbell in "Troilus and Cressida"

James Eichelberger, Richard Kneeland in "Down by the River ..." Above: Michael Gorrin, George Martin, Barbara Orson, William Cain in "The Price"

William Cain, William Damkoehler, Richard Kneela in "Child's Play" Above: William Dankoehler, Barbara Orson in "School for Wives"

212

WASHINGTON THEATER CLUB
Washington, D.C.
September 23, 1971—June 25, 1972

Executive Director, Hazel H. Wentworth; Managing Director, Bill Walton; Artistic Director, Davey Marlin-Jones; Press, Lillian Miller; Designers, T. C. Behrens, John H. Paull; Costumes, Madeleine Grigg; Lighting, Michael J. Rosati; Stage Manager, B. C. May; Stage Directors, Joel Friedman, Leland Ball, Thomas Gruenewald, Davey Marlin-Jones, Bill Walton, Douglas Seale

PRODUCTIONS AND CASTS

ADAPTATION with Joseph Daly, Ronn Robinson, Jamie Donnelly, Armand Assante

NEXT with Benjamin H. Slack, and Victoria Zussin

ALL OVER with Carmen Mathews, Barbara Caruso, Al Christy, Don Lochner, Gina Petrushka, Ronn Robinson, Victoria Zussin, John Jackson, Mark Rodgers, Scott Schofield

CURSE YOU, SPREAD EAGLE with Marshall Borden, Carleton Carpenter, Donna Liggitt Forbes, Ann Hodapp, Marcia Lewis, Joshua Mostel

THE PHILANTHROPIST with Ralph Cosham, Marjorie Lynne Feiner, Ted Graeber, Nancy Reardon, Holland Taylor, Edward Zang, Howard Zielke

LEMON SKY with James Broderick, Michael Christopher, Marjorie Lynne Feiner, Trinity Thompson, Jennifer Warren, Liam Clark, Mark Clark, Paul Mandelbaum, Sidney Zagri

WASHINGTON SQUARE with book, music, and lyrics by Kenneth Jerome and Jerome Walman from Henry James' novel; Director, Davey Marlin-Jones; with Jeannie Carson, Hurd Hatfield, Biff McGuire, Lois Holmes (World Premiere)

FOUR MINUS ONE with James Brochu, Edmund Day, Bruce A. Goldstein, Lucy Lee Flippen, Jack Halstead, Mickey Hartnett, Susan Lipton, Ronn Robinson, John Seitz, Nelson Smith, Eric Tavaris

LADY AUDLEY'S SECRET with Douglas Seale, Russell Nype, Donna Curtis, June Gable, Lu Ann Post, Danny Sewell, Richard Curnock, Ann Ault, James Carrington, Ronn Robinson

Cynthia Brumback Photos

**Left: Edward Zang, Nancy Reardon in
"The Philanthropist"**

**Lois Holmes, Biff McGuire, Jeannie Carson
in "Washington Square" Top: Russell Nype, Donna
Curtis in "Lady Audley's Secret"**

**Al Christy, Barbara Caruso, Carmen Mathews
in "All Over"**

YALE REPERTORY THEATRE
New Haven, Conn.
October 14, 1971—June 3, 1972

Artistic Director, Robert Brustein; Managing Director, Sheldon Kleinman; Press, David Conte; Designer, Steven Rubin; Stage Managers, Frank S. Torok, Carol M. Waaser; Production Supervisors, John Hood, Al Kibbe; Technical Directors, George Moredock, Edgar Swift; Photographer, Michael Shane; Stage Directors, Tom Haas, Robert Brustein, Alvin Epstein, Michael Posnick, Roger Hendricks Simon, Jacques Brudick

COMPANY

Sarah Albertson, Thomas Barbour, James Brick, Stephanie Cotsirilos, Carmen de Lavallade, Tony de Santis, Robert Drivas, Alvin Epstein, Jeremy Geidt, David Hurst, Stephen Joyce, Frank Langella, Maxine Lieberman, Stephen Mendillo, Joan Pape, Elizabeth Parrish, Dick Shawn, Charles Turner, Christopher Walken, Joan Welles, Nancy Wickwire, Henry Winkler, Charles Bletson, Meredith Burns, Lisa Carling, Herb Downer, William Gearhart, Andrew Johnson, Marty Lafferty, Hannibal Penney, Jr., William Peters, Dean Radcliffe, Paul Schierhorn, Yannis Simonides, Rosemary Stewart

PRODUCTIONS

"When We Dead Awaken," "The Big House," "Caligula," "The Seven Deadly Sins," "The Little Mahagonny," "Passion," "Stops," "Jacques Brel: Songs," "I Married You for the Fun of It," "Life Is a Dream," "Happy End"

Michael Shane Photos

Right: Carmen DeLavallade in "Seven Deadly Sins"

Alvin Epstein, Elizabeth Parrish in "I Married You . . ."
Above: Christopher Walken, David Hurst in "Caligula"

Stephen Joyce, Elizabeth Parrish in "Happy End"
Above: Jeremy Geidt, Tony de Santis, Bill Peters, Dick Shawn in "Big House"

PULITZER PRIZE PLAYS

1918-Why Marry?, **1919**-No award, **1920**-Beyond the Horizon, **1921**-Miss Lulu Bett, **1922**-Anna Christie, **1923**-Icebound, **1924**-Hell-Bent Fer Heaven, **1925**-They Knew What They Wanted, **1926**-Craig's Wife, **1927**-In Abraham's Bosom, **1928**-Strange Interlude, **1929**-Street Scene, **1930**-The Green Pastures, **1931**-Alison's House, **1932**-Of Thee I Sing, **1933**-Both Your Houses, **1934**-Men in White, **1935**-The Old Maid, **1936**-Idiot's Delight, **1937**-You Can't Take It With You, **1938**-Our Town, **1939**-Abe Lincoln in Illinois, **1940**-The Time of Your Life, **1941**-There Shall Be No Night, **1942**-No award, **1943**-The Skin of Our Teeth, **1944**-No award, **1945**-Harvey, **1946**-State of the Union, **1947**-No award, **1948**-A Streetcar Named Desire, **1949**-Death of a Salesman, **1950**-South Pacific, **1951**-No award, **1952**-The Shrike, **1953**-Picnic, **1954**-The Teahouse of the August Moon, **1955**-Cat on a Hot Tin Roof, **1956**-The Diary of Anne Frank, **1957**-Long Day's Journey into Night, **1958**-Look Homeward, Angel, **1959**-J. B., **1960**-Fiorello!, **1961**-All the Way Home, **1962**-How to Succeed in Business without Really Trying, **1963**-No award, **1964**-No award, **1965**-The Subject Was Roses, **1966**-No award, **1967**-A Delicate Balance, **1968**-No award, **1969**-The Great White Hope, **1970**-No Place to Be Somebody, **1971**-The Effect of Gamma Rays on Man-in-the-Moon Marigolds, **1972**-No award

NEW YORK DRAMA CRITICS CIRCLE AWARD PRODUCTIONS

1936-Winterset, **1937**-High Tor, **1938**-Of Mice and Men, Shadow and Substance, **1939**-The White Steed, **1940**-The Time of Your Life, **1941**-Watch on the Rhine, The Corn is Green, **1942**-Blithe Spirit, **1943**-The Patriots, **1944**-Jacobowsky and the Colonel, **1945**-The Glass Menagerie, **1946**-Carousel, **1947**-All My Sons, No Exit, Brigadoon, **1948**-A Streetcar Named Desire, The Winslow Boy, **1949**-Death of a Salesman, The Madwoman of Chaillot, South Pacific, **1950**-The Member of the Wedding, The Cocktail Party, The Consul, **1951**-Darkness at Noon, The Lady's Not for Burning, Guys and Dolls, **1952**-I Am a Camera, Venus Observed, Pal Joey, **1953**-Picnic, The Love of Four Colonels, Wonderful Town, **1954**-Teahouse of the August Moon, Ondine, The Golden Apple, **1955**-Cat on a Hot Tin Roof, Witness for the Prosecution, The Saint of Bleecker Street, **1956**-The Diary of Anne Frank, Tiger at the Gates, My Fair Lady, **1957**-Long Day's Journey into Night, The Waltz of the Toreadors, The Most Happy Fella, **1958**-Look Homeward Angel, Look Back in Anger, The Music Man, **1959**-A Raisin in the Sun, The Visit, La Plume de Ma Tante, **1960**-Toys in the Attic, Five Finger Exercise, Fiorello!, **1961**-All the Way Home, A Taste of Honey, Carnival, **1962**-Night of the Iguana, A Man for All Seasons, How to Succeed in Business without Really Trying, **1963**-Who's Afraid of Virginia Woolf?, **1964**-Luther, Hello, Dolly!, **1965**-The Subject was Roses, Fiddler on the Roof, **1966**-The Persecution and Assassination of Marat as Performed by the Inmates of the Asylum of Charenton under the Direction of the Marquis de Sade, Man of La Mancha, **1967**-The Homecoming, Cabaret, **1968**-Rosencrantz and Guildenstern Are Dead, Your Own Thing, **1969**-The Great White Hope, 1776, **1970**-The Effect of Gamma Rays on Man-in-the-Moon Marigolds, Borstal Boy, Company, **1971**-Home, Follies, The House of Blue Leaves, **1972**-That Championship Season, Two Gentlemen of Verona

AMERICAN THEATRE WING ANTOINETTE PERRY (TONY) AWARD PRODUCTIONS

1948-Mister Roberts, **1949**-Death of a Salesman, Kiss Me, Kate, **1950**-The Cocktail Party, South Pacific, **1951**-The Rose Tattoo, Guys and Dolls, **1952**-The Fourposter, The King and I, **1953**-The Crucible, Wonderful Town, **1954**-The Teahouse of the August Moon, Kismet, **1955**-The Desperate Hours, The Pajama Game, **1956**-The Diary of Anne Frank, Damn Yankees, **1957**-Long Day's Journey into Night, My Fair Lady, **1958**-Sunrise at Campobello, The Music Man, **1959**-J. B., Redhead, **1960**-The Miracle Worker, Fiorello! tied with Sound of Music, **1961**-Becket, Bye Bye Birdie, **1962**-A Man for All Seasons, How to Succeed in Business without Really Trying, **1963**-Who's Afraid of Virginia Woolf?, A Funny Thing Happened on the Way to the Forum, **1964**-Luther, Hello, Dolly!, **1965**-The Subject Was Roses, Fiddler on the Roof, **1966**-The Persecution and Assassination of Marat as Performed by the Inmates of the Asylum of Charenton under the Direction of the Marquis de Sade, Man of La Mancha, **1967**-The Homecoming, Cabaret, **1968**-Rosencrantz and Guildenstern Are Dead, Hallelujah, Baby!, **1969**-The Great White Hope, 1776, **1970**-Borstal Boy, Applause, **1971**-Sleuth, Company, **1972**-Sticks and Bones, Two Gentlemen of Verona

Julie Andrews

Warren Beatty

Carol Channing

Marlon Brando

Eileen Heckart

PREVIOUS THEATRE WORLD AWARD WINNERS

1944–45: Betty Comden, Richard Davis, Richard Hart, Judy Holliday, Charles Lang, Bambi Linn, John Lund, Donald Murphy, Nancy Noland, Margaret Phillips, John Raitt
1945–46: Barbara Bel Geddes, Marlon Brando, Bill Callahan, Wendell Corey, Paul Douglas, Mary James, Burt Lancaster, Patricia Marshall, Beatrice Pearson
1946–47: Keith Andes, Marion Bell, Peter Cookson, Ann Crowley, Ellen Hanley, John Jordan, George Keane, Dorothea MacFarland, James Mitchell, Patricia Neal, David Wayne
1947–48: Valerie Bettis, Edward Bryce, Whitfield Connor, Mark Dawson, June Lockhart, Estelle Loring, Peggy Maley, Ralph Meeker, Meg Mundy, Douglass Watson, James Whitmore, Patrice Wymore
1948–49: Tod Andrews, Doe Avedon, Jean Carson, Carol Channing, Richard Derr, Julie Harris, Mary McCarty, Allyn Ann McLerie, Cameron Mitchell, Gene Nelson, Byron Palmer, Bob Scheerer
1949–50: Nancy Andrews, Phil Arthur, Barbara Brady, Lydia Clarke, Priscilla Gillette, Don Hanmer, Marcia Henderson, Charlton Heston, Rick Jason, Grace Kelly, Charles Nolte, Roger Price
1950-51: Barbara Ashley, Isabel Bigley, Martin Brooks, Richard Burton, James Daly, Cloris Leachman, Russell Nype, Jack Palance, William Smithers, Maureen Stapleton, Marcia Van Dyke, Eli Wallach
1951–52: Tony Bavaar, Patricia Benoit, Peter Conlow, Virginia de Luce, Ronny Graham, Audrey Hepburn, Diana Herbert, Conrad Janis, Dick Kallman, Charles Proctor, Eric Sinclair, Kim Stanley, Marian Winters, Helen Wood
1952–53: Edie Adams, Rosemary Harris, Eileen Heckart, Peter Kelley, John Kerr, Richard Kiley, Gloria Marlowe, Penelope Munday, Paul Newman, Sheree North, Geraldine Page, John Stewart, Ray Stricklyn, Gwen Verdon
1953–54: Orson Bean, Harry Belafonte, James Dean, Joan Diener, Ben Gazzara, Carol Haney, Jonathan Lucas, Kay Medford, Scott Merrill, Elizabeth Montgomery, Leo Penn, Eva Marie Saint
1954–55: Julie Andrews, Jacqueline Brookes, Shirl Conway, Barbara Cook, David Daniels, Mary Fickett, Page Johnson, Loretta Leversee, Jack Lord, Dennis Patrick, Anthony Perkins, Christopher Plummer
1955–56: Diane Cilento, Dick Davalos, Anthony Franciosa, Andy Griffith, Laurence Harvey, David Hedison, Earle Hyman, Susan Johnson, John Michael King, Jayne Mansfield, Sarah Marshall, Gaby Rodgers, Susan Strasberg, Fritz Weaver
1956–57: Peggy Cass, Sydney Chaplin, Sylvia Daneel, Bradford Dillman, Peter Donat, George Grizzard, Carol Lynley, Peter Palmer, Jason Robards, Cliff Robertson, Pippa Scott, Inga Swenson
1957–58: Anne Bancroft, Warren Berlinger, Colleen Dewhurst, Richard Easton, Tim Everett, Eddie Hodges, Joan

Hovis, Carol Lawrence, Jacqueline McKeever, Wynne Miller, Robert Morse, George C. Scott
1958–59: Lou Antonio, Ina Balin, Richard Cross, Tammy Grimes, Larry Hagman, Dolores Hart, Roger Mollien, France Nuyen, Susan Oliver, Ben Piazza, Paul Roebling, William Shatner, Pat Suzuki, Rip Torn
1959–60: Warren Beatty, Eileen Brennan, Carol Burnett, Patty Duke, Jane Fonda, Anita Gillette, Elisa Loti, Donald Madden, George Maharis, John McMartin, Lauri Peters, Dick Van Dyke
1960-61: Joyce Bulifant, Dennis Cooney, Nancy Dussault, Robert Goulet, Joan Hackett, June Harding, Ron Husmann, James MacArthur, Bruce Yarnell
1961–62: Elizabeth Ashley, Keith Baxter, Peter Fonda, Don Galloway, Sean Garrison, Barbara Harris, James Earl Jones, Janet Margolin, Karen Morrow, Robert Redford, John Stride, Brenda Vaccaro
1962–63: Alan Arkin, Stuart Damon, Melinda Dillon, Robert Drivas, Bob Gentry, Dorothy Loudon, Brandon Maggart, Julienne Marie, Liza Minnelli, Estelle Parsons, Diana Sands, Swen Swenson
1963–64: Alan Alda, Gloria Bleezarde, Imelda De Martin, Claude Giraud, Ketty Lester, Barbara Loden, Lawrence Pressman, Gilbert Price, Philip Proctor, John Tracy, Jennifer West
1964–65: Carolyn Coates, Joyce Jillson, Linda Lavin, Luba Lisa, Michael O'Sullivan, Joanna Pettet, Beah Richards, Jaime Sanchez, Victor Spinetti, Nicholas Surovy, Robert Walker, Clarence Williams III
1965–66: Zoe Caldwell, David Carradine, John Cullum, John Davidson, Faye Dunaway, Gloria Foster, Robert Hooks, Jerry Lanning, Richard Mulligan, April Shawhan, Sandra Smith, Lesley Ann Warren
1966–67: Bonnie Bedelia, Richard Benjamin, Dustin Hoffman, Terry Kiser, Reva Rose, Robert Salvio, Sheila Smith, Connie Stevens, Pamela Tiffin, Leslie Uggams, Jon Voight, Christopher Walken
1967–68: Pamela Burrell, Sandy Duncan, Julie Gregg, Bernadette Peters, Alice Playten, Brenda Smiley, David Birney, Jordan Christopher, Jack Crowder, Stephen Joyce, Mike Rupert, Russ Thacker
1968–69: Jane Alexander, David Cryer, Ed Evanko, Blythe Danner, Ken Howard, Lauren Jones, Ron Leibman, Marian Mercer, Jill O'Hara, Ron O'Neal, Al Pacino, Marlene Warfield
1969–70: Susan Browning, Donny Burks, Catherine Burns, Len Cariou, Bonnie Franklin, David Holliday, Katharine Houghton, Melba Moore, David Rounds, Lewis J. Stadlen, Kristoffer Tabori, Fredricka Weber
1970–71: Clifton Davis, Michael Douglas, Julie Garfield, Martha Henry, James Naughton, Tricia O'Neil, Kipp Osborne, Roger Rathburn, Ayn Ruymen, Jennifer Salt, Joan Van Ark, Walter Willison

Richard Burton

Liza Minelli

Anthony Perkins

Gwen Verdon

Cliff Roberts

216

1972 THEATRE WORLD AWARD WINNERS

JONELLE ALLEN
of "Two Gentlemen of Verona"

WILLIAM ATHERTON
of "Suggs"

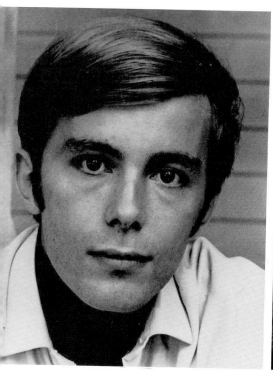

RICHARD BACKUS
of "Promenade, All!"

MAUREEN ANDERMAN
of "Moonchildren"

ADRIENNE BARBEAU
of "Grease"

ROBERT FOXWORTH
of "The Crucible"

JESS RICHARDS
of "On the Town"

CARA DUFF—MacCORMICK
of "Moonchildren"

ELAINE JOYCE
of "Sugar"

BEN VEREEN
of "Jesus Christ Superstar"

BEATRICE WINDE
of "Ain't Supposed to Die a Natural Death"

JAMES WOODS
of "Moonchildren"

1972 THEATRE WORLD AWARD PARTY

Van Williams Photos

Robert Morse, Richard Backus

Robert Morse, Adrienne Barbeau

Robert Morse, Robert Foxwort

Below: Robert Morse, Beatrice Winde

Below: William Atherton

Below: Robert Morse, Elaine Jo

William Schelble, Richard Backus,
Paul Lipson, Keene Curtis

Robert Morse

Ben Vereen, Jonelle Allen, Bhaskar

Below: James Coco, Robert Drivas, Terrence McNally

John Simon, Adrienne Barbeau

Below: Gene Nelson, Elaine Joyce, Robert Morse

Barbara Marshall, Jess Richards, Scott Chelius,
rs Gavon, Mary Ann Niles, Pepper Powell, David Rounds

Lauren Jones, James Woods, John Anderman,
Maureen Anderman

Gregory Abels   Andra Akers   Paul Ainsley   Cindy Ames   Don Amendolia

BIOGRAPHIES OF THIS SEASON'S CAST

AARON, JACK. Born May 1, 1933 in NYC. Attended Hunter Col., Actors Workshop. Off-Bdwy in "Swim Low Little Goldfish," "Journey of the Fifth Horse," "The Nest," "One Flew Over the Cuckoo's Nest."

ABELS, GREGORY. Born Nov. 6, 1941 in Jersey City, NJ. Studied with Stella Adler. Debut OB 1970 in NYSF's "War of Roses," followed by "Macbeth," "Phoebus," "Oedipus at Colonus"(ELT).

ABRAHAM, F. MURRAY. Born Oct. 24, 1939 in Pittsburgh. Attended UTex. Off-Bdwy bow 1967 in "The Fantasticks," followed by "An Opening in the Trees," "Fourteenth Dictator," "Young Abe Lincoln," "Tonight in Living Color," "Adaptation," "Survival of St. Joan," "The Dog Ran Away," "Fables," "Richard III," "Little Murders," "Scuba Duba," "Where Has Tommy Flowers Gone?," Bdwy debut "The Man In The Glass Booth" (1968).

ACKERMAN, LONI ZOE. Born Apr. 10, 1949 in NYC. Attended New School. Bdwy debut 1968 in "George M!", followed by "Dames at Sea" (OB), "No, No, Nanette."

ACKROYD, DAVID. Born May 30, 1940 in Orange, NJ. Bucknell and Yale graduate. Bdwy debut 1971 in "Unlikely Heroes."

ADAMS, MASON. Born Feb. 26, 1919 in NYC. Graduate U. Wisc. Neighborhood Playhouse. Appeared in "Get Away, Old Man," "Public Relations," "Career Angel," "Violet," "A Shadow of My Enemy," "Tall Story," "Inquest," "Trial of Catonsville 9," "Sign in Sidney Brustein's Window."

ADRIAN, JAMES. Born Feb. 28 in Breckenridge, Tex. Attended TCU. Debut 1966 OB in "Winterset," followed by "DuBarry Was a Lady"(ELT).

AGRESS, TED. Born Apr. 20, 1945 in Bklyn. Attended Adelphi U. Bdwy debut 1965 in "Hello, Dolly!," followed by "Dear World," "Look Me Up" (OB).

AINSLEY, PAUL. Born Apr. 11, 1945 in Boston. Graduate San Fernando State Col. Bdwy bow 1971 in "Jesus Christ Superstar."

AKERS, ANDRA. Born Sept. 16, 1946 in NYC. Attended Sarah Lawrence Col., HB Studio. Bdwy debut 1970 in "Charley's Aunt," followed by "Wanted" (OB).

ALDREDGE, TOM. Born Feb. 28, 1928 in Dayton, O. Attended Dayton U., Goodman Theatre. Bdwy bow 1959 in "The Nervous Set," followed by "UTBU," "Slapstick Tragedy," "Everything In The Garden," "Indians," "Engagement Baby," "How the Other Half Loves," "Sticks and Bones." OB in "The Tempest," "Between Two Thieves," "Henry V," "The Premise," "Love's Labour's Lost," "Troilus and Cressida," "Butter and Egg Man," "Ergo," "Boys In The Band," "Twelfth Night," "Colette," "Hamlet" (NYSF).

ALEXANDER, C. K. Born May 4, 1920 in Cairo, Egypt. Graduate American U. Bdwy debut 1946 in "Hidden Horizon," followed by "The Happy Time," "Flight into Egypt," "Mr. Pickwick," "Can-Can," "Fanny," "The Matchmaker," "La Plume de Ma Tante," "Rhinoceros," "Carnival," "Tovarich," "The Dragon" (OB), "Corruption in the Palace of Justice" (OB), "Poor Bitos," "Ari," "Justice Box" (OB).

ALEXANDER, TERRY. Born Mar. 23, 1947 in Detroit, Mich. Graduate Wayne State U. Bdwy debut 1971 in "No Place to Be Somebody."

ALICE, MARY. Born Dec. 3, 1941 in Indianola, Miss. Studied with NEC, and appeared in its "Trials of Brother Jero" and "The Strong Breed" (1967); Bdwy debut 1971 in "No Place to Be Somebody," followed by "Duplex"(LC).

ALLEN, JONELLE. Born July 18, 1944 in NYC. Attended Professional Children's School. Bdwy debut 1949 in "The Wisteria Trees," followed by "Hair," "George M!," "Two Gentlemen of Verona" for which she received a Theatre World Award, OB in "Someone's Coming Hungry," "5 on the Blackhand Side," "Bury the Dead," "Moon on a Rainbow Shawl."

ALLEN, JUDY. Born Aug. 14, 1945 in NYC. Graduate Brandeis U. Debut OB 1967 in "Now Is the Time for All Good Men," followed by "Carving a Statue," "Dance Wi' Me."

ALLEN, NORMAN. Born Dec. 24, 1939 in London. Bdwy bow 1963 in "Chips with Everything," followed by "Half a Sixpence," "Rockefeller and the Red Indians," "Get Thee to Canterbury" (OB), "Borstal Boy," "Vivat! Vivat Regina!"

ALLEN, SETH. Born July 13, 1941 in Bklyn. Attended Musical Theatre Acad. OB in "Viet Rock," "Futz," "Hair," "Candaules Commissioner," LC in "Mary Stuart" and "Narrow Road to the Deep North," Bdwy debut 1972 in "Jesus Christ Superstar."

ALLSBROOK, BILL. Born May 21, 1945 in Roanoke Rapids, NC. Graduate Temple U. Bdwy bow 1968 in "Cabaret," followed by "Applause."

AMAN, JOHN. Born Sept. 28 in Hollywood, Fla. Attended U. Miami. Bdwy bow 1962 in "Mr. President," followed by "Darling of the Day," CC's "Brigadoon" and "South Pacific," OB in "Hit the Deck," "Golden Apple," "Now," "Happy Hypocrite," "Of Thee I Sing," "Don't Walk on the Clouds."

AMENDOLIA, DON. Born Feb. 1, 1945 in Woodbury, NJ. Attended Glassboro State Col., AADA. Debut OB 1966 in "Until the Monkey Comes," followed by "Park"(ELT).

AMES, CINDY. Born in Brooklyn. Attended Actors Lab. Debut OB 1970 in "Hedda Gabler," followed by "Death of J.K."

ANANIA, JOHN. Born July 12, 1923 in Sicily. Attended HB Studio. Bdwy bow 1947 in "Sweethearts," followed by "Christine," "What A Killing" (OB), "Little Me," "Fly Blackbird" (OB), "Cafe Crown," "Skyscraper," "Breakfast at Tiffany's," "Golden Rainbow," "The Penny Wars," "Applause."

ANDERMAN, MAUREEN. Born Oct. 26, 1946 in Detroit. Graduate UMich. Bdwy debut 1970 in ASF's "Othello," followed by "Moonchildren" for which she received a Theatre World Award, "An Evening with Richard Nixon and . . ."

ANDERS, KATIE. Born Oct. 15, 1942 in Chicago. UCalif. graduate. Attended Am. Musical Acad. Debut OB 1969 in "Of Thee I Sing," followed by "DuBarry Was a Lady"(ELT).

ANDERSON, THOMAS. Born Nov. 28, 1906 in Pasadena, Cal. Attended Pasadena Jr. Col., Am. Theatre Wing. Bdwy debut 1934 in "4 Saints in 3 Acts," followed by "Roll Sweet Chariot," "Cabin In The Sky," "Native Son," "Set My People Free," "How Long Till Summer," "A Hole In The Head," "The Great White Hope," "70, Girls, 70," OB in "Conquering Thursday," "The Peddler," "The Dodo Bird," "Don't Play Us Cheap."

ANDREWS, GEORGE LEE. Born Oct. 13, 1942 in Milwaukee, Wisc. Debut OB 1970 in "Jacques Brel Is Alive. . . ."

Katie Anders   Jerome Anello   Osceola Archer   Tom Atkins   Catherine Bacon

ANELLO, JEROME. Born Feb. 14, 1939 in NYC. Graduate CCNY, Yale. Debut OB 1971 in "Charlie Was Here and Now He's Gone."

ANTHONY, ROBERT. Born May 10, 1941 in Newark, NJ. Attended Boston U, AADA. Off-Bwdy in "Jerico-Jim Crow," "Bugs and Veronica," "Dirty Old Man," "Hamlet" and "Othello" (NYSF), "Scuba Duba," Bdwy in "The Man in the Glass Booth" ('68), "Butterflies Are Free."

ANTONIADOU, KOULA. Born Jan 28, 1945 in Cyprus. Studied at Greek Art Theatre School (Athens), Yale, Theatre Inst. Debut 1969 OB in "House of Bernarda Alba," followed by "The Father," "Interrogation of Havana."

APLON, BORIS. Born July 14 in Chicago. Attended U. Chicago, Goodman Theatre. OB in "Makrapoulos Secret," "King of the Whole Damn World," at CC in "Carousel" and "Show Boat," on Bdwy in "Candide," "Anya," "Fiddler on the Roof."

ARCHER, OSCEOLA. Born in Albany, Ga. Graduate Howard U., NYU. Bdwy debut 1934 in "Between Two Worlds," followed by "Panic," "The Cat Screams," "Hippolytus," "Romeo and Juliet," "Ring Round the Moon," "The Crucible," "The Seagull," "The Guide," "The Screens" (OB).

ARMEN, JOHNNY. Born Jan. 4, 1938 in NYC. Graduate Fordham U. Bdwy debut 1971 in "Lenny."

ARNOLD, JEANNE. Born July 30 in Berkeley, Calif. Graduate U. Cal. NY debut OB 1955 in "Threepenny Opera," followed by "Take Five," "Demi-Dozen," "Medium Rare," "Put It In Writing," "Beggar's Opera," on Bdwy in "The Happy Time," "Coco."

ARNOLD, VICTOR. Born July 1, 1936 in Herkimer, NY. NYU graduate. OB in "Shadow of Heroes," "Merchant of Venice," "3x3," "Lovey," "Fortune and Men's Eyes," "Time for Bed, Take Me to Bed," on Bdwy in "The Deputy," "Malcolm" "We Bombed in New Haven," "Fun City."

ASHLEY, ELIZABETH. Born Aug. 30, 1939 in Ocala, Fla. Attended Neighborhood Playhouse. Bdwy debut 1959 in "The Highest Tree," followed by "Take Her, She's Mine" for which she received a Theatre World Award, "Barefoot in the Park," "Ring Round the Bathtub."

ASTREDO, HUMBERT ALLEN. Born in San Francisco. Attended SFU. NY debut in "Arms and the Man" (OB'67), followed by "Fragments," "Murderous Angels," Bdwy in "Les Blancs," "An Evening with Richard Nixon and . . ."

ATHERTON, WILLIAM. Born July 30, 1947 in New Haven, Conn. Carnegie Tech graduate. Debut 1971 OB in "House of Blue Leaves," followed by "Basic Training of Pavlo Hummel," "Suggs" (LC) for which he received a Theatre World Award; Bdwy bow 1972 in "The Sign in Sidney Brustein's Window."

ATKINS, EILEEN. Born June 16, 1934 in London. Attended Guildhall School. Bdwy debut 1966 in "The Killing of Sister George," followed by "The Promise," "Vivat! Vivat Regina!"

ATKINS, TOM. Born in Pittsburgh. Graduate Duquesne U., AADA. With LCRep in "Unknown Soldier and His Wife," and "Cyrano," Bdwy in "Keep It in the Family," "Front Page," OB in "Whistle in the Dark," "Nobody Hears a Broken Drum," "Long Day's Journey into Night."

ATKINSON, DAVID. Born in Montreal, Oct. 20, 1921. Attended McGill U., Pasadena Playhouse. Credits: "Inside U.S.A.," "Girl In Pink Tights," "The Vamp," CC revivals of "Carousel," "Kiss Me, Kate," "Brigadoon," and "Annie Get Your Gun," "Man of La Mancha."

ATTLE, JOHN C. Born in Tacoma, Wash. Graduate U. Wash. Bwdy bow 1964 in "Fiddler On The Roof," followed by "Jacques Brel Is Alive and Well and Living In Paris" (OB).

ATTLES, JOSEPH. Born Apr. 7, 1903 in Charleston, SC. Attended Harlem Musical Conserv. Bdwy bow in "Blackbirds of 1928," followed by "John Henry," "Porgy and Bess," "Kwamina," "Tambourines to Glory," OB in "Jerico-Jim Crow," "Cabin in the Sky," "Prodigal Son," "Day of Absence," with LCRep in "Cry of Players," "King Lear," and "Duplex."

AUBERJONOIS, RENE. Born June 1, 1940 in NYC. Graduate Carnegie Inst. With LCRep in "A Cry of Players," "King Lear," and "Twelfth Night," on Bdwy in "Fire," "Coco."

AUMONT, JEAN-PIERRE. Born Jan 5, 1913 in Paris. Attended Ntl. School of Dramatic Art. Bdwy bow 1942 in "Rose Burke," followed by "My Name Is Aquilon," "Heavenly Twins," "Second String," "Tovarich," "Camino Real"(LC), "Murderous Angels"(OB).

AVALOS, LUIS. Born Sept. 2, 1946 in Havana. Graduate NYU. Debut at CC in "Never Jam Today," followed by "Rules for the Running of Trains" (OB), and LC's "Camino Real," "Beggar on Horseback," "Good Woman of Setzuan," "Kool Aid."

BACALL, LAUREN. Born Sept. 16, 1924 in NYC. Attended AADA. Bdwy debut 1942 in "Johnny 2 x 4," followed by "Goodbye Charlie," "Cactus Flower," "Applause."

BACKUS, RICHARD. Born Mar. 28, 1945 in Goffstown, NH. Harvard graduate. Bdwy debut 1971 in "Butterflies Are Free," followed by "Promenade, All!" for which he received a Theatre World Award.

BACON, CATHERINE. Born Sept. 7, 1947 in Chelsea, Mass. Attended AADA. Bdwy debut 1969 in "Penny Wars," followed by "Cold Feet"(OB).

BAIN, CONRAD. Born Feb. 4, 1923 in Lethbridge, Can. Attended AADA. Bdwy in "Sixth Finger In A Five Finger Glove," "Candide," "Hot Spot," "Advise and Consent," "The Cuban Thing," "Twigs," Off-Bdwy: "The Makropoulous Secret," "The Queen and The Rebels," "Hogan's Goat," "The Kitchen," "Scuba Duba," "Nobody Hears A Broken Drum," "Steambath," "Play Strindberg"(LC).

BAKER, BENNY. Born May 5, 1907 in St. Joseph, Mo. Bdwy debut 1931 in "You Said It," followed by "DuBarry Was a Lady," "Let's Face It," "The Tempest," "No, No, Nanette."

BAKER, MARK. Born Oct. 2, 1946 in Cumberland, Md. Attended Wittenberg U., Carnegie-Mellon U., Neighborhood Playhouse, AADA. Debut 1971 OB in "Love Me, Love My Children."

BALABAN, ROBERT. Born Aug. 16, 1945 in Chicago. Attended Colgate, NYU. Debut OB 1967 in "You're a Good Man, Charlie Brown," followed by "Plaza Suite" (Bdwy '68), "Up Eden," "White House Murder Case," "Basic Training of Pavlo Hummel."

BARAGREY, JOHN. Born Apr. 15, 1918 in Haleyville, Ala. Attended UAla. Credits: "Sons and Soldiers," "Twilight Bar," "The Enchanted," "Pride's Crossing," "Royal Family," "The Crucible," "The Devils," "Elizabeth the Queen"(CC), "The Grass Harp," "Murderous Angels"(OB).

BARBEAU, ADRIENNE. Born June 11, 1945 in Sacramento, Cal. Attended Foothill Col. Bdwy debut 1968 in "Fiddler on the Roof," followed by "Stag Movie"(OB), "Grease" for which she received a Theatre World Award.

Lenny Bari

Noreen Bartolomeo

David Beckman

Joan Bassie

Joe Bellomo

BARI, LENNY. Born Mar. 1, 1955 in The Bronx. Bdwy debut 1971 in "The Me Nobody Knows."

BARNES, VERONA. Attended Winston-Salem State Col. Bdwy debut 1968 in "Great White Hope," followed by "Sleep"(OB).

BARNEY, JAY. Born Mar. 14, 1918, in Chicago. Attended Chicago U., Theatre Wing, Actors Studio. Bdwy in "The Respectful Prostitute," "Hope's the Thing with Feathers," "Detective Story," "The Number," "Grass Harp," "Richard III," "Stockade," "The Immoralist," "The Trial," "Young and Beautiful," "Eugenia," "Fig Leaves Are Falling," "All the Girls Came out to Play," OB in "A Certain Young Man," "Beyond Desire," "Goa," "The David Show," "Man with a Flower in His Mouth."

BARON, SANDY. Born in Bklyn in 1938. Bklyn.Col. grad. Appeared in "Second City," "The Premise," "Tchin-Tchin," "One Flew over the Cuckoo's Nest," "Arturo Ui," "Generation," "Muzeeka"(OB), "Lenny."

BARRETT, RAINA. Born Jan. 5, 1941 in Detroit. Graduate Ithaca Col. Debut 1968 Off-Bdwy in "Recess," followed by "Oh! Calcutta!"

BARRIE, BARBARA. Born May 23, 1931 in Chicago. Graduate UTex. Bdwy debut 1955 in "The Wooden Dish" followed by "Happily Never After," "Company," "Selling of the President," "Prisoner of Second Avenue," OB in "The Crucible," "The Beaux Stratagem." "Taming of The Shrew" and "All's Well That Ends Well" (CP), "Horseman, Pass by," "Twelfth Night" (CP).

BARRS, NORMAN. Born Nov. 6, 1917 in London. NY debut 1948 with Dublin Gate Co. in "The Old Lady Says No!" and "Where Stars Walk," followed by "Now I Lay Me Down To Sleep," "The Little Glass Clock," "The Apple Cart," "The Little Moon of Alban," "Kwamina," "Poor Bitos," "The Zulu and the Zayda," "Hostile Witness," "Loot," OB in "Little Boxes," "Saved," "Homecoming."

BARTENIEFF, GEORGE. Born Jan 24, 1933 in Berlin. Bdwy debut 1947 in "The Whole World Over," followed by "Venus Is," "All's Well That Ends Well," "Walking to Waldheim" (OB), "Memorandum" (OB), "Quotations From Chairman Mao Tse-Tung," "Death of Bessie Smith," "CopOut," "The Increased Difficulty of Concentration"(LC), "Room Service," "Trelawny of The Wells"(OB), "Unlikely Heroes."

BARTLETT, MICHAEL. Born Aug. 23, 1901 in North Oxford, Mass. Attended Princeton. Bdwy debut 1930 in "Through the Years," followed by "Three Waltzes," "Cat and the Fiddle," "Schoo! for Husbands," "Follies."

BARTOLOMEO, NOREEN. Born July 12, 1947 in Fairfield, Conn. Graduate UConn., Catholic U. Debut OB 1972 in "DuBarry Was a Lady"(ELT).

BASSIE, JOAN. Born July 22, 1939 in Chicago. Attended RADA. NY debut 1964 in "Arms and the Man"(OB), followed by Bdwy bow 1967 in "The Imaginary Invalid" and "Tonight at 8:30," "Not Now, Darling," "Taming of the Shrew"(OB).

BAVAN, YOLANDE. Born June 1, 1942 in Ceylon. Attended U. Colombo. NY debut 1964 in "A Midsummer Night's Dream" (CP), followed by OB's "Jonah," "House of Flowers," "Salvation," "Tarot," "Back Bog Beast Bait," "Leaves of Grass," "Heathen" (Bdwy '72).

BAXTER, ANNE. Born May 7, 1923 in Michigan City, Ind. Studied at Irvine School. Bdwy debut 1936 in "Seen but not Heard," followed by "There's Always a Breeze," "Mme. Capet," "Square Root of Wonderful," "Applause."

BAXTER, KEITH. Born Apr. 29, 1935 in Newport, Wales. Graduate RADA. Bdwy debut 1961 in "A Man for All Seasons" for which he received a THEATRE WORLD Award, followed by "The Affair," "Avanti," "Sleuth."

BEAL, JOHN. Born Aug. 13, 1909 in Joplin, Mo. Graduate U. Pa. Many credits include "Wild Waves," "Another Language," "She Loves Me Not," "Russet Mantle," "Soliloquy," "Miss Swan Expects," "Liberty Jones," "Voice of The Turtle," "Lend An Ear," "Teahouse of The August Moon," "Calculated Risk," "Billy," "Our Town" (1970). Off-Bdwy in "Our Town," "Wilder's Triple Bill," "To Be Young, Gifted and Black," "Candyapple," "Long Day's Journey into Night."

BEAN, REATHAL. Born Aug. 24, 1942 in Mo. Graduate Duke U. Appeared (OB) in "America Hurrah," "San Francisco's Burning," "The Love Cure," "Henry IV" (CP), "In Circles," "Peace," "Journey of Snow White," "Wanted."

BEARDSLEY, ALICE. Born Mar. 28, 1927 in Richmond, Va. UIowa graduate. Bdwy debut 1960 in "The Wall," OB in "Eastward in Eden," "In Good King Charles' Golden Days," "Leave it to Jane," "Camino Real," "A Man's a Man," "Cindy," "Boy on a Straight-back Chair," "Things."

BECKER, RAY. Born May 18, 1934 in NYC. Attended HB Studio. Bdwy bow in "How To Suceed . . . ," followed by "Curley McDimple"(OB), "George M!" "Appiause."

BECKMAN, DAVID. Born May 26, 1944 in Jamestown, NY. Graduate BrownU. Debut OB 1968 in "To Change a River," followed by "Something for Kitty Genovese," "Oedipus at Colonus"(ELT).

BEDFORD, BRIAN. Born Feb. 16, 1935 in Morley, Eng. Attended RADA. NY bow 1960 in "Five Finger Exercise," followed by "Lord Pengo," "The Private Ear," "The Knack" (OB). "The Astrakhan Coat," "The Unknown Soldier and His Wife," "Seven Descents of Myrtle," with APA in "Misanthrope," "Cocktail Party," and "Hamlet," "Private Lives," "School for Wives."

BELL, MARY. Born Nov. 17, 1904 in Austin, Tex. Attended UTex. Many credits include "The Shrike," "Cat on a Hot Tin Roof," "Cloud 7," "Miracle Worker," "Beyond Desire," "Passion of Antigona Perez"(OB).

BELLOMO, JOE. Born Apr. 12, 1938 in NYC. Attended Manhattan Sch. of Music. Bdwy bow 1960 in "New Girl in Town," followed by CC's "South Pacific" and "Guys and Dolls," OB in "Cindy," "Fantasticks."

BENJAMIN, FRED. Born Sept. 8, 1944 in Boston. Has appeared in "We're Civilized" (OB), "Hello Dolly!," "Promises, Promises."

BENJAMIN, RICHARD. Born May 22, 1938 in NYC. Graduate Northwestern U. Bdwy debut 1966 in "Star Spangled Girl" for which he received a Theatre World Award, followed by "Little Black Book."

BENSON, ROBBY. Born Jan. 21, 1956 in Dallas, Tex. Attended AADA. Bdwy bow 1969 in "Zelda," followed by "The Rothschilds."

BEN-ZALI, SIDNEY. Born Dec. 20, 1945 in Rio de Janeiro. NY debut OB 1965 in "Lorenzaccio," Bdwy bow 1971 in "The Rothschilds."

Margo Ann
Berdeshevsky   Robert Berdeen   Verna Bloom   Dick Bonelle   Joan Blondell

BERDEEN, ROBERT. Born Aug. 6 in Arlington Va. Attended Neighborhood Playhouse. Credits: "A Dream of Swallows"(OB), "The Passion of Josef D." "Fiddler on the Roof," "Royal Hunt of the Sun," "Billy," "Me and Juliet"(ELT), "Ballad of Johnny Pot"(OB).

BERDESHEVSKY, MARGO ANN. Born May 29, 1945 in NYC. Attended Northwestern U. OB in "Mary of Nijmeghen," "Objective Case," "Necessity of Being Polygamous," "Yerma"(LC), "The Basement," "Middle of the Night"(ELT).

BERGMAN, INGRID. Born Aug. 29, 1917 in Stockholm. Studied at Royal Dramatic Theatre. Bdwy debut 1940 in "Liliom," followed by "Joan of Lorraine," "More Stately Mansions," "Capt. Brassbound's Conversion."

BERNHEIM, SHIRL. Born Sept 21, 1921 in NYC. Studied with Ouspenskaya. Debut OB 1967 in "A Different World," followed by "Stag Movie," "Middle of the Night"(ELT).

BERRY, ERIC. Born Jan. 9, 1913 in London. Graduate RADA. NY debut 1954 in "The Boy Friend," followed by "Family Reunion," "The Power and the Glory," "Beaux Stratagem," "Broken Jug," "Pictures in the Hallway," "Peer Gynt," "Great God Brown," "Henry IV," "The White House," "White Devil," "Charley's Aunt," "The Homecoming" (OB), "Capt. Brassbound's Conversion."

BERRY, JOHN. Born in NYC; studied at Mercury Theatre. Bdwy debut 1950 in "All You Need Is One Good Break," followed by "Love Suicide at Schofield Barracks."

BINGHAM, BOB. Born Oct 29, 1946 in Seattle, Wash. Attended UWash. Bdwy debut 1971 in "Jesus Christ Superstar."

BIRNEY, DAVID. Born Apr. 23, 1939 in Washington, D.C. Graduate Dartmouth, UCLA OB with NYSF in "Comedy of Errors," "Titus Andronicus," and "King John," "MacBird," "Crimes of Passion," "Ceremony of Innocence," LC's "Summertree" for which he received a THEATRE WORLD Award, "The Miser," "Playboy of The Western World," "Good Woman of Setzuan," "An Enemy of The People," and "Antigone"(LC).

BLACKBURN, ROBERT. Born Jan. 21, 1925 in Montgomery, Ala. Attended Columbia U. Credits: "As You Like It," "King Lear," "The Misanthrope," "Volpone," "Henry IV," "Octoroon," "Hamlet," "Black Wednesday," "An Evening with Richard Nixon and . . ."

BLACKTON, JACK. Born Mar. 16, 1938 in Colorado Springs. Graduate U. Colo. Off-Bdwy in "The Fantasticks," "Put It In Writing," "Jacques Brel Is Alive . . ." "Hark," Bdwy bow 1966 in "Mame."

BLAINE, VIVIAN. Born Nov. 21, 1923 in Newark, NJ. Bdwy debut 1950 in "Guys and Dolls," followed by "Hatful of Rain," "Say, Darling," "Enter Laughing," "Guys and Dolls" (CC'66), "Company."

BLOCK, CHAD. Born May 1, 1938 in Twin Falls, Ida. Bdwy bow 1954 in "The Vamp," followed by "Li'l Abner," "Destry Rides Again," "Take Me Along," "Do Re Mi," "Come On Strong," "Hello, Dolly!," "Walking Happy," "Hallelujah, Baby!" "Coco," "A Funny Thing Happened on the Way to the Forum."

BLOCK, LARRY. Born Oct. 30, 1942 in NYC. Graduate URI. Bdwy bow 1966 in "Hail Scrawdyke," followed by "La Turista," OB in "Eh?," "Fingernails Blue as Flowers."

BLONDELL, JOAN. Born Aug. 30, 1912 in NYC. Bdwy debut 1929 in "Maggie the Magnificent," followed by "Penny Arcade," "Naked Genius," "Rope Dancers," OB in "A Palm Tree in a Rose Garden," and "Effect of Gamma Rays on Man-in-the-moon Marigolds."

BLOOM, CLAIRE. Born Feb. 15, 1931 in London. Bdwy debut 1956 with Old Vic in "Romeo and Juliet" and "Richard II," followed by "Rashomon," OB in "A Doll's House," and "Hedda Gabler," "Vivat! Vivat Regina!"

BLOOM, VERNA. Born Aug. 7, in Lynn, Mass. Graduate Boston U. Bdwy debut 1967 in "Marat/deSade," followed by "Kool Aid"(LC).

BLYDEN, LARRY. Born June 23, 1925 in Houston, Tex. Bdwy bow 1949 in "Mr. Roberts," followed by "Wish You Were Here," "Oh, Men! Oh, Women!," "Italian Straw Hat" (OB), "Who Was that Lady I Saw You With?" "Flower Drum Song," "Foxy," "Blues for Mr. Charlie," "Luv," "Apple Tree," "Mother Lover," "You Know I Can't Hear You When the Water's Running," "A Funny Thing Happened on the Way to the Forum."

BOBBIE, WALTER. Born Nov. 18, 1945 in Scranton, Pa. Graduate UScranton, Catholic U. Bdwy bow 1971 in "Frank Merriwell," followed by "Grass Harp," "Grease," "Drat!" (OB).

BOGERT, WILLIAM. Born Jan. 25, 1936 in NYC. Yale graduate. On Bdwy in "Man for All Seasons," "Hamlet," "Star Spangled Girl," "Cactus Flower," "Sudden and Accidental Re-education of Horse Johnson," OB in "Country Wife," "Taming of the Shrew," "Henry V," "Love's Labour's Lost," "A Gun Play."

BOND, RUDY. Born Oct. 1, 1915 in Philadelphia. Attended UPa. On Bdwy in "Streetcar Named Desire," "Bird Cage," "Two Blind Mice," "Romeo and Juliet," "Glad Tidings," "Golden Boy," "Fiorello," "Illya Darling," "Night Watch," OB in "O'Daniel," LCRep's "After the Fall" and "Incident at Vichy," "Big Man," "Match-Play," "Papp."

BONELLE, DICK. Born Apr. 11, 1936 in Houston, Tex. Graduate UHouston. Debut OB 1970 in "Lyle," followed by "Sugar" (Bdwy).

BOOTH, SHIRLEY. Born Aug. 30, 1907 in NYC. Bdwy debut 1925 in "Hell's Bells," followed by "Bye Bye Baby," "Laff That Off," "War Song," "Too Many Heroes," "Three Men on a Horse," "Excursion," "Philadelphia Story," "My Sister Eileen," "Tomorrow the World," "Hollywood Pinafore," "Land's End," "Goodbye, My Fancy," "Love Me Long," "Come Back, Little Sheba," "A Tree Grows in Brooklyn," "Time of the Cuckoo," "By the Beautiful Sea," "Miss Isobel," "Juno," "Second String," "Look to the Lilies," "Hay Fever."

BORDO, ED. Born Mar. 3, 1931 in Cleveland, O. Graduate Allegheny Col. Bdwy bow 1964 in "Last Analysis," followed by "Inquest," OB in "The Dragon," "Waiting for Godot."

BORRELLI, JIM. Born Apr. 10, 1948 in Lawrence, Mass. Graduate Boston Col. NY debut Off-Bdwy 1971 in "Subject to Fits," followed by "Grease."

Mary Boylan

Martin Brandfon

Anna Brennen

Alan Braunstein

Susan Brick

BOSCO, PHILIP. Born Sept. 26, 1930 in Jersey City, NJ. Graduate Catholic U. Credits: "Auntie Mame," "Rape of The Belt," "Ticket of Leave Man"(OB), "Donnybrook," "Man For All Seasons," with LCRep in "The Alchemist," "East Wind," "Galileo," "St. Joan," "Tiger At The Gates," "Cyrano," "King Lear," "A Great Career," "In The Matter of J. Robert Oppenheimer," "The Miser," "The Time of Your Life," "Camino Real," "Operation Sidewinder," "Amphitryon," "An Enemy of the People," "Playboy of the Western World," "Good Woman of Setzuan," "Antigone," "Mary Stuart," "Narrow Road to the Deep North," "The Crucible," "Twelfth Night."

BOSTWICK, BARRY. Born Feb. 24, 1945 In San Mateo, Cal. Graduate Cal-Western, NYU. Bdwy debut with APA in "War and Peace," "Pantagleize," "Misanthrope." "Cock-A-Doodle Dandy," "Hamlet," OB in "Salvation," "Colette," "Soon," "Screens," "Grease."

BOVA, JOSEPH. Born May 25 in Cleveland, O. Graduate Northwestern U. Debut OB 1959 in "On the Town," followed by "Once upon a Mattress, "House of Blue Leaves," NYSF's "Taming of the Shrew," "Richard III," "Comedy of Errors," "Invitation to a Beheading," on Bdwy in "Rape of the Belt," "Irma La Douce," "Hot Spot," "The Chinese."

BOVASSO, JULIE. Born Aug. 1, 1930 in Bklyn. Attended CCNY. On Bdwy in "Monique," "Minor Miracle," "Gloria and Esperanza," OB in "Naked," "The Maids," "The Lesson," "The Typewriter," "Screens."

BOYLAN, MARY. Born in Plattsburg, NY. Attended Mt. Holyoke Col. Bdwy debut 1938 in "Dance Night," followed by "Susannah and the Elders," "The Walrus and the Carpenter," "Our Town," "Live Life Again," OB in "To Bury a Cousin," "Curley McDimple," "Blood," "Middle of the Night"(ELT).

BRAHA, HERB. (formerly Herb Simon) Born Sept. 18, 1946 in Hyannis, Mass. Attended Carnegie Tech. Debut 1971 OB in "Godspell."

BRANDFON, MARTIN. Born June 14, 1949 in Islip, NY. Graduate SUNY Binghamton. Debut 1972 OB in "Oedipus at Colonus."

BRASWELL, CHARLES. Born Sept. 7 in McKinney, Tex. Attended Arlington State Col. Bdwy bow 1960 in "A Thurber Carnival," followed by "Wildcat," "Sail Away," "Hot Spot," "Here's Love," "I Had A Ball," "Me and Thee," "Mame," "Company."

BRAUNSTEIN, ALAN. Born Apr. 30, 1947 in Bklyn. Debut OB 1962 in "Daddy Come Home," followed by Bdwy bow 1970 in "Hair," "Jesus Christ Superstar."

BREMERS, BEVERLY ANN. Born Mar. 10, 1950 in Chicago. Attended HB Studio. NY debut 1969 in "Hair," followed by "The Me Nobody Knows."

BRENNEN, ANNA. Born in Elko, Nev. UCal. graduate. Debut 1972 OB in "Eros and Psyche."

BREZANY, EUGENE. Born Aug. 12, 1945 in St. Louis, Mo. Graduate Northwestern U. Bdwy bow 1970 in "Othello," followed by "There's One in Every Marriage."

BRICKELL, SUSAN. Born June 11, 1950 in NYC. Graduate Queen's Coll. Debut OB 1969 in "Cosmic Compulsion," followed by "Eros and Psyche."

BRIGHT, RICHARD. Born June 28, 1937 in Bklyn. Off-Bdwy in "The Balcony," "Does A Tiger Wear a Necktie?" "The Beard," "Survival of St. Joan," "Kool Aid"(LC).

BROCKSMITH, ROY. Born Sept. 15, 1945 in Quincy, Ill. Debut OB 1971 in "Whip Lady," followed by "The Workout," "Beggar's Opera."

BROOKES, JACQUELINE. Born July 24, 1930 in Montclair, NJ. Graduate UIowa, RADA. Bdwy debut 1955 in "Tiger at the Gates," followed by "Watercolor," "Abelard and Heloise," OB in "The Cretan Woman" for which she received a THEATRE WORLD Award, "The Clandestine Marriage," "Measure for Measure," "Duchess of Malfi," "Ivanov," "Six Characters in Search of an Author," "An Evening's Frost," "Come Slowly, Eden," "The Increased Difficulty of Concentration"(LC), "The Persians," "Sunday Dinner," "House of Blue Leaves."

BROOKS, DAVID. Born Sept. 24, 1917 in Portland, Ore. Attended UWash, Curtis Inst. Bdwy bow 1944 in "Bloomer Girl," followed by "Brigadoon," "Mr. President," "Sunday Man," "Park," "The Last Analysis"(OB).

BROWN, KERMIT. Born Feb. 3, 1937 in Asheville, NC. Graduate Duke U. With APA in "War and Peace," "Judith," "Man and Superman," "The Show-Off," "Pantagleize," "The Cherry Orchard," OB in "The Millionairess," "Things."

BROWN, PENDLETON. Born Sept. 17, 1948 in Corry, Pa. Studied at HB Studio. Bdwy bow 1971 in "Soon," followed by "The Sign in Sidney Brustein's Window."

BROWN, TALLY. Born Aug. 1, 1934 in NYC. Graduate NYU, Juilliard. On Bdwy in "Pajama Game," "Tenderloin," "Mame," OB in "Jackass," "Justice Box."

BROWNING, SUSAN. Born Feb. 25, 1941 in Baldwin, NY. Graduate Penn. State. Bdwy bow 1963 in "Love and Kisses," followed by "Company" for which she received a Theatre World Award, Off-Bdwy in "Jo," "Dime A Dozen," "Seventeen," "Boys from Syracuse," "Collision Course."

BROWNLEE, DELL. Born in Paris. Attended Marymount Neighborhood Playhouse. Bdwy debut 1961 in "The Unsinkable Molly Brown," followed by "Carnival," "Here's Love," "Fade Out, Fade In," "Man of La Mancha."

BRUCE, SAMUEL. Born Aug. 3, 1936 in Kingston, Ont. Can. Graduate Queen's U. (Can.). Debut OB 1967 with American Savoyards in repertory, followed by "Oedipus at Colonus."

BRUNO, JEAN. Born Dec. 7, 1926 in Bklyn. Attended Hofstra Col., Feagin School. Bdwy debut 1960 in "Beg, Borrow or Steal," followed by "Midgie Purvis," "Music Man," "Family Affair," "Minnie's Boys," OB in "All That Fall," "Hector," "Hotel Paradiso," "Pidgeons in the Park," "Ergo," "Trelawny of the Wells," "Song for the First of May."

BULOS, YUSEF. Born Sept. 14, 1940 in Jerusalem. Attended Beirut Am. U., AADA. NY debut 1965 OB with Am. Savoyards in repertory, followed by Bdwy's "Indians," "Capt Brassbound's Conversion."

BURR, ROBERT. Born in Jersey City, NJ. Attended Colgate U. Has appeared in "Cradle Will Rock," "Mister Roberts," "Romeo and Juliet," "Picnic," "The Lovers," "Anniversary Waltz," "Top Man," "Remains to Be Seen" "The Wall," "Andersonville Trial," "A Shot in the Dark," "A Man for All Seasons," "Luther," "Hamlet," "Bajour," "White Devil," "Royal Hunt of the Sun," "Dinner at 8," "King John" "Henry VI"(CP), "Love Suicide at Schofield Barracks," "Wild and Wonderful."

ichael Cavanaugh   Tina Chen   Carleton Carpenter   Barbara Cason   Stephen Cheng

BURROWS, VINIE. Born Nov. 15, 1928 in NYC. Graduate NYU. On Bdwy in "Wisteria Trees," "Green Pastures," "Mrs. Patterson," "The Skin of Our Teeth," "The Ponder Heart," OB in her one-woman "Walk Together Children."

BUSH, NORMAN. Born Apr. 11, 1933 in Louisville, Ky. Attended AADA. OB 1960 in "The Goose," followed by "The Connection," "Funny House of a Negro," "The Toilet," "Daddy Goodness," "Kongi's Harvest," "Summer of the 17th Doll," "Song of the Lusitanian Bogey," "God Is A(Guess What?)," "Malcochon," "Man Better Man," "Day of Absence," "Brotherhood," "Akokawe," "In New England Winter," "Sleep."

BYRNE, GAYLEA. Born in Baltimore, Md. Graduate Peabody Conservatory. Debut 1961 OB in "All In Love," followed by "Music Man" (CC), "Man of La Mancha."

BYRNES, MAUREEN. Born May 14, 1944 in Chicago. Bdwy debut 1965 in "La Grosse Valise," followed by "Oh, Calcutta!"

CAHILL, JAMES. Born May 31, 1940 in Bklyn. Bdwy bow 1967 in "Marat/deSade," OB in "The Hostage," "The Alchemist," "Johnny Johnson," NYSF's "Peer Gynt" and "Timon of Athens," LC's "Evening for Merlin Finch" and "Disintegration of James Cherry," "Crimes of Passion," "Rain," "Screens."

CAMPANELLA, PHILIP. Born May 24, 1948 in Jersey City, NJ. Graduate St. Peter's Col., HB Studio. Debut OB 1970 in "Lady from Maxim's," followed by "Hamlet," "Tug of War," "Charles Abbott & Son," "She Stoops to Conquer," "Taming of the Shrew," "Misalliance."

CANNING, JAMES J. Born July 2, 1946 in Chicago, Graduate DePaul U. Debut OB 1972 in "Grease."

CARA, IRENE. Born Mar. 18, 1959 in NYC. Bdwy debut 1968 in "Maggie Flynn," followed by "The Me Nobody Knows."

CAREY, FRANK. Born Oct. 12, 1934 in Tarrytown, NY. Attended AADA. Debut OB 1960 in "Nat Turner," followed by "The Brick and the Rose," "Black Quartet," Bdwy bow 1972 in "Don't Play Us Cheap."

CARIOU, LEONARD. Born Sept. 30, 1939 in Winnipeg, Can. Bdwy debut 1968 with Minn. Theatre Co. in "House of Atreus," followed by "Henry V.," "Applause" for which he received a THEATRE WORLD Award, "Night Watch."

CARLIN, CHET. Born Feb. 23, 1940 in Malverne, NY. Graduate Ithaca Col., Catholic U. Bdwy bow 1972 in "An Evening with Richard Nixon and ...," OB in "Under Gaslight" (ELT), "Lou Gehrig Did Not Die of Cancer," "Graffiti!"

CARNEY, ART. Born Nov. 4, 1918 in Mt. Vernon, NY. Bdwy bow 1957 in "Rope Dancers," followed by "Take Her, She's Mine," "Odd Couple," "Lovers," "Prisoner of Second Avenue."

CARPENTER, CARLETON. Born July 10, 1926 in Bennington, Vt. Attended Northwestern U. Bdwy bow 1944 in "Bright Boy," followed by "Career Angel," "3 to Make Ready," "Magic Touch," "John Murray Anderson's Almanac," "Hotel Paradiso," "Box of Watercolors," "Hello, Dolly!," OB in "A Stage Affair," "Boys in the Band," "Lyle," "Dylan."

CARROLL, HELENA. Born in Glasgow, Scot, Attended Weber-Douglas School, London. US debut with Dublin Players. Founded, directed, acted with Irish Players Off-Bdwy. Bdwy debut 1956 in "Separate Tables," followed by "Happy as Larry," "A Touch of the Poet," "Little Moon of Alban," "The Hostage," "Oliver!," "Pickwick," "Three Hand Reel" (OB), "Something Different," "Georgy," "Borstal Boy," "Pictures in the Hallway" (LC), "Small Craft Warnings" (OB).

CASH, ROSALIND. Born Dec. 31, 1938 in Atlantic City, NJ. Attended CCNY. Bdwy debut 1966 in "The Wayward Stork," OB in "Junebug Graduates Tonight," "Fiorello" (CC). "To Bury A Cousin," "Song of The Lusitanian Bogey," "Kongi's Harvest," "Ceremonies In Dark Old Men," "An Evening of One Acts," "Man Better Man," "The Harangues," "Day of Absence," "Brotherhood," "Charlie Was Here and Now He's Gone."

CASON, BARBARA. Born Nov. 15, 1933 in Memphis, Tenn. Graduate Iowa U. Bdwy debut 1967 in "Marat/Sade," followed by "Jimmy Shine," "Night Watch," OB in "Firebugs," "Spitting Image," "Enemy of the People" (LC).

CASTANOS, LUZ. Born July 15, 1935 in NYC. Graduate CUNY. Debut OB 1959 in "Last Visit," followed by "Eternal Sabbath," "Finis for Oscar Wilde," "Young and Fair," "La Dama Duende," "A Media Luz Los Tres," "Yerma."

CATLETT, MARY JO. Born Sept. 2, 1938 in Denver, Colo. Graduate Loretto Hts. Col. Has appeared in "Along Came A Spider" (OB), "New Girl In Town," "Fiorello," "Pajama Game," "Hello, Dolly!" "Canterbury Tales," "Promenade" (OB), "Greenwillow" (ELT), "Different Times."

CAVANAUGH, MICHAEL. Born in NYC. Attended San Francisco State Col. NY bow 1969 in "Oh! Calcutta!"

CHACE, DOROTHY. Born in North Bergen, NJ. Attended SF State Col., Stanford, Yale, Bdwy debut 1969 in "3 Men on a Horse," LCRep's "Caucasian Chalk Circle," and "Cyrano," "Screens" (OB).

CHANG, TISA. Born Apr. 5 in Chungking, China. Attended CCNY. Bdwy debut 1970 in "Lovely Ladies, Kind Gentlemen," followed by "Brothers" (OB).

CHARISSE, ZAN. Born Nov. 14, 1951 in NYC. Debut 1971 OB in "Look Me Up."

CHARNEY, JORDAN. Born in NYC. Graduate Bklyn Col. Off-Bdwy in "Harry, Noon and Night," "A Place for Chance," "Hang Down Your Head and Die," "The Pinter Plays," "Telemachus Clay," "Zoo Story," "Viet Rock," "MacBird," "Red Cross," "The Glorious Ruler," "Waiting for Godot," "Slow Memories," "One Flew over the Cuckoo's Nest;" Bdwy in "Slapstick Tragedy," "The Birthday Party."

CHEN, TINA. Born Nov. 2 in Chung King, China. Attended U Hartford, Hartt Col. Bdwy debut 1972 in "Love Suicide at Schofield Barracks."

CHENG, STEPHEN. Born in Shanghai. Colombia graduate. Bdwy bow 1959 in "World of Suzie Wong," followed by "Harold," "Holly Golightly," "Opening," "Ballet behind the Bridge" (OB).

CHRIS, MARILYN. Born May 19, 1939 in NYC. Attended CCNY. Appeared in "The Office," "Birthday Party," "7 Descents of Myrtle," "Lenny," OB in "Nobody Hears a Broken Drum," "Fame," "Judas Applause," "Junebug Graduates Tonight," "Man Is Man," "In the Jungle of Cities," "Good Soldier Schweik," "The Tempest," "Ride a Black Horse," "Screens," "Kaddish."

Jerry Clark

Crickett Coan

John Clarkson

Barbara Coggin

David Connell

CHRISTIAN, ROBERT. Born Dec. 27, 1939 in Los Angeles. Attended UCLA. Off-Bdwy in "The Happening," "Hornblend," "Fortune and Men's Eyes," "Boys in The Band," "Behold! Cometh The Vanderkellans," LCRep's "Mary Stuart," "Narrow Road to the Deep North," and "Twelfth Night," Bdwy in "We Bombed In New Haven," "Does A Tiger Wear a Necktie?," "An Evening with Richard Nixon and . . ."

CLANTON, RALPH. Born Sept. 11, 1914 in Fresno, Cal. Attended Pasadena Playhouse. On Bdwy in "Victory Belles," "Macbeth," "Richard III," "Othello," "Lute Song," "Cyrano," "Antony and Cleopatra," "Design for a Stained Glass Window," "Taming of the Shrew," "Burning Glass," "Vivat Regina!," OB in "Ceremony of Innocence," "Endecott and the Red Cross."

CLARK, JERRY. Born Oct. 11 in Dallas, Tex. Yale graduate. Debut 1967 OB in "Macbird!," followed by "Babes in Arms," "Photo Finish," "The Way It Is," "Wanted."

CLARKSON, JOHN. Born Jan. 19, 1932 in London. Graduate Oxford U. NY debut OB 1971 in "Murderous Angels."

COAN, CRICKETT. Born Oct. 28 in Raleigh, NC. Graduate Hollins Col., Sorbonne, ULausanne, Neighborhood Playhouse. Debut 1969 OB in "The Square," followed by "Hatful of Rain" (ELT), "Universal Nigger," LCRep's "Mary Stuart."

COATES, CAROLYN. Born Apr. 29, 1930 in Oklahoma City. Attended UCLA. OB in "The Innocents," "The Balcony," "Electra," "Trojan Women" for which she received a THEATRE WORLD Award, "A Whitman Portrait," "Party On Greenwich Avenue," "Club Bedroom," "A Scent of Flowers," "The Effect of Gamma Rays on Man-in-the-Moon Marigolds," LCRep's "Country Wife," "Condemned of Altona," "Caucasian Chalk Circle," and "The Disintegration of James Cherry," on Bdwy in "Death of Bessie Smith," "American Dream," "Fire!," "All Over."

COE, JOHN. Born Oct. 19, 1925 in Hartford, Conn. Graduate Boston U. On Bdwy in "Passion of Josef D," "Man in the Glass Booth," "La Strada," OB in "Marrying Maiden," "Thistle in My Bed," "John," "Wicked Cooks," "June Bug Graduates Tonight," "Drums in the Night," "America Hurrah," "Father Uxbridge Wants to Marry," "Nobody Hears a Broken Drum," "Dylan," "Screens."

COFFIELD, PETER. Born July 17, 1945 in Evanston, Ill. Graduate of Northwestern, UMich. With APA in "The Misanthrope," "Cock-A-Doodle Dandy" and "Hamlet," followed by "Abelard and Heloise," "Vivat! Vivat Regina!"

COFFIN, FREDERICK. Born Jan. 16, 1943 in Detroit. Graduate UMich. Debut 1971 OB in "Basic Training of Pavlo Hummel."

COGGIN, BARBARA. Born Feb. 27 in Chattanooga, Tenn. Attended Peabody Col. Bdwy debut 1970 in "Lovely Ladies, Kind Gentlemen," OB in "The Drunkard," "One for the Money etc."

COHEN, MARGERY. Born June 24, 1947 in Chicago. Attended UWisc., UChicago, HB Studio, Bdwy debut 1968 in "Fiddler on the Roof," followed by "Jacques Brel Is Alive and Well . . ."

COLBY, BARBARA. Born July 2, 1940 in NYC. Attended Carnegie Tech, Sorbonne. Bdwy debut 1965 in "The Devils," OB in "Under Milkwood," "Six Characters in Search of an Author," "Murderous Angels."

COLE, DENNIS. Born July 19, 1943 in Detroit, Mich. Attended UDetroit. Bdwy debut 1972 in "All the Girls Came out to Play."

COLE, KAY. Born Jan. 13, 1948 in Miami, Fla. Bdwy debut 1961 in "Bye Bye Birdie," followed by "Stop the World I Want to Get Off," "Roar of the Greasepaint . . .," "Hair," "Jesus Christ Superstar," OB in "The Cradle Will Rock," "Two if by Sea."

COLLINS, DOROTHY. Born 1927 in Windsor, Ont., Can. Bdwy debut 1971 in "Follies."

COLLINS, STEPHEN. Born Oct. 1, 1947 in Des Moines, I. Graduate Amherst Col. Bdwy debut 1972 in "Moonchildren," OB in "Twelfth Night."

COLON, MIRIAM. Born 1945 in Ponce, PR. Attended UPR, Actors Studio. Bdwy debut 1953 in "In the Summer House," OB in "Me, Candido," "The Ox Cart," "Passion of Antigona Perez."

COLSON, C. DAVID. Born Dec. 23, 1941 in Detroit. Graduate UMich. Debut 1970 in "The Last Sweet Days of Isaac" (OB), followed by "Masquerade," "Ballet behind the Bridge," Bdwy debut 1970 in "Purlie."

COLTON, CHEVI. Born in NYC. Attended Hunter Col. Off-Bdwy in "Time of Storm," "Insect Comedy" (CC). "The Adding Machine," "O Marry Me," "Penny Change," "The Mad Show," "Jacques Brel Is Alive . . .," on Bdwy in "Cabaret."

CONDOS, DIMO. Born Feb. 29, 1932 in NYC. Off-Bdwy in "The Celebration," "O'Flaherty," "The Cannibals," "Moths," "Pinkville."

CONNELL, DAVID. Born Nov. 24, 1935 in Cleveland, O. Attended Kent State U. Bdwy bow 1968 in "Great White Hope," followed by "Don't Play Us Cheap," OB in "Ballet behind the Bridge."

CONNELL, GORDON. Born Mar. 19, 1923 in Berkeley, Cal. Graduate UCal., NYU. Bdwy bow 1961 in "Subways Are for Sleeping," followed by "Hello, Dolly!," OB in "Beggar's Opera."

CONNELL, JANE. Born Oct. 27, 1925 in Berkeley, Cal. Attended UCal. Off-Bway in "Shoestring Revue," "Threepenny Opera," "Pieces of Eight," "Demi-Dozen," "She Stoops to Conquer," "Drat!," "The Real Inspector Hound," on Bdwy in "New Faces of 1956," "Drat! The Cat!," "Mame," "Dear World."

CONWAY, KEVIN. Born May 29, 1942 in NYC. Debut 1968 OB in "Muzeeka," on Bdwy 1969 in "Indians," followed by "Saved" (OB), "Moonchildren."

COOK, BARBARA. Born Oct. 25, 1927 in Atlanta, Ga. Bdwy debut 1951 in "Flahooley," followed by "Plain and Fancy" for which she received a Theatre World Award, "Candide," "Music Man," CC's "Carousel" and "The King and I," "The Gay Life," "She Loves Me," "Something More," "Any Wednesday," "Show Boat" (LC), "Little Murders," "Man of La Mancha," "Grass Harp."

COONAN, SHEILA. Born June 28, 1922 in Montreal, Can. Attended McGill U. Appeared in "Red Roses For Me," "A Taste of Honey," "The Hostage," "Hogan's Goat" (OB), "The Great White Hope," "Macbeth" (OB), "A Song for the First of May" (OB).

| Peggy Cooper | Frank Coppola | Jacqueline Coslow | Don Croll | Tandy Cronyn |

COOPER, MARILYN. Born Dec. 14, 1936 in NYC. Attended NYU. Appeared in "Mr. Wonderful," "West Side Story," "Brigadoon" (CC), "Gypsy," "I Can Get It For You Wholesale," "The Mad Show" (OB), "Hallelujah, Baby!", "Golden Rainbow;" "Mame," "A Teaspoon Every 4 Hours," "Two by Two," "On the Town," "Look Me Up" (OB).

COOPER, PEGGY. Born Mar. 31, 1931 in Huntington, W Va. Graduate Baldwin-Wallace Conserv. Bdwy debut 1968 in "Zorba," followed by "La Strada," "The Rothschilds."

COPELAND, JOAN. Born June 1, 1922 in NYC. Attended Bklyn Col., AADA. Appeared in "How I Wonder," "Sundown Beach," "Detective Story," "Handful of Fire," "Tovarich," "Something More," "The Price," "Two by Two."

COPPOLA, FRANK. Born May 16, 1944 in Cleveland O. Attended Kent State U. Debut 1966 in CC's "Most Happy Fella" followed by "Guys and Dolls," followed by "Fiddler on the Roof," "No Place to Be Somebody," OB in "Wanted."

CORBETT, GRETCHEN. Born Aug. 13, 1947 in Portland, Ore. Attended Carnegie Tech. Off-Bdwy in "Arms and The Man," "The Bench," "Iphigenia In Aulis," "Henry VI," "Survival of St. Joan," "Justice Box," on Bdwy in "After The Rain," "Forty Carats."

CORBIN, BARRY. Born Oct. 16, 1940 in LaMesa, Tex. Attended Tex. Tech. Appeared with ASF's "Othello" on Bdwy in 1969, OB in "Masquerade."

CORY, KENNETH. Born July 21, 1941 in Hanover, Pa. Studied with Meisner, Adler. Bdwy debut 1971 in "Company."

COSLOW, JACQUELINE. Born Feb. 19, 1943 in Hollywood, Cal. Attended Mills Col., ULondon, RADA. Debut 1960 OB in "Borak," followed by "Androcles and the Lion," "Arms and the Man," "Shadow of a Gunman," "Trial of the Catonsville 9."

COSTER, NICOLAS. Born Dec. 3, 1934 in London. Attended Neighborhood Playhouse. Bdwy bow 1960 in "Becket," followed by "90 Day Mistress," "But Seriously," "Twigs," Off-Bway in "Epitaph for George Dillon," "Shadow and Substance," "Thracian Horses," "O, Say Can You See," "Happy Birthday, Wanda June."

COTSWORTH, STAATS. Born Feb. 17, 1908 in Oak Park, Ill. Attended Philadelphia Col. NY debut 1932 with Civic Rep. Co. Credits include "Romeo and Juliet," "Alice in Wonderland," "Rain from Heaven," "Murder at the Vanities," "Mme. Capet," "Macbeth," "She Stoops to Conquer," "Richard III," "Advise and Consent," "Hamlet," "Right Honourable Gentleman," "Weekend," "A Patriot for Me," "Lost in the Stars," OB in "Madwoman of Chaillot," "A Place without Mornings."

COWAN, GRANT. Born Aug. 20, 1935 in Winnipeg, Can. Attended U. Manitoba, Bristol Old Vic. Bdwy bow 1971 in "You're a Good Man, Charlie Brown."

COX, RICHARD. Born May 6, 1948 in NYC. Yale graduate. Debut OB 1970 in "Saved," followed by "Fuga," Bdwy 1972 in "The Sign in Sidney Brustein's Window."

CRAIG, NOEL. Born Jan. 4 in St. Louis, Mo. Attended Northwestern, Goodman Theatre, Guildhall School London. Bdwy debut 1967 in "Rosencrantz and Guildenstern Are Dead," followed by "A Patriot for Me," "Conduct Unbecoming," "Vivat! Vivat Regina!"

CREST, ROBERT. Born July 21, 1938 in Peco, Tex. Attended Trinity U., Pasadena Playhouse. Debut 1969 OB in "The Fantasticks," followed by "Servant of Two Masters" (ELT).

CROFT, PADDY. Born in Worthing, Eng. Attended Avondale Col. Off-Bdwy 1961 "The Hostage," followed by "Billy Liar," "Live Like Pigs," "Hogan's Goat," "Long Day's Journey into Night," "Shadow of a Gunman," on Bdwy in "The Killing of Sister George," "The Prime of Miss Jean Brodie."

CROLL, DON. Born Apr. 3, 1947 in Buffalo, NY. Graduate Ithaca Col. Bdwy debut 1971 in "On the Town."

CROMWELL, JOHN. Born Dec. 23, 1887. Bdwy debut 1910 in "Baby Mine," followed by "Little Women," "Man Who Came Back," "Major Barbara," "The World We Live In," "Silver Cord," "Gentlemen of the Press," "Yankee Point," "Point of No Return," "Climate of Eden," "Sabrina Fair," "Solitaire."

CROMWELL, J. T.. Born Mar. 4, 1935 in Ann Arbor, Mich. Graduate UCinn. Bdwy bow 1965 in "Half A Sixpence," followed by "Jacques Brel Is Alive . . ." (OB).

CRONYN, HUME. Born July 18, 1911 in London, Ont., Can. Attended McGill U., AADA. Bdwy debut 1934 in "Hipper's Holiday," followed by "Boy Meets Girl," "High Tor," "Room Service," "There's Always a Breeze," "Escape This Night," "Off to Buffalo," "Three Sisters," "Weak Link," "Retreat to Pleasure," "Mr. Big," "Survivors," "Four-poster," "Madam, Will You Walk" (OB), "The Honeys," "A Day by the Sea," "Man in the Dog Suit," "Triple Play," "Big Fish, Little Fish," "Hamlet," "Physicists," "Delicate Balance," "Hadrian VII," "Promenade, All!"

CROWLEY, EDWARD. Born Sept. 5, 1926 in Lewiston, Me. Attended AADA. Bdwy bow 1958 in "Make A Million," followed by "Family Way," OB in "Admirable Bashville," "Evening with GBS," "Once around the Block," "I Want You," "Lion in Love," "Telemachus Clay," "Hair," "How to Steal an Election," LCRep's "In the Matter of J. Robert Oppenheimer" and "An Evening for Merlin Finch," "Dylan."

CRYER, DAVID. Born Mar. 8, 1936 in Evanston, Ill. Attended DePauw U. Off-Bdwy in "The Fantasticks," "Streets of New York," "Now Is The Time For All Good Men" and "Whispers on The Wind," on Bdwy in "110 In The Shade," "Come Summer," for which he received a Theatre World Award, "1776," "Ari."

CULLUM, JOHN. Born Mar. 2, 1930 in Knoxville, Tenn. Graduate U.Tenn. Bdwy bow 1960 in "Camelot," followed by "Infidel Caesar," "The Rehearsal," "Hamlet," "On A Clear Day You Can See Forever" for which he received a Theatre World Award, "Three Hand Reel" (OB), "Man of LaMancha," "1776," "Vivat! Vivat Regina!" "The King and I" (JB).

CUNLIFFE, JERRY. Born May 16, 1935 in Chicago. Attended UChicago. Debut OB 1957 in "Anatol," followed by "Antigone," "Difficult Woman," "Tom Paine," "Futz," Bdwy 1972 in "Elizabeth I."

CUNNINGHAM, JOHN. Born June 22, 1932 in Auburn, NY. Graduate of Dartmouth and Yale. Off-Bdwy in "Love Me Little," "Pimpernel," "The Fantasticks," "Love and Let Love," on Bdwy in "Hot Spot," "Zorba," "Company," "1776."

CURNOCK, RICHARD. Born May 9, 1922 in London. Bdwy bow 1964 in "Oh! What a Lovely War," followed by "The Cherry Orchard," "There's One in Every Marriage."

| Philip Cusack | John Cutts | Jack Dabdoub | Jeff David | Diana Davila |

CURTIS, KEENE. Born Feb. 15, 1925 in Salt Lake City. Graduate U.Utah. Bdwy bow 1949 in "Shop At Sly Corner," with APA in "School For Scandal," "The Tavern," "Anatole," "Scapin," "Right You Are," "The Importance of Being Earnest," "Twelfth Night," "King Lear," "The Seagull," "Lower Depths," "Man and Superman," "Judith," "War and Peace," "You Can't Take It With You," "Pantagleize," "The Cherry Orchard," "Misanthrope," "Cocktail Party," "Cock-A-Doodle Dandy," and "Hamlet," followed by "A Patriot for Me," "Colette" (OB), "The Rothschilds," "Ride across Lake Constance" (LC), "Night Watch."

CUSACK, PHILIP. Born May 10, 1934 in Boston. Attended Emerson Col. Bdwy bow 1966 in "3 Bags Full," followed by "Gingerbread Lady," OB in "Boys in the Band."

CUTTS, JOHN. Born in Eng. Trained at Old Vic. Bdwy bow 1972 in "There's One in Every Marriage."

DABDOUB, JACK. Born Feb. 5 in New Orleans. Graduate Tulane U. OB in "What's Up," "Time For The Gentle People," "The Peddler," "The Dodo Bird," on Bdwy in "Paint Your Wagon," "My Darlin' Aida," "Happy Hunting," "Hot Spot," "Camelot," "Baker Street," "Anya," "Annie Get Your Gun" (LC), "Her First Roman," "Coco," "Man of LaMancha" (also LC).

DABNEY, KATHLEEN. Born Nov. 10, 1942 in Brownwood, Tex. Graduate Stephens Col., UMiss. Bdwy debut 1967 in "You Know I Can't Hear You When the Water's Running," OB in "Sara B. Devine," "Unknown Soldier and His Wife" (LC), "Where Has Tommy Flowers Gone?"

DAMON, CATHRYN. Born Sept. 11 in Seattle, Wash. Bdwy debut 1954 in "By The Beautiful Sea," followed by "The Vamp," "Shinbone Alley," "A Family Affair," "Foxy," "Flora, The Red Menace," "UTBU," "Come Summer," "Criss-Crossing," "A Place for Polly," "Last of the Red Hot Lovers," OB in "Boys from Syracuse," "Secret Life of Walter Mitty," "Show Me Where The Good Times Are," "Effect of Gamma Rays on Man-in-the-Moon Marigolds".

DANA, LEORA. Born Apr. 1, 1923 in NYC. Attended Barnard Col., RADA. Bdwy debut 1947 in "Madwoman of Chaillot," followed by "Happy Time," "Point of No Return," "Sabrina Fair," Best Man," "Beekman Place," OB in "In the Summer House," "Wilder's Triple Bill," "Collision Course," "Bird of Dawning Singeth All Night Long," "Increased Difficulty of Concentration" (LC), "Place without Mornings."

DANIELE, GRACIELA. Born Dec. 8, 1939 in Buenos Aires. Bdwy debut 1964 in "What Makes Sammy Run?" followed by "Here's Where I Belong," "Promises, Promises," "Follies."

DANIELS, WILLIAM. Born Mar. 31, 1927 in Brooklyn. Graduate Northwestern U. Bdwy bow 1943 in "Life With Father," followed by "Richard II," "Seagulls Over Sorrento," "Legend of Lizzie," "Cat On A Hot Tin Roof," "A Thousand Clowns," "The Zoo Story" (OB), "The Iceman Cometh" (OB), "Look Back in Anger" (OB), "Dear Me, The Sky Is Falling," "One Flew Over The Cuckoo's Nest," "On A Clear Day You Can See Forever," "Daphne In Cottage D," "1776."

DANNER, BLYTHE. Born in Philadelphia. Graduate of Bard Col. Debut OB 1966 in "The Infantry," followed by "Collision Course," "Summertree," "Up Eden," "Someone's Comin' Hungry," LCRep "Cyrano," and "The Miser" for which she received a THEATRE WORLD Award, Bdwy debut 1969 in "Butterflies Are Free," "Twelfth Night" (LC)

DARNELL, ROBERT. Born Sept. 26, 1929 in Los Angeles. Bdwy bow 1962 in "Irma La Douce," followed by "Spoon River," "Luv," "You Know I Can't Hear You . . . ," "Selling of the President," OB in "Threepenny Opera," "Young Abe Lincoln," "Tempest," "On the Town," "In White America," "Who's Happy Now?"

DA SILVA, HOWARD. Born May 4, 1909 in Cleveland, O. Attended Carnegie Tech. Debut with Civic Rep Co., followed by "Ten Million Ghosts," "Golden Boy," "The Cradle Will Rock," "Casey Jones," "Abe Lincoln In Illinois," "Summer Night," "Two On An Island," "Oklahoma!," "Shootin' Star," "Burning Bright," "The Unknown Soldier and His Wife," "Compulsion," "Fiorello," "Romulus," "In The Counting House," "Dear Me, The Sky Is Falling," "Hamlet" (CP), "1776." Off-Bdwy in "World of Sholom Aleichem," "The Adding Machine," "Diary of A Scoundrel," and "Volpone."

DAVID, CLIFFORD. Born June 30, 1932 in Toledo, O. Attended Toledo U., Actors Studio. Bdwy bow 1960 in "Caligula," followed by "Wildcat," "The Aspern Papers," "Boys From Syracuse" (OB), "On A Clear Day You Can See Forever," "A Joyful Noise," "1776," "Camino Real" (LC).

DAVID, JEFF. Born Sept 16, 1940 in Philadelphia. Graduate Carnegie Tech. OB in "Arms and the Man," "Phaedra," "Country Wife," "Caucasian Chalk Circle," "Butter and Egg Man," "Francesca de Remini," "Hamlet," "Pequod," "Memory Bank," "Perry's Mission," "Interrogation of Havana."

DAVIDSON, JACK. Born July 17, 1936 in Worcester, Mass. Boston U. graduate. Debut OB 1968 in "Moon for the Misbegotten," Bdwy bow 1972 in "Capt. Brassbound's Conversion."

DAVILA, DIANA. Born Nov. 5, 1947 in NYC. Bdwy debut 1967 in "Song of The Grasshopper," followed by "The Prime of Miss Jean Brodie," OB in "What the Butler Saw," "The Refrigerators," "People Are Living There" (LC), "Two Gentlemen of Verona," "Last Analysis."

DAVIS, CHERRY. Born in Independence, Mo. Attended RADA. OB in "Young Abe Lincoln," "Threepenny Opera," "Corner of the Morning," "As You Like It," "Your Own Thing," "Small Craft Warnings," on Bdwy in "Gypsy," "Oliver," "George M!"

DAVIS, CLIFTON. Born Oct. 4 in Chicago. Attended Oakwood Col. Debut OB 1968 in "How to Steal an Election," followed by "Horseman, Pass By," "To Be Young, Gifted and Black," "No Place to Be Somebody," "Do It Again!" for which he received a Theatre World Award, on Bdwy in "Hello, Dolly!" "Jimmy Shine," "Look to the Lilies," "The Engagement Baby," "Two Gentlemen of Verona."

Mark Dawson

Connie Day

Joseph della Sorte

Sally De May

Mark Dempsey

DAVIS, OSSIE. Born in Cogdell, Ga., in 1917. Attended Howard U. Bdwy bow 1946 in "Jeb," followed by "Anna Lucasta," "Leading Lady," "Smile of the World," "Wisteria Trees," "Royal Family" (CC), "Green Pastures," "Remains to Be Seen," "Touchstone," "No Time for Sergeants," "Jamaica," "Raisin in the Sun," "Purlie Victorious," which he wrote, "Ballad of Bimshire" (OB), "The Zulu and the Zayda," "Ain't Supposed to Die a Natural Death."

DAWSON, MARK. Born Mar. 23, 1920 in Philadelphia. Studied at Phila. Cons. Bdwy bow 1942 in "By Jupiter," followed by "Dancing in the Streets," "Sweethearts," "High Button Shoes" for which he received a Theatre World Award, "Great to Be Alive," "Me and Juliet," "Ankles Aweigh," "New Girl in Town," "Fiorello," "Riot Act," "Odd Couple," "Twigs."

DAY, CONNIE. Born Dec 26. 1940 in NYC. Debut OB 1971 in "Look Me Up."

DAY, DINAH. Born Jan 5, 1945 in Flushing, NY. Attended Hunter Col., HB Studio. Debut OB 1972 in "No Strings" (ELT).

DeCARLO, YVONNE. Born Sept. 1, 1924 in Vancouver, BC. Attended Vancouver School of Drama. Bdwy debut 1971 in "Follies."

DECKARD, DIANE. Born Jan. 16 in Berkeley, Cal. Attended Bennington Col. Bdwy debut 1966 in "The Devils," OB in "Sweeney Todd," "Witches' Sabbath," "Dark Horses," "June Moon" (ELT).

DEEBLE, DEBORAH. Born Oct. 27 1945 in Plainfield, NJ. Attended Carnegie Tech. Debut 1968 OB in "Up Eden," followed by "Beggar's Opera."

DeHETRE, KATHERINE. Born Sept. 18, 1946 in Compton, Cal. Graduate Emerson Col., Yale. Bdwy debut 1972 in "Love Suicide at Schofield Barracks."

DELEGALL, BOB. Born July 24, 1945 in Philadelphia. Debut Off-Bdwy 1971 in "The Basic Training of Pavlo Hummel," followed by "The Corner."

DELL, GABRIEL. Born Oct. 7, 1930 in Barbados, BWI. On Bdwy in "Dead End," "Tickets, Please," "Ankles Aweigh," CC's "Can-Can," "Wonderful Town," and "Oklahoma!," "Marathon '33," "Anyone Can Whistle," "Sign in Sidney Brustein's Window," "Luv," "Something Different," "Fun City," OB in "Chocolates," "Adaptation."

della SORTE, JOSEPH. Born May 5, 1940 in Yonkers, NY. Graduate Boston U., Neighborhood Playhouse. Bdwy bow 1961 in "Ross," followed by "Taming of the Shrew" (CP), "South Pacific" (LC), "Billy," "The Man with the Flower in His Mouth" (OB), "Ari," "Screens" (OB), "Water Hen" (OB).

DEMAS, CAROLE. Born May 26, 1940 in Bklyn. Attended UVt., NYU. OB in "Morning Sun," "The Fantasticks," "How to Steal an Election," "Rondelay," "Grease," Bdwy debut 1965 in "Race of Hairy Men."

DeMAY, SALLY. Born Jan 17, 1922 in Philadelphia. On Bdwy in "Li'l Abner," "Golden Rainbow," "How Now Dow Jones," "70 Girls 70," OB in "We're Civilized," "Cold Feet."

DEMPSEY, JEROME. Born Mar. 1, 1929 in St. Paul, Minn. Graduate Toledo U. Bdwy bow 1959 in "West Side Story," followed by "The Deputy," "Spofford," "Room Service," "Love Suicide at Schofield Barracks," LCRep's "Cry of Players," "Year Boston Won the Pennant," and "The Crucible," OB in "Justice Box."

DEMPSEY, MARK. Born Jan. 29, 1936 in Hollywood, Calif. Graduate U.Wash. Debut 1969 in "Oh! Calcutta!", followed by "Lost in the Stars."

DeNIRO, ROBERT. Born Aug. 17, 1943 in NYC. Studied with Stella Adler. Debut, OB 1970 in "One Night Stands of a Noisy Passenger," followed by "Kool Aid" (LC).

DENNEN, BARRY. Born Feb. 22, 1938 in Chicago. UCLA graduate. Bdwy debut 1971 in "Jesus Christ Superstar."

DESPO. Born July 13, 1920 in Piraeus, Greece. Bdwy bow 1967 in "Illya, Darling." followed by "Istanboul" (OB), "Screens" (OB).

DEVLIN, JOHN. Born Jan. 26, 1937 in Cleveland, O. Carnegie Tech. graduate. Bdwy bow 1964 in "Poor Bitos," followed by "Billy," "Vivat! Vivat Regina!," NYSF's "Richard III," "King Lear" (LC).

DEWHURST, COLLEEN. Born in Montreal, Can. Attended Downer Col., AADA. Bdwy debut 1952 in "Desire under the Elms," followed by "Tamburlaine the Great," "Country Wife," "Caligula," "All the Way Home," "Great Day in the Morning," "Ballad of the Sad Cafe," "More Stately Mansions," "All Over," Off-Bdwy in "Taming of the Shrew," "The Eagle Has Two Heads," "Camille," "Macbeth," "Children of Darkness" for which she received a THEATRE WORLD Award, "Antony and Cleopatra" (CP), "Hello and Goodbye," "Good Woman of Setzuan" (LC), "Hamlet" (NYSF).

DeYOUNG, CLIFF. Born Feb 12, 1971 in Los Angeles. Graduate Cal. State, Ill. U., HB Studio. Bdwy bow 1970 in "Hair," followed by "Sticks and Bones."

DIAMOND, MATTHEW. Born Nov. 26, 1951 in NYC. Attended CCNY. Debut 1971 OB in "Love Me, Love My Children."

DIAMOND, MICHAEL. Born July 18, 1945 in Bklyn. Attended UNH. Bdwy bow 1969 OB in "King Lear," followed by "Henry V," "Heloise" (ELT), "Capt. Brassbound's Conversion" (Bdwy '72).

DIENER, JOAN. Born Feb. 24, 1934 in Cleveland, O. Attended Sarah Lawrence Col. Bdwy debut 1948 in "Small Wonder," followed by "Season in the Sun," "Kismet" for which she received a Theatre World Award, "Cry for Us All," "Man of La Mancha" (also LC).

DIETRICH, DENA. Born Dec. 4, 1928 in Pittsburgh. Attended AADA. Debut 1962 OB in "Out of This World," followed by "Cindy," "Rimers of Eldritch," Bdwy in "Funny Girl," "Here's Where I Belong," "Freaking out of Stephanie Blake," "Prisoner of Second Avenue."

DIETZ, EILEEN. Born in NYC; attended Neighborhood Playhouse, AADA. Appeared OB in "Come Back, Little Sheba," "Steambath," "Ontological Proof of My Existence."

DIXON, MacINTYRE. Born Dec. 22, 1931 in Everett, Mass. Graduate Emerson Col. Off-Bdwy in "Quare Fellow," "Plays for Bleecker St.," "Stewed Prunes," "Cat's Pajamas," "Three Sisters," "3 X 3," "Second City," "Mad Show," "Meeow!," on Bdwy in "Xmas in Las Vegas," "Cop-Out," "Story Theatre," "Metamorphoses," "Twigs."

Peter Donat   Sandra Dorsey   Pi Douglass   Kathleen Doyle   Don Draper

DODGE, JERRY. Born Feb. 1, 1937 in New Orleans. Graduate Notre Dame. Bdwy bow 1961 in "Bye Bye Birdie," followed by "110 in the Shade," "Hello, Dolly!," "George M!," OB in "Sap of Life," "One Flew over the Cuckoo's Nest."

DONAT, PETER. Born Jan 20, 1928 in Nova Scotia, Can. Attended Acadia U., Yale. On Bdwy in "Highlights of the Empire," "First Gentleman" for which he received a Theatre World Award, "Country Wife," " The Entertainer," "Chinese Prime Minister," "One in Every Marriage," OB in "A God Slept Here," "Three Sisters."

DONHOWE, GWYDA. Born Oct. 20, 1933 in Oak Park, Ill. Attended Drake U. Goodman Theatre, Bdwy debut 1957 in "Separate Tables," followed by "Half a Sixpence," "The Flip Side," "Paris Is Out," "Applause," with APA in "The Showoff," "War and Peace," "Right You Are . . . ," "You Can't Take It with You," Off-Bdwy in "Philosophy in the Boudoir," "Rondelay."

DONNELLY, DONAL. Born July 6, 1931 in Bradford, Eng. Bdwy debut 1966 in "Philadelphia, Here I Come!," followed by "A Day in the Death of Joe Egg," "Sleuth."

DONNELLY, RUTH. Born May 17, 1896 in Trenton, NJ. Bdwy debut 1914 in "A Scrap of Paper," followed by "Going Up," "A Prince There Was," "As YouWere," "Meanest Man in the World," "Madeleine and the Movies," "Riot Act," "No, No, Nanette."

D'ORSAY, FIFI. Born Apr. 16, 1904 in Montreal, Can. After long and successful film career, made Bdwy debut 1971 in "Follies."

DORSEY, SANDRA. (formerly Sandy Ellen) Born Sept. 28, 1939 in Atlanta, Ga. Graduate Oglethorpe U. Bdwy debut 1965 in "Drat! The Cat!," followed by "Illya, Darling," "Gantry," "On the Town."

DOUGLASS, PI. Born in Sharon, Conn. Attended Boston Cons. Bdwy debut 1969 in "Fig Leaves Are Falling," followed by "Hello, Dolly!," "Georgy," "Purlie," "Ari," "Jesus Christ Superstar," "Selling of the President," OB in "Of Thee I Sing."

DOVA, NINA. Born Jan. 15, 1926 in London. Attended Neighborhood Playhouse. Debut OB in "I Feel Wonderful," followed by Bdwy in "Zorba," "The Rothschilds."

DOWD, M'EL. Born Feb. 2, in Chicago. Attended Goodman Theatre. OB in "Macbeth," "A Midsummer Night's Dream," "Romeo Juliet," " Julius Caesar," "Royal Gambit," "The Emperor," "Invitation To A Beheading," "Mercy Street," "Gun Play," Bdwy debut 1958 in "Methuselah," followed by "A Case of Libel," "Sweet Bird of Youth," "Camelot," "The Right Honourable Gentleman," "The Sound of Music" (CC), LCRep "Unknown Soldier and His Wife," and "Tiger At The Gates," "Everything In The Garden," "Dear World," "Not Now, Darling."

DOWNING, DAVID. Born July 21, 1943 in NYC. OB in "Day of Absence," "Happy Ending," "Song of The Lusitanian Bogey," "Ceremonies in Dark Old Men," "Man Better Man," "The Harangues," "Brotherhood," "Perry's Mission," "Rosalee Pritchett," "Dream on Monkey Mt.," "Ride a Black Horse," "Ballet behind the Bridge."

DOYLE, KATHLEEN. Born Nov. 7, 1947 in Hyattsville, Md. Graduate Goodman Sch. NY debut 1971 with LCRep in "Ride across Lake Constance," "Mary Stuart," "Twelfth Night," "The Crucible."

DRAPER, DON. Born Sept. 25, 1929 in Modesto, Cal. Attended AADA. Bdwy bow 1960 in "Advise and Consent," OB in "Madam, Will You Walk," "Coriolanus," "Nightride."

DRIVAS, ROBERT. Born Oct. 7, 1938 in Chicago. Bdwy debut 1958 in "The Firstborn," followed by "One More River," "The Wall," "Lorenzo," "Irregular Verb to Love," "And Things That Go Bump in the Night," OB in "Diff'rent," "Mrs. Dally Has a Lover" for which he received a Theatre World Award, "Sweet Eros," "Where Has Tommy Flowers Gone?"

DRUMMOND, ALICE. Born May 21, 1929 in Pawtucket R.I. Attended Pembroke Col. OB in "Royal Gambit," "Go Show Me A Dragon," "Sweet of You to Say So," "Gallows Humor," "American Dream," "Giants' Dance," "The Carpenters," "Charles Abbott & Son," "God Says There Is No Peter Ott," Bdwy debut 1963 in "Ballad of the Sad Cafe," followed by "Malcolm," "The Chinese."

DUELL, WILLIAM. Born Aug. 30, 1923 in Corinth, NY. Attended Ill. Wesleyan, Yale. OB in "Threepenny Opera," "Portrait of the Artist as a Young Man," "Barroom Monks." "A Midsummer Night's Dream," "Henry IV," "Taming of the Shrew," "The Memorandum," on Bdwy in "A Cook for Mr. General," "Ballad of the Sad Cafe," "Ilya, Darling," "1776."

DUFF-MacCORMICK, CARA. Born Dec. 12 in Woodstock, Can. Attended AADA. Debut 1969 OB in "Love Your Crooked Neighbor," Bdwy 1972 in "Moonchildren" for which she received a Theatre World Award.

DUGAN, DENNIS. Born Sept 5, 1946 in Wheaton, Ill. Graduate Goodman Theatre. Debut 1971 OB in "The House of Blue Leaves."

DUNN, MICHAEL. Born Oct. 20, 1934 in Shattuck, Okla. Graduate UMich. Bdwy bow 1960 in "Here Come the Clowns," followed by "How to Make a Man," "Ballad of the Sad Cafe," "Inner Journey," OB in "Two by Saroyan," "Hop, Signor," "Timon of Athens" (NYSF).

DURNING, CHARLES. Born Feb 28, 1933 in Highland Falls, NY. Attended Columbia. NYU. Bdwy credits: "Poor Bitos," "Drat! The Cat!," "Pousse Cafe," "The Happy Time," "Indians," OB in "Two By Saroyan," "The Child Buyer," "An Album of Gunther Grass," "Huui, Huui," "An Invitation To A Beheading," "Lemon Sky," "Henri VI," "Happiness Cage," "That Championship Season," "Hamlet" (NYSF).

arbara eda-Young   **Larry Ellis**   **Suellen Estey**   **Ed Evanko**   **Pat Evans**

EAGLE, JEFF. Born Apr. 26, 1947 in Bklyn. Graduate Victor Valley Col. Debut 1971 OB in "Timon of Athens" (NYSF), followed by "Dylan."

EASTON, EDWARD. Born Oct. 21, 1942 in Moline, Ill. Graduate Lincoln Col., UIll., Neighborhood Playhouse. Debut 1967 OB in "Party on Greenwich Avenue," followed by "Middle of the Night" (ELT).

EASTON, RICHARD. Born Mar. 22, 1933 in Montreal, Can. Bdwy bow 1957 in "The Country Wife" for which he received a Theatre World Award, followed by "Back to Methuselah," with APA in "Anatol," "Man and Superman," "The Seagull," "Exit the King," "Pantagleize," "Cherry Orchard," "Misanthrope," "Cock-a-doodle Dandy," and "Hamlet," OB in "Salad Days," "Murderous Angels."

EBERT, JOYCE. Born June 26, 1933 in Homestead, Pa. Graduate Carnegie Tech. Debut 1956 OB in "Liliom," followed by "Sign of Winter," "Asmodee," "King Lear," "Hamlet," "Under Milkwood," "Trojan Women," "White Devil," "Tartuffe" (LC), Bdwy 1971 in "Solitaire/Double Solitaire."

eda-YOUNG, BARBARA. Born Jan. 30, 1945 in Detroit, Mich. Bdwy debut 1968 in "Lovers and Other Strangers," OB in "The Hawk," LCRep's "Time of Your Life," "Camino Real," "Operation Sidewinder," and "Kool Aid."

EDELSTEIN, RAY. Born Sept. 6, 1937 in Roanoke, Va. Debut 1970 in "Candyapple" (OB), followed by "Oh! Calcutta!"

EDWARDS, RONNIE CLAIRE. Born Feb. 9, 1933 in Oklahoma City. Graduate U Okla. Debut 1963 in "Paint Your Wagon," followed by "Trial of the Catonsville 9."

ELIAS, HECTOR. Born Sept. 24 in Buenos Aires. Studied at HB Studio. Debut 1968 OB in "Grab Bag," followed by Puerto Rican Traveling Theatre, Bdwy bow 1972 in "Sticks and Bones."

ELLIOTT, PATRICIA. Born July 21, 1942 in Gunnison, Colo. Graduate U. Colo., London Academy. Debut with LCRep 1968 in "King Lear," and "A Cry of Players," followed by OB in "Henry V," "The Persians", "A Doll's House," "Hedda Gabler," "In Case of Accident," "Water Hen."

ELLIS, LARRY. Born July 28, 1939 in NYC. Bdwy debut 1966 in "Slapstick Tragedy," followed by "Frank Merriwell," "No, No, Nanette."

ELLSWORTH, ELINOR. Born Jan. 21 in Simsbury, Conn. Attended Sarah Lawrence Col., Hartt Col., Juilliard. Debut 1967 OB in "Once upon a Mattress," followed by "Who Stole the American Crown Jewels," "Confessions of a Spent Youth," "Jacques Brel Is Alive and Well . . . "

ELSTON, ROBERT. Born May 29, 1934 in NYC. Graduate Hunter Col., CCNY. Bdwy debut 1958 in "Maybe Tuesday," followed by "Tall Story," "Golden Fleecing," "Spoon River Anthology," "You Know I Can't Hear You When the Water's Running," "Vivat! Vivat Regina!," OB in "Undercover Man," "Conditioned Reflex."

ENSERRO, MICHAEL. Born Oct. 5, 1918 in Soldier, Pa. Attended Allegheny Col., Pasadena Playhouse. On Bdwy in "Me and Molly," "Passion of Josef D," "Song of the Grasshopper," "Mike Downstairs," "Camino Real" (LC), OB in "Penny Change," "Fantasticks," "The Miracle," "The Kitchen," "Rome, Rome."

ENTEN, BONI. Born Feb. 20, 1947 in Baltimore, Md. Attended TCU. Bdwy debut 1965 in "The Roar of the Greasepaint," OB in "You're a Good Man, Charlie Brown," "Oh! Calcutta," "Salvation," "The Real Inspector Hound."

EPSTEIN, PIERRE. Born July 27, 1930 in Toulouse, France. Graduate UParis, Columbia. Bdwy bow 1962 in "A Shot in the Dark," followed by "Enter Laughing," "Incident at Vichy" (LC), "Bajour," "Black Comedy," "Fun City," OB in "Threepenny Opera," "Too Much Johnson," "Second City," "People vs. Ranchman," "Promenade."

ESTEY, SUELLEN. Born Nov. 21, in Mason City, Ia. Graduate Stephens Col., Northwestern U. Debut 1970 OB in "Some Other Time," followed by "June Moon" (ELT), Bdwy 1972 in "The Selling of the President."

EVANKO, ED. Born in Winnipeg, Can. Studied at Bristol Old Vic. Bdwy debut 1969 in "Canterbury Tales" for which he received a Theatre World Award, followed by OB "Love Me, Love My Children," "Leaves of Grass."

EVANS, DAMON. (formerly Dickie Evans) Born Nov. 24, 1950 in Baltimore, Md. Studied at Boston Cons. Debut 1971 OB in "A Day in the Life of Just about Everyone," followed by "Love Me, Love My Children," Bdwy 1971 in "The Me Nobody Knows," "Lost in the Stars."

EVANS, DILLON. Born Jan. 2, 1921 in London. Attended RADA. Bdwy bow 1950 in "The Lady's Not for Burning," followed by "School for Scandal," "Hamlet," "Ivanov," "Vivat! Vivat Regina!," OB in "Druid's Rest," "Rondelay," "Little Boxes."

EVANS, HARVEY. Born Jan. 7, 1941 in Cincinnati, O. Bdwy debut 1957 in "New Girl in Town," followed by "West Side Story," "Redhead," "Gypsy," "Anyone Can Whistle," "Hello Dolly!," "George M!," "Our Town," "The Boy Friend," "Follies,"

EVANS, PAT. Born Dec. 29, 1940 in NYC. Debut OB 1971 in "A Gun Play."

EVERHART, REX. Born June 13, 1920 in Watseka, Ill. Graduate U. Mo., NYU. Bdwy bow 1955 in "No Time for Sergeants," followed by "Tall Story," "Moonbirds," "Tenderloin," "A Matter of Position," "Rainy Day in Newark," "Skyscraper," "How Now, Dow Jones?," "1776."

EWER, DONALD. Born Sept. 10, 1923 in London. Attended RADA. Bdwy debut 1957 in "Under Milk Wood," followed by "Alfie," "Billy Liar" (OB), "Saved" (OB), "There's One in Every Marriage."

FAIRCHILD, CHARLOTTE. Born June 3, 1930 in Dayton, O. Attended Western Reserve U., Cleveland Playhouse. Bdwy debut 1957 in "Damn Yankees," followed by "Fiorello," "Mr. President," "Mame," "All the Girls Came out to Play," OB in "Penny Friend."

Arthur Faria

Geraldine Fitzgerald

Ike Feather

Beth Fortenberry

Robin Field

FALK, PETER. Born Sept. 16, 1927 in NYC. Graduate New School, Syracuse U. Debut OB 1956 in "Don Juan," followed by "The Changeling," "The Iceman Cometh," "St. Joan," "Diary of a Scoundrel," "The Lady's Not for Burning," "Purple Dust," "Bonds of Interest," "Comic Strip," Bdwy bow 1964 in "Passion of Josef D," subsequently "Prisoner of Second Avenue."

FARIA, ARTHUR. Born Nov. 24, 1944 in Fall River, Mass. Studied at SMTI, Boston Cons. Bdwy bow 1970 in "Georgy," followed by "The Boy Friend," "Sugar."

FASCIANO, RICHARD. Born Mar. 18, 1943 in Ansonia, Conn. Graduate U Conn. Bdwy debut 1970 in "Butterflies Are Free."

FAY, BRENDAN. Born in NYC; attended Maritime Acad. On Bdwy in "Legend of Lizzie," "First Love," "Borstal Boy," OB in "Heloise," "Threepenny Opera," "Donogoo," "King of the Whole Damned World," "Wretched the Lion-Hearted," "Time of the Key," "Thistle in My Bed," "Posterity for Sale," "Stephen D," LCRep's "King Lear" and "Cry of Players," "Brothers."

FEATHER, IKE. Born Dec. 5, 1949 in Buffalo, NY. Graduate Towson State Col. Debut 1972 OB in "DuBarry Was a Lady."

FELLOWS, DON. Born Dec. 2 1922 in Salt Lake City. Attended UWisc. Appeared in "Mister Roberts," "South Pacific," "Only in America," "Marathon '33," "Generation," OB in "Friday Night," "My House Is Your House," "Sleep."

FENNO, WILL. Born May 22, 1948 in Milwaukee, Wisc. Attended UWisc., Goodman Theatre. Bdwy debut 1971 in "Solitaire/Double Solitaire."

FERNANDEZ, JOSE. Born Aug. 19, 1948 in Havana, Cuba. Attended HB Studio. OB in "Dark of the Moon," "The Me Nobody Knows."

FIELD, ROBIN. Born Apr. 13, 1947 in Los Angeles. Attended USCal. Debut 1968 OB in "Your Own Thing," followed by "Look Me Up."

FITZGERALD, GERALDINE. Born Nov. 24, 1914 in Dublin, Ire. Bdwy debut 1938 in "Heartbreak House," followed by "Sons and Soldiers," "Doctor's Dilemma," "King Lear," "Hide and Seek," OB in "The Cave Dwellers," "Pigeons," "Long Day's Journey into Night," "Everyman and Roach."

FITZGERALD, NEIL. Born Jan. 15, 1898 in Tipperary, Ire. Attended Trinity Col. Appeared in "Leave Her To Heaven," "The Wookey," "Without Love," "Ten Little Indians," "Plan M," "You Touched Me," "The Play's the Thing," "Design For a Stained Glass Window," "The High Ground," "To Dorothy, a Son," "Mr. Pickwick," "Witness for the Prosecution," "Little Moon of Alban" "Hadrian VII," "The Mundy Scheme," "All Over," OB in "Portrait of the Artist as a Young Man," "Three Hand Reel," "Carricknabauna." "Murderous Angels."

FLANAGAN, FIONNUALA. Born Dec. 10, 1941 in Dublin, Ire. Attended Fribourg U. NY debut 1968 in "Lovers" (LC), followed by "The Incomparable Max."

FLANAGAN, PAULINE. Born June 29, 1925 in Sligo, Ire. Debut OB 1958 in "Ulysses in Nighttown," followed by "Pictures in the Hallway," "Antigone" (LC), on Bdwy in "God and Kate Murphy," "The Living Room," "The Crucible" (LC).

FLYNN, THOMAS F. Born Dec. 16, 1946 in Albany, NY. Graduate Union Col., Neighborhood Playhouse. Debut 1970 OB in "House of Blue Leaves."

FORD, DAVID. Born Oct. 30, 1929 in LaJolla, Calif. Attended Ariz. State, US.Dak. Debut OB 1958 in "Billy Budd," followed by "Tea Party," on Bdwy in "The Physicists," "1776."

FORD, PAUL. Born Nov. 2, 1901 in Baltimore, Md. Attended Dartmouth. Bdwy bow 1944 in "Decision," followed by "Lower North," "Kiss Them for Me," "Flamingo Road," "On Whitman Avenue," "Another Part of the Forest," "Command Decision," "Teahouse of the August Moon," "Whoop-Up," "Music Man," "Thurber Carnival," "Never Too Late," "3 Bags Full," "What Did We Do Wrong?," "3 Men on a Horse," "Front Page," "Fun City."

FORD, RUTH. Born July 7, 1915 in Hazelhurst, Miss. Attended UMiss. Bdwy debut 1938 in "Shoemaker's Holiday," followed by "Danton's Death," "Swingin' the Dream," "No Exit," "This Time Tomorrow," "Clutterbuck," "House of Bernarda Alba," "Island of Goats," "Requiem for a Nun," "The Milk Train Doesn't Stop Here Anymore," "Grass Harp," OB in "Glass Slipper," "Miss Julie."

FORLOW, TED. Born Apr. 29 1931 in Independence, Mo. Attended Baker U. Bdwy debut 1957 in "New Girl in Town," followed by "Juno," "Destry Rides Again," "Subways Are for Sleeping," "Can-Can," "Wonderful Town" (CC), "A Funny Thing Happened on the Way to the Forum," "Milk and Honey," "Carnival" (CC'68), "Man of La Mancha." (also LC).

FORSYTHE, HENDERSON. Born Sept. 11, 1917 in Macon, Mo. Attended UIowa. OB in "The Iceman Cometh," "The Collection," "The Room," "A Slight Ache," "Happiness Cage", "Waiting for Godot", "In Case of Accident." Bdwy in "The Cellar and the Well," "Miss Lonelyhearts," "Who's Afraid of Virginia Woolf?," "Malcolm," "Right Honourable Gentleman," "Delicate Balance," "Birthday Party," "Harvey," "Engagement Baby."

FORTENBERRY, BETH. Born Mar. 24, 1948 in Gainesville, Tex. Attended Okla.U. Debut 1972 OB in "One for the Money etc."

FOSTER, FRANCES. Born June 11 in Yonkers, NY. Bdwy debut 1955 in "The Wisteria Trees," followed by "Nobody Loves an Albatross," "Raisin in the Sun," OB in "Take a Giant Step," "Edge of the City," "Tammy and the Doctor," "The Crucible," "Happy Ending," "Day of Absence," "An Evening of One Acts," "Man Better Man," "Brotherhood," "Akokawe," "Rosalee Pritchett," "Sty of the Blind Pig," and "Ballet behind the Bridge," "Good Woman of Setzuan" (LC), "Behold! Cometh the Vanderkellans."

FOSTER, GLORIA. Born Nov. 15, 1936 in Chicago. Attended Ill. State U., Goodman Theatre. OB in "In White America," "Medea" for which she received a Theatre World Award, "Yerma" (LC), "A Hand Is on the Gate," "Black Visions."

234

Conard Fowkes   **Dorothy Frank**   **Jim Frank**   **Bruce French**   **Dick Fuchs**

FOWKES, CONARD. Born Jan. 4, 1933 in Washington, D.C. Yale Graduate. Bdwy bow 1958 in "Howie," followed by "The Wall," "Minor Miracle," "All the Girls Came out to Play," OB in "Look Back in Anger," "That Thing at the Cherry Lane," "America Hurrah," "The Reckoning," "Istanboul," "Sleep."

FOXWORTH, ROBERT. Born Nov. 1, 1941 in Houston, Tex. Carnegie Tech. graduate. Bdwy debut 1969 in "Henry V," followed by "The Crucible" (LCRep) for which he received a Theatre World Award.

FRANCIS, GERALD G. Born Mar. 22, 1950 in NYC. CCNY graduate. Bdwy debut 1972 in "Don't Bother Me I Can't Cope."

FRANK, DOROTHY. Born July 8, 1942 in St. Louis, Mo. Bdwy debut 1960 in "Tenderloin," followed by "Sail Away," "No Strings," "New Faces," "Once upon a Mattress," "Coco," "Different Times," "Beggar on Horseback" (LC), "Boys from Syracuse" (OB).

FRANK, JIM. Born June 1 in Houston, Tex. Attended Lon Morris Col. Debut 1972 OB in "No Strings" (ELT).

FRANKLIN, BONNIE. Born Jan. 6, 1944 in Santa Monica, Cal. Attended Smith Col. UCLA. Debut Off-Bdwy 1968 in "Your Own Thing," followed by "Dames at Sea," "Drat!," Bdwy bow 1970 in "Applause" for which she received a Theatre World Award.

FRANKLIN HUGH. Born Aug. 24, 1916 in Muskogee, Okla. Attended Northwestern U. Bdwy bow 1938 in "Gloriana," followed by "Harriet," "Alice in Wonderland," "Medea," "Best Man," "Luther," "A Shot in the Dark," "Arturo Ui," "The Devils," "What Did We Do Wrong?," OB in "How Much, How Much?," "Misalliance."

FREEMAN, ARNY. Born Aug. 28, 1908 in Chicago. Bdwy bow 1949 in "Streetcar Named Desire," followed by "Great Sebastians," "Tall Story," "Hot Spot," "What Makes Sammy Run?," "Cactus Flower," "Minnie's Boys," OB in "Gay Divorcee," CC's "Dream Girl" and "The Shrike," "A Gun Play."

FREEMAN, MORGAN. Born June 1, 1937 in Memphis, Tenn. Attended LACC. Bdwy bow 1967 in "Hello, Dolly!," OB in "Ostrich Feathers," "Niggerlovers," "Exhibition," "Black Visions."

FRENCH, ARTHUR. Born in NYC. Attended Bklyn Col. OB in "Raisin' Hell In the Sun," "Ballad of Bimshire," "Day of Absence," "Happy Ending," "Jonah," "Black Girl," "Ceremonies In Dark Old Men," "An Evening of One Acts," "Man Better Man," "Brotherhood," "Perry's Mission," "Rosalee Pritchett." Bdwy 1971 in "Ain't Supposed to Die a Natural Death."

FRENCH, ARTHUR W. III. Born Apr. 30, 1965 in NYC. Debut OB 1971 in "Black Girl."

FRENCH, BRUCE. Born July 4, 1945 in Reinbeck, Ia. Graduate Iowa U. Debut 1972 OB in "Shadow of a Gunman."

FREY, LEONARD. Born Sept. 4, 1938 in Bklyn. Attended Cooper Union, Neighborhood Playhouse. OB in "Little Mary Sunshine," "Funny House of a Negro," "Boys in the Band," LCRep's "Time of Your Life," "Beggar on Horseback," "People Are Living There," and "Twelfth Night," on Bdwy in "Fiddler on the Roof."

FRY, RAY. Born Feb. 22, 1923 in Hebron, Ind. Graduate SF State Col.,Northwestern. Bdwy bow 1944 in "Hickory Stick," followed by "Cyrano," "The Cradle Will Rock," LCRep's "Danton's Death," "Country Wife," "Caucasian Chalk Circle," "Alchemist," "Galileo," "St. Joan," "Tiger At The Gates," "Cyrano," "A Cry of Players," "Bananas," "The Miser," "Operation Sidewinder," "Beggar on Horseback," "Playboy of the Western World," "Good Woman of Setzuan," "Birthday Party," "Antigone," "Mary Stuart," "Twelfth Night."

FUCHS, DICK. Born Feb. 23, 1944 in St. Louis, Mo. Graduate UMo. Debut 1972 OB in "Anna K."

FULLER, PENNY. Born 1940, in Durham, NC. Attended Northwestern. Appeared in "Barefoot in the Park," "Cabaret," NYSF's "Richard III," "As You Like It," and "Henry IV," "Applause."

GABLE, JUNE. Born June 5, 1945 in NY. Graduate Carnegie Tech. Off-Bdwy in "MacBird," "Jacques Brel Is Alive and Well and Living In Paris," "A Day in the Life of Just about Everyone," "Mod Donna," "Wanted."

GALICI, VINCENT MICHAEL. Born Dec. 13, 1945 in Detroit, Mich. Graduate AADA. Debut 1972 OB in "Rain."

GALLAGHER, HELEN. Born in Brooklyn, 1926. Bdwy debut 1947 in "Seven Lively Arts," followed by "Mr. Strauss Goes to Boston," "Billion Dollar Baby," "Brigadoon," "High Button Shoes," "Touch and Go," "Make a Wish," "Pal Joey," "Hazel Flagg," CC's "Guys and Dolls," "Finian's Rainbow," and "Oklahoma," "Pajama Game," "Bus Stop," "Portofino," "Sweet Charity," "Mame," "Cry For Us All," "No, No, Nanette."

GAMBOA, MARCELO. Born Apr. 2, 1939 in Buenos Aires. On Bdwy in "Flora the Red Menace," "La Grosse Valise," "Annie Get Your Gun," "Illya, Darling," "Carnival" (CC), "Minnie's Boys," "The Boy Friend," "Wild and Wonderful."

GANTRY, DONALD. Born June 11, 1936 in Philadelphia. Attended Temple U. Bdwy debut 1961 in "One More River," OB in "The Iceman Cometh," "Children of Darkness," "Here Come the Clowns," "Seven at Dawn," "Long Day's Journey into Night."

GARDENIA, VINCENT. Born Jan. 7 in Italy. Debut OB 1956 in "Man With The Golden Arm," followed by "Brothers Karamazov," "Power of Darkness," "Machinal," "Gallows Humor," "Endgame," "Little Murders," "Passing through from Exotic Places," "Carpenters," on Bdwy in "The Visit" (1957), "The Cold Wind and The Warm," "Rashomon," "Only in America," "The Wall," "Daughters of Silence," "Siedman and Son," "Dr. Fish," "Prisoner of Second Avenue."

| Linda Gerard | Kurt Garfield | Asa Gim | Igors Gavon | Karen Gorney |

GARFIELD, DAVID. Born Feb. 6, 1941 in Brooklyn. Graduate Columbia, Cornell. OB in "Hang Down Your Head and Die," Bdwy bow 1967 in "Fiddler on the Roof," followed by "The Rothschilds."

GARFIELD, KURT. Born Jan. 10, 1931 in The Bronx. Attended Goodman Theatre. Bdwy debut 1970 in "Sheep on the Runway," OB in "Dylan," "The Screens."

GARLAND, GEOFF. Born June 10, 1932 Warrington, Eng. Debut OB 1961 in "The Hostage," on Bdwy in "Hamlet," "The Imaginary Invalid," "A Touch of The Poet," "Tonight At 8:30," "Front Page," "Capt. Brassbound's Conversion," OB in "Trelawney of the Wells," "Timon of Athens" (NYSF), "Waiting for Godot."

GARNER, MARTIN. Born July 9, 1927 in Bklyn. Attended New School, HB studio, Theatre Wing. Bdwy debut 1959 in "The Tenth Man," followed by "Seidman & Son," "Gideon," "Dylan," OB in "Jacknife," "The Kitchen," "Dybbuk," "Golem," "Last Analysis."

GARRETT, JOY. Born Mar. 2, 1945 in Ft. Worth, Tex. Graduate Tex. Wesleyan, AADA. NY bow Off-Bdwy 1969 in "Gertrude Stein's First Reader," followed by "The Drunkard," "Candyapple," "One for the Money," Bdwy 1971 in "Inner City."

GARY, HAROLD. Born May 7, 1910 in NYC. Bdwy bow 1928 in "Diamond Lil," followed by "Crazy with the Heat," "A Flag Is Born," "Guys and Dolls," "Oklahoma!," "Arsenic and Old Lace," "Billion Dollar Baby," "Fiesta," "The World We Make," "Born Yesterday," "Will Success Spoil Rock Hunter?," "Let It Ride," "Counting House," "Arturo Ui," "A Thousand Clowns," "Enter Laughing," "Illya, Darling," "The Price," "Rosebloom" (OB).

GAVON, IGORS. Born Nov. 14, 1937 in Latvia. Bdwy bow 1961 in "Carnival," followed by "Hello, Dolly!" "Marat/DeSade," "Billy," "Sugar," OB in "Your Own Thing," "Promenade," "Exchange," "Nevertheless, They Laugh."

GAYNES, EDMUND. Born May 14, 1947 in Brooklyn. Graduate CCNY. Bdwy bow 1958 in "Body Beautiful," followed by "Greenwillow," "The Fig Leaves Are Falling," OB in "Bartleby," "Best Foot Forward," "Promenade," "Now Is the Time," "F. Jasmine Addams," "Plagueship."

GeBAUER, GENE. Born June 28, 1934 in Ord, Neb. NY bow 1960 in "Machinal" (OB), followed by "Once Upon a Mattress," "Stag Movie," on Bdwy in "Camelot," "No Strings," "Hello, Dolly!," "Oh! Calcutta!," "Sugar."

GELFAND, CAROL. Born Aug. 16, 1937 in Chicago. Attended U. Ill, Columbia. Debut off-Bdwy 1961 in "The Cage," Bdwy bow 1970 in "Company."

GENEST, EDMOND. Born Oct. 27, 1943 in Boston. Attended Suffolk U. Debut 1972 OB in "The Real Inspector Hound."

GERACI, FRANK. Born Sept. 8, 1939 in Bklyn. Attended Yale, HB Studio. Debut 1961 OB in "Color of Darkness," followed by "Mr. Grossman," "Balm in Gilead," "Fantasticks," "Tom Paine," "End of All Things Natural," Bdwy bow 1972 in "Love Suicide at Schofield Barracks."

GERARD, LINDA. Born Dec. 24, 1938 in Trenton, NJ. Attended Finch Col., Am. Theatre Wing. Bdwy debut 1965 in "Funny Girl," OB in "Look Me Up."

GERSTAD, JOHN. Born Sept. 3, 1925 in Boston. Attended Harvard. Bdwy debut 1943 in "Othello," followed by "Dark of The Moon," "Joy To The World," "Not For Children," "The Male Animal" (CC'52), "Golden Fleecing," "Trial of Lee Harvey Oswald," "Come Summer," "Penny Wars," "Oklahoma!" (LC), "All Over," "All the Girls Came out to Play."

GIBSON, JUDY. Born Sept. 11, 1947 in Trenton, NJ. Graduate Rider Col. Bdwy debut 1970 in "Purlie," followed by "Sensations," "Manhattan Arrangement," "Two if by Sea."

GILFORD, JACK. Born July 25 in NYC. Bdwy bow 1940 in "Meet the People," followed by "They Should Have Stood in Bed," "Count Me In," "The Live Wire," "Alive and Kicking," "Once Over Lightly," "Diary of Anne Frank," "Romanoff and Juliet," "The Tenth Man," "A Funny Thing Happened . . .," "Cabaret," "3 Men on a Horse," "No, No, Nanette."

GIM, ASA. Born May 30, 1945 in Korea. NYU graduate. Debut 1971 OB in "Basic Training of Pavlo Hummel," followed by "Sticks and Bones."

GLOVER, JOHN. Born Aug. 7, 1944 in Kingston, NY. Attended Towson State Col. Debut OB 1969 in "A Scent of Flowers," followed by "Subject to Fits," "House of Blue Leaves," Bdwy 1972 in "The Selling of the President."

GOLDSMITH, MERWIN. Born Aug. 7, 1937 in Detroit, Mich. Graduate UCLA. Studied at Old Vic. Bdwy debut 1970 in "Minnie's Boys," OB in "Hamlet as a Happening," "The Chickencoop Chinaman," "Wanted."

GOODFRIEND, LYNDA. Born Oct. 31, 1950 in Miami, Fla. Graduate SMU. Debut 1972 OB in "No Strings" (ELT).

GORDON, CARL. Born Jan. 20, 1932 in Richmond, Va. Bdwy bow 1966 in "Great White Hope," OB in "Day of Absence," "Happy Ending," "Strong Breed," "Trials of Brother Jero," "Kongi's Harvest," "Ain't Supposed to Die a Natural Death" (Bdwy '71).

GORDON, PEGGY. Born Dec. 26, 1949 in NYC. Attended Carnegie Tech. Debut OB 1971 in "Godspell."

GORMAN, CLIFF. Born Oct. 13, 1936 in NYC. Attended UCLA. OB in "Hogan's Goat," "Boys in the Band," "Ergo," Bdwy bow 1971 in "Lenny."

GORNEY, KAREN. Born Jan. 28, 1945 in Los Angeles. Graduate Carnegie Tech., Brandeis U. Debut 1972 OB in "Dylan."

GORWIN, PETER. Born June 26, 1948 in Duluth, Minn. Attended Loyola U. Bdwy debut 1971 in "Trial of the Catonsville 9."

Harold Gould

Harry Goz

John Granger

Del Green

Allan Gruet

GOSSETT, LOUIS. Born May 27, 1936 in Bklyn. NYU graduate. Bdwy bow 1953 in "Take a Giant Step," followed by "Desk Set," "Lost in the Stars" (CC), "Raisin in the Sun," "Tambourines to Glory," "The Zulu and the Zayda," "My Sweet Charlie," "Carry Me Back to Morningside Heights," OB in "The Blacks," "Telemachus Clay," "Bloodknot," "Murderous Angels."

GOULD, HAROLD. Born Dec. 10, 1923 in Schenectady, N.Y. Graduate SUNY, Cornell. NY bow 1969 in LC's "The Increased Difficulty of Concentration," and "Amphitryon," followed by "House of Blue Leaves" (OB).

GOZ, HARRY G. Born June 23, 1932 in St. Louis. Attended St. Louis Inst. Debut 1957 in "Utopia Limited," followed by "Bajour," "Fiddler on the Roof," "Two by Two."

GRANGER, JOHN. Born Feb. 21, 1924 in Okla. Attended Culver U., Rice U. Bdwy debut 1953 in "The Little Hut," OB in "The Screens."

GRANT, LEE. Born Oct. 31, 1927 in NYC. Attended Neighborhood Playhouse. Bdwy debut 1948 in "Joy to the World," followed by "Detective Story," "Arms and the Man," "Lo and Behold!," "Wedding Breakfast," "A Hole in the Head," "Two for the Seesaw," "The Captains and the Kings," "The Maids" (OB), "Electra" (NYSF), "Prisoner of Second Avenue."

GRANT, MICKI. Born June 30 in Chicago. Attended U. Ill., Geller School. Bdwy debut 1963 in "Tambourines to Glory," OB in "Fly Blackbird," "The Blacks," "Brecht on Brecht," "Jerico-Jim Crow," "The Cradle Will Rock," "Leonard Bernstein's Theatre Songs," "To Be Young, Gifted and Black," "Don't Bother Me, I Can't Cope."

GRASSLE, KAREN. Born in Albany, Cal. Graduate UCal., London Acad., Pasadena Playhouse. Bdwy debut 1969 in "The Gingham Dog," followed by "Cymbeline" (NYSF), "Butterflies Are Free."

GREEN, DEL. Born July 8, 1938 in Pocatello, Ida. Bdwy debut 1967 in "Illya, Darling," followed by "Love Suicide at Schofield Barracks."

GREEN, MARTYN Born Apr. 22, 1899 in London. Attended Royal Col. Appeared with D'Oyly Carte (1934–51), Chartok's Gilbert & Sullivan Co., "Misalliance," "Shangri-La," "Child of Fortune," "A Visit to a Small Planet," "Black Comedy," "Canterbury Tales," "Charley's Aunt," "The Incomparable Max," Off-Bdwy in "Drums under the Windows," "Red Roses for Me," "Carricknabauna."

GREENE, JAMES. Born Dec. 1, 1926 in Lawrence, Mass. Graduate Emerson Col. OB in "The Iceman Cometh," "American Gothic," "The King and the Duke," "The Hostage," "Plays for Bleecker St.," "Moon in the Yellow River," "Misalliance," with LCRep 2 years, with APA in "You Can't Take It with You," "School for Scandal," "Wild Duck," "Right You Are," "The Show-Off" and "Pantagleize." on Bdwy in "Romeo and Juliet," "Girl on Via Flaminia," "Compulsion," "Inherit the Wind," "Shadow of a Gunman," "Andersonville Trial," "Night Life," "School for Wives," "Ring Round the Bathtub."

GREENE, RICHARD. Born Jan. 8, 1946 in Miami, Fla. Graduate Fla. Atlantic U. Debut 1971 with LCRep in "Macbeth," "Play Strindberg," "Mary Stuart," "Narrow Road to the Deep North," "Twelfth Night," "The Crucible."

GREENHOUSE, MARTHA. Born June 14 in Omaha, Neb. Attended Hunter Col., Am. Th. Wing. Appeared in "Sons and Soldiers," "Clerambard" (OB), "Our Town" (OB), "Dear Me, the Sky is Falling," "Family Way," "Woman Is My Idea," "3 by Ferlinghetti" (OB), "No Strings" (ELT).

GRIGAS, JOHN. Born Feb. 16, 1930 in Shenandoah, Pa. Bdwy debut 1956 in "Plain and Fancy," followed by "My Fair Lady," "Milk and Honey," "Baker Street," "It's Superman," "Man of La Mancha," "Dear World," "Follies."

GRIZZARD, GEORGE. Born Apr. 1, 1928 in Roanoke Rapids, Va. Graduate UNC. Bdwy bow 1954 in "All Summer Long," followed by "Desperate Hours," "Happiest Millionaire" for which he received a Theatre World Award, "Disenchanted," "Big Fish, Little Fish," with APA 1961–62, "Who's Afraid of Virginia Woolf?," "Glass Menagerie," "You Know I Can't Hear You When the Water's Running," "Noel Coward's Sweet Potato," "Gingham Dog," "Inquest," "The Country Girl."

GROVER, STANLEY. Born Mar. 28, 1926 in Woodstock, Ill. Attended UMo. Appeared in "Seventeen," "Wish You Were Here," "Time Remember'd," "Candide," "13 Daughters," "Mr. President," CC's "South Pacific," "Finian's Rainbow," and "King and I," "Lyle" (OB), "Company."

GRUET, ALLAN. Born Mar. 22, 1945 in Paterson, NJ. Graduate Boston U. Bdwy debut 1968 in "Fiddler on the Roof," followed by "The Rothschilds."

GUERRERO, DANNY. Born Oct. 14, 1945 in Tucson, Ariz. Attended UCLA, Pasadena Playhouse. OB in "Hello, Tourista," "Two Gentlemen of Verona," "Devil's Disciple," "Who's Who, Baby," "Manhattan Arrangement," "Hark!"

GUEST, CHRISTOPHER. Born Feb. 5, 1948 in NYC. Attended Bard Col., NYU. Bdwy bow 1970 in "Room Service," followed by "Moonchildren," OB in "Little Murders."

GUNN, MOSES. Born Oct. 2, 1929 in St. Louis, Mo. Graduate Tenn. AIU, UKan. OB in "Measure for Measure," "Bohikee Cree," "Day of Absence," "Happy Ending," "Baal," "Hard Travelin'," Lonesome Train," "In White America," "The Blacks," "Titus Andronicus" (NYSF), "Song of the Lusitanian Bogey," "Summer of the 17th Doll," "Kongi's Harvest," "Daddy Goodness," "Cities in Bezique," "To Be Young, Gifted and Black," "Sty of the Blind Pig," "Twelfth Night" (LC), Bdwy in "A Hand Is on the Gate" ('66), "Othello."

GUSS, LOUIS. Born Jan. 4 in NYC. Credits: "Girl on the Via Flaminia," "Handful of Fire," "One More River," "Once There Was a Russian," "Night of the Iguana," "Odd Couple," "Flora the Red Menace," "But Seriously," "Gandhi" (OB), "Capt. Brassbound's Conversion."

GWILLIM, JACK. Born Dec. 15, 1915 in Canterbury, Eng. Attended Central Sch. of Speech. Bdwy debut 1956 with Old Vic in "Macbeth," "Romeo and Juliet," "Richard II," "Troilus and Cressida," followed by "Laurette," "Ari," "Lost in the Stars."

| Michael Hadge | Lois Ann Hall | Jack Hallett | Katie Hanley | Ben Hammer |

HACKETT, JOAN. Born Mar. 1 in NYC. Attended Actors Studio. OB debut 1959 in "A Clearing in the Woods," followed by "Call Me by My Rightful Name" for which she received a Theatre World Award, Bdwy bow 1959 in "Much Ado about Nothing," followed by "Peterpat," "Park," "Night Watch."

HADGE, MICHAEL. Born June 6, 1932 in Greensboro, NC. Bdwy bow 1958 in "The Cold Wind and the Warm," followed by "Lady of the Camellias," "Impossible Years," OB in "Local Stigmatic," "The Hunter."

HAID, CHARLES. Born June 2, 1943 in Palo Alto, Cal. Graduate Carnegie-Mellon U. Bdwy debut 1972 in "Elizabeth I."

HAILEY, MARIAN. Born Feb. 1, 1941 in Portland, Ore. U. Wash graduate. Bdwy debut 1965 in "Mating Dance," followed by "Any Wednesday," "Best Laid Plans," "Keep It In The Family," "Harvey," "Company," OB in "Under the Yum Yum Tree," "Thornton Wilder's Triple Bill," "Castro Complex."

HAINES, A. LARRY. Born Aug. 3, 1917 in Mt. Vernon, NY. Attended CCNY. Bdwy bow 1962 in "A Thousand Clowns," followed by "Generation," "Promises, Promises," "Last of the Red Hot Lovers," "Twigs."

HALL, ALBERT. Born Nov. 10, 1937 in Boothton, Ala. Columbia graduate. Debut 1971 OB in "Basic Training of Pavlo Hummel," followed by "Duplex" (LC), Bdwy 1971 "Ain't Supposed to Die a Natural Death."

HALL, BRIAN. Born June 27, 1959 in Paterson, NJ. Studied at HB Studio. Debut 1970 OB in "Peanut Butter and Jelly," followed by Bdwy bow 1971 in "The Rothschilds."

HALL, GEORGE. Born Nov. 19, 1916 in Toronto, Can. Attended Neighborhood Playhouse. Bdwy debut 1946 in "Call Me Mister," followed by "Lend an Ear," "Touch and Go," "Live Wire," "The Boy Friend," "There's a Girl in My Soup," "An Evening with Richard Nixon and ...," OB in "Balcony," "Ernest in Love," "A Round with Ring."

HALL, LOIS ANN. Born Mar. 31, 1947 in Philadelphia. Graduate Fla. Atlantic U. Debut 1972 OB in "DuBarry Was A Lady."

HALL, PAMELA. Born Oct. 16, 1947 in Champaign, Ill. Attended UIll. OB in "Harold Arlen Songbook," "Frere Jacques," "A Month of Sundays," on Bdwy in "Dear World," "1776," "A Funny Thing Happened on the Way to the Forum."

HALLETT, JACK. Born Nov. 7, 1948 in Philadelphia. Attended AADA. Debut OB 1972 in "Servant of Two Masters" (ELT).

HAMILTON, ROGER. Born in San Diego, Cal., May 2, 1928. Attended San Diego Col., RADA. OB in "Merchant of Venice," "Hamlet," "Live Like Pigs," "Hotel Passionato," "Sjt. Musgrove's Dance," on Bdwy in "Someone Waiting," "Separate Tables," "Little Moon of Alban," "Luther," "The Deputy," "Rosencrantz and Guildenstern Are Dead," "The Rothschilds."

HAMMER, BEN. Born Dec. 8, 1925 in Bklyn. Graduate Bklyn Col. Bdwy bow 1955 in "The Great Sebastians," followed by "Diary of Anne Frank," "The Tenth Man," "Mother Courage," "The Deputy," "Royal Hunt of the Sun," OB in "Crucible" (LC), "Murderous Angels."

HANEY, SONJA. Born May 24, 1943 in Portsmouth, Va. Attended LACC. Bdwy debut 1972 in "A Funny Thing Happened on the Way to the Forum."

HANLEY, ELLEN. Born May 15, 1926 in Lorain, O. Attended Juilliard. Bdwy debut 1946 in "Annie Get Your Gun," followed by "Barefoot Boy with Cheek" for which she received a Theatre World Award, "High Button Shoes," "Two's Company," "First Impressions," "Fiorello!", "The Boys from Syracuse" (OB), "1776."

HANLEY, KATIE. Born Jan. 17, 1949 in Evanston, Ill. Attended Carnegie-Mellon U. Debut 1971 OB in "Godspell," followed by "Grease."

HANNING, GERALDINE. Born in Cleveland, O. Graduate Conn. Col., Western Reserve U. Debut 1954 OB in "Praise of Folly," followed by "In Good King Charles' Golden Days," "Philanderer," "Lysistrata," "Alcestis Comes Back," "Under the Gaslight," "One for the Money."

HANSEN, RONN. Born Oct. 18, 1939 in Madison, Wisc. Graduate UWisc. Bdwy bow 1965 in "Slapstick Tragedy," followed by "Minnie's Boys," OB "No Strings" (ELT).

HARDY, JOSEPH. Born Aug. 10, 1918 in Arlington, Mass. Attended Leland Powers Sch. Bdwy bow 1942 in "R.U.R.," followed by "The Tempest," "Small Hours," "Mr. Roberts" (CC), "Freaking out of Stephanie Blake," OB in "Career," "Respectful Prostitute," "Mutilation."

HARE, WILL. Born Mar. 30, 1919 in Elkins, WVa. Attended Am. Actors Theatre. Credits: "The Eternal Road," "The Moon Is Down," "Suds in Your Eye," "Only the Heart," "The Visitor," "Trip to Bountiful," "Witness for the Prosecution," "Marathon '33," OB in "The Viewing," "Winter Journey," "Dylan," "Older People."

HARKEY, JAMES. Born Apr. 10, 1934 in Plainview, Ark. Attended UArk., Carnegie Tech. Debut 1972 OB in "Oedipus at Colonus" (ELT).

HARMON, JENNIFER. Born Dec. 3, 1943 in Pasadena, Cal. Attended UMiss., UMich. With APA (1960-69) in "Right You Are," "You Can't Take It with You," "War and Peace," "Wild Duck," "School for Scandal," OB in "Effect of Gamma Rays on Man-in-the-moon Marigolds."

HARMON, JILL. Born in NYC, Apr. 25, 1949. Attended Northwestern. Debut 1962 OB in "Black Monday," followed by "Rate of Exchange," Bdwy in "Fiddler on the Roof."

HARNEY, BEN. Born Aug. 29, 1952 in Bklyn. Bdwy debut 1971 in "Purlie," OB in "Don't Bother Me, I Can't Cope."

HARRIS, CYNTHIA. Born in NYC. Graduate Smith Col. Bdwy debut 1963 in "Natural Affection," followed by "Any Wednesday," "Best Laid Plans," "Company," OB in "The Premise," "Three by Wilder," "America Hurrah," "White House Murder Case."

Geraldine Hanning

Joseph Hardy

Cynthia Harris

Winston DeWitt Hemsley

Katherine Helmond

HARRIS, JULIE. Born Dec. 2, 1925 in Grosse Point, Mich. Attended Yale. Bdwy debut 1945 in "It's a Gift," followed by "Henry V," "Oedipus," "The Playboy of the Western World," "Alice in Wonderland," "Macbeth," "Sundown Beach" for which she received a Theatre World Award, "The Young and The Fair," "Magnolia Alley," "Montserrat," "The Member of the Wedding." "I Am a Camera," "Mlle. Colombe," "The Lark," "Country Wife," "Warm Peninsula," "Little Moon of Alban," "A Shot in the Dark," "Marathon '33," "Ready When You Are, C.B," "Hamlet" (CP), "Skyscraper," "40 Carats," "And Miss Reardon Drinks A Little," "Voices."

HARRIS, ROSEMARY. Born Sept. 19, 1930 in Ashby, Eng. Attended RADA. Bdwy debut 1952 in "Climate of Eden" for which she received a Theatre World Award, followed by "Troilus and Cressida," "Interlock," "The Disenchanted," "The Tumbler," APA's "The Tavern," "School for Scandal," "Seagull," "Importance of Being Earnest," "War and Peace," "Man and Superman," "Judith," and "You Can't Take It with You," "Lion in Winter," "Old Times."

HAYESON, JIMMY. Born June 27, 1924 in Carthage, NC. Graduate NC Col. Debut 1969 OB in "Black Quartet," followed by "Black Girl," Bdwy 1971 in "Ain't Supposed to Die a Natural Death."

HECHT, PAUL. Born Aug. 16, 1941 in London. Attended McGill U. OB in "Sjt. Musgrave's Dance" and "MacBird," on Bdwy in "Rosencrantz and Guildenstern Are Dead," "1776," "The Rothschilds," "The Ride Across Lake Constance" (LC).

HEFFERNAN, JOHN. Born May 30, 1934 in NYC. Attended CCNY, Columbia, Boston U. OB in "The Judge," "Julius Caesar," "Great God Brown," "Lysistrata," "Peer Gynt," "Henry IV," "Taming of the Shrew," "She Stoops to Conquer," "The Plough and the Stars," "Octoroon," "Hamlet," "Androcles and the Lion," "A Man's a Man," "Winter's Tale," "Arms and the Man," "St. Joan" (LCRep), "Peer Gynt" (CP), "Memorandum," "Invitation to a Beheading," "Shadow of a Gunman," on Bdwy in "Luther," "Tiny Alice," "Postmark Zero," "Woman Is My Idea," "Morning, Noon and Night," "Purlie."

HEFLIN, MARTA. Born Mar. 29, 1945 in Washington, DC. Attended Northwestern, Carnegie Tech. Debut 1967 in "Life With Father" (CC), followed by OB in "Salvation," "Soon," "Wedding of Iphigenia," Bdwy debut 1972 in "Jesus Christ Superstar."

HEFLIN, NORA. Born Feb. 2, 1950 in Los Angeles. Bdwy debut 1968 in "The Prime of Miss Jean Brodie," followed by "The Crucible" (LC).

HELMOND, KATHERINE. Born in Galveston, Tex. OB in "Orpheus Descending," "Trip to Bountiful," "The Time of Your Life," "Another Part of the Forest," "Mousetrap," "House of Blue Leaves."

HEMSLEY, SHERMAN. Born Feb. 1, 1938 in Philadelphia. Attended Phila. Academy of Dramatic Arts. Debut 1968 OB in "The People vs. Ranchman," Bdwy 1970 in "Purlie."

HEMSLEY, WINSTON DeWITT. Born May 21, 1947 in Bklyn. Bdwy bow 1965 in "Golden Boy," followed by "A Joyful Noise," "Hallelujah, Baby," "Hello, Dolly!," OB in "Buy Bonds Buster."

HENDERSON, MELANIE. Born Sept. 20, 1957 in NYC. Debut 1970 in "The Me Nobody Knows."

HENRITZE, BETTE. Born May 3 in Betsy Layne, Ky. Graduate U. Tenn. OB in "Lion in Love," "Abe Lincoln in Illinois," "Othello," "Baal," "Long Christmas Dinner," "Queens of France," "Rimers of Eldritch," "Displaced Person," "Acquisition," "Crime of Passion," "Happiness Cage," NYSF's "Henry VI," "Richard III," "Older People," Bdwy in "Jenny Kissed Me," "Pictures in the Hallway," "Giants, Sons of Giants," "Ballad of a Sad Cafe," "The White House," "Dr. Cook's Garden," "Here's Where I Belong."

HENRY, MARTHA. Born Feb. 17, 1938 in Detroit, Mich. Graduate Carnegie Tech. Debut 1971 with LCRep's "Playboy of the Western World," "Scenes from American Life," "Antigone" for which she received a Theatre World Award, "Narrow Road to the Deep North," "Twelfth Night," and "The Crucible."

HEPPLE, JEANNE. Born in London; attended ULondon. Bdwy debut 1965 in "Inadmissable Evidence," followed by "A Touch of the Poet," "Tonight at 8:30," "Imaginary Invalid," NYSF's "Henry VI," and "Richard III," "How the Other Half Loves," "Night Watch," OB in "Sjt. Musgrave's Dance," "Early Morning," "Reliquary of Mr. and Mrs. Potterfield."

HERRMANN, EDWARD. Born July 21, 1943 in Washington, DC. Graduate Bucknell U., London AMDA. Debut 1970 OB in "Basic Training of Pavlo Hummel," Bdwy 1972 in "Moonchildren."

HEUMAN, BARBARA. Born Feb. 24, 1944 in Montrose, Pa. Graduate UWash. Debut 1970 OB in "Dames at Sea," Bdwy 1971 in "No, No, Nanette."

HEYMAN, BARTON. Born Jan. 24, 1937 in Washington, DC. Attended UCLA. OB 1967 in "A Midsummer Night's Dream," Bdwy debut 1969 in "Indians," followed by "Trial of Catonsville 9," "Sleep" (OB).

HICKEY, WILLIAM. Born in Bklyn. Studied at HB Studio. Bdwy bow 1951 in "St. Joan," followed by "Tovarich," "Miss Lonelyhearts," "Body Beautiful," "Make a Million," "Not Enough Rope," "Moonbirds," "Step on a Crack," OB in "On the Town," "Next," "Happy Birthday, Wanda June," "Small Craft Warnings."

HIGGINS, MICHAEL. Born Jan. 20, 1922 in Bklyn. Attended Manhattan Col., Theatre Wing. Bdwy bow 1946 in "Antigone," followed by "Our Lan'," "Romeo and Juliet," "The Crucible," "The Lark," OB in "White Devil," "Carefree Tree," "Easter," "The Queen and the Rebels," "Sally, George and Martha."

HIGH, BOLEN. Born Nov. 27, 1945 in Houston, Tex. Graduate U Denver, Goodman Theatre. Bdwy debut 1969 in "Henry V," OB in "Meeow!," "Intense Family."

HILL, RALSTON. Born Apr. 24, 1927 in Cleveland, O. Graduate Oberlin Col. OB in "The Changeling," "Streets of New York," "Valmouth," "Carousel," (LC'65) "Beggar's Opera," on Bdwy in "1776."

David Hooks   Ann Hodges   Douglas Houston   Illa Howe   Erik Howell

HINGLE, PAT. Born July 19, 1923 in Denver. Graduate Tex. U. Bdwy bow 1953 in "End As A Man," followed by "Festival," "Cat On A Hot Tin Roof," "Girls of Summer," "Dark At The Top of The Stairs," "J.B.," "Deadly Game," "Strange Interlude," "Blues For Mr. Charlie," "A Girl Could Get Lucky," "The Glass Menagerie," "Johnny No Trump," "The Price," "Child's Play," "The Selling of the President."

HINNANT, BILL. Born Aug. 28, 1935 on Chincoteague Island, Va. Yale graduate. Appeared in "No Time for Sergeants," followed by "Here's Love," "Frank Merriwell," OB in "All Kinds of Giants," "Put It in Writing," "You're A Good Man, Charlie Brown," "American Hamburger League," "God Bless Coney."

HODAPP, ANN. Born May 6, 1946 in Louisville, Ky. Attended Hunter, NYU. Debut OB 1968 in "You're A Good Man, Charlie Brown," followed by "A Round with Ring," "House of Leather," "Shoestring Revue" (ELT), "God Bless Coney."

HODGES, ANN. Born in Elizabethtown, Ky. Bdwy debut 1962 in "No Strings," followed by "The Rothschilds," OB in "Bella," "Boys from Syracuse."

HOFFMAN, JANE. Born July 24 in Seattle, Wash. Attended U. Cal. Bdwy debut 1940 in "Tis of Thee," followed by "Crazy with the Heat," "Something for the Boys," "One Touch of Venus," "Calico Wedding," "Mermaids Singing," "A Temporary Island," "Story for Strangers," "Two Blind Mice," "The Rose Tattoo," "The Crucible," "Witness for the Prosecution," "Third Best Sport," "Rhinoceros," "Mother Courage and Her Children," "Fair Game for Lovers," "A Murderer among Us," OB in "American Dream," "Sandbox," "Picnic on the Battlefield," "Theatre of The Absurd," "Child Buyer," "A Corner of The Bed," "Someone's Comin' Hungry," "Increased Difficulty of Concentration" (LC), "American Hamburger League," "Slow Memories." "Last Analysis."

HOLBROOK, HAL. Born Feb. 17, 1925 in Cleveland, O. Graduate Denison U. Bdwy bow 1961 in "Do You Know the Milky Way?," followed by "Glass Menagerie," "Mark Twain Tonight!," "Apple Tree," "I Never Sang for My Father," "Man of La Mancha," "Does a Tiger Wear a Necktie?," OB in "Henry IV" and "Richard II" (ASF), "Abe Lincoln in Illinois," LCRep's "Marco Millions," "Incident at Vichy," "Tartuffe," and "After the Fall," "Lake of the Woods."

HOLGATE, RONALD. Born May 26, 1937 in Aberdeen, S.D. Attended Northwestern U., New Eng. Cons. Debut 1961 OB in "Hobo," followed by "A Funny Thing Happened On The Way To The Forum," "Milk and Honey," "Hooray, It's A Glorious Day" (OB), "1776."

HOLLAND, ANTHONY. Born Oct. 17, 1933 in Brooklyn. Graduate U Chicago. OB in "Venice Preserved," "Second City," "Victim of Duty," "New Tenant," "Dynamite Tonight," "Quare Fellow," "White House Murder Case," "Waiting For Godot," on Bdwy in "My Mother, My Father and Me," "We Bombed in New Haven."

HOLLIDAY, DAVID. Born Aug. 4, 1937 in Illinois. Attended Carthage Col. After appearing in London, made Bdwy bow 1968 in "Man of La Mancha," followed by "Coco" for which he received a Theatre World Award, "Nevertheless, They Laugh" (OB).

HOOKS, DAVID. Born Jan. 9, 1920 in Smithfield, NC. Graduate UNC. Bdwy debut 1950 in "Pride's Crossing," followed by "Golden Apple," "Gideon," "Gantry," OB in "Ardele," "Antigone," "Zoo Story," "American Dream," "Corruption in the Palace of Justice," "Medea," APA's "Seagull," "Tavern," "School for Scandal," NYSF's "Antony and Cleopatra," and "Henry IV," "Small Craft Warnings."

HOREN, LEAH. Born June 22, 1942 in Philadelphia. Graduate Curtis Inst. Bdwy debut 1969 in "Celebration," followed by "No Strings" (ELT).

HORTON, CLAUDE. Born in London; attended Guildhall Sch. Bdwy debut 1938 in "Come Across," followed by "There Shall Be No Night," "Witness for the Prosecution," "Constant Wife," "Anne of the Thousand Days," "Rebecca," "A Call on Kuprin," "Not Now, Darling," "The Incomparable Max."

HOUSE, JANE. Born in 1946 in Panama City, Pan. Attended Stanford U. Bdwy debut 1971 in "Lenny."

HOUSTON, DOUGLAS. Born Aug. 13, 1946 in Coos Bay, Ore. Graduate UOre. Debut 1972 OB in "One for the Money."

HOWARD, ALAN. Born Mar. 21, 1951 in Rockville Centre, NY. Bdwy bow 1960 in "The Wall," followed by "Garden of Sweets," "A Gift of Time," "Playroom," OB in "King of the Whole Damn World," "Square in the Eye," "Titus Andronicus" (NYSF), "A Certain Young Man," "Whitsuntide."

HOWE, ILLA CAMERON. Born June 18, 1948 in Washington, DC. Graduate Northwestern U. Debut 1971 OB in "Middle of the Night" (ELT).

HOWELL, ERIK. Born in Dothan, Ala. Attended Wm. & Mary Col. Debut 1966 OB in "The Fantasticks," followed by "Who's Who, Baby?"

HOWELL, MARGARET. Born Sept. 9, 1947 in Raleigh, NC. Graduate UNC. Debut OB 1970 in "Dark of the Moon," followed by "Ride across Lake Constance" (LC).

HOWLAND, BETH. Born May 28, 1941 in Boston. Debut OB 1960 in "Once Upon A Mattress," followed by Bdwy in "Bye, Bye, Birdie," "High Spirits," "Drat! The Cat!," "Darling of the Day," "Company."

HUBBARD, ELIZABETH. Born Dec. 22 in NYC. Graduate Radcliffe Col., RADA. Bdwy debut 1960 in "The Affair," followed by "The Passion of Josef D," "The Physicists," "A Time for Singing," "A Day in the Death of Joe Egg," "Children, Children," OB in "Threepenny Opera," "Boys from Syracuse."

HUFFMAN, DAVID. Born May 10, 1945 in Berwin, Ill. Bdwy debut 1971 in "Butterflies Are Free," followed by OB's "Small Craft Warnings."

Barnard Hughes   Leonard Jackson   Jim Jacobs   Dorothy Dorian James   William Jay

HUGHES, BARNARD. Born July 16, 1915 in Bedford Hills, N.Y. Attended Manhattan Col. OB in "Rosmersholm," "A Doll's House," "Hogan's Goat," "Line," "Older People," "Hamlet" (NYSF), on Bdwy in "The Ivy Green," "Dinosaur Wharf," "Teahouse of The August Moon" (CC'56), "A Majority of One," "Advise and Consent," "The Advocate," "Hamlet," "I Was Dancing," "Generation," "How Now, Dow Jones?," "Wrong Way Light Bulb," "Sheep On The Runway," "Abelard and Heloise."

HUGHES, TRESA. Born Sept. 17, 1929 in Washington, DC. Attended Wayne U. OB in "Electra," "The Crucible," "Hogan's Goat," "Party On Greenwich Avenue," "Fragments," "Passing Through from Exotic Places," "Beggar On Horseback" (LC), "Early Morning," on Bdwy in "Miracle Worker," "Devil's Advocate," "Dear Me, The Sky Is Falling," "Last Analysis," "Spofford," "Man In The Glass Booth," "Prisoner of Second Avenue."

HUNT, CARL. Born June 21, 1941 in Boston. Graduate U Minn., Temple U. Debut OB 1971 in "The House of Blue Leaves."

HUSMANN, RON. Born June 30, 1937 in Rockford, Ill. Attended Northwestern, On Bdwy in "Fiorello!" "Greenwillow," "Tenderloin" for which he received a Theatre World Award, "All American," "Lovely Ladies, Kind Gentlemen," "Look Where I'm At" (OB). "On the Town."

HYMAN, ELAINE. Born in Detroit. Columbia Graduate. Bdwy debut 1962 in "General Seeger," followed by "Say Darling," OB in "Javelin," "Night of the Dunce," "What the Butler Saw," "Children, Children."

ING, ALVIN. Born May 26, 1938 in Honolulu. Columbia Graduate. Bdwy debut 1959 in "World of Suzie Wong," OB in "Tenth of an Inch," "Cranes and Peonies," "Coffins for Butterflies," "Six."

IRVING, GEORGE S. Born Nov. 1, 1922 in Springfield, Mass. Attended Leland Powers Sch. Bdwy bow 1943 in "Oklahoma!," followed by "Call Me Mister," "Along Fifth Avenue," "Two's Company," "Me and Juliet," "Can-Can," "Shinbone Alley," "Bells Are Ringing," "The Good Soup," "Tovarich," "A Murderer Among Us," "Alfie," "Anya," "Galileo" (LC), "The Happy Time," "Up Eden" (OB), "4 on a Garden," "An Evening with Richard Nixon and . . ."

IVES, ANNE. Born in Providence, RI. Attended Sargent's School, Am. Th. Wing. Bdwy debut 1906 in "The Chorus Lady," after many years in London returned in 1952 to Bdwy in "Point of No Return," followed by "Masquerade," "The Crucible" (OB), "Effect of Gamma Rays on Man-in-the-Moon Marigolds," (OB), "Good Woman of Setzuan" (LC).

JACKSON, ANNE. Born Sept. 3, 1926 in Allegheny, Pa. Attended Neighborhood Playhouse, Actors Studio. Bdwy debut 1945 in "Signature," followed by "Yellow Jack," "John Gabriel Borkman," "Last Dance," "Summer and Smoke," "Magnolia Alley," "Love Me Long," "Lady from the Sea," "Never Say Never," "Oh, Men! Oh, Women!" "Rhinoceros," "Luv," "The Exercise," "Inquest," "Promenade, All!," OB in "Brecht on Brecht," "The Tiger" and "The Typists."

JACKSON, LEONARD. (formerly L. Errol Jaye) Born Feb. 7, 1928 in Jacksonville, Fla. Graduate Fisk U. Debut 1965 OB in "Troilus and Cressida" (NYSF), followed by "Henry V," "Happy Ending," "Day of Absence," "Who's Got His Own?," "Electronic Nigger and Others," "Black Quartet," "Five on the Blackhand Side," "Boesman and Lena," "Murderous Angels," "Chickencoop Chinaman," Bdwy bow in 1968 in "Great White Hope," "Lost in the Stars."

JACKSON, MARY. Born Nov. 22, 1915 in Milford, Mich. Graduate Western Col. Bdwy debut 1944 in "Kiss and Tell," followed by "Eastward in Eden," "Flowering Cherry," "Trial of Catonsville 9" (OB).

JACOBI, LOU. Born Dec. 28, 1913 in Toronto, Can. Bdwy bow 1955 in "Diary of Anne Frank," followed by "The Tenth Man," "Come Blow Your Horn," "Fade Out-Fade In," "Don't Drink the Water," "A Way of Life," "Norman, Is That You?," "Unlikely Heroes."

JACOBS, JIM. Born Oct. 7, 1942 in Chicago. Attended Chi. City Col. Bdwy debut 1971 in "No Place to Be Somebody."

JAMES, DOROTHY DORIAN. Born in Conn; attended Northwestern U. Debut 1960 OB in "The Lady's Not for Burning," followed by "River Line," "Mercy Street," on Bdwy in "Hostile Witness," "Man for All Seasons," "An Evening with Richard Nixon and . . ."

JARRETT, JERRY. Born Sept. 9, 1918 in Brooklyn. Attended New Theatre School. OB in "Waiting for Lefty." "Nat Turner," "Me Candido," "That 5 A.M. Jazz," Bdwy bow 1948 in "At War with the Army," followed by "Gentlemen Prefer Blondes," "Stalag 17," "Fiorello," "Fiddler on the Roof."

JAY, DAVID. Born June 4, 1961 in Worcester, Mass. Debut OB 1971 in "Waiting for Godot," Bdwy 1972 "Lost in the Stars."

JAY, WILLIAM Born May 15, 1935 in Baxter Springs, Kan. Attended Omaha U. Debut OB 1963 in "Utopia," followed by "The Blacks," "Loop The Loop," "Happy Ending," "Day of Absence," "Hamlet" and "Othello" (CP), "Song of The Lusitanian Bogey", "Ceremonies In Dark Old Men," "Man Better Man," "The Harangues," "Brotherhood," "Perry's Mission," "Rosalee Pritchett," "Sister Sadie."

JENS, SALOME. Born May 8, 1935 in Milwaukee, Wisc. Bdwy debut 1956 in "Sixth Finger in a Five-Finger Glove," followed by "The Disenchanted," "A Far Country," "Night Life," "I'm Solomon," "A Patriot for Me," OB in "Bald Soprano," "Jack," "Deidre of the Sorrows," "USA," "Balcony," "Desire under the Elms," "Posterity for Sale," "Moon for the Misbegotten," "LCRep's" "After the Fall," "But for Whom Charlie," "Tartuffe," "Mary Stuart," and "Ride across Lake Constance."

JENSEN, STERLING Born Mar. 15, 1925 in San Diego, Cal. Bdwy debut 1955 in "Desk Set," followed OB by "Mime Theatre," "The Father," "The Miser," "Peleas and Melisande," "The Bond," "King Lear," "Journey's End," "Dance of Death," "Trumpets and Drums," "Macbeth," "Oedipus," "Lady from Maxim's," "Uncle Vanya," "Master Builder," "Taming of the Shrew."

Page Johnson

Onni Johnson

James Earl Jones

Jane A. Johnston

James Karen

JETHRO, PHIL. Born Sept. 10, 1947 in Minneapolis, Minn. Attended UCLA. Bdwy debut 1971 in "Jesus Christ Superstar."

JOHANN, JOHN. Born Dec. 23, 1942 in Madison, Wisc. Attended LA State Col. Debut 1966 in "Autumn's Here," followed by "My Fair Lady" (CC), "Me and Juliet" (ELT), Bdwy in "Come Summer," "Follies."

JOHNS, CLAY. Born June 6, 1934 in Lima, O. Off Bdwy in "Tiger at the Gates," "The Disenchanted," "Under the Gaslight," "The Queen and the Rebels," "The Drunkard," "Johnny Johnson," "They Don't Make 'em like that Anymore."

JOHNSON, ONNI. Born Mar. 16, 1949 in NYC. Graduate Brandeis U. Debut 1964 in "Unfinished Business," followed by "She Stoops to Conquer," "22 Years," Bdwy bow 1971 in "Oh! Calcutta!"

JOHNSON, PAGE. Born Aug. 25, 1930 in Welch, W.Va. Graduate Ithaca Col. Bdwy bow 1951 in DeHavilland's "Romeo and Juliet," followed by "Electra," "Oedipus," "Camino Real," "In April Once" for which he received a Theatre World Award, "Red Roses for Me," "The Lovers," OB in "Military Taps," "The Enchanted," "Guitar," " 4 in 1," "Journey of the Fifth Horse," "Yucca Trail," "Ruby's Revenge," APA's "School for Scandal," "The Tavern" and "The Seagull," "Odd Couple," "Boys In The Band."

JOHNSTON, JANE A. Born Aug. 4, 1934 in Akron, O. Attended Briarcliff, Theatre Wing, Neighborhood Playhouse. Bdwy debut 1956 in "Happy Hunting," followed by "Company," CC's "Wonderful Town" and "The Cradle Will Rock," OB in "Billy Barnes Revue," "Greenwich Village USA."

JOHNSTON, JUSTINE. Born June 13 in Evanston, Ill. OB in "Little Mary Sunshine," "The Time of Your Life" (LC), on Bdwy in "Pajama Game," "Milk and Honey," "Follies."

JONES, CHARLOTTE. Born Jan. 1 in Chicago. Attended Loyola, DePaul U. OB in "False Confessions," "Sign of Jonah," "Girl on the Via Flaminia," "Red Roses for Me," "Night Is Black Bottles," "Camino Real," "Plays for Bleecker St.," "Pigeons," "Great Scot!" "Sjt. Musgrave's Dance," "Papers," "Johnny Johnson," on Bdwy in "Camino Real," "Buttrio Square," "Mame," "How Now Dow Jones."

JONES, JAMES EARL. Born Jan. 17, 1931 in Arkabutla, Miss. Graduate Mich U. OB in "The Pretender," "The Blacks," "Clandestine on the Morning Line," "The Apple," "A Midsummer Night's Dream," "Moon on a Rainbow Shawl" for which he received a Theatre World Award. "PS 193," "Last Minstrel," "Love Nest," "Bloodknot," "Othello," "Baal," "Danton's Death" (LC), "Boesman and Lena," "Hamlet" (NYSF) on Bdwy in "The Egghead," "Sunrise at Campobello," "The Cool World," "A Hand is on the Gate," "Great White Hope," "Les Blancs."

JONES, LAUREN. Born Sept. 7 in Boston. Bdwy debut 1964 in "Ben Franklin in Paris," followed by "Skyscraper," "Does a Tiger Wear a Necktie?" for which she received a Theatre World Award, "Ain't Supposed to Die a Natural Death," "Wise Child," OB in "Ballad of Bimshire," "Trials of Brother Jero," "Ballet behind the Bridge."

JONES, NEIL. Born May 6, 1942 in Boston. Attended Boston Cons. On Bdwy in "The Music Man," "Hello, Dolly!," "Promises, Promises."

JOYCE, ELAINE. Born Dec. 19, 1945 in Cleveland, O. Attended UCLA. Bdwy debut 1972 in "Sugar" for which she received a Theatre World Award.

JULIA, RAUL. Born Mar. 9, 1940 in San Juan, PR. Graduate UPR. OB in "Macbeth" "Titus Andronicus" (CP), "Theatre in the Streets," "Life Is a Dream" "Blood Wedding," "Ox Cart," "No Exit," "Memorandum," "Frank Gagliano's City Scene," "Your Own Thing," "Persians," "Castro Complex," "Pinkville," "Hamlet" (NYSF), Bdwy bow 1968 in "The Cuban Thing," followed by "Indians," "Two Gentlemen of Verona."

KAHL, HOWARD. Born Sept. 17, 1930 in New Albany, Ind. Graduate Ind. U. Bdwy bow 1962 in "Camelot," followed by "Hot Spot," "Fade Out-Fade In," "Pleasure and Palaces," "Anya," "On A Clear Day You Can See Forever," "Cabaret," "Applause."

KAHN, MADELINE. Born Sept. 29, 1942 in Boston. Graduate Hofstra U. Bdwy in "New Faces of 1968," followed by "Promenade" (OB), "2 by 2."

KAPLAN, JEANNE. Born in Bklyn. Bdwy debut 1968 in "The Cuban Thing," OB in "A View from the Bridge," "Ox Cart," "Electronic Nigger," "Rome, Rome."

KAREN, JAMES. Born Nov. 28, 1923 in Wilkes-Barre, Pa. Attended Neighborhood Playhouse. Bdwy bow 1948 in "Streetcar Named Desire," followed by "Enemy of the People," "Third Best Sport," "A Cook for Mr. General," "Who's Afraid of Virginia Woolf?," "Tiny Alice," "Cactus Flower," "Birthday Party," "Everything in the Garden," "Only Game in Town," "Time of Storm"(OB), "Engagement Baby," "Country Girl."

KARIN, RITA. Born Oct. 24, 1919 in Warsaw, Poland. Bdwy debut 1960 in "The Wall," followed by "A Call on Kuprin," "Penny Wars," OB in "Pocket Watch," "Scuba Duba," "House of Blue Leaves."

KARM, MICHAEL. Born Oct. 24, 1941 in Chicago. Attended U Ill. NY bow 1963 OB in "Best Foot Forward," followed by "South Pacific" (CC), "How to Succeed . . ." (CC), "South Pacific" (LC), "Mad Show" (OB), "Salvation" (OB), Bdwy debut 1970 in "Two by Two."

KARR, PATTI. Born July 10 in St. Paul, Minn. Attended TCU. On Bdwy in "Maggie," "Carnival in Flanders," "Pipe Dream," "Bells Are Ringing," "New Girl in Town," "Body Beautiful," "Bye Bye Birdie," "New Faces of 1962," "Come on Strong," "Look to the Lilies," "Different Times," OB in "A Month of Sundays," "Up Eden."

KASON, CORINNE. Born Mar. 10 in San Francisco. Attended San Jose State Col. Debut 1968 OB in "Futz" followed by "By Jupiter," "Unfair to Goliath," Bdwy bow 1969 in "Fiddler on the Roof."

Laura Kenyon

Alan Kass

Elaine Kerr

Walter Klavun

Sally Kirkland

KASS, ALAN. Born Apr. 23, 1928 in Chicago. Graduate CCNY. Bdwy bow 1968 in "Golden Rainbow," followed by "Sugar," OB in "Guitar."

KAVANAUGH, DORRIE. Born July 12, Attended Tulane U. Graduate Neighborhood Playhouse. Bdwy debut 1969 in "Fire," OB in "Saved," "Soft Core," "Sleep."

KAYE, DANNY. Born Jan. 18, 1913 in Bklyn. Bdwy debut 1939 in "Left of Broadway," followed by "Straw Hat Revue," "Lady in the Dark," "Let's Face It," "Two by Two."

KEACH, STACY. Born June 2, 1941 in Savannah, Ga. Graduate U.Cal. Yale, London Acad. OB in "MacBird," "Niggerlovers," "Henry IV" (CP), LCRep's "Country Wife," "King Lear," "Peer Gynt" (CP), "Long Day's Journey into Night," "Hamlet" (NYSF), Bdwy debut in "Indians" (1969).

KEELER, RUBY. Born Aug. 25, 1910 in Halifax, N.S., Can. Bdwy debut 1923 in "The Rise of Rosie O'Reilly," followed by "Show Girl," "Bye Bye, Bonnie," "Lucky," "Sidewalks of New York" "Hold on to Your Hats," films, retirement, and "No, No, Nanette" in 1970.

KEES, JOHN DAVID. Born in Brookhaven, Miss. Graduate La. State U., Columbia. Debut 1972 OB in "Small Craft Warnings."

KEITH, LAWRENCE. Born Mar. 4, 1931 in Bklyn. Graduate Bklyn Col., Ind.U. Bdwy debut 1960 in "My Fair Lady," followed by "High Spirits," "I Had a Ball," "Best Laid Plans," "Mother Lover," OB in "The Homecoming."

KELLOGG, RILEY. Born May 5, 1961 in NYC. Debut 1972 OB in "And They Put Handcuffs on the Flowers."

KELLY, PATSY. Born Jan. 12, 1910 in Bklyn. Bdwy debut 1928 in "Three Cheers," followed by "Earl Carroll's Sketch Book," "Vanities," "Wonder Bar," "Flying Colors," long career in films, "Dear Charles," "No, No, Nanette."

KELTON, GENE. Born Oct. 21, 1938 in Flagstaff, Ariz. Appeared in "Once upon a Mattress," "Destry Rides Again," "Subways Are for Sleeping," "Here's Love," "Fade Out-Fade In," "Skyscraper," "Mame," "Dear World," "Applause."

KENYON, LAURA. Born Nov. 23, 1947 in Chicago. Graduate USCal. Bdwy debut 1969 in "Man of La Mancha," followed by "On the Town," OB in "Peace."

KERCHEVAL, KEN. Born July 15, 1935 in Indiana. Attended Pacific U., Neighborhood Playhouse. OB in "Dead End," "Young Abe Lincoln," "Black Monday," "A Man's a Man," "23 Pat O'Brien Movies," "Father Uxbridge Wants to Marry," "Horseman, Pass By," "Who's Happy Now?," on Bdwy in "Something about a Soldier," "Fiddler on the Roof," "Happily Never After," "The Apple Tree," "Cabaret," "Father's Day."

KERR, ELAINE. Born Apr. 20, 1942 in Indianapolis, Ind. Graduate Ind.U. Bdwy debut 1971 in "No Place to Be Somebody," followed by "Night Watch," OB in "Trojan Women."

KERT, LARRY. Born Dec. 5, 1934 in Los Angeles. Attended LACC. Bdwy bow 1953 in "John Murray Anderson's Almanac," followed by "Ziegfeld Follies," "Mr. Wonderful," "Walk Tall," "Look Ma, I'm Dancin'," "Tickets, Please," "West Side Story," "A Family Affair," "Breakfast at Tiffany's," "Cabaret," "La Strada," "Company."

KILEY, RICHARD. Born Mar. 31, 1922 in Chicago. Attended Loyola U. Bdwy debut 1953 in "Misalliance" for which he received a Theatre World Award, followed by "Kismet,'" "Sing Me No Lullaby," "Time Limit!" "Redhead," "Advise and Consent," "No Strings," "Here's Love," "I Had a Ball," "Man of La Mancha" (also LC), "Her First Roman," "The Incomparable Max," "Voices."

KIM, CHRISTAL. Born Sept. 25, 1916 in Kalamazoo, Mich. Attended Professional Children's School, NYC. Bdwy debut 1953 in "Teahouse of the August Moon," followed by "Basic Training of Pavlo Hummel"(OB).

KIMBROUGH, CHARLES. Born May 23, 1936 in St. Paul, Minn. Graduate Ind. U., Yale. OB in "All in Love," "Struts and Frets," Bdwy bow 1969 in "Cop-Out," followed by "Company."

KIMMINS, KENNETH. Born Sept. 4, 1941 in Bklyn. Graduate Catholic U. Debut 1966 OB in "The Fantasticks," followed by "Adaptation," Bdwy "Fig Leaves Are Falling" (1969), "Gingerbread Lady," "Company."

KING, JOHN MICHAEL. Born May 13, 1926 in NYC. Attended AADA. Bdwy debut 1951 in "Courtin' Time," followed by "Music in the Air," "Of Thee I Sing," "Buttrio Square," "Me and Juliet," "Ankles Aweigh," "Hit the Trail," "Fanny," "My Fair Lady" for which he received a Theatre World Award, "Anya," "On a Clear Day You Can See Forever," OB "Have I Got One for You," "Sound of Music" (JB).

KING, ROBERT. Born June 15, 1936 in NYC. Graduate Juilliard. Bdwy debut 1972 in "An Evening with Richard Nixon . . ."

KIRKLAND, SALLY. Born Oct. 31, 1944. Member Actors Studio. Bdwy debut 1961 in "Step on a Crack," followed by "Bicycle Ride to Nevada," "Marathon '33," OB in "Midsummer Night's Dream," "Fitz," "Bitch of Waverly Place," "Tom Paine," "Futz," "Sweet Eros," "Witness," "One Night Stands of a Noisy Passenger," "Justice Box," "Delicate Champions," "Where Has Tommy Flowers Gone?," "Chickencoop Chinaman."

KISER, TERRY. Born Aug. 1, 1939 in Omaha, Neb. Graduate U. Kan. Debut 1966 OB in "Night of The Dance," followed by "Fortune and Men's Eyes" for which he received a Theatre World Award, "Horseman, Pass By," "Frank Gagliano's City Scene," "The Ofay Watcher," "Castro Complex," "In Case of Accident," Bdwy debut 1970 in "Paris Is Out."

KLAVUN, WALTER. Born May 8, 1906 in NYC. Yale graduate. Bdwy debut 1928 in "Say When," followed by "No More Ladies," "Arms for Venus," "Annie Get Your Gun," "Twelfth Night," "Dream Girl," "Auntie Mame," "Say, Darling," "Desert Incident," "How to Succeed in Business . . . ," "What Makes Sammy Run," "Twigs," OB in "Mornings at 7," "Dandy Dick."

rene Frances Kling   Richard Kline   Judy Knaiz   William Knight   Elaine Kussack

KLINE, RICHARD. Born Apr. 29, 1944 in NYC. Graduate Queen's Col., Northwestern U. Debut 1971 in LCRep's "Mary Stuart," "Narrow Road to the Deep North," "Twelfth Night," "The Crucible."

KLING, IRENE FRANCES. Born Mar. 25, 1947 in Bklyn. Graduate NYU, AADA. Debut 1966 OB in "Miss Julie," followed by "The Stronger," "Death of Bessie Smith," "Don Juan in Hell," "Hands of God," "Beggar's Opera."

KNAIZ, JUDY. Born Nov. 7, 1940 in Pittsburgh, Pa. Attended Pittsburgh Playhouse. Debut 1967 OB in "Shoemaker's Holiday," followed by "Arabian Nights," "Dames at Sea," "Now Is the Time for All Good Men" (ELT), "That's Entertainment."

KNIGHT, WILLIAM. Born Dec. 6, 1934 in Los Angeles. Graduate LACC. debut 1970 in "Oh! Calcutta!", followed by "An Evening with Richard Nixon and . . ."

KOLAS, MARY LYNN. Born Sept. 13, 1950 in East Chicago, Ill. Attended Chicago Cons., Northwestern U. Debut 1971 OB in "Look Me Up."

KROSS, RONALD. Born Feb. 24, 1936 in Nanticoke, Pa. Graduate Wilkes Col., Penn. State. Bdwy debut 1969 in "1776."

KUHNER, JOHN. Born Dec. 27, 1942 in Cleveland, O. Graduate Denison U. Debut 1968 OB in "Your Own Thing," followed by "House of Leather," "Tarot," "Wanted."

KUPPERMAN, ALVIN. Born Oct. 14, 1945 in Brooklyn. Graduate Emerson Col. OB in "If We Grow Up," Bdwy debut 1970 in "Minnie's Boys," "A Dream Out of Time" (OB), "Unlikely Heroes."

KURTZ, SWOOSIE. Born Sept. 6, 1944 in Omaha, Nebr. Attended USCal. London Acad. Debut OB 1968 in "The Firebugs," followed by "The Effect of Gamma Rays on Man-in-the-moon Marigolds."

KUSSACK, ELAINE. Born Dec. 30 in Brooklyn. Graduate Hunter, Col., Columbia. Bdwy debut 1969 in "Fiddler on the Roof."

LACY, TOM. Born Aug. 30, 1933 in NYC. Debut OB 1965 in "The Fourth Pig," followed by "Fantasticks," "Shoemaker's Holiday," "Love and Let Love," "Millionairess," "Crimes of Passion," "The Real Inspector Hound."

LAMONT, ROBIN. Born June 2, 1950 in Boston, Attended Carnegie-Mellon U. Debut OB 1971 in "Godspell."

LAMOS, MARK. Born Mar. 10, 1946 in Chicago. Attended Northwestern U. Bdwy debut 1972 in "The Love Suicide at Schofield Barracks."

LaMOTTA, JOHNNY. Born Jan. 8, 1939 in Bklyn. Bdwy bow 1967 in "Illya, Darling," followed by "I'm Solomon," "Zorba," OB in "Dead Survivors," "God Bless Coney."

LAMPERT, ZOHRA. Born May 13, 1936 in NYC. Attended Chicago U. Bdwy debut 1956 in "Major Barbara," followed by "Maybe Tuesday," "Look, We've Come Through," "First Love," "Mother Courage," "Nathan Weinstein, Mystic, Conn." "Lovers and Other Strangers," "The Sign in Sidney Brustein's Window," OB in "Venus Observed," "Diary of a Scoundrel," LCRep's "After the Fall" and "Marco Millions."

LANDIS, JEANETTE. Born Apr. 4, in Eng. Studied at Ntl. Theatre. Bdwy debut 1966 in "Marat/de Sade," followed by "There's One in Every Marriage," "Elizabeth I."

LANNING, JERRY. Born May 17, 1943 in Miami, Fla. Graduate USCal. Bdwy debut 1966 in "Mame" for which he received a Theatre World Award, followed by "1776," OB in "Memphis Store Bought Teeth."

LARKIN, DONALD B. Born Apr. 13, 1943 in The Bronx. Studied at HB Studio. OB in "The Victim," "The Form," "Cry in the Streets," "Eros and Psyche," "James Joyce Memorial Liquid Theatre."

LARSEN, WILLIAM. Born Nov. 20, 1927 in Lake Charles, La. Attended UTex. On Bdwy in "Ballad of the Sad Cafe," "Half a Sixpence," "Funny Girl," "Halfway up a Tree," "There's a Girl in My Soup," "Dear World," OB in "The Crucible," "Fantasticks," "Legend of Lovers," "Twelfth Night," APA's "Tavern," "Lower Depths," and "School for Scandal," "Troilus and Cressida," "Murderous Angels."

LARSON, PHILIP. Born Feb. 10, 1942 in Grand Island, Neb. Graduate UNeb., UIowa. Debut 1971 OB in "Nightride."

LAUGHLIN, SHARON Graduate U. Wash., Bdwy debut 1964 in "One by One," OB in "Henry IV" (NYSF), "Huui, Huui," "Mod Donna," "Subject to Fits," "Murderous Angels."

LaVALLEE, BILL. Born June 13, 1943 in Baton Rouge, La. Attended LSU. Debut OB 1968 in "Redhead," followed by "God Bless You, Harold Fineberg," "Shoestring Revue" (ELT), "The Web."

LAVIZZO, VALCOUR. Born Sept. 7, 1953 in Atlanta, Ga. Attended AADA, HB Studio. Debut 1971 OB in "The Screens," followed by "Kaddish," "Rain."

LAWRENCE, DELPHI. Born Mar. 23, 1932 in London. Attended RADA. Debut 1972 OB in "The Divorce of Judy and Jane," followed by "Dylan."

LAWRIE, TED. Born May 22, 1923 in NYC. Attended Columbia. Bdwy debut 1948 in "Ballet Ballads," followed by "Follies," OB in "Jacques Brel Is Alive . . ."

LAWSON, LEE. Born Oct. 14, 1941 in NYC. Attended Bost U. Columbia. OB in "Firebugs," "The Knack," "Birthday Party" (LC), "Scenes from American Life" (LC), Bdwy bow 1966 in "Agatha Sue, I Love You," followed by "Cactus Flower," "My Daughter, Your Son," "Suggs" (LC).

LEBOWSKY, STANLEY. Born Nov. 29, 1926 in Minneapolis, Minn. Graduate UCLA. Bdwy debut 1959 in "Whoop-Up," followed by "Irma La Douce," "Family Affair," "Tovarich," "Half a Sixpence," "Breakfast at Tiffany's," "Gantry," "Ari," "Jesus Christ Superstar."

LeCLAIR, HENRY. Born July 27 in Cranston, RI. On Bdwy in "Flora, The Red Menace," "A Time For Singing," "Wonderful Town" (CC'67), "1776."

LeMASSENA, WILLIAM. Born May 23, 1916 in Glen Ridge, NJ. Attended NYU. Bdwy bow 1940 in "Taming of the Shrew," followed by "There Shall Be No Night," "The Pirate," "Hamlet," "Call Me Mister," "Inside USA," "I Know, My Love," "Dream Girl," "Nina," "Ondine," "Fallen Angels," "Redhead," "Conquering Hero," "Beauty Part," "Come Summer," "Grin and Bare it," OB in "The Coop," CC's "Brigadoon" and "Life with Father," "F. Jasmine Addams."

Joseph Leon

Zoya Leporska

LeRoy Lessane

Renee Lippin

Bill Linton

LeNOIRE, ROSETTA. Born Aug. 8, 1911 in NYC. Attended Theatre Wing. Bdwy debut 1936 in "Macbeth," followed by "Bassa Moona," "Hot Mikado," "Marching with Johnny," "Janie," "Decision," "Three's a Family," "Destry Rides Again," "Finian's Rainbow," "South Pacific," "Sophie," "Tambourines to Glory," "Blues for Mr. Charlie," "Great Indoors," "Show Boat" (LC), "Lost in the Stars," "A Cry of Players" (LC), OB in "Bible Salesman," "Double Entry," "Clandestine on the Morning Line," "Cabin in the Sky."

LENS, PATRICIA. Born May 3, 1947 in Philadelphia. Attended Northwestern U. Bdwy debut 1969 in "Celebration," followed by "Man of LaMancha."

LEON, GEOFF. Born in Long Beach, Cal. Graduate UCal. Bdwy debut 1970 in "Georgy," OB in "Gertrude Stein's First Reader," "One for the Money."

LEON, JOSEPH. Born June 8, 1923 in NYC. Attended NYU, CCNY, UCLA, UNev. Bdwy debut 1950 in "Bell, Book and Candle," followed by "Seven Year Itch," "Pipedream," "Fair Game," "Gazebo," "Julia, Jake and Uncle Joe," "Beauty Part," "Merry Widow," "Henry Sweet Henry," "Jimmy Shine," OB in "Come Share My House," "Dark Corners," "Interrogation of Havana."

LEONTOVICH, EUGENIE. Born in Moscow in 1894. Bdwy debut 1928 in "And So to Bed," followed by "Grand Hotel," "Twentieth Century," "Dark Eyes," "Obsession," "Anastasia," "Cave Dwellers," OB in "Anna K."

LEPORSKA, ZOYA. Born Dec. 19, 1920 in Siberia. Bdwy debut 1953 in "Pajama Game," followed by "Damn Yankees," "New Girl in Town," "Sound of Music," "Bravo Giovanni," "On the Town."

LeROUX, MADELEINE. Born May 28, 1946 in Laramie, Wyo. Graduate UCape Town. Debut OB 1969 in "The Moondreamers," followed by "Dirtiest Show in Town," "Rain."

LeROY, KEN. Born Aug. 17, 1927 in Detroit. Attended Neighborhood Playhouse. On Bdwy in "The American Way," "Morning Star," "Anne of England," "Oklahoma!," "Carousel," "Brigadoon," "Call Me Madam," "Pajama Game," "West Side Story," "Fiddler on the Roof."

LESSANE, LEROY. Born Aug. 5, 1942 in NYC. Debut 1970 OB in "Gandhi," followed by "Snowbound King," "Ballad of Johnny Pot," "A Man Is a Man," Bdwy 1972 in "Capt. Brassbound's Conversion."

LESTER, BARBARA. Born Dec. 27, 1928 in London. Graduate Columbia U. Bdwy debut 1956 in "Protective Custody," followed by "Legend of Lizzie," "Luther," "Inadmissible Evidence," "Johnny No-Trump," "Grin and Bare It," OB in "Electra," "Queen after Death," "Summer of the 17th Doll," "Richard II" and "Much Ado About Nothing" (NYSF), "One Way Pendulum," "Abelard and Heloise," "There's One in Every Marriage."

LEVERIDGE, LYNN ANN. Born Mar. 16, 1948 in NYC. Attended Hofstra U. Debut 1970 in "Saved," followed by "Beggar's Opera."

LEVI, BARUK. Born June 14, 1947 in Bklyn. Graduate Bklyn Col. Debut 1972 OB in "And They Put Handcuffs on the Flowers."

LEWIS, GILBERT. Born Apr. 6, 1941 in Philadelphia. Attended Morgan State Col. Bdwy bow 1969 in "Great White Hope," OB in "Who's Got His Own," "Transfers," "Ballet behind the Bridge."

LEWIS, MARCIA. Born Aug. 18, 1938 in Melrose, Mass. Attended UCinn. OB in "Impudent Wolf," "Who's Who, Baby?," "The Time of Your Life" (LC), "God Bless Coney," Bdwy debut in "Hello, Dolly!"

LEYDEN, LEO. Born Jan. 28 1929 in Dublin, Ire. Attended Abbey Theatre School. Bdwy debut 1960 in "Love and Libel," followed by "Darling of the Day," "The Mundy Scheme," "The Rothschilds." "Capt. Brassbound's Conversion."

LIBERTO, DON. Born June 10, 1915 in Pittsburgh, Pa. Bdwy debut 1936 in "Babes in Arms," followed by "DuBarry Was a Lady," "By Jupiter," "Jackpot," "Annie Get Your Gun," "Look, Ma, I'm Dancin'," OB in "Look Me Up."

LIGON, TOM. Born Sept. 10, 1945 in New Orleans, La. Bdwy debut 1969 in "Angela," followed by "Love Is a Time of Day," OB in "Your Own Thing," "A Place Without Mornings," "God Says There Is No Peter Ott."

LINDEN, HAL. Born Mar. 20, 1931 in NYC. Attended CCNY, Am. The. Wing. On Bdwy in "Strip for Action." "Bells Are Ringing," "Wildcat," "Subways Are for Sleeping," "Anything Goes" (OB), "Something More," "Apple Tree," "Education of Hyman Kaplan," "The Rothschilds," "The Sign in Sidney Brustein's Window."

LINDSAY, KEVIN-JOHN. Born Sept. 7, 1957 in NYC. Debut 1970 in "The Me Nobody Knows."

LINDSTROM, CARL. Born Dec. 9, 1938 in Portland, Ore. Bdwy debut 1972 in "A Funny Thing Happened on the Way to the Forum."

LINN, MARGARET. Born Aug. 21, 1934 in Richmond, Ind. Attended Northwestern U., Denver U. OB in "Pale Horse Pale Rider," "The Room," "Billy Liar," "Huui, Huui," "Disintegration of James Cherry" (LC), "House of Blue Leaves," on Bdwy in "How's the World Treating You?," "Halfway Up the Tree," "Ring Round the Bathtub."

LINTON, WILLIAM. Born Dec. 16, 1935 in Edinburgh, Scot. Attended Pasadena Playhouse. Bdwy debut 1960 in "Beg, Borrow or Steal," followed by "Wildcat," "Family Affair," "DuBarry Was a Lady" (ELT).

LiPARI, MARJORIE. Born June 1, 1945 in Brooklyn, Bdwy debut 1968 in "Hair."

LIPPIN, RENEE. Born July 26, 1946 in NYC. Graduate Adlephi U. Debut 1970 OB in "The Way It Is," Bdwy bow 1971 in "Fun City."

LIPSON, CLIFFORD. Born Feb. 10, 1947 in Providence, RI. Attended Neighborhood Playhouse, AMDA. OB in "Great Scot!," "Hooray, It's A Glorious Day," "The Indian Wants the Bronx," "Salvation," Bdwy bow 1970 in "Hair," followed by "Jesus Christ Superstar."

LIPSON, PAUL. Born Dec. 23, 1913 in Brooklyn. Attended Ohio State, Theatre Wing. Bdwy bow 1942 in "Lily of the Valley," followed by "Heads or Tails," "Detective Story," "Remains to Be Seen," "Carnival in Flanders," "I've Got Sixpence," "The Vamp," "Bells Are Ringing," "Fiorello" (CC), "Sound of Music," "Fiddler on the Roof."

245

Peter Lombard   Peggy Longo   Rod Loomis   Debra Lyman   Alvin Lum

LIPTON, MICHAEL. Born Apr. 27, 1925 in NYC. Attended Queen's Col. Appeared in "Caesar and Cleopatra," "Moon Is Blue," "Sing Me No Lullaby," "Wake Up, Darling," "Tenth Man," "Separate Tables," "Inquest," OB in "Lover," "Trigon," "Long Christmas Dinner," "Hamp," "Boys in the Band," "Justice Box."

LISA, LUBA. Born in Bklyn. Attended Theatre Wing. Bdwy debut 1961 in "Carnival," followed by "I Can Get It for You Wholesale," "West Side Story" (CC), "I Had a Ball" for which she received a Theatre World Award, OB in "Your Own Thing," "They Don't Make 'Em Like That Anymore."

LITTLE, CLEAVON. Born June 1, 1939 in Chickasha, Okla. Attended San Diego State U, AADA. Debut OB 1967 in "MacBird," followed by "Hamlet" (NYSF), "Someone's Coming Hungry," "Ofay Watcher," "Scuba Duba," Bdwy debut 1968 in "Jimmy Shine" followed by "Purlie." "Narrow Road to the Deep North," (LC)

LOMBARD, PETER. Born Oct. 12, 1935 in Spokane, Wash. Graduate UAriz. Bdwy debut 1960 in "Conquering Hero," followed by "Carnival," "Generation," "Sweet Charity," "1776," OB in "Will the Mail Train Run Tonight?," "Wanted."

LONG, AVON. Born June 18, 1910 in Baltimore, Md. Studied at New Eng. Cons. Bdwy debut 1942 in "Porgy and Bess," followed by "Memphis Bound," "Carib Song," "Beggar's Holiday," "Don't Play Us Cheap," OB in "Ballad of Jazz Street."

LONGO, PEGGY. Born Oct. 1, 1943 in Brooklyn. Graduate Ithaca Col. With NYC Opera before 1967 Bdwy debut in "Fiddler on the Roof."

LOOMIS, ROD. Born Apr. 21, 1942 in St. Albans, Vt. Graduate Boston U, Brandeis U. Debut 1972 OB in "Two if by Sea."

LOWERY, MARCELLA. Born Apr. 27, 1946 in Jamaica, NY. Graduate Hunter Col. Debut 1967 OB in "Day of Absence," followed by "American Pastoral," "Ballet behind the Bridge," "Jamimma."

LOWRY, JUDITH. Born July 27, 1890 in Morristown, NJ. Bdwy debut 1915 in "Romeo and Juliet," followed by many productions. Currently in "The Effect of Gamma Rays on Man-in-the-Moon Marigolds" (OB).

LUDWIG, SALEM. Born July 31, 1915 in Bklyn. Attended Bklyn Col. Bdwy bow 1946 in "Miracle in the Mountains," followed by "Camino Real," "Enemy of the People," "All You Need Is One Good Break," "Inherit the Wind," "Disenchanted," "Rhinoceros," "Three Sisters," "Zulu and the Zayda," "Moonchildren," OB in "Brothers Karamazov," "Victim," "Troublemaker," "Man of Destiny," "Night of the Dunce," "Corner of the Bed," "Awake and Sing."

LUM, ALVIN. Born May 28, 1931 in Honolulu. Attended U. Hawaii. Debut 1969 OB in "In the Bar of a Tokyo Hotel," followed by Bdwy bow 1970 in "Lovely Ladies, Kind Gentlemen," "Two Gentlemen of Verona."

LUMLEY, TERRY. Born Mar. 24, 1945 in Oakland, Cal. Graduate San Jose State Col., Brandeis U. Bdwy debut 1971 in "No Place to Be Somebody."

LUSTIK, MARLENA. Born Aug. 22, 1944 in Milwaukee, Wisc. Attended Marquette U. Bdwy debut 1966 in "Pousse Cafe," followed by "Effect of Gamma Rays on Man-in-the-Moon Marigolds" (OB).

LYMAN, DEBRA. Born July 17, 1940 in Philadelphia. Graduate Phil. Col. Debut 1967 OB in "By Jupiter," followed by Bdwy bow 1972 in "Sugar."

LYMAN, PEGGY. Born June 28, 1950 in Cincinnati, O. Attended UCinn. Bdwy debut 1972 in "Sugar."

LYNDE, JANICE. Born Mar. 28, 1947 in Houston, Tex. Attended UInd. Bdwy debut 1971 in "The Me Nobody Knows," followed by "Applause," "Butterflies Are Free," OB in "Sambo."

LYNDECK, EDMUND. Born Oct. 4, 1925 in Baton Rouge, La. Graduate Montclair State Col., Fordham U. Bdwy debut 1969 in "1776."

MacCAULEY, MARK. Born Dec. 11, 1948 in NYC. Attended UInd. Debut 1969 OB in "Crimes of Passion," followed by "Anna K."

MacGOWRAN, JACK. Born Oct. 13, 1918 in Dublin, Ire. Trained at Abbey Theatre. Bdwy debut 1958 in "Juno," followed OB by "Gandhi," "MacGowran in the Works of Beckett."

MacMAHON, ALINE. Born May 3, 1899 in McKeesport, Pa. Attended Barnard Col. Bdwy debut 1921 in "Madras House," followed by "Green Ring," "Exciters," "Grand Street Follies," "Beyond the Horizon," "Maya," "Once in a Lifetime," "Heavenly Express," "Eve of St. Mark," "Confidential Clerk," "A Day by the Sea," "I Knock at the Door," "Pictures in the Hallway," "All the Way Home," LCRep's "The Alchemist," "Yerma," "East Wind," "Galileo," "Walking to Waldheim," "Tiger at the Gates," "Cyrano," "Pictures in the Hallway," "Mary Stuart," "The Crucible."

MAGGART, BRANDON. Born Dec. 12, 1933 in Carthage, Tenn. Graduate U. Tenn. OB in "Sing, Muse!," "Like Other People," "Put It In Writing" for which he received a Theatre World Award, Bdwy debut 1965 in "Kelly," followed by "New Faces of 1968," "Applause."

MAGUIRE, KATHLEEN. Born Sept. 27 in NYC. Attended Neighborhood Playhouse. Bdwy debut 1948 in "Sundown Beach," followed by "Greatest Man Alive," "Miss Isobel," "Sudden and Accidental Re-education of Horse Johnson," "Ring Round the Bathtub."

MAHER, JOSEPH. Born Dec. 29, 1933 in Westport, Ire. Bdwy bow 1964 in "Chinese Prime Minister," followed by "Prime of Miss Jean Brodie," "Henry V," "There's One in Every Marraige," OB in "The Hostage," "Live Like Pigs," "Importance of Being Earnest," "Eh?," "Local Stigmatic," "Mary Stuart" (LC)

MAHONEY, TRISH. Born Feb. 1, 1946 in Cairo, Egy. Attended Long Beach City Col. Bdwy debut 1972 in "A Funny Thing Happened on the Way to the Forum."

MAITLAND, MICHAEL. Born Aug. 27, 1956 in Ft. Lauderdale, Fla. Debut OB 1963 in "Trojan Women," followed by Bdwy in "Music Man," "Mame," "The Rothschilds."

MAITLAND, RUTH. Born Apr. 16, 1926 in NYC. Bdwy debut 1940 in "Walk with Music," followed by "Johnny 2X4," "Junior Miss," "Burlesque," "No, No, Nanette," OB in "Solid Gold Cadillac," "Pullman Car Hiawatha," "Spiral Staircase."

Ruth Maitland   **Sid Marshall**   **Victoria Mallory**   **Winston May**   **Leila Martin**

MALLORY, VICTORIA. Born Sept. 20, 1948 in Virginia. Graduate AMDA. Debut 1968 in "West Side Story" (LC), followed by "Carnival" (CC'68), "Follies."

MALONE, NANCY. Born Mar. 19, 1935 in Queens Village, NY. Bdwy debut 1952 in "Time Out for Ginger," followed by "Major Barbara," "Makropoulis Secret" (OB), "A Touch of the Poet," "Trial of the Catonsville 9" (OB).

MANCINI, RIC. Born Apr. 16, 1933 in Bklyn. Attended Bklyn Col. Debut OB 1966 in "A View from the Bridge." followed by "All My Sons," "Night of the Iguana," "5 Finger Exercise," "Heloise" (ELT), "Soon Jack November."

MANDAN, ROBERT. Born Feb. 2, 1932 in Clever, Mo. Attended Pomona Col. on Bdwy in "Debut," "Speaking of Murder," "No Exit" (OB), "Maggie Flynn," "But Seriously," "Applause."

MARCHAND, NANCY. Born June 19, 1928 in Buffalo, NY. Graduate Carnegie Tech. Debut in "The Taming of the Shrew" (CC), followed by "Merchant of Venice," "Much Ado About Nothing," "The Balcony,"(OB) "Three Bags Full," "After The Rain," LCRep's "The Alchemist," "Yerma," "Cyrano," and "Mary Stuart," "Forty Carats," "And Miss Reardon Drinks A Little."

MARKLIN, PETER. Born Dec. 22, 1939 in Buffalo, NY. Graduate Northwestern U. Appeared in "The Brig" (OB), "Fiddler on the Roof."

MARSHALL, MORT. Born Aug. 17, 1918, in NYC. Graduate Rollins Col., Yale. Bdwy bow 1947 in "Crime and Punishment," followed by "Gentlemen Prefer Blondes," "Of Thee I Sing," "Best House in Naples," "Men of Distinction," "Ziegfeld Follies," "All American," "Little Me," "Gypsy," "Music Man," "Minnie's Boys," "A Funny Thing Happened on the Way to the Forum."

MARSHALL, NORMAN THOMAS. Born Apr. 28, 1939 in Richmond, Va. Attended UVa., Hunter, CCNY. Debut 1966 OB in "The Gorilla Queen," followed by "Boy on the Straightback Chair," "Charlie Was Here and Now He's Gone."

MARSHALL, SID. Born July 15, 1941 in Mt. Pleasant, NY. Attended Dramatic Workshop. Bdwy debut 1972 in "Lost in the Stars," OB in "Bachelor Toys," "Sambo," "Armored Dove," "Your Own Thing."

MARTEL, TOM. Born Sept. 28, 1949 in Long Beach, Cal. Graduate U.S. Intl. U. Debut 1972 OB in "Hard Job Being God."

MARTIN, LEILA. Born Aug. 22, 1932 in NYC. Bdwy debut 1944 in "Peepshow," followed by "Two on the Aisle," "Wish You Were Here," "Guys and Dolls" (CC), "Best House in Naples," "Ernest in Love" (OB), "Henry Sweet Henry," "The Wall," "Visit to a Small Planet," "The Rothschilds."

MARTIN, PAM. Born May 8 in Omaha, Neb. Attended UDenver. Debut 1972 OB in "One for the Money."

MARTIN, RON. Born June 23, 1947 in NYC. Attended Queens Col. Bdwy debut 1968 in "Red, White and Maddox," followed by "Child's Play," OB in "Sensations," "Small Craft Warnings."

MARTIN, VIRGINIA. Born Dec. 2, 1932 in Chattanooga, Tenn. Studied at Theatre Wing. Appeared in "South Pacific," "Pajama Game," "Ankles Aweigh," "New Faces of 1956," "How to Succeed in Business . . . ," "Little Me," OB in "Buy Bonds Buster."

MARYE, DONALD. Born Apr. 7, 1905 in Chicago. Bdwy debut 1952 in "The Crucible," followed by "Make a Million," "Luther," "Philadelphia, Here I Come!," "The Incomparable Max."

MASIELL, JOE. Born Oct. 27, 1939 in Bklyn. Studied at HB Studio. Debut 1964 OB in "Cindy," followed by "Jacques Brel Is Alive . . . ," "Sensations," "Leaves of Grass," Bdwy in "Dear World" (1969), "Different Times."

MASCOLO, JOSEPH. Born Mar. 13, 1935 in Hartford, Conn. Appeared in "Night Life," "A View from the Bridge," "Dinner at 8," "To Clothe the Naked" (OB), LCRep's "The Time of Your Life" "Camino Real," "Good Woman of Setzuan," "Murderous Angels" (OB).

MASTERS, BENJAMIN. Born May 6, 1947 in Corvallis, Ore. Graduate U Ore. Debut 1970 OB in "Boys in the Band," followed by "What the Butler Saw," Bdwy bow 1972 in "Capt. Brassbound's Conversion."

MATHEWS, CARMEN. Born May 8, 1918 in Philadelphia. Graduate RADA. Bdwy debut 1938 in "Henry IV," followed by "Hamlet," "Richard II," "Harriet," "Cherry Orchard," "The Assassin," "Man and Superman," "Ivy Green," "Courtin' Time," "My Three Angels," "Holiday for Lovers," "Night Life," "Lorenzo," "The Yearling," "Delicate Balance," "I'm Solomon," "Dear World," "Ring Round the Bathtub."

MATTHAEI, KONRAD. Born in Detroit; Yale graduate. Debut 1961 OB in "She Stoops to Conquer," followed by "Thracian Horses," "Trelawney of the Wells," "King of the Dark Chamber," "Don Carlos," "A Man's a Man," "Riverwind," "Boys in the Band," "The Real Inspector Hound," Bdwy in "13 Daughters," "The Milk Train Doesn't Stop Here Anymore," "A Place for Polly."

MAY, WINSTON. Born Feb. 3, 1937 in Mammoth Spring, Ark. Graduate Ark. State U., Am. Th. Wing. Debut OB 1967 in "Man Who Washed His Hands," followed by "King Lear," "Candida," "Trumpets and Drums," "Otho the Great," "Uncle Vanya," "Servant of Two Masters" (ELT).

McADAMS, STACY. Born Aug. 23, 1938 in Memphis, Tenn. Attended UBrussels, Georgetown U. Debut 1968 OB in "Up Eden," followed by "Blind Guy."

McCALL, JANET. Born June 26, 1935 in Washington, DC. Graduate Penn. State. Debut 1960 OB in "Golden Apple," followed by "Life Is a Dream," "Tatooed Countess," "The Bacchantes," "Jacques Brel Is Alive . . . ," Bdwy in "Camelot" ('60), "1776," "Two by Two."

McCAMBRIDGE, MERCEDES. Born Mar. 17, 1918 in Joliet, Ill. Graduate Mundelein Col. Bdwy debut 1945 in "A Place of Our Own," followed by "Woman Bites Dog," "The Young and Fair," "Who's Afraid of Virginia Woolf?," "Love Suicide at Schofield Barracks," OB in "Cages."

McCARTHER, AVIS. Born May 6, 1947 in NC. Attended New School. Bdwy debut 1969 in "Penny Wars," OB in "A Roof over Your Head," "Pig Pen," "Middle of the Night" (ELT).

McCARTY, MARY. Born 1923 in Kan. Bdwy debut 1948 in "Sleepy Hollow" for which she received a Theatre World Award, followed by "Small Wonder," "Miss Liberty," "Bless You All," "A Rainy Day in Newark," "Follies."

247

Tanny McDonald

Don McGrath

Faye Menken

Don McHenry

Joanna Miles

McCLANAHAN, RUE. Born Feb. 21 in Healdton, Okla. Bdwy debut 1965 in "Best Laid Plans," followed by "Jimmy Shine," "Father's Day," OB in "Secret Life of Walter Mitty," "Big Man," "Macbird!," "Tonight in Living Color," "Who's Happy Now?," "Dark of the Moon," "God Says There Is No Peter Ott," "Dylan."

McDONALD, JAMES. Born June 23 in Jersey City, NJ. Attended Rutgers U. OB in "The Trojan Women," "White Devil," "Fortune and Men's Eyes," Bdwy bow 1970 in "Fiddler on the Roof."

McDONALD, TANNY. Born Feb. 13, 1939 in Princeton, Ind. Vassar graduate. Debut OB with Am. Savoyards, followed by "All in Love," "To Broadway with Love," "Carricknabauna," "Beggar's Opera," "Brand," "Goodbye, Dan Bailey," on Bdwy in "Fiddler on the Roof," "Come Summer."

McGRATH, DON. Born Mar. 3, 1940 in Pittsburgh, Pa. Graduate Duquesne U., NYU, AMDA. Debut 1970 OB in "Madwoman of Chaillot," followed by "Oedipus at Colonus."

McGREEVEY, ANNIE. Born in Bklyn; AADA graduate. Bdwy debut in "Company," OB in "Booth Is Back in Town."

McGUIRE, BIFF. Born Oct. 25, 1926 in New Haven, Conn. Attended Mass. State Col. Bdwy in "Make Mine Manhattan," "South Pacific," "Dance Me a Song," "The Time of Your Life" (CC&LC), "A View from the Bridge," "Greatest Man Alive," "The Egghead," "Triple Play," "Happy Town," "Beg, Borrow or Steal," "Finian's Rainbow" (CC), "Beggar on Horseback" (LC), "Father's Day," "Trial of the Catonsville 9."

McGUIRE, MITCHELL. Born Dec. 26, 1936 in Chicago. Attended Goodman Th. School, Santa Monica City Col. OB in "The Rapists," "Go, Go, Go, God is Dead," "Waiting for Lefty," "The Bond," "The Guns of Carrar," "Oh, Calcutta."

McHATTIE, STEPHEN. Born Feb. 3 in Antigonish, N.S. Graduate Acadia U, AADA. With NYSF in "Henry IV," on Bdwy in "The American Dream" ('68), OB in "Richard III," "The Persians," "Pictures in The Hallway" (LC), "Now There's Just the Three of Us," "Anna K.," "Twelfth Night" (LC).

McHENRY, DON. Born Feb. 25, 1908 in Paterson, NJ. Attended Rutgers U. Bdwy bow 1938 in "Don't Throw Glass Houses," followed by "Medea," "Tower beyond Tragedy," "The Crucible," "Fanny," "Destry Rides Again," "Tovarich," "Elizabeth the Queen" (CC'66), "King Lear" and "A Cry of Players" (LC), "Hamlet" (OB), "Vivat! Vivat Regina!"

McKECHNIE, DONNA. Born Nov. 1944 in Detroit. Bdwy debut 1961 in "How To Succeed . . . ," followed by "Promises, Promises," "Company," "On the Town."

McMARTIN, JOHN. Born in Warsaw, Ind. Attended Columbia. Debut OB 1959 in "Little Mary Sunshine" for which he received a Theatre World Award, followed by (Bdwy bow 1968) "The Conquering Hero," "Blood, Sweat and Stanley Poole," "Children from Their Games," "Rainy Day in Newark," "Too Much Johnson" (OB), "Sweet Charity," "Follies."

McNEELEY, GALE. Born Feb. 21, 1946 in Cleveland, O. Graduate Carroll U., Neighborhood Playhouse. Debut OB in "Two Gentlemen of Verona" (NYSF), followed by "Oedipus at Colonus" (ELT).

McWILLIAMS, CAROLINE. Born Apr. 4 in Seattle, Wash. Attended Carnegie Tech, Pasadena Playhouse. Bdwy debut 1971 in "The Rothschilds," OB in "An Ordinary Man."

MEEKER, RALPH. Born Nov. 21, 1920 in Minneapolis, Minn. Attended Northwestern U. Bdwy bow 1945 in "Strange Fruit," followed by "Cyrano de Bergerac," "Mr. Roberts" for which he received a Theatre World Award, "Streetcar Named Desire," "Picnic," "Cloud 7," "Rhinoceros," "Something about a Soldier," "Mrs. Dally," LCRep's "After the Fall" and "But for Whom Charlie," OB in "House of Blue Leaves."

MENKEN, FAYE. Born Feb. 19, 1947 in NYC. Graduate NYU. Bdwy debut 1969 in "Fiddler on the Roof."

MERENSKY, JOHN. Born Nov. 4, 1943 in NYC. Attended Neighborhood Playhouse, HB Studio. With APA in "Man and Superman," "Judith," and "War and Peace," OB in "Something for Kitty Genovese," "The Nun," "Two Gentlemen of Verona," "As You Like It," "Are You Prepared to Be a U.S. Marine?," "Disintegration of James Cherry" (LC), "Twentieth Century Tar."

MERRIMAN, DAN. Born July 10, 1929 in Ft. Worth, Tex. Attended TCU, Juilliard. Bdwy debut 1954 in "Saint of Bleecker Street," followed by "Hello, Dolly!," "Heathen," OB in "Pirates of Penzance," "Ransom of Red Chief."

MERRITT, LARRY. Born Nov. 27, 1937 in Ballston Spa, NY. Bdwy debut 1961 in "No Strings," followed by "No Where to Go but Up," "Golden Rainbow," "Dear World," "On the Town."

MICHAELS, LAURA. Born Nov. 17, 1953 in NYC. Attended HB Studio. Bdwy debut 1962 in "Sound of Music," followed by "Roar of the Greasepaint . . . ," "A Time For Singing," "The Me Nobody Knows," "Jesus Christ Superstar."

MICHAELS, STUART. Born Oct. 31, 1940 in Manchester, Conn. Attended Emerson Col., HB Studio. Debut 1971 OB in "June Moon" (ELT).

MICKEY, JERED. Born July 29, 1934 in Moscow, Ida. Graduate Carnegie-Mellon U. Bdwy bow 1963 in "Andorra," followed by "Barefoot in the Park," "The Homecoming," OB in "Boys in the Band," "House of Blue Leaves."

MILES, JOANNA. Born Mar. 6, 1940 in Nice, France. Studied at Actors Studio. Bdwy debut 1963 in "Marathon '33," followed by "Lorenzo," OB in "Walk-up," "Cave Dwellers," "Once in a Life Time," "Home Free," "Drums in the Night," "Dylan."

MILES, SYLVIA. Born Sept. 9, 1934 in NYC. Attended Pratt Inst., Actors Studio. Debut 1954 OB in "A Stone for Danny Fisher," followed by "Iceman Cometh," "The Balcony," "Chekhov Sketch Book," "Matty, Moron, Madonna," "The Kitchen," "Rosebloom," Bdwy "The Riot Act" (1963).

MILLER, DROUT. Born Sept. 18, 1942 in Trenton, NJ. Attended Lafayette Col. Bdwy debut 1970 in "Borstal Boy," followed by "Tall and Rex" (OB).

MILLER, HAROLD. Born Aug. 25, 1935 in NYC. Graduate CCNY. Debut 1962 OB in "Color Scheme," followed by "Limits," "Perfect Party," LCRep's "Narrow Road to the Deep North," and "Twelfth Night."

MILLER, JASON. Born 1940 in Scranton, Pa. Graduate UScranton. Appeared OB in "Subject to Fits," "That Championship Season" which he wrote.

MILLER, KATHLEEN. Born July 1, 1945 in Los Angeles. Attended U Cal., AADA Debut OB in "House of Leather," followed by Bdwy bow (1970) in "Butterflies Are Free."

Michael Miller

Page Miller

Robert Moberly

Marcia Mohr

Robert G. Murch

MILLER, MICHAEL. Born Sept. 1, 1931 in Los Angeles. Attended Bard Col. OB debut 1961 in "Under Milk Wood," followed by "The Lesson," "A Memory of 2 Mondays," "Little Murders," "Tom Paine," "Morning, Noon and Night," "Enemy of the People" (LC). "Whitsuntide," on Bdwy in "Ivanov," "Black Comedy," "Trial of Lee Harvey Oswald."

MILLER, PAGE. Born Apr. 13, 1947 in Circleville, O. Attended AMDA. Debut 1971 OB in "F. Jasmine Addams."

MINER, JAN. Born Oct. 15, 1919 in Boston. Debut 1958 OB in "Obligato," followed by "Decameron," "Dumbbell People," "Autograph Hound," on Bdwy in "Viva Madison Avenue," (1960) "Lady of the Camellias," "Freaking out of Stephanie Blake," "Othello," "Milk Train Doesn't Stop Here Anymore," "Butterflies Are Free."

MISITA, MICHAEL. Born Jan. 10, 1947 aboard HMS Queen Mary. Graduate Boston Cons. Bdwy debut 1968 in "Fig Leaves Are Falling," followed by "Mame," "Applause," "Follies."

MITCHELL, ANN. Born Oct. 23 in Providence, RI. Bdwy debut 1958 in "Make a Million," OB in "Threepenny Opera," "Once upon a Mattress," "Amorous Flea," "Anna K."

MIXON, ALAN. Born Mar. 15, 1933 in Miami, Fla. Attended UMiami. Bdwy bow 1962 in "Something about a Soldier," followed by "Sign in Sidney Brustein's Window," "The Devils," "Unknown Soldier and His Wife," "Love Suicide at Schofield Barracks," OB in "Suddenly Last Summer," "Desire under the Elms," "Trojan Women," "Alchemist," "Child Buyer," "Mr. and Mrs. Lyman," "A Whitman Portrait," "Iphigenia in Aulis," "Small Craft Warnings."

MOBERLY, ROBERT. Born Apr. 15, 1939 in Excelsior Springs, Mo. UKan. graduate. Debut 1967 OB in "Arms and the Man," followed by "The Millionairess," "A Gun Play," "Shadow of a Gunman," Bdwy bow 1970 in "A Place for Polly."

MOHR, MARCIA. Born Feb. 3, 1935 in Boston. Attended Syracuse U. Debut 1967 OB in "Harold Arlen Songbook," followed by "Georgie Porgie," "Soon Jack November."

MOORE, JONATHAN. Born Mar. 24, 1923 in New Orleans. Attended Piscator's Workshop. Debut 1961 OB in "After the Angels," followed by "Dylan," "1776."

MORRIS, GARRETT. Born Feb. 1, 1944 in New Orleans. Graduate Dillard U. OB in "Bible Salesman," "Slave Ship," "Transfers," "Operation Sidewinder" (LC), "In New England Winter," "Basic Training of Pavlo Hummel," on Bdwy in "Porgy and Bess," "Hallelujah, Baby," "I'm Solomon," "The Great White Hope," "Ain't Supposed to Die a Natural Death."

MORROW, KAREN. Born Dec. 15, 1936 in Chicago. Attended Clarke Col. Debut 1961 OB in "Sing, Muse!" for which she received a Theatre World Award, followed by "Boys from Syracuse," CC's, "Oklahoma!," "Most Happy Fella," "Brigadoon," and "Carnival," Bdwy in "I Had a Ball" (1964), "A Joyful Noise," "I'm Solomon'" "Grass Harp," "The Selling of the President."

MORSE, RICHARD. Born May 31 in Brookline, Mass. Attended Principia Col., Neighborhood Playhouse. Debut 1955 OB in "Teach Me How To Cry," followed by "Thor With Angels," "Makropoulos Secret," "All Kinds of Giants," "Mime Theatre," on Bdwy in "Mother Courage," "Fiddler on the Roof."

MORSE, ROBERT. Born May 18, 1931 in Newton, Mass. Bdwy debut 1955 in "The Matchmaker," followed by "Say, Darling" for which he received a Theatre World Award, "Take Me Along," "How to Succeed in Business ..." "Sugar."

MOSS, ARNOLD. Born Jan. 28, 1910 in Bklyn. Attended CCNY, Columbia. With LeGallienne's Repertory Co., on Bdwy in "Fifth Column," "Hold on to Your Hats," "Journey to Jerusalem," "Flight to the West," "The Land Is Bright," "The Tempest," "Front Page," "Twelfth Night," "King Lear," "Measure for Measure," "Follies."

MULLIGAN, RICHARD. Born Nov. 13, 1932 in The Bronx. Bdwy bow 1961 in "All the Way Home," followed by "Nobody Loves an Albatross," "Never Too Late," "Mating Dance" for which he received a Theatre World Award, "Hogan's Goat" (OB), "How the Other Half Loves," "Ring Round the Bathtub."

MURCH, ROBERT G. Born Apr. 17, 1935 in Jefferson Barracks, Mo. Graduate Wash. U. Bdwy bow 1966 in "Hostile Witness," followed by "The Harangues" (NEC), "Conduct Unbecoming," OB in "Charles Abbott & Son," "She Stoops to Conquer."

MURPHY, CHRISTOPHER. Born June 1944 in Troy, NY. Fordham, NYU graduate. Debut 1961 OB in "The Hostage," followed by "Heloise," "The Tavern."

MURPHY, GERRY. Born Aug. 14, 1934 in Portland, Ore. Columbia graduate. Debut 1962 OB in "Portrait of the Artist ...," followed by "Hop, Signor," "Barroom Monks," "Trial of the Catonsville 9," "Murderous Angels."

MURRAY, BRIAN. Born Oct. 9, 1939 in Johannesburg, SA. Debut 1964 OB in "The Knack," followed by "King Lear" (LC), Bdwy in "All in Good Time" (1964), "Rosencrantz and Guildenstern Are Dead," "Sleuth."

MURRAY, PEG. Born in Denver, Colo. Attended Western Reserve U. OB in "Children of Darkness," "A Midsummer Night's Dream," "Oh, Dad, Poor Dad ...," on Bdwy in "Great Sebastians," "Gypsy," "Blood, Sweat and Stanley Poole," "She Loves Me," "Anyone Can Whistle," "The Subject Was Roses," "Something More," "Cabaret," "Fiddler on the Roof."

MUSANTE, TONY. Born June 30, 1936 in Bridgeport, Conn. Graduate Oberlin Col. Debut 1960 OB in "Borak," followed by "Balcony," "Theatre of the Absurd," "Half-past Wednesday," "The Collection," "The Tender Heel," "Kiss Mama," "Mme. Mousse," "Zoo Story," "Match-Play," "Night of the Dunce," "A Gun Play."

MYERS, PAMELA. Born July 15, 1947 in Hamilton, O. Graduate Cincinnati Cons. of Music. In "Upstairs At The Downstairs" before Bdwy debut 1970 in "Company," followed by "The Selling of the President."

MYLES, LYNDA. Attended Mich. State Col. Columbia. OB in "Two Gentlemen of Verona." "Trojan Women," "Rocking Chair," "No Exit," "Iphigenia in Aulis," on Bdwy in "Plaza Suite."

Joan Nelson

Joseph Napoli

Mary Ann Niles

Tim Noble

Cecelia Norflee

NAPOLI, JOSEPH. Born Aug. 1940 in New Orleans. Attended Fordham, Tulane, Sorbonne. Debut OB 1971 in "One Flew Over the Cuckoo's Nest."

NAUGHTON, JAMES. Born Dec. 6, 1945 in Middletown, Conn. Graduate Brown, Yale. Debute OB 1971 in "Long Day's Journey into Night" for which he received a Theatre World Award, followed by "The Web and the Rock."

NELSON, CHRISTOPHER. Born Apr. 29, 1944 in Duluth, Minn. Bdwy debut 1968 in "Cabaret," followed by "Promises, Promises," "Follies."

NELSON, GENE. Born Mar 24, 1920 in Seattle, Wash. Bdwy debut 1942 in "This is the Army," followed by "Lend an Ear" for which he won a Theatre World Award, "Follies."

NELSON, JOAN. Born June 7, 1943 in LaGrande, Ore. Graduate Redlands U. Bdwy debut in "Here's Where I Belong," followed by "Wonderful Town" (CC), "Lovely Ladies, Kind Gentlemen," OB in "Beggar's Opera."

NELSON, RUTH. Born Aug. 2, 1905 in Saginaw, Mich. Studied at Am. Lab. Theatre. Bdwy debut 1931 with Group Theatre in "House of Connolly," and in Group productions until 1941, followed by "Grass Harp," "Collette" (OB), "Solitaire."

NEWMAN, PHYLLIS. Born Mar. 19, 1935 in Jersey City, NJ. Attended Western Reserve U. Bdwy debut 1953 in "Wish You Were Here," followed by "Bells Are Ringing," "I Feel Wonderful" (OB), "First Impressions," "Subways Are for Sleeping," "Apple Tree," "On the Town."

NEWMAN, STEPHEN D. Born Jan. 20, 1943 in Seattle, Wash. Stanford Graduate. Debut 1971 OB in Judith Anderson's "Hamlet," followed by "School for Wives," Bdwy bow 1972 in "An Evening with Richard Nixon and ...," "Beggar's Opera" (OB).

NICHOLLS, ALLAN. Born Apr. 8, 1945 in Montreal, Can. Bdwy debut 1969 in "Hair," followed by "Inner City."

NILES, MARY ANN. Born May 2, 1933 in NYC. Attended Miss Finchley's, Ballet Acad. Bdwy debut in "Girl from Nantucket," followed by "Dance Me a Song," "Call Me Mister," "Make Mine Manhattan," "La Plume de Ma Tante," "Carnival," "Flora the Red Menace," "Sweet Charity," "George M!," "No, No, Nanette." OB in "The Boys from Syracuse," "Little Brown Road," "Big Spender," "Your Sister Rose," "Wonderful Town" (CC '67), "Carnival" (CC '68).

NOBLE, JAMES. Born Mar. 5, 1922 in Dallas, Tex. Attended SMU. Bdwy bow 1949 in "The Velvet Glove," followed by "Come of Age," "A Far Country," "Strange Interlude," "1776," OB in "Wilder's Triple Bill," "Night of the Dunce," "Rimers of Eldritch," "The Acquisition," "A Scent of Flowers."

NOBLE, TIM. Born Feb. 22, 1945 in Indianapolis, Ind. Attended Butler U., Ball State U. Bdwy debut 1972 in "The Selling of the President."

NOLEN, JOYCE. Born Oct. 5, 1949 in Philadelphia, Pa. Debut OB 1967 in "Curley McDimple," Bdwy bow 1972 in "Different Times."

NORFLEET, CECELIA. Born Sept. 18, 1949 in Chicago. Graduate Roosevelt U. Bdwy debut 1969 in "Hair," followed by "Jesus Christ Superstar," "Ain't Supposed to Die a Natural Death."

NYE, CARRIE. Attended Stephens Col., Yale. Bdwy debut 1960 in "A Second String," followed by "Mary, Mary," "Half a Sixpence," "A Very Rich Woman," "Cop-out," OB in "Ondine," "Ghosts," "Importance of Being Earnest," "Trojan Women," "The Real Inspector Hound."

OAKES, GARY. Born Feb. 22, 1936 in North Adams, Mass. Attended Columbia, Neighborhood Playhouse. Debut OB 1963 in "Boys from Syracuse," followed by "Shoemaker's Holiday," on Bdwy in "1776."

OAKLAND, SIMON. Born Aug. 28, 1920 in Bklyn. Attended Columbia. Appeared in "Skipper Next to God," "Light up the Sky," "Caesar and Cleopatra," "Harvey," "The Shrike," "Sands of Negev," "The Great Sebastians," "Angela," "Twigs."

O'BRIEN, FRANK. Born Apr. 28 in NYC. Graduate Georgetown U. Bdwy debut 1971 in "Two Gentlemen of Verona."

O'CONNELL, PATRICIA. Born Mar. 27 in NYC. Studied at Theatre Wing. Debut 1958 OB in "The Saintliness of Margery Kemp," followed by "Time Limit," "An Evening's Frost," "Mrs. Snow," "Electric Ice," "Survival of St. Joan," "Rain," Bdwy debut 1970 in "Criss-crossing."

O'CONNOR, KEVIN. Born May 7, 1938 in Hololulu. Attended UHawaii, Neighborhood Playhouse. Debut 1964 OB in "Up to Thursday," followed by "Six from LaMama," "Rimers of Eldritch," "Tom Paine," "Boy on the Straight-back Chair," "Dear Janet Rosenberg," "Eyes of Chalk," Bdwy (1970) "Gloria and Esperanza," "Kool Aid" (LC).

O'HARA, JENNY. Born Feb. 24 in Sonora, Cal. Attended Carnegie Tech. Bdwy debut 1964 in "Dylan," followed by "Fig Leaves Are Falling," "Criss-Crossing," "Promises, Promises," OB in "Hang Down Your Head and Die," "Play with a Tiger," "Arms and the Man," "Sambo," "My House Is Your House."

O'HARA, JILL. Born Aug. 23, 1947 in Warren, Pa. Attended Edinburgh State Teachers Col. OB in "Hang Down Your Head and Die," "Hair," "Master Builder," Bdwy debut 1968 in "George M!" followed by "Promises, Promises," for which she received a Theatre World Award.

OLIVER, JODY. Born Aug. 6, 1954 in Forest Hills, NY. Bdwy debut 1967 in "The Happy Time," followed by "Lenny."

OMENS, ESTELLE. Born Oct. 11, 1928 in Chicago. Graduate U Iowa. OB in "Summer and Smoke," "Grass Harp," "Legend of Lovers," "Plays of Bleecker Street," "Pullman Car Hiawatha," "Brownstone Urge," "Gandhi," "Shadow of a Gunman," Bdwy debut 1969 in "The Watering Place."

O'NEIL, TRICIA. Born Mar. 11, 1945 in Shreveport, La. Graduate Baylor U. Bdwy debut 1970 in "Two by Two" for which she received a Theatre World Award.

O'NEILL, DICK. Born Aug. 29, 1928 in The Bronx. Attended Utica Col. Bdwy bow 1961 in "The Unsinkable Molly Brown," followed by "Skyscraper," "Have I Got One for You" (OB), "Promises, Promises," "Tough to Get Help."

ORFALY, ALEXANDER. Born Oct. 10, 1935 in Brooklyn. Appeared in "South Pacific" (LC), "How Now, Dow Jones," "Ari," "Sugar," OB in "The End of All Things Natural," "Mahagonny," "Johnny Johnson."

Autris Paige

Elizabeth Owens

Ron Panvini

Marion Paone

Wilbur Patterson, Jr.

OSBORNE, KIPP. Born Oct. 17, 1944 in Jersey City, NJ. Attended UMich., Neighborhood Playhouse. Bdwy debut 1970 in "Butterflies Are Free" for which he received a Theatre World Award.

OTTO, LIZ. Born in Coral Gables, Fla. Graduate U. Fla. Debut 1963 OB in "The Plot against the Chase Manhattan Bank," followed by "I Dreamt I Dwelt in Bloomingdale's," "One for the Money."

OWENS, ELIZABETH. Born Feb. 26, 1938 in NYC. Attended New School, Neighborhood Playhouse. Debut 1955 OB in "Dr. Faustus Lights the Lights," followed by "The Lovers" (Bdwy), "Chit Chat on a Rat," "The Miser," "The Father," "The Importance of Being Earnest," "Candida," "Trumpets and Drums," "Oedipus," "Macbeth," "Not Now Darling" (Bdwy), "Uncle Vanya," "Misalliance," "Master Builder."

OWEN, REGINALD. Born Aug. 5, 1887 in Wheathampstead Herts, Eng. Graduate RADA. Bdwy debut 1924 in "The Carolinian," followed by "Androcles and the Lion," "Importance of Being Earnest," "The Play's the Thing," "Skin Deep," "The Marquise," "Three Musketeers," "Candle Light," "Out of a Blue Sky," "Petticoat Influence," "Child of Manhattan," "Affairs of State," "A Funny Thing Happened on the Way to the Forum."

PAGE, EVELYN. Born in Fremont, Neb. Attended UNeb. Debut 1958 OB in "The Boy Friend," followed by "Brothers," Bdwy in "Plain and Fancy" (1956), "Mr. Wonderful," "Little Me," "On a Clear Day You Can See Forever," "Canterbury Tales."

PAGLIA, GINA. Born Sept. 6, 1955 in NYC. Bdwy debut 1967 in "Henry Sweet Henry," followed by "Happy Time," "On the Town."

PAIGE, AUTRIS. Born Aug. 17, 1941 in Houston, Tex. Graduate San Francisco State. Bdwy debut 1972 in "Lost in the Stars."

PALMER, LELAND. Born in Port Washington, NY. Bdwy debut 1966 in "Joyful Noise," followed by "Applause," OB in "Your Own Thing," "Dames at Sea."

PALMER, STACY. Born in 1930 in Little Valley, NY. Attended UBuffalo, AADA. Debut 1971 OB in "Middle of the Night" (ELT).

PALMIERI, JOSEPH. Born Aug. 1, 1939 in Bklyn. Attended Catholic U. Appeared with NYSF 1965-6, "Cyrano de Bergerac" (LCRep), OB in "Butter and Egg Man," "Boys in the Band," "Beggar's Opera."

PANKIN, STUART. Born Apr. 8, 1946 in Philadelphia, Pa. Graduate Dickinson Col, Columbia. With NYSF (1968–71) in "Wars of the Roses," "Richard III," "Timon of Athens," "Cymbeline," LCRep's "Mary Stuart," "Narrow Road to the Deep North," "Twelfth Night," "The Crucible."

PANVINI, RON. Born Mar. 6, 1945 in NYC. Graduate NYU. Studied at HB Studio. Debut 1971 OB in "Lake of the Woods."

PAONE, MARION. Born Mar. 12 in NYC. Bklyn Col. graduate. Appeared OB in "Witness," "Where Has Tommy Flowers Gone?"

PAPE, JOAN. Born Jan. 23, 1944 in Detroit, Mich. Graduate Purdue U., Yale. Debut 1972 in "Suggs" (LC).

PARKER, LARA. Born Oct. 27, 1942 in Knoxville, Tenn. Graduate Southwestern U., UIowa. Bdwy debut 1968 in "Woman Is My Idea," followed OB by "Lulu," "A Gun Play."

PARKS, TRINA. Born Dec. 26 in Bklyn. Debut 1964 OB in "Prodigal Son," followed by "House of Flowers," "Never Jam Today," on Bdwy in "Her First Roman" ('68), "Selling of the President."

PARSONS, ESTELLE. Born Nov. 20, 1927 in Lynn, Mass. Attended Boston U., Conn. Col., Actors Studio. OB in "Threepenny Opera," "Automobile Graveyard," "Mrs. Dally Has A Lover" for which she received a Theatre World Award, "In the Summer House," "Monopoly," "Peer Gynt" (CP), "Mahagonny," "Silent Partner," with LC Rep's "East Wind," "Galileo," "People Are Living There," on Bdwy in "Happy Hunting," "Whoop-Up!" "Beg, Borrow or Steal," "Ready When You Are, C.B." "Malcolm," "The Seven Descents of Myrtle," "A Way of Life," "And Miss Reardon Drinks a Little."

PASSELTINER, BERNIE. Born Nov. 21, 1931 in NYC. Graduate Catholic U. OB "Square in the Eye," "Sourball," "As Virtuously Given," "Now Is the Time for All Good Men," "Rain," "Kaddish," on Bdwy in "The Office" ('66).

PATRICK, DENNIS. Born Mar. 14, 1918 in Philadelphia, Pa. Appeared in "Harvey," "Cock-a-doodle-doo," "Liar," "Wayward Saint" for which he received a Theatre World Award, "St. Joan," "Marat/deSade," "Children Children."

PATTERSON, WILBUR, JR. Born May 25, 1946 in NYC. Attended AMDA. Debut OB 1971 in "One Flew over the Cuckoo's Nest."

PATTON, LUCILLE. Born in NYC; attended Neighborhood Playhouse. Bdwy debut 1946 in "Winter's Tale," followed by "Topaze," "Arms and the Man," "Joy to the World," "All You Need Is One Good Break," "Fifth Season," "Heavenly Twins," "Rhinoceros," "Marathon '33," "Last Analysis," "Dinner at 8," "La Strada," "Unlikely Heroes," "Love Suicide at Schofield Barracks," OB in "Ulysses in Nighttown," "Failures," "Three Sisters," "Yes, Yes, No, No," "Tango."

PAULSEN, ALBERT. Born Dec. 13, 1927 in Ecuador. Attended Neighborhood Playhouse, Actors Studio. Bdwy debut 1958 in "Night Circus," followed by "Three Sisters," OB in "Don Juan," "Papp," "Fingernails Blue as Flowers."

PAYTON-WRIGHT, PAMELA. Born Nov. 1, 1941 in Pittsburgh. Graduate Birmingham Southern Col. RADA. Bdwy debut 1967 with APA in "The Show-Off," "Exit The King," and "The Cherry Orchard," "Jimmy Shine," OB in "The Effect of Gamma Rays on Man-in-the-Moon Marigolds," "Crucible" (LC).

PEARSON, SCOTT. Born Dec. 13, 1941 in Milwaukee. Attended Valparaiso U., UWisc. Bdwy debut 1966 in "A Joyful Noise," followed by "Promises, Promises."

PEARSON, SUSAN G. Born Jan. 3, 1941 in Minneapolis. Attended U. Minn. Debut 1969 in "No Place to Be Somebody."

PEERCE, JAN. Born June 3 in NYC. Studied at NY Col. of Music. Leading opera and concert tenor before Bdwy debut Dec. 14, 1971 in "Fiddler on the Roof."

Edward Penn   Elaine Petricoff   Kurt Peterson   Carla Pinza   Rick Podell

PELHAM, JIMMY. Born in Goldsboro, NC. Graduate NYU. Bdwy debut 1968 in "Great White Hope," followed by "Tough to Get Help."

PENDLETON, WYMAN. Born Apr. 18, 1916 in Providence, RI. Graduate Brown U. OB in "Gallows Humor," "American Dream," "Zoo Story," "Corruption in the Palace of Justice," "Giant's Dance," "Child Buyer," "Happy Days," "Butter and Egg Man," on Bdwy in "Tiny Alice," "Malcolm," "Quotations From Chairman Mao Tse-Tung," "Happy Days," "Henry V," "Othello," "There's One in Every Marriage."

PENN, EDWARD. Born in Washington, DC. Studied at HB Studio. Debut 1965 OB in "The Queen and the Rebels," followed by "My Wife and I," "Invitation to a March" (ELT), "Of Thee I Sing," "Fantasticks," "Greenwillow" (ELT), "One for the Money."

PENTECOST, GEORGE. Born July 15, 1939 in Detroit. Graduate Wayne State, UMich. With APA in "Scapin," "Lower Depths," "The Tavern," "School for Scandal," "Right You Are," "War and Peace," "The Wild Duck," "The Show-Off," "Pantagleize," and "The Cherry Orchard," "The Boys in the Band" (OB), "School for Wives," "Twelfth Night" (LC).

PENZNER, SEYMOUR. Born July 29, 1915 in Yonkers, NY. Attended CCNY. OB in "Crystal Heart," "Guitar" on Bdwy in "Oklahoma," "Finian's Rainbow," "Call Me Madam," "Paint Your Wagon," "Can-Can," "Kean," "Baker Street," "Man of La Mancha."

PETERS, BERNADETTE. Born Feb 28, 1948 in Jamaica, NY. OB in "Penny Friend," "Curley McDimple," "Most Happy Fella"(CC), "Dames at Sea," "Nevertheless, They Laugh," Bdwy debut 1967 in "Girl in the Freudian Slip," followed by "Johnny No Trump," "George M" for which she received a Theatre World Award, "La Strada," "On the Town."

PETERS, BROCK. Born July 2, 1927 in NYC. Attended Chicago U., CCNY. Bdwy bow 1943 in "Porgy and Bess," followed by "South Pacific," "Anna Lucasta," "My Darlin' Aida," "Mr. Johnson," "Kwamina," "Caucasian Chalk Circle"(LC), "Lost in the Stars."

PETERS, STEPHEN. Born Feb 3, 1944 in NYC. With LCRep in "The Changeling," "Incident at Vichy," and "Tartuffe," "Royal Hunt of the Sun"(Bdwy '65), APA's "School for Scandal," "Wild Duck," and "War and Peace," OB in "Ten Nights in a Barroom," "Smudge."

PETERSEN, ERIKA. Born Mar. 24, 1949 in NYC. Attended NYU. Debut 1963 OB in "One Is a Lonely Number," followed by "I Dreamt I Dwelt in Bloomingdale's," "F. Jasmine Addams."

PETERSON, KURT. Born Feb 12, 1948 in Stevens Point, Wisc. Attended AMDA. Appeared in "An Ordinary Miracle"(OB), "West Side Story"(LC'68), Bdwy debut 1969 in "Dear World," followed by "Dames at Sea"(OB), "Follies."

PETRICOFF, ELAINE. Born in Cincinnati, O. Graduate Syracuse U. Bdwy debut 1971 in "The Me Nobody Knows," OB in "Hark!"

PETRO, MICHAEL. Born July 1, 1944 in Westfield, NY. Graduate Slippery Rock Col., HB Studio. Bdwy debut 1971 in "Fiddler on the Roof."

PHALEN, ROBERT. Born May 10, 1937 in San Francisco. Attended CCSF. UCal. With LCRep in "Danton's Death," "Country Wife," "Caucasian Chalk Circle," "Alchemist," "Yerma," "Galileo," "St. Joan," "Tiger at the Gates," "Cyrano," "King Lear," "Cry of Players," "In the Matter of J. Robert Oppenheimer," "Operation Sidewinder," "Beggar on Horseback," "Good Woman of Setzuan," "Birthday Party," "Silence," "Mary Stuart," "Narrow Road to the Deep North," "Twelfth Night," and "The Crucible."

PHILLIPS, MARY BRACKEN. Born Aug. 15, 1946 in Kansas City, Mo. Attended Kansas U. Debut 1969 OB in "Perfect Party," Bdwy bow in "1776," followed by "Look Where I'm At" (OB), "Different Times."

PHILLIPS, WENDELL K. Born Nov. 27, 1907 in Bladinsville, Ill. Attended UWisc. Bdwy bow 1931 in "Incubator," followed by "Mother Sings," "Many Mansions," "Abe Lincoln in Illinois," "Fifth Column," "Anne of the Thousand Days," "Solid Gold Cadillac," "The Investigation," OB in "Death of J.K."

PINCUS, WARREN. Born Apr. 13, 1938 in Bklyn. Attended CCNY. OB in "Miss Nepertiti Regrets," "Circus," "Magician," "Boxcars," "Demented World," "Give My Regards," "Electronic Nigger," "Last Pad," "Waiting for Godot," "In the Time of Harry Harass."

PINZA, CARLA. Born Feb. 2, 1942 in Puerto Rico. Attended Hunter Col. OB in "The Ox Cart," "House of Flowers," Bdwy debut 1968 in "The Cuban Thing," followed by "Two Gentlemen of Verona."

PLEASENCE, DONALD. Born Oct. 5, 1919 in Nottingham, Eng. On Bdwy in "Antony and Cleopatra," "Caesar and Cleopatra," "The Caretaker," "Poor Bitos," "Man in the Glass Booth," "Wise Child."

PLUMLEY, DON. Born Feb. 11, 1934 in Los Angeles. Graduate Pepperdine Col. Debut OB 1961 in "The Cage," followed by NYSF's "Midsummer Night's Dream," "Richard II," "Cymbeline," and "Much Ado about Nothing," "Saving Grace," "A Whistle in the Dark," "Operation Sidewinder" and "Enemy of The People"(LC), "Back Bog Beast Bait."

PODELL, RICK. Born Nov. 16, 1946 in Los Angeles. Attended San Francisco State. Debut 1972 OB in "Two if by Sea," followed by "Buy Bonds Buster."

POINTER, PRISCILLA. Born in NYC. With LCRep from 1965, in "Summertree," "An Evening for Merlin Finch," "Inner Journey," "Disintegration of James Cherry," "Time of Your Life," "Camino Real," "Amphitryon," "Good Woman of Setzuan," "Scenes from American Life," "Play Strindberg," "Ride Across Lake Constance."

POLITO, PHILIP. Born Feb. 17, 1944 in Hackensack, NJ. Graduate Ill. Wesleyan U., Yale. Bdwy debut 1969 in "1776."

PONAZECKI, JOE. Born Jan. 7, 1934 in Rochester, NY. Attended Rochester U., Columbia. Bdwy bow 1959 in "Much Ado about Nothing," followed by "Send Me No Flowers," "A Call On Kuprin," "Take Her, She's Mine," "The Dragon" (OB), "Fiddler on the Roof," "Xmas in Las Vegas," "3 Bags Full," "Love in E-Flat," "90 Day Mistress," "Muzeeka"(OB), "Witness"(OB), "Harvey," "Trial of the Catonsville 9," "Country Girl."

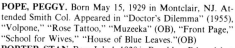

Lizabeth Pritchett   Joseph Ragno   Victoria Racimo   Richard Ramos   Sheilah Rae

POPE, PEGGY. Born May 15, 1929 in Montclair, NJ. Attended Smith Col. Appeared in "Doctor's Dilemma" (1955), "Volpone," "Rose Tattoo," "Muzeeka" (OB), "Front Page," "School for Wives."(OB)

PORTER, STAN. Born July 1, 1928 in Brooklyn. Bdwy debut 1967 in "Hello, Solly!," Off-Bdwy in "Jacques Brel Is Alive and Well . . ."

POTTER, ANDREW. Born Mar. 5, 1944 in NYC. Attended Cornell U. Debut 1972 OB in "Eros and Psyche."

PRICE, GILBERT. Born Sept. 10, 1942 in NYC. Attended Am Th. Wing. Bdwy bow 1965 in "Roar of the Greasepaint . . .," followed by "Lost in the Stars," OB in "Kicks & Co.," "Fly Blackbird," "Jerico-Jim Crow" for which he received a Theatre World Award, "Promenade," "Slow Dance on the Killing Ground," "Six," "Melodrama Play."

PRIMROSE, ALEK. Born Aug. 20, 1934 in San Joaquin, Cal. Attended Col. of the Pacific. OB in "In Good King Charles' Golden Days," "Golem," "Leave It to Jane," "The Balcony," "Rules of the Game," "A Man's a Man," "In White America," "Kitchen," LCRep's "Incident at Vichy" and "Tartuffe," Bdwy in "A Cook for Mr. General," "House of Atreus," "Arturo Ui," "Room Service," "Ring Round the Bathtub."

PRITCHETT, LIZABETH. Born Mar. 12, 1920 in Dallas, Tex. Attended SMU. Bdwy debut 1959 in "Happy Town," followed by "Sound of Music," "Maria Golovin," "The Yearling," "A Funny Thing Happened on the Way to the Forum," OB in "Cindy."

PURNELL, ROGER. Born June 11, 1943 in Spartanburg, SC. Graduate Middlebury Col., Yale. Bdwy debut 1970 in "Sleuth."

QUARRY, RICHARD. Born Aug. 9, 1944 in Akron, O. Graduate UAkron, NYU. Bdwy bow 1970 in "Georgy," followed by "Oh! Calcutta!"

QUAYLE, ANTHONY. Born Sept. 7, 1913 in Ainsdale, Eng. Attended RADA. Bdwy debut 1936 in "Country Wife," followed by "Tamburlaine the Great," "The Firstborn," "Galileo" (LC) "Halfway up the Tree," "Sleuth."

RACHINS, ALAN. Born Oct. 3, 1942 in Brookline, Mass. Attended U. Pa. Bdwy debut 1967 in "After The Rain," followed by "Hadrian VII," "Oh! Calcutta!"

RACIMO, VICTORIA. Born Dec. 26, 1945 in NYC. Attended Juilliard, Columbia. Bdwy debut 1959 in "Flower Drum Song," OB in "The Basic Training of Pavlo Hummel."

RAE, SHEILAH. Born Apr. 27, 1946 in Chicago, UMich. graduate. Bdwy debut 1967 in "Fiddler on the Roof," followed by "Applause," "The Selling of the President," OB in "Horror Show," "Iphigenia."

RAGNO, JOSEPH. Born Mar. 11, 1936 in Bklyn. Attended Allegheny Col. Debut 1960 OB in "Worm in the Horseradish," followed by "Elizabeth the Queen" (ELT), "A Country Scandal," "The Shrike," (ELT), "Cymbeline" (NYSF), "Love Me, Love My Children," "Interrogation of Havana," Bdwy bow 1969 in "Indians."

RAHN, PATSY. Born Jan. 10, 1950 in Mich. Studied at Studio Lab Theatre. Debut 1971 OB in "Love me, Love My Children."

RALSTON, TERI. Born Feb. 16, 1943 in Holyoke, Colo. Graduate SF State Col. Debut 1969 OB in "Jacques Brel Is Alive . . .," Bdwy bow 1970 in "Company."

RAMOS, RICHARD. Born Aug. 23, 1941 in Seattle, Wash. Graduate UMinn. Bdwy debut 1968 in "House of Atreus," followed by "Arturo Ui," OB in "Screens."

RAMSAY, REMAK. Born Feb. 2, 1937 in Baltimore, Md. Princeton graduate. OB in "Hang Down Your Head and Die," "The Real Inspector Hound," Bdwy bow in 1965 in "Half a Sixpence," followed by "Sheep on the Runway," "Lovely Ladies, Kind Gentlemen," "On the Town."

RAMSEY, MARION. Born May 10, 1947 in Philadelphia. Bdwy bow 1969 in "Hello, Dolly!," followed OB by "The Me Nobody Knows," "Soon," "Do It Again," "Wedding of Iphigenia."

RANDALL, CHARLES. Born Mar. 15, 1923 in Chicago. Attended Columbia. Bdwy bow 1953 in "Anastasia," followed by "Enter Laughing," "Trial of Lee Harvey Oswald," OB in "Adding Machine," "Cherry Orchard," "Brothers Karamazov," "Susan Slept Here," "Two for Fun," "Timon of Athens" (NYSF).

RANDOLPH, MIMI. Born Dec. 26, 1922 in Montreal, Can. Debut OB 1962 in "All in Love," followed by "Jo," "Pocketwatch," on Bdwy in "Dear Me, the Sky Is Falling," "Fiddler on the Roof."

RATCLIFFE, SAMUEL D. Born Mar. 30, 1945 in Eagle Lake, Fla. Graduate Birmingham Southern Col. Debut 1969 OB in "The Fantasticks," followed by Bdwy bow in "Fiddler on the Roof."

RATHBURN, ROGER. Born Nov. 11, 1940 in Perrysburg, O. Attended Ohio State, Neighborhood Playhouse. Bdwy debut 1971 in "No, No, Nanette" for which he received a Theatre World Award.

RAVEN, ELSA. Born Sept. 21, 1929 in Charleston, SC. Attended Charleston Col. Bdwy debut 1959 in "Legend of Lizzie," OB in "Taming of the Shrew" (NYSF), "In a Bar in a Tokyo Hotel," "The Web and the Rock."

RAWLINS, LESTER. Born Sept. 24, 1924 in Farrell, Pa. Attended Carnegie Tech. Appeared in "Othello," "King Lear," "The Lovers," "Man for All Seasons," OB in "Endgame," "Quare Fellow," "Camino Real," "Hedda Gabler," "Old Glory," "Child Buyer," "Winterset," "In the Bar of a Tokyo Hotel," "The Reckoning," "Nightride."

REAMS, LEE ROY. Born Aug. 23, 1942 in Covington, Ky. Graduate U. Cinn. Cons. Bdwy debut 1966 in "Sweet Charity," followed by "Oklahoma!" (LC), "Applause."

REDFIELD, WILLIAM. Born Jan. 26, 1927 in NYC. Bdwy bow 1936 in "Swing Your Lady," followed by "Excursion," "Virginia," "Stop-over," "Our Town," "Second Helping," "Junior Miss," "Snafu," "Barefoot Boy with Cheek," "Montserrat," "Miss Liberty," "Out of This World," "Misalliance," "Double in Hearts," "Man for All Seasons," "Minor Adjustment," "Love Suicide at Schofield Barracks," OB in "Making of Moo."

Alexander Reed

Antonia Rey

Paul Richards

Jane Robertson

Ralph Roberts

REDWOOD, JOHN HENRY. Born Sept. 10, 1942 in Bklyn. Attended U Kan. Debut OB 1970 in "Cartouche," followed by "One Flew over the Cuckoo's Nest," "Black Visions."

REED, ALEXANDER. Born June 9, 1916 in Clearfield, Pa. Graduate Columbia. Debut 1956 OB in "Lady from the Sea," followed by "All the King's Men," "Death of Satan," "The Balcony," "Call Me by My Rightful Name," Bdwy in "Man for All Seasons" (1962), "The Physicists," "Hostile Witness," "Lost in the Stars."

REILEY, ORRIN. Born Aug. 12, 1946 in Santa Monica, Cal. Graduate UCLA. Bdwy debut 1969 in "Dear World," followed by "Man of La Mancha," "Applause," "On the Town."

REMME, JOHN. Born Nov. 21, 1935 in Fargo, NDak. Attended UMinn. Debut 1972 OB in "One for the Money."

REVILL, CLIVE. Born Apr. 18, 1930 in Wellington, NZ. Attended Rongotai Col. Bdwy debut 1952 in "Mr. Pickwick," followed by "Irma La Douce," "Oliver!," "Sherry!," "The Incomparable Max."

REY, ANTONIA. Born Oct. 12, 1927 in Havana, Cuba. Graduate Havana U. Bdwy debut 1964 in "Bajour," followed by "Yerma" (OB), "Mike Downstairs," "Fiesta In Madrid" (CC), "Engagement Baby," "Camino Real" (LC), "Back Bog Beast Bait" (OB), "Rain" (OB).

RICH, DORIS. Born Aug. 14, 1905 in Boston. Attended AADA. Bdwy debut 1927 in "Getting in the Movies," followed by "Mad Hopes," "Taming of the Shrew," "Sophie," "Flamingo Road," "Strange Bedfellows," "Madwoman of Chaillot," "Affair of Honor," "Redhead," "The Physicists," "UTBU," "We Have Always Lived in the Castle," "A Warm Body," "The Crucible" (LC).

RICHARDS, JESS. Born Jan. 23, 1943 in Seattle, Wash. Attended UWash. Bdwy debut 1966 in "Walking Happy," followed by "South Pacific" (LC), "Blood Red Roses," "Two by Two," "On the Town" for which he received a Theatre World Award, OB in "One for the Money."

RICHARDS, JON. Born in Wilkes Barre, Pa. Appeared in "Tobacco Road," "Arsenic and Old Lace," "Love or Money," "Gramercy Ghost," "Bad Seed," "Leave It to Jane" (OB), "Sunrise at Campobello," "Sail Away," "A Murderer among Us," "A Very Rich Woman," "Roar like a Dove," "Elizabeth the Queen," "3 Bags Full," "Woman Is My Idea," "Does a Tiger Wear a Necktie?," "One Flew over the Cuckoo's Nest" (OB).

RICHARDS, PAUL. Born Aug. 31, 1934 in Bedford, Ind. Graduate Ind. U. Bdwy debut 1960 in "Once Upon A Mattress," followed by "Camelot," "It's Superman," "A Joyful Noise," "1776."

RIFKIN, RON. Born Oct. 31, 1939 in NYC. Graduate NYU. Member Actors Studio. Bdwy debut 1960 in "Come Blow Your Horn," OB in "Rosebloom."

RITCHARD, CYRIL. Born Dec. 1, 1897 in Sydney, Austr. Attended Sydney U. Bdwy debut 1947 in "Love for Love," followed by "Make Way for Lucia," "The Relapse," "Peter Pan," "Visit to a Small Planet," "The Pleasure of His Company," "Happiest Girl in the World," "Romulus," "Too True to Be Good," "Irregular Verb to Love," "Roar of the Greasepaint . . .," "Peter and the Wolf," "Sugar."

ROBARDS, JASON. Born July 26, 1922 in Chicago. Attended AADA. Bdwy debut 1947 with D'Oyly Carte, followed by "Stalag 17," "The Chase," "Long Day's Journey into Night" for which he received a Theatre World Award, "The Disenchanted," "Toys in the Attic," "Big Fish, Little Fish," "A Thousand Clowns," "Hughie," "The Devils," "We Bombed in New Haven," "Country Girl," OB in "American Gothic," "Iceman Cometh," LCRep's "After the Fall," and "But for Whom Charlie."

ROBERTS, ARTHUR. Born Aug. 10, 1938 in NYC. Harvard graduate. Debut 1964 OB in "Hamlet" (NYSF), followed by "Galileo" (LC), "Boys in the Band," "Anna K.," Bdwy bow 1970 in "Borstal Boy."

ROBERTS, DAVIS. Born Mar. 7, 1917 in Mobile, Ala. Attended U Chicago, UCLA, Actors Lab. Debut 1971 in "Trial of the Catonsville 9."

ROBERTS, RALPH. Born Aug. 17 in Salisbury, NC. Attended UNC. Debut 1948 in "Angel Street," followed by "4 Chekhov Comedies," "S.S. Glencairn," "Madwoman of Chaillot," "Witness for the Prosecution," "The Lark," "Bells Are Ringing," "The Milk Train Doesn't Stop Here Anymore," "Love Suicide at Schofield Barracks."

ROBERTS, TONY. Born Oct. 22, 1939 in NYC. Graduate Northwestern. Bdwy bow 1962 in "Something about a Soldier," followed by "Take Her, She's Mine," "Last Analysis," "The Cradle Will Rock" (OB), "Never Too Late," "Barefoot in the Park," "Don't Drink the Water," "How Now, Dow Jones," "Play It Again, Sam," "Promises, Promises," "Sugar."

ROBERTSON, JANE. Born May 17, 1948 in Bartlesville, Okla. Attended U Okla. Debut OB 1970 in "Shoestring Revues" (ELT), followed by "DuBarry Was a Lady" (ELT), "Buy Bonds Buster."

ROBERTSON, HAMISH. Born Feb. 17, 1943 in Glasgow, Scot. Attended Queen's U. (Can.). Bdwy debut 1972 in "There's One in Every Marriage."

ROBINSON, ANDY. Born Feb. 14, 1942 in NYC. Graduate New School, LAMDA. Debut 1967 OB in "MacBird," followed by "Cannibals," "Futz," "Young Master Dante," "Operation Sidewinder" (LC), "Subject to Fits," LCRep's "Mary Stuart," and "Narrow Road to the Deep North."

ROBINSON, ROGER. Born May 2, 1941 in Seattle, Wash. Attended USCal. Bdwy debut 1969 in "Does a Tiger Wear a Necktie?," OB in "Walk in Darkness," "Jerico-Jim Crow," "Who's Got His Own," "Trials of Brother Jero," "The Miser" (LC), "Interrogation of Havana."

RODGERS, SHEV. Born Apr. 9, 1928 in Holister, Cal. Attended SF State Col. Bdwy bow 1959 in "Redhead," followed by "Music Man," "Man of La Mancha" (also LC), OB in "Get Thee to Canterbury," "War Games."

ROGAN, PETER. Born May 11, 1939 in County Leitrim, Ire. Bdwy debut 1966 in "Philadelphia, Here I Come!," OB in "The Kitchen," "Nobody Hears a Broken Drum," "Picture of Dorian Gray," "Macbeth," "Sjt. Musgrave's Dance," "Stephen D.," "People Are Living There" (LC).

Steven Rosenthal   **Jan Ross**   **Hansford Rowe**   **Diana Sands**   **Ian Sander**

ROGERS, PAUL. Born Mar. 22, 1917 in Plympton, Eng. Attended Chekhov Theatre Sch. Bdwy debut with Old Vic (1956-7) in "Macbeth," "Romeo and Juliet," "Troilus and Cressida," and "Richard II," subsequently in "Photo Finish," "The Homecoming," "Here's Where I Belong," "Sleuth."

ROLLE, ESTHER. Born Nov. 8 in Pompano Beach, Fla. Attended Hunter Col. Bdwy debut 1964 in "Blues for Mr. Charlie," followed by "Purlie Victorious," "Amen Corner," "Don't Play Us Cheap," OB in "The Blacks," "Happy Ending," "Day of Absence," "Evening of One Acts," "Man Better Man," "Brotherhood," "Okakawe," "Rosalee Pritchett," "Dream on Monkey Mt.," "Ride a Black Horse," "Ballet behind the Bridge."

RONAN, ROBERT. Born Feb. 17, 1938 in Richmond Hills, NY. Attended Hofstra U. OB in "Dr. Faustus," "Colombe," NYSF's "Love's Labour's Lost," "All's Well That Ends Well," "Comedy of Errors," "Twelfth Night" and "Henry IV," "The Memorandum," "Invitation To A Beheading," "Trelawny of the Wells," "Timon of Athens" (NYSF).

ROSE, GEORGE. Born Feb. 19, 1920 in Bicester, Eng. Debut with Old Vic 1946 in "Henry IV," followed by "Much Ado About Nothing," "A Man For All Seasons," "Hamlet" "Royal Hunt of the Sun," "Walking Happy," "Loot," "My Fair Lady" (CC'68), "Canterbury Tales," "Coco," "Wise Child."

ROSENTHAL, STEVEN. Born May 3, 1946 in NYC. Graduate Emerson Col. Bdwy debut 1972 in "Capt. Brassbound's Conversion."

ROSQUI, TOM. Born June 12, 1928 in Oakland, Calif. Graduate Col. of Pacific. With LCRep in "Danton's Death," "Condemned of Altona," "Country Wife," "Caucasian Chalk Circle," "Alchemist," "Yerma," and "East Wind," OB in "Collision Course," "Day of Absence," "Brotherhood," "What the Butler Saw." "Waiting for Godot," "Unlikely Heroes" (Bdwy '71).

ROSS, JAMIE. Born May 4, 1939 in Markinch, Scot. Attended RADA. Bdwy debut 1962 in "Little Moon of Alban," followed by "Moon Besieged," "Penny Friend" (OB), "Ari," "Different Times."

ROSS, JAN. Born Feb. 5, 1948 in Long Beach, Cal. Graduate Brandeis U. Debut 1972 OB in "Two if by Sea."

ROUNDS, DAVID. Born Oct. 9, 1938 in Bronxville, NY. Attended Denison U. OB in "You Never Can Tell," "Money," "The Real Inspector Hound," Bdwy debut 1965 in "Foxy" followed by "Child's Play" for which he received a Theatre World Award, "The Rothschilds."

ROUNSEVILLE, ROBERT. Born Mar. 25, 1919 in Attleboro, Mass. Attended Tufts U. Bdwy bow 1937 in "Babes In Arms," followed by "Two Bouquets," "Knickerbocker Holiday," "Higher and Higher," "Up In Central Park," "Show Boat" "Merry Widow," "Candide," "Brigadoon" (CC), "Man of La Mancha" (also LC).

ROWE, HANSFORD. Born May 12, 1924 in Richmond, Va. Graduate URichmond. Bdwy debut 1968 in "We Bombed in New Haven," OB in "Curley McDimple," "Fantasticks," "Last Analysis," "God Says There Is No Peter Ott."

ROWLES, POLLY. Born Jan. 10 in Philadelphia, Pa. Carnegie Tech graduate. Bdwy debut 1938 in "Julius Caesar," followed by "Richard III," "Anne of the Thousand Days," "Golden State," "Small Hours," "Gertie," "Time out for Ginger," "Wooden Dish," "Goodbye Again," "Auntie Mame," "Look after Lulu," "A Mighty Man Is He," "No Strings," "The Killing of Sister George," "Forty Carats," OB in "Older People."

RUSKIN, SHIMEN. Born Feb. 25, 1907 in Vilno, Poland. Bdwy debut 1937 in "Having Wonderful Time," OB in "Saturday Night," "Little Murders," "7 Days of Mourning," "Last Analysis."

RUSSELL, JANE. Born June 21, 1921 in Bemidji, Minn. Attended Max Reinhardt Sch. Bdwy debut 1971 in "Company."

RUSSOM, LEON. Born Dec. 6, 1941 in Little Rock, Ark. Attended Southwestern U. OB in "Futz," (LCRep), "Boys In The Band," "Oh! Calcutta!" "Trial of the Catonsville 9," NYSF's "Henry VI," and "Richard III," "Shadow of a Gunman."

RYAN, CHARLENE. Born in NYC. Bdwy debut 1964 in "Never Live Over a Pretzel Factory," followed by "Sweet Charity," "Fig Leaves Are Falling," "Coco," "A Funny Thing Happened on the Way to the Forum."

RYAN, JOHN P. Born July 30, 1938 in NYC. Graduate CCNY. Bdwy debut 1967 in "Daphne in Cottage D," followed by "Love Suicide at Schofield Barracks," OB in "Big Man," "Nobody Hears a Broken Drum."

ST. JOHN, MARCO. Born May 7, 1939 in New Orleans. Fordham graduate. Bdwy bow 1964 in "Poor Bitos," followed by "And Things That Go Bump in the Night," "Unknown Soldier and His Wife," "Weekend," "Forty Carats," APA's "We Comrades Three," and "War and Peace," OB in "Angels of Anadarko," "Man of Destiny," "Timon of Athens" (NYSF)

SALMON, SCOTTY. Born Jan. 13, 1943 in Wichita Falls, Tex. Bdwy bow 1966 in "Pousse Cafe," followed by "Mame," "George M!," "That's Entertainment"(OB).

SANDER, IAN. Born in NYC; graduate USCal., AADA. Bdwy debut 1971 in "No Place to Be Somebody."

SANDERS, HONEY. Born Dec. 24, 1928 in Bklyn. Attended Hofstra U. Bdwy debut 1961 in "13 Daughters," followed by "Mame," "Education of Hyman Kaplan," "Heathen," CC's "South Pacific" and "Rose Tattoo," OB in "She Shall Have Music," "Tobacco Road."

SANDS, DIANA. Born Aug. 22, 1934 in NYC. Bdwy debut 1958 in "A Raisin in the Sun," followed by "Tiger, Tiger, Burning Bright" for which she received a Theatre World Award, "Blues for Mr. Charlie," "The Owl and the Pussycat," "We Bombed in New Haven," "Gingham Dog," "Ain't Supposed to Die a Natural Death," LCRep's "St. Joan" and "Tiger at the Gate," OB in "An Evening with Will Shakespeare," "World of Sholom Aleichem," "Major Barbara," "Man with the Golden Arm," "Land beyond the River," "The Egg and I," "Another Evening with Harry Stoones," "Black Monday," "Brecht on Brecht," "The Living Premise."

SANTANGELO, MELODY. Born Jan. 25, 1946 in Chicago. Attended Goodman Theatre, UCLA. Bdwy debut 1970 in "Hair," followed by "Lenny."

Fay Sappington

Stephen Scott

Lea Scott

Norman Shelly

Peg Shirley

SAPPINGTON, FAY. Born May 22, 1906 in Galveston, Tex. Attended UTex., Pasadena Playhouse. On Bdwy in "Southern Exposure," "The Cellar and the Well," "Glad Tidings," "J.B.," "The Yearling," "Golden Rainbow," OB in "Campbells of Boston," "In Case of Accident."

SARANDON, CHRIS. Born July 24, 1942 in Beckley, WVa. Graduate UWVa., Catholic U. Bdwy debut 1970 in "The Rothschilds."

SARANDON, SUSAN. Born Oct. 4, 1946 in NYC. Graduate Catholic U. Bdwy debut 1972 in "An Evening with Richard Nixon and . . ."

SAUNDERS, LANNA. Born Dec. 22, 1941 in NYC. Bdwy debut 1957 in "Sunrise at Campobello," followed by "Milk and Honey," "Never Live over a Pretzel Factory," "Philadelphia, Here I Come," OB "Marcus in the High Grass," LCRep's "After the Fall," and "The Changeling," "Anna K."

SAUNDERS, MARILYN. Born Apr. 28, 1948 in Brooklyn. Attended Bklyn Col. OB in "Dames at Sea," Bdwy debut 1970 in "Company."

SCHINDLER, ELLEN. Born Oct. 26, 1942 in Sioux City, I. Graduate Syracuse U. Debut 1969 OB in "The Serpent," followed by "Red Burning Light," "Terminal," "And They Put Handcuffs on the Flowers."

SCHNABEL, STEFAN. Born Feb. 2, 1912 in Berlin, Ger. Attended UBonn, Old Vic. Bdwy bow 1937 in "Julius Caesar," followed by "Shoemaker's Holiday," "Glamour Preferred," "Land of Fame," "Cherry Orchard," "Around the World," "Now I Lay Me Down to Sleep," "Idiot's Delight" (CC), "Love of Four Colonels," "Plain and Fancy," "Small War on Murray Hill," "A Very Rich Woman," "In the Matter of J. Robert Oppenheimer" (LC), "A Patriot for Me," OB in "Tango," "Older People."

SCHROCK, ROBERT. Born June 28, 1945 in Wolf Lake, Ind. Attended Goodman Sch. Debut OB 1970 in "The Dirtiest Show in Town," followed by "The Fantasticks."

SCIORTINO, PAT. Born Oct. 17, 1951 in Lakeland, Fla. Attended Manatee Col. Debut 1972 OB in "No Strings" (ELT).

SCOTT, LEA. Born Oct. 5 in NYC. Debut 1962 OB in "The Blacks," followed by "No Place to Be Somebody," "Black Electra," "Soon Jack November."

SCOTT, STEPHEN. Born Feb. 8, 1928 in London. Attended Central Speech School. Bdwy debut 1967 in "There's a Girl in My Soup," followed by "Borstal Boy," "Vivat! Vivat Regina!"

SCOURBY, ALEXANDER. Born Nov. 13, 1913 in Bklyn. Attended UWVa. Bdwy bow 1936 in "Hamlet," followed by "Henry IV," "Richard II," "A Flag Is Born," "Crime and Punishment," "St. Joan," "Detective Story," "Darkness at Noon," "Tonight in Samarkand," "Vivat! Vivat Regina!," OB "A Month in the Country," "Tovarich," "A Whitman Portrait."

SEKI, HOSHIN. Born Mar. 21, 1941 in NYC. Attended URI, Harvard. Debut 1971 OB in "Basic Training of Pavlo Hummel."

SEVRA, ROBERT. Born Apr. 15, 1945 in Kansas City, Mo. Graduate Stanford U., UMich. Debut 1972 OB in "Servant of Two Masters" (ELT).

SHAKAR, MARTIN. Born in Detroit, Jan. 1, 1940. Attended Wayne State U. OB in "Lorenzaccio," "Macbeth," "The Infantry," "Americana Pastoral," "No Place To Be Somebody," "The World of Mrs. Solomon," "And Whose Little Boy Are You?," "Investigation of Havana," "Night Watch." Bdwy bow 1969 in "Our Town."

SHANNON, MICHAEL. Born Jan. 24, 1943 in Chicago. Graduate Northwestern U. Bdwy bow 1971 in "Butterflies Are Free," OB in "Orestes," "In Case of Accident."

SHARKEY, SUSAN. Born Dec. 12, 1948 in NYC. Graduate U Ariz. Debut OB 1968 in "Guns of Carrar" and "Cuba Si," with LCRep in "Playboy of the Western World," "Good Woman of Setzuan," "Enemy of the People," "People Are Living There" and "Narrow Road to the Deep North."

SHARP, SAUNDRA. Born Dec. 21, 1942 in Cleveland, O. Graduate Bowling Green State U. Bdwy debut 1967 in "Hello, Dolly!," followed OB by "Five on the Black Hand Side," "Black Girl."

SHAW, ROBERT. Born Aug. 9, 1927 in Westhoughton, Eng. RADA graduate. Bdwy debut 1961 in "The Caretaker," followed by "The Physicists," "Gantry," "Old Times."

SHAWN, MICHAEL. Born July 3, 1944 in Springfield, Ill. Bdwy debut 1968 in "Golden Rainbow" followed by "Promises, Promises."

SHELLY, NORMAN. Born May 3, 1921 in Denver, Colo. Attended New School. Bdwy bow 1950 in "Peter Pan," followed by "Daughter of Silence," "Promises, Promises."

SHELTON, REID. Born Oct. 7, 1924 in Salem, Ore. Graduate UMich. Bdwy bow 1952 in "Wish You Were Here," followed by "Wonderful Town," "By the Beautiful Sea," "Saint of Bleecker St." "My Fair Lady," "Oh! What a Lovely War," "Carousel" (CC), "Canterbury Tales," "The Rothschilds," OB in "Phedre," "Butterfly Dream," "Man with a Load of Mischief," "Beggar's Opera."

SHELTON, SLOANE. Born Mar. 17, 1934 in Asheville, NC. Attended Berea Col., RADA. Bdwy bow 1967 in "Imaginary Invalid," "Touch of the Poet," "Tonight at 8:30," "I Never Sang for My Father," OB in "Androcles and the Lion," "The Maids," "Way of the World," "Dark of the Moon," "Basic Training of Pavlo Hummel."

SHEPARD, RED. Born Aug. 20, in Martinez, Cal. Bdwy debut 1970 in "Hair."

SHERWOOD, MADELEINE. Born Nov. 13, 1926 in Montreal, Can. Attended Yale. OB in "Brecht on Brecht," "Medea," "Hey You, Light Man," "Friends and Relations," "Older People," Bdwy in "The Chase," "The Crucible," "Cat on a Hot Tin Roof," "Invitation to a March," "Camelot," "Arturo Ui," "Do I Hear a Waltz?," "Inadmissible Evidence," "All Over."

SHERWOOD, WAYNE. Born in Olivia, Minn. Graduate UOre. Bdwy bow 1955 in "Catch a Star," followed by "Wonderful Town" (CC), OB in "Jacques Brel Is Alive . . .," "Johnny Johnson."

SHIRLEY, PEG. Born Oct. 6 in Philadelphia, Pa. Studied at HB Studio. Bdwy debut 1956 in "Middle of the Night," followed by "The Hostage," "All the Girls Came out to Play," OB in "The Maids," "The Tiger" and "The Typists."

| Harvey Siegel | Ethel Shutta | Stuart Silver | Helen Stenborg | Josef Sommer |

SHOWALTER, MAX. Born June 2, 1917 in Caldwell, Kan. Attended Pasadena Playhouse. Bdwy bow 1938 in "Knights of Song," followed by "Very Warm for May," "My Sister Eileen," "Show Boat," "John Loves Mary," "Make Mine Manhattan," "Hello, Dolly!," "Grass Harp."

SHUTTA, ETHEL. Born Dec. 1, 1896 in NYC. On Bdwy in "Ziegfeld Follies," "Passing Show of 1923," "Marjorie," "Louis XIV," "Whoopee," "My Dear Public," "Jennie," "Follies."

SIEBERT, CHARLES. Born Mar. 9, 1938 in Kenosha, Wisc. Graduate Marquette U., LAMDA. Appeared in "Richard III" (CP), "Galileo" (LC), on Bdwy in "Jimmy Shine," "Gingerbread Lady," "Sticks and Bones."

SIEGEL, HARVEY. Born Feb. 28, 1945 in NYC. Attended Stella Adler Studio. Debut 1971 OB in "Out of the Death Cart," followed by "The Team," "June Moon" (ELT).

SILVER, JOE. Born Sept. 28, 1922 in Chicago. Attended U Wisc., Am. Th. Wing. Bdwy bow 1942 in "Tobacco Road," followed by "Doughgirls," "Heads or Tails," "Nature's Way," "Gypsy," "The Heroine," "The Zulu and the Zayda," "You Know I Can't Hear You When the Water's Running," "Lenny," OB in "Blood Wedding," "Lamp at Midnight," "Joseph and His Brethren," "The Victors," and "Shrinking Bride."

SILVER, STUART. Born June 29, 1947 in Hollywood, Cal. Attended URochester, AADA. Debut 1969 OB in "Little Murders," followed by "Seven Days of Mourning," "Dance Wi' Me," "Wanted."

SILVERS, PHIL. Born May 11, 1911 in Bklyn. In vaudeville before 1939 Bdwy bow in "Yokel Boy," followed by "High Button Shoes," "Top Banana," "Do Re Mi," "How the Other Half Loves," "A Funny Thing Happened on the Way to the Forum."

SIMMS, DONALD. Born Aug. 5, 1934 in NYC. Debut 1964 OB in "Kiss Mama," followed by Bdwy bow 1969 in "3 Men on a Horse," "All the Girls Came out to Play."

SIMONIAN, RONALD. Born Dec. 19, 1948 in Lawrence, Mass. Studied at Intnl. School of Dance. Debut 1972 OB in "DuBarry Was a Lady" (ELT).

SINCLAIR, BETTY. Born Feb. 7, 1907 in Liverpool, Eng. Bdwy debut 1947 in "Winslow Boy," followed by "Deep Blue Sea," "Doctor's Dilemma," "Sleeping Prince," "Apple Cart," "Lord Pengo," "Ivanov," "The Incomparable Max."

SKLAR, MICHAEL. Born July 12, 1944 in Hollywood, Cal. Graduate UCLA. Debut 1971 OB in "June Moon" (ELT).

SLACK, BEN. Born July 23, 1937 in Baltimore, Md. Graduate Catholic U. Debut 1971 OB in "Oedipus at Colonus," followed by "Interrogation of Havana," "Rain."

SLAUGHTER, HARRIET. Born Apr. 2, 1937 in Ft. Worth, Tex. Graduate U Tex. Bdwy debut 1960 in "The Hostage," followed by "Fiddler on the Roof."

SMALL, NEVA. Born Nov. 12, 1952 in NYC. Bdwy debut 1964 in "Something More," followed by "The Impossible Years," "Henry, Sweet Henry," "Frank Merriwell," OB in "Ballad for a Firing Squad," "Tell Me Where the Good Times Are," "How Much, How Much?," "F. Jasmine Addams."

SMITH, ALEXIS. Born June 8, 1921 in Penticton, Can. Attended LACC. Bdwy debut 1971 in "Follies."

SMITH, SHEILA. Born Apr. 3, 1933 in Conneaut, O. Attended Kent State U., Cleveland Playhouse. Bdwy debut 1963 in "Hot Spot," followed by "Mame" for which she received a Theatre World Award, "Follies," "Company," "Sugar," OB in "Taboo Revue," "Anything Goes," "Best Foot Forward," and "Sweet Miani," "Fiorello" (CC'62).

SNYDER, ARLEN DEAN. Born Mar 3, 1933 in Rice, Kan. Graduate U Tulsa, U Iowa. Bdwy bow 1965 in "The Family Way," followed OB in "Benito Cereno," "Hogan's Goat," "Miss Pete," "Open 24 Hours," "Candyapple," "June Moon" (ELT)

SNYDER, DREW. Born Sept. 25, 1946 in Buffalo, NY. Graduate Carnegie Tech. Bdwy debut 1968 with APA in "Pantagleize," "Cocktail Party" "Cock-a-doodle Dandy," and "Hamlet," followed by NYSF's "Henry VI," "Richard III," "Sticks and Bones."

SOMMER, JOSEF. Born June 26, 1934 in Greifswald, Ger. Graduate Carnegie Tech. Bdwy bow 1970 with ASF's "Othello," followed by "Children, Children," "Trial of the Catonsville 9."

SPIELBERG, DAVID. Born Mar. 6, 1940 in Mercedes, Tex. Graduate UTex. Debut 1963 OB in "A Man's a Man," followed by "Two Executioners," "Funnyhouse of a Negro," "MacBird," "Persians," "Trial of the Catonsville 9," "Sleep."

SPIVAK, ALICE. Born Aug. 11, 1935 in Bklyn. Attended HB Studio. Debut 1954 OB in "Early Primrose," followed by "Of Mice and Men," "Secret Concubine," "Port Royal," "Time for Bed—Take Me to Bed," "House of Blue Leaves."

STALEY, JAMES. Born May 20, 1948 in Oklahoma City. Graduate Okla. U. Bdwy debut 1972 in "Promenade, All!"

STANLEY, FLORENCE. Born July 1 in Chicago. Graduate Northwestern. OB in "Machinal," "Electra," Bdwy debut 1965 in "Glass Menagerie," followed by "Fiddler On The Roof," "Prisoner of Second Avenue."

STAPLETON, MAUREEN. Born June 21, 1925 in Troy, NY. Attended HB Studio. Bdwy debut 1946 in "Playboy of the Western World," followed by "Antony and Cleopatra," "Detective Story," "Bird Cage," "Rose Tattoo" for which she received a Theatre World Award, "The Emperor's Clothes," "The Crucible," "Richard III," "The Seagull," "27 Wagons Full of Cotton," "Orpheus Descending," "The Cold Wind and the Warm," "Toys in the Attic," "Glass Menagerie" ('65), "Plaza Suite," "Norman, Is That You?," "Gingerbread Lady," "Country Girl."

STARR, BILL. Born July 6 in San Francisco. Studied at HB Studio. Bdwy debut 1959 in "Take Me Along," followed by "Molly Brown," "All American," "Nowhere to Go but Up," "Something More," "Fade Out—Fade In," "High Spirits," "It's Superman," "Illya, Darling," "Drat! The Cat!," "A Funny Thing Happened on the Way to the Forum."

STENBORG, HELEN. Born Jan. 24, 1925 in Minneapolis, Minn. Attended Hunter Col. OB in "A Doll's House," "A Month in the Country," "Say Nothing," "Rosmersholm," "Rimers of Eldritch," "Trial of the Catonsville 9," Bdwy "Sheep on the Runway" ('69).

Garn Stephens   John Stratton   Pat Stevens   Liam Sullivan   Alexandra Stoddar

STEPHENS, GARN. Born in Tulsa, Okla. Graduate Calif. Western U., Pasadena Playhouse. Debut 1972 OB and Bdwy in "Grease."

STERLING, PHILIP. Born Oct. 9, 1922 in NYC. Graduate UPa. Bdwy bow 1955 in "Silk Stockings," followed by "Interlock," "An Evening with Richard Nixon and . . .," OB "Victims of Duty," "Opening of a Window," "Trojan Women," "Party for Divorce," "Party on Greenwich Ave.," "Peddler," "Summertree," "Older People."

STERN, JOSEPH. Born Sept. 3, 1940 in Los Angeles. Graduate UCLA. Debut 1967 OB in "MacBird!," followed by "Homecoming," "Henry IV," "Last Analysis," "Cymbeline" (NYSF)

STERNHAGEN, FRANCES. Born Jan. 13, 1932 in Washington, DC. Vassar graduate. OB in "Admirable Bashful," "Thieves' Carnival," "Country Wife," "Ulysses in Nighttown," "Saintliness of Margery Kemp," "The Room," "A Slight Ache," "Displaced Person," "Playboy of the Western World" (LC), Bdwy in "Great Day In the Morning," "Right Honourable Gentleman," with APA in "Cocktail Party" and "Cock-a-doodle Dandy," "The Sign in Sidney Brustein's Window."

STEVENS, FRAN. Born Mar. 8 in Washington, DC. Attended Notre Dame, Cleveland Playhouse. Has appeared in "Pousse Cafe," "Most Happy Fella," "A Funny Thing Happened on the Way to the Forum," "How Now Dow Jones," "Her First Roman," "Cry for Us All," "On the Town," OB "Frank Gagliano's City Scene."

STEVENS, PAT. Born in Linden, NJ. Attended HB Studio. Bdwy debut 1967 in "Hello, Dolly!," followed by "Manhattan Arrangement" (OB), "DuBarry Was a Lady" (ELT).

STEVENS, TONY. Born May 2, 1948 in St. Louis, Mo. Debut 1967 CC revival of "Wonderful Town," followed by "Fig Leaves Are Falling," "Billy," "Jimmy," "Boy Friend," "Ballad of Johnny Pot" (OB), "On the Town."

STEWART, RAY. Born Apr. 21, 1932 in San Benito, Tex. Graduate UTex., Pasadena Playhouse. OB in "Black Monday," "Conerico Was Here to Stay," "Second City," "Play," "Experiment," "Fantasticks," LCRep's "King Lear," "A Cry of Players," "Inner Journey," "Mary Stuart," and "Narrow Road to the Deep North," Bdwy bow 1970 in "Postcards."

STOCKING, ROBERT. Born Sept. 3, 1941 in Vicksburg, Miss. Attended Chicago City Col. Debut 1967 OB in "Trials of Brother Jero," followed by "Candaules Commissioner," "The Strong Breed," "No Place to Be Somebody," "Ballet behind the Bridge."

STOCKWELL, JEREMY. Born in Houston, Tex. Graduate UTex. Debut 1969 OB in "Fortune and Men's Eyes," followed by "Nightride."

STODDART, ALEXANDRA. Born Sept. 16, 1947 in La-Grange, Ill. Graduate Northwestern U. Debut 1972 in "The Crucible" (LC).

STOLBER, DEAN. Born Sept. 2, 1944 in Philadelphia, Pa. Graduate Harvard, NYU. Bdwy debut 1960 in "Bye Bye Birdie," followed by "You're a Good Man, Charlie Brown," OB in "The Singing Guitar."

STONEBURNER, SAM. Born Feb. 24, 1934 in Fairfax County, Va. Graduate Georgetown U., AADA. Debut 1960 OB in "Ernest in Love," followed by "Foreplay," Bdwy bow 1972 in "Different Times."

STORM, HOWARD. Born Dec. 11, 1939 in NYC. Bdwy debut 1969 in "The Committee," followed by "Fun City."

STRATTON, JOHN. Born Apr. 15 in San Francisco. Attended HB Studio. Debut 1955 OB in "The Chair," followed by "Leave It to Jane," "Two if by Sea," Bdwy bow "Sweet Charity."

STRITCH, ELAINE. Born Feb. 2, 1925 in Detroit, Mich. Attended Dramatic Workshop. Bdwy debut in "Loco," followed by "Made in Heaven," "Angel in the Wings," "Call Me Madam," "Pal Joey," "On Your Toes," "Bus Stop," "The Sin of Pat Muldoon," "Goldilocks," "Sail Away," "Who's Afraid of Virginia Woolf?," "Wonderful Town" (CC), "Private Lives" (OB), "Company."

STRUDWICK, SHEPPERD. Born Sept. 22, 1907 in Hillsboro, NC. Graduate UNC. Bdwy bow 1929 in "Yellow Jacket," followed by "Both Your Houses," "Let Freedom Ring," "End of Summer," "As You Like It," "Christopher Blake," "Affairs of State," "Ladies of the Corridor," "Doctor's Dilemma," "The Seagull," "Night Circus," "Desert Incident," "Only in America," "J.B.," "Who's Afraid of Virginia Woolf?," "The Devils," "The Price," "Galileo" (LC), NYSF's "Measure for Measure" and "Timon of Athens."

STUART, IAN JOHN. Born May 25, 1940 in London. Attended St. Ignatius Col. Debut 1972 OB in "Misalliance."

STUART, LAURA. Born May 26, 1938 in Philadelphia. Attended Catholic U. OB in "Electra," "Trojan Women," "Women at the Tomb," Bdwy debut 1968 in "Fiddler on the Roof."

STUCKMANN, EUGENE. Born Nov. 16, 1917 in NYC. Bdwy bow 1943 in "Richard III," followed by "Counsellor-at-law," "Othello," "The Tempest," "Foxhole in the Parlor," "Henry VIII," "Androcles and the Lion," "Yellow Jack," "Skipper Next to God," "A Patriot for Me," OB "The Web and the Rock."

STUTHMAN, FRED. Born June 27, 1919 in Long Beach, Cal. Attended UCal. Debut 1970 OB in "Hamlet," followed by "Uncle Vanya," "Charles Abbot & Son," "She Stoops to Conquer," "Master Builder," "Taming of the Shrew," "Misalliance," "Merchant of Venice," "Conditions of Agreement."

SULLIVAN, JEREMIAH. Born Sept. 22, 1937 in NYC. Harvard graduate. Appeared in "Compulsion" (1957), "Ardele" (OB), "Astrakhan Coat," "Philadelphia, Here I Come!," "Lion In Winter," "Hamlet," "A Scent of Flowers" (OB), "House of Blue Leaves" (OB).

SULLIVAN, JOSEPH. Born Nov. 29, 1918 in NYC. Attended Fordham, Am. Theatre Wing. Appeared in "Sundown Beach," "Command Decision," "The Live Wire," "Country Girl," "Oh, Men! Oh, Women!," "The Rainmaker," "Best Man," "Fiddler on the Roof."

SULLIVAN, LIAM. Born May 18, 1923 in Jacksonville, Ind. Attended Harvard. Bdwy bow 1951 in "The Constant Wife," followed by "Little Foxes," OB in "Anna K."

SUTORIUS, JAMES. Born Dec. 14, 1944 in Euclid, O. Graduate Ill. Wesleyan, AMDA. Bdwy debut 1970 in "The Cherry Orchard," OB in "Servant of Two Masters" (ELT).

Donald Symington

Caryl Tenney

Geoffrey Taylor

Brenda Thomson

Rex Thompson

SUTTON, DOLORES. Born in NYC; graduate NYU. Bdwy debut 1962 in "Rhinoceros," followed by "General Seeger," OB in "Man with the Golden Arm," "Machinal," "Career," "Brecht on Brecht," "To Be Young, Gifted and Black," "The Web and the Rock."

SWANSON, GLORIA. Born Mar. 27, 1898 in Chicago. Bdwy debut 1945 in "A Goose for the Gander," followed by "Twentieth Century," "Nina," "Butterflies Are Free."

SWANSON, LARRY. Born Nov. 10, 1930 in Roosevelt, Okla. Graduate Okla.U. Bdwy debut 1966 in "Those That Play the Clowns," followed by "Great White Hope," OB in "Dr. Faustus Lights the Lights," "A Thistle in My Bed," "A Darker Flower," "Vincent," "MacBird!," "Unknown Soldier and His Wife" (LC), "Sound of Music" (CC, JB).

SWEET, DOLPH. Born July 18, 1920 in NYC. Columbia graduate. Bdwy debut 1960 in "Rhinoceros," followed by "Romulus," "The Advocate," "Sign in Sidney Brustein's Window," "The Great Indoors," "Natural Look," "Billy," "Penny Wars," OB in "The Dragon," "Too Much Johnson," "Sjt. Musgrave's Dance," "Ceremony of Innocence," "Death of J. K."

SYMINGTON, DONALD. Born Aug. 30, 1925 in Baltimore, Md. Debut 1947 in "Galileo," followed by CC's "Caesar and Cleopatra," "Dream Girl," and "Lute Song," "A Girl Can Tell," OB in "Suddenly Last Summer," "Lady Windermere's Fan," "Rate of Exchange," "Shrinking Bride," "Murderous Angels."

SYMONDS, ROBERT. Born Dec. 1, 1926 in Bristow, Okla. Attended Tex. U, UMo. With LC Rep in "Danton's Death," "County Wife," "The Alchemist," "Galileo," "St. Joan," "Tiger at the Gates," "Cyrano," "Cry of Players," "Inner Journey," "The Miser," "Time of Your Life," "Camino Real," "Disintegration Of James Cherry," "Silence," "Landscape," "Amphitryon," "Birthday Party," "Landscape," "Silence," "Scenes from American Life," "Play Strindberg," "Mary Stuart," "Narrow Road to the Deep North."

TARLOW, FLORENCE. Born Jan. 19, 1929 in Philadelphia. Graduate Hunter Col. OB in "Beautiful Day," "Istanbul," "Gorilla Queen," "American Hurrah," "Red Cross," "Promenade," Bdwy debut 1968 in "Man in the Glass Booth," "Good Woman of Setzuan" (LC), "Inner City."

TASK, MAGGIE. Born July 4 in Marion, O. Attended Wright Col. Bdwy debut 1960 in "Greenwillow," followed by "Family Affair," "Tovarich," CC's "Most Happy Fella" and "Carousel," "Funny Girl," "Kelly," "Anya," "Time for Singing," "Darling of the Day," "Education of Hyman Kaplan," "Sound of Music."

TAYLOR, CLARICE. Born Sept 20, in Buckingham County, Va. Attended New Theater School. Debut 1943 OB in "Striver's Row," followed by "Major Barbara," "Family Portrait," "Trouble in Mind," "The Egg and I," "A Medal for Willie," "Nat Turner," "Simple Speaks His Mind," "Gold through the Trees," "The Owl Answers," "Song of the Lusitanian Bogey," "Summer of the 17th Doll," "Kongi's Harvest," "Daddy Goodness," "God Is a (Guess What?)," "An Evening of One Acts," "5 on the Black Hand Side," "Man Better Man," "Day of Absence," "Brotherhood," "Akokawe," "Rosalee Pritchett," "Sty of the Blind Pig," "Duplex" (LC).

TAYLOR, GEOFFREY. Born July 1, 1945 in Washington, Iowa. Attended UIowa. Debut OB in "You're a Good Man, Charlie Brown," followed by "The Fantasticks."

TEAGUE, ANTHONY. Born Jan. 4, 1940 in Jacksboro, Tex. Bdwy debut 1963 in "110 in the Shade," followed by "No, No, Nanette."

TENNEY, CARYL. Born July 11 in Thatcher, Ariz. Bdwy debut 1968 in "I'm Solomon," followed by "Two by Two."

THACKER, RUSS. Born June 23, 1946 in Washington, DC. Attended Montgomery Col. Debut 1967 in "Life with Father" (CC), followed OB by "Your Own Thing" for which he received a Theatre World Award, Bdwy bow 1971 in "Grass Harp," "Heathen."

THOMA, CARL. Born Aug. 29, 1947 in Manila, PI. Attended SUNY at Buffalo. Debut 1970 in "The Me Nobody Knows."

THOMAS, PHILIP M. Born May 26, 1949 in Columbus, O. Attended UCal. Bdwy debut 1971 in "No Place to Be Somebody," followed by "The Selling of the President."

THOMPSON, REX. Born Dec. 14, 1942 in NYC. On Bdwy in "Alive and Kicking," "Wisteria Trees," "The King and I," "Escapade," "King of Hearts," "First Love," "Charley's Aunt," "The Incomparable Max."

THOMPSON, SADA. Born Sept. 27, 1929 in Des Moines, Iowa. Graduate Carnegie Tech. Debut OB 1953 in "Under Milk Wood," followed by "Clandestine Marriage," "Murder in the Cathedral," "White Devil," "Carefree Tree," "The Misanthrope," "USA," "River Line," "Ivanov," "The Last Minstrel," "An Evening for Merlin Finch," "The Effect of Gamma Rays On The Man-in-the-Moon Marigolds," on Bdwy in "Festival," "Juno," "Johnny No-Trump," "The American-Dream," "Happy Days." "Twigs."

THOMSON, BRENDA. Born Mar. 2, 1944 in Savannah, Ga. Attended Sarah Lawrence Col. Bdwy debut 1971 in "Company."

THURSTON, TED. Born Jan. 9, 1920 in St. Paul, Minn. Attended Drake U., Wash. U. Debut 1951 in "Paint Your Wagon," followed by "Girl in Pink Tights," "Kismet," "Buttrio Square," "Seventh Heaven," "Most Happy Fella," "Li'l Abner," "13 Daughters," "Happiest Girl in Town," "Let It Ride," "Sophie," "Luther," "Cafe Crown," "I Had a Ball," "Wonderful Town" (CC), "Bible Salesman" (OB), "Celebration," "Gantry," "Wild and Wonderful."

TOBIN, MATTHEW. Born Aug. 10, 1933 in Indianapolis, Ind. Carnegie Tech graduate. Debut OB 1959 in "The Hasty Heart," followed by "Boys from Syracuse," "Mad Show," "Boys in the Band," "Empire Builders," "Lyle," "Survival of St. Joan," "Any Resemblance to Persons Living or Dead," Bdwy bow 1960 in "Redhead," "Love Suicide at Schofield Barracks."

TOLAN, MICHAEL. Born in Detroit, Mich. Graduate Wayne U. Bdwy debut 1955 in "Will Success Spoil Rock Hunter?," followed by "A Hatful of Rain," "The Genius and the Goddess," "Romanoff and Juliet," "A Majority of One," "A Far Country," "Unlikely Heroes," OB in "Coriolanus," "Journey of the Fifth Horse."

John Travolta   Virginia Vestoff   Stephen Van Benschoten   Sasha von Scherler   Ed VanNuys

TOWERS, CONSTANCE. Born May 20, 1933 in Whitefish, Mont. Attended Juilliard, AADA. Bdwy debut 1965 in "Anya," "Show Boat" (LC), CC's "Carousel," "Sound of Music," and "The King and I," "Engagement Baby," JB's "Sound of Music," and "The King and I."

TRACEY, PAUL. Born June 5, 1939 in Durban, SA. Attended Malvern Col. Bdwy debut 1966 in "Wait a Minim!," followed by "The Rothschilds."

TRAPANI, LOU. Born Dec. 17, 1947 in Bklyn. Graduate Hofstra U. Debut 1970 OB in "Journey to Bahia," followed by "Hamlet," "She Stoops to Conquer," "Taming of the Shrew," "Misalliance," "Merchant of Venice," "And They Put Handcuffs on the Flowers."

TRAVOLTA, JOHN. Born Feb. 18, 1954 in Englewood, NJ. Debut 1972 OB in "Rain."

TRIBUSH, NANCY. Born Dec. 18, 1940 in NYC. Graduate Bklyn. Col. Bdwy debut 1961 in "Bye, Bye, Birdie," followed by "Happily Never After," "Oh, Calcutta," OB in "Riverwind," "Hang Down Your Head and Die."

TRONTO, RUDY. Born July 14, 1928 in Peekskill, NY. Bdwy debut 1960 in "Irma La Douce," followed by "Carnival," "Man of La Mancha," OB in "Boys from Syracuse," "Secret Life of Walter Mitty."

TROOBNICK, GENE. Born Aug. 23, 1926 in Boston. Attended Ithaca Col., Columbia. Bdwy bow 1960 in "Second City," followed by "The Odd Couple," "Before You Go," "The Time of Your Life" (LC), OB in "Dynamite Tonight," "A Gun Play."

TUPOU, MANU. Born in 1939 in Fiji Islands. Attended San Francisco State, ULondon. Bdwy bow 1969 in "Indians," followed by "Othello," "Capt. Brassbound's Conversion," OB "Madwoman of Chaillot," "Passion of Antigona Perez," "Wedding of Iphigenia."

TWOMEY, JOHN. Born July 17, 1948 in Salem, Mass. Graduate Brandeis U. Debut 1972 OB in "Hard Job Being God!"

URE, MARY. Born in 1933 in Glasgow, Scot. Attended Central School of Speech. Bdwy debut 1957 in "Look Back in Anger," followed by "Duel of Angels," "Old Times."

URICH, TOM. Born Mar. 26 in Toronto, O. Attended Cin. Cons. OB in "Streets Of New York," "Fantasticks," "Shoemaker's Holiday," Bdwy bow 1970 in "Applause."

VALE, MICHAEL. Born June 28, 1922 in Bklyn. Attended New School. Bdwy bow 1961 in "The Egg," followed by "Cafe Crown," "The Last Analysis," "Impossible Years," OB in "Autograph Hound," "The Moths," "Now There's the Three of Us," "Tall and Rex," "Kaddish."

VAN, BOBBY. Born Dec. 6, 1930 in The Bronx. Bdwy debut 1950 in "Alive and Kicking," followed by "On Your Toes," "No, No, Nanette."

VAN AKEN, GRETCHEN. Born Nov. 15, 1940 in Ridgeway, Pa. Graduate Emerson Col., Central Sch. of Speech, London. Bdwy debut 1964 in "Oliver!," followed by "Walking Happy," OB in "Digging for Apples," "Wanted."

VAN BENSCHOTEN, STEPHEN. Born Aug. 27, 1943 in Washington, DC. Graduate LaSalle Col., Yale. Debut 1967 OB in "King John" (NYSF), Bdwy bow 1971 in "Unlikely Heroes."

VANDIS, TITOS. Born Nov. 7, 1917 in Athens, Greece. Attended Ntl. Theatre Drama School. Bdwy bow 1965 in "On a Clear Day You Can See Forever," followed by "Illya, Darling," "The Guide," "Look to the Lilies," "Man of La Mancha."

VANISON, DOLORES. Born Mar. 25, 1942 in Lynchburg, Va. Graduate Bklyn Col., LIU. Bdwy debut 1969 in "Hello, Dolly!," followed by "Greenwillow" (ELT), "Black Terror" (OB).

VANLEER, JAY. Born June 24, 1931 in Cleveland, O. Graduate Western Reserve U. Bdwy debut 1972 in "Don't Play Us Cheap."

VANNUYS, ED. Born Dec. 28, 1930 in Lebanon, Ind. Attended Ind.U. Debut 1969 OB in "No Place to Be Somebody," Bdwy bow 1971 in same, followed by "Black Terror."

VARRATO, EDMOND. Born Nov. 25, 1919 in Blairsville, Pa. Attended State U., Theatre Wing. Bdwy debut 1948 in "Ballet Ballads," followed by "La Plume de Ma Tante," "Something More," "Pickwick," "Marat/deSade," "St. Joan," "Mike Downstairs," "Man of La Mancha" (also LC).

VERDON, GWEN. Born Jan. 13, 1926 in Culver City, Cal. Bdwy debut 1950 in "Alive and Kicking," followed by "Can-Can" for which she received a Theatre World Award, "Damn Yankees," "New Girl in Town," "Redhead," "Sweet Charity," "Children, Children."

VEREEN, BEN. Born Oct. 10, 1946 in Miami, Fla. Graduate HS Performing Arts. Debut 1965 OB in "Prodigal Son," followed by Bdwy bow in "Hair," then "Jesus Christ Superstar" for which he received a Theatre World Award.

VERNON, HARVEY. Born June 20, 1927 in Flint, Mich. Graduate Wayne State, UMich. Bdwy debut 1971 in "Grass Harp."

VESTOFF, VIRGINIA. Born Dec. 9, 1940 in NYC. OB in "The Boy Friend," "Crystal Heart," "Fall Out," "New Cole Porter Revue," "Man with a Load of Mischief," "Love and Let Love," on Bdwy in "From A to Z" (1960), "Irma La Douce," "Baker Street," "1776."

VIGODA, ABE. Born Feb. 24, 1921 in NYC. OB in "Dance of Death," "Feast of Panthers," "Witches' Sabbath," "Cherry Orchard," "Mrs. Warren's Profession," "A Darker Flower," "The Cat and the Canary," on Bdwy in "Marat/deSade," "Man in the Glass Booth," "Inquest," "Tough to Get Help."

VILLECHAIZE, HERVE. Born Apr. 23, 1943 in Paris. Debut 1969 OB in "Moondreamers," followed by "Young Master Dante," "Honest-to-God Schnozzola," Bdwy bow 1970 in "Gloria and Esperanza." then "Elizabeth I."

VITA, MICHAEL. Born in 1941 in The Bronx. Studied at HB Studio. Bdwy debut 1967 in "Sweet Charity," followed by "Golden Rainbow," "Promises Promises," OB in "Sensations," "That's Entertainment."

VON SCHERLER, SASHA. Born Dec. 12 in NYC. Bdwy debut 1959 in "Look after Lulu," followed by "Rape of the Belt," "The Good Soup," "Great God Brown," "First Love," "Alfie," "Harold," OB in "Admirable Bashville," "The Comedian," "Conversation Piece," "Good King Charles' Golden Days," "Under Milkwood," "Plays for Bleecker Street," "Ludlow Fair," "Twelfth Night" (CP), "Sondra," "Cyrano" (LC), "Crimes of Passion," "Henry VI," "Trelawny of the Wells," "Screens," "Soon Jack November."

| Michael Wager | Art Wallace | George Wallace | Ruth Warrick | Frederick Warriner |

WAGER, MICHAEL. Born Apr. 29, 1925 in NYC. Harvard graduate. Bdwy bow 1949 in "Streetcar Named Desire," followed by "Small Hours," "Bernardine," "Merchant of Venice," "Misalliance," "Remarkable Mr. Pennypacker," "Othello," "Henry IV," "St. Joan," "Firstborn," "The Cradle Will Rock," "Three Sisters," "The Cuban Thing," OB in "Noontide," "Brecht on Brecht," "Sunset," "Penny Friend," "Trelawny of the Wells," "Taming of the Shrew."

WALKEN, CHRISTOPHER. Born Mar. 31, 1943 in Astoria, NY. Attended Hofstra U. Bdwy debut 1958 in "J.B.," followed by "Best Foot Forward" (OB), "High Spirits," "Baker Street," "The Lion In Winter," "Measure For Measure" (CP), "Rose Tattoo" (CC'66) for which he received a Theatre World Award, "Unknown Soldier and His Wife," "Iphigenia In Aulis" (OB), "Rosencrantz and Guildenstern Are Dead," "Lemon Sky" (OB), "Scenes from American Life," (LC), "Cymbeline" (NYSF).

WALKER, SYDNEY. Born May 4, 1921 in Philadelphia. Attended Conservatoire Nationale, Paris, Bdwy bow 1960 in "Becket," OB in "Volpone," "Julius Caesar," "King Lear," "The Collection," "A Scent of Flowers," "The Nuns," with APA in "You Can't Take It with You," "War and Peace," "Right You Are," "School for Scandal," "We Comrades Three," "The Wild Duck," "Pantagleize," "The Cherry Orchard," "The Misanthrope," "Cocktail Party," and "Cock-A-Doodle Dandy," "Blood Red Roses," with LCRep in "Playboy of the Western World," "Good Woman of Setzuan," "Enemy of the People," "Antigone," Mary Stuart," "Narrow Road to the Deep North," "Twelfth Night," "The Crucible."

WALLACE, ART. Born Sept. 21, 1935 in Oklahoma City. Attended Wash.U., Actors Studio./Bdwy debut 1963 in "No Place to Go but Up," followed by "A Joyful Noise," "Music Man" (CC), "Purlie," OB in "Tattooed Countess," "Flaholley" (ELT), "Hotel Passionato," "Now Is the Time for All Good Men," "Perfect Party."

WALLACE, GEORGE. Born June 8, 1917 in NYC. Studied at Ben Bards Drama Sch. Bdwy debut 1955 in "Pipe Dream," followed by "Pajama Game," "New Girl in Town," "Jennie," "Company."

WALLACE, LEE. Born July 15, 1930 in NYC. Attended NYU. Debut OB 1966 in "Journey of the Fifth Horse," followed by "Saturday Night," "Evening with Garcia Lorca," "Macbeth" (NYSF), "Booth Is Back in Town," "Awake and Sing," "Shepherd of Avenue B," "Basic Training of Pavlo Hummel."

WALLACH, ELI. Born Dec. 7, 1915 in Bklyn. Graduate UTex., CCNY. Attended Actors Studio, Neighborhood Playhouse. Bdwy bow 1945 in "Skydrift," followed by "Henry VIII," "Androcles and the Lion," "Alice in Wonderland," "Yellow Jack," "What Every Woman Knows," "Antony and Cleopatra," "Mr. Roberts," "Lady from the Sea," "Rose Tattoo" for which he received a Theatre World Award, "Mlle. Colombe," "Teahouse of the August Moon," "Major Barbara," "The Cold Wind and the Warm," "Rhinoceros," "Luv," "The Staircase," "Promenade, All!," OB in "The Chairs," "The Tiger" and "The Typists."

WARD, DOUGLAS TURNER. (also uses Douglas Turner) Born May 5, 1930 in Burnside, La. Attended UMich. Bdwy bow 1959 in "A Raisin in the Sun," OB in "The Iceman Cometh," "The Blacks," "Pullman Car Hiawatha," "Bloodknot," "Happy Ending," "Day of Absence," "Kongi's Harvest," "Ceremonies in Dark Old Men," "The Harangues," "The Reckoning," "Frederick Douglass through His Own Words."

WARD, JANET. Born Feb. 19 in NYC. Attended Actors Studio. Bdwy bow 1945 in "Dream Girl," followed by "Anne of the Thousand Days," "Detective Story," "King of Friday's Men," "Middle of the Night," "Miss Lonelyhearts," "J.B.," "Cheri," "The Egg," "Impossible Years," "Of Love Remembered," OB in "Chapparal," "The Typists" and "The Tiger," "Summertree," "Dream of a Blacklisted Actor," "Cruising Speed 600 MPH," "One Flew over the Cuckoo's Nest."

WARE, BILL. Born Jan. 30, 1943 in NYC. Bdwy debut 1970 in "Les Blancs," OB in "Masks in Brown," "Slave Ship."

WARRICK, RUTH. Born June 29 in St. Joseph, Mo. Attended UMo. Bdwy debut 1957 in "Miss Lonelyhearts," followed by "Take Me Along," OB in "Single Man at a Party," "Any Resemblance to Persons Living or Dead," "Misalliance," "Conditions of Agreement."

WARRINER, FREDERIC. Born June 2, 1916 in Pasadena, Cal. Graduate Pasadena Playhouse. Bdwy debut 1950 in "King Lear," followed by "Speak of the Devil," "Mr. Pickwick," "Taming of the Shrew," "Getting Married," "St. Joan," "A Pin to See the Peepshow," "Wayward Saint," "Caligula," "Major Barbara," "Time Remembered," "Oliver," "Man for All Seasons," "Portrait of a Queen," "Two Gentlemen of Verona" (NYSF), OB in "Invitation to a Beheading," "Trelawny of the Wells."

WATERSTON, SAM. Born Nov. 15, 1940 in Cambridge, Mass. Graduate Yale. Bdwy bow 1963 in "Oh, Dad, Poor Dad . . .," followed by "First One Asleep Whistle," "Halfway up the Tree," "Indians," "Hay Fever," OB in "As You Like It," "Thistle in My Bed," "The Knack," "Fitz," "Biscuit," "La Turista," "Posterity For Sale," "Ergo," "Muzeeka," "Red Cross," "Henry IV" (CP), "Spitting Image," "I Met A Man," "Brass Butterfly" "Trial of the Catonsville 9," "Cymbeline," "Hamlet" and "Much Ado about Nothing" (NYSF).

WATSON, DOUGLASS. Born Feb. 24, 1921 in Jackson, Ga. Graduate UNC. Bdwy bow 1947 in "The Iceman Cometh," followed by "Antony and Cleopatra" for which he received a Theatre World Award, "Leading Lady," "Richard III," "Happiest Years," "That Lady," "Wisteria Trees," "Romeo and Juliet," "Desire under the Elms," "Sunday Breakfast," "Cyrano de Bergerac," "Confidential Clerk," "Portrait of a Lady," "Miser," "Young and Beautiful," "Little Glass Clock," "Country Wife," "Man for All Seasons," "Chinese Prime Minister," "Marat/deSade," "Prime of Miss Jean Brodie," "Pirates of Penzance," "The Hunter" (OB).

Susan Watson	Jim Weston	Billie Lou Watt	Walter Willison	Jane Whitehill

WATSON, SUSAN. Born Dec. 17, 1938 in Tulsa, Okla. Attended Juilliard. OB in "The Fantasticks," "Lend an Ear," "Follies of 1910," "Carousel" (LC), CC's "Oklahoma!," and "Where's Charley?," on Bdwy in "Bye Bye Birdie," "Carnival," "Ben Franklin In Paris," "A Joyful Noise," "Celebration," "Beggar on Horseback" (LC), "No, No, Nanette."

WATT, BILLIE LOU. Born June 20, 1924 in St. Louis, Mo. Attended Northwestern U. Bdwy bow 1945 in "Little Women," followed by "Barefoot Boy with Cheek," "King of Hearts," "Tough to Get Help."

WEEMS, NANCY. Born Dec. 30, 1948 in Glendale, Cal. Attended Stephens Col. Debut 1972 OB in "Servant of Two Masters" (ELT).

WEIL, ROBERT E. Born Nov. 18, 1914 in NYC. Attended NYU. Bdwy bow in "New Faces of 1942," followed by "Burlesque," "Becket," "Once upon a Mattress," "Blood, Sweat and Stanley Poole," "Night Life," "Arturo Ui," "Love Your Crooked Neighborhood" (OB), "Beggar on Horseback" (LC), "Lenny."

WEISS, KENNETH. Born Sept. 16, 1947 in Newark, NJ. Graduate UPittsburgh, NYU. Debut 1972 OB in "Eros and Psyche."

WELBES, GEORGE M. Born Sept, 14, 1934 in Sioux Falls, SD. Graduate USD. Debut 1968 OB in "Oh Say Can You See L.A.," followed by "The Other Man," "Oh! Calcutta!"

WELCH, CHARLES. Born Feb. 2, 1921 in New Britain, Conn. Attended Am. Th. Wing. Bdwy bow 1948 in "Cloud 7," followed by "Make a Million," "Donnybrook," "Golden Boy," "Breakfast at Tiffany's," "Married Alive," "Darling of the Day," "Dear World," "Follies."

WELDON, CHARLES. Born June 1, 1940 in Wetumka, Okla. Bdwy debut 1969 in "Big Time Buck White," followed OB by "Ride a Black Horse," "Long Time Coming and a Long Time Gone," "Jamimma."

WESTCOTT, LYNDA. Born June 17, 1942 in Muskegon, Mich. Attended City Col. OB in "Deep Are the Roots," "Finian's Rainbow," "International Wrestling Match," "No Place to Be Somebody," "Murderous Angels."

WESTON, JIM. Born Aug. 2, 1942 in Montclair, NJ. Attended Manchester Col., AADA. Bdwy bow 1969 in "Red, White and Maddox," followed by "Lovely Ladies, Kind Gentlmen," OB in "She Loves Me" (ELT), "Ballad of Johnny Pot," "A Gun Play."

WHEEL, PATRICIA. Born in NYC. Has appeared in "Cyrano," "The Tempest," "Arms and the Man," "Little Brown Jug," "Stars Weep," "Browning Version," "Cry of the Peacock," "Gertie," "Sacred Flame," "Soldiers," "Butterflies Are Free," "Voices."

WHITE, JANE. Born Oct. 30, 1922 in NYC. Attended Smith Col. Bdwy debut 1942 in "Strange Fruit," followed by "Climate of Eden," "Take a Giant Step," "Jane Eyre," "Once upon a Mattress," "Cuban Thing," OB in "Razzle Dazzle," "Insect Comedy," "The Power and the Glory," "Hop, Signor," "Trojan Women," "Iphigenia in Aulis," "Cymbeline" (NYSF).

WHITEHILL, JANE. Born Nov. 9 in Durham, NC. Graduate UChicago. Debut 1968 OB in "People vs. Ranchman," followed by "Young Master Dante," "War Games," "Dance Wi' Me."

WHYTE, DONN. Born Feb. 23, 1941 in Chicago. Attended Northwestern. Debut 1969 OB in "The Brownstone Urge," followed by "Foreplay," "One Flew over the Cuckoo's Nest."

WIDDOES, KATHLEEN. Born Mar. 21, 1939 in Wilmington, Del. Attended Paris' Theatre des Nations. Bdwy debut 1958 in "The Firstborn," followed by "World of Suzie Wong," OB "Three Sisters," "The Maids," "You Can't Take It with You," "To Clothe the Naked," "World War 2-1/2," "Beggar's Opera," "Much Ado About Nothing" (NYSF).

WIEBEN, MICHAEL. Born Aug. 17, 1944 in El Centro, Cal. Graduate Cal-State. Debut 1972 OB in "Dylan."

WILCOX, RALPH. Born Jan. 30, 1951 in Milwaukee, Wisc. Attended UWisc. Debut 1971 OB in "Dirtiest Show in Town," Bdwy bow 1971 in "Ain't Supposed to Die a Natural Death."

WILDER, DAVID. Born Dec. 26, 1936 in The Bronx. Graduate CCNY. Studied at Juilliard. Bdwy debut 1968 in "Zorba," followed by "Man of La Mancha," "1776," "On the Town."

WILKERSON, ARNOLD. Born Apr. 6, 1943 in San Francisco. Attended RADA. Bdwy debut 1968 in "Jimmy Shine," OB in "Hair," "Don't Bother Me, I Can't Cope."

WILKINSON, KATE. Born Oct. 25 in San Francisco. Attended San Jose State Col. Bdwy debut 1967 in "Little Murders," followed by "Johnny No-Trump," "Watercolor," "Postcards," "Ring Round the Bathtub," OB in "La Madre," "Earnest in Love," "Story of Mary Surratt" (ELT), "Bring Me a Warm Body," "Child Buyer," "Rimers of Eldritch," "A Doll's House," "Hedda Gabler."

WILLIAMS, BARBARA. Born May 24 in Milwaukee, Wisc. Attended Northwestern U. On Bdwy in "Damn Yankees," "Music Man," "Different Times," OB in "Streets of NY."

WILLIAMS, DICK. Born Aug. 9, 1938 in Chicago. Debut 1968 OB in "Big Time Buck White," followed by "Jamimma," Bdwy (1971) in "Ain't Supposed to Die a Natural Death."

WILLIAMS, ELLWOODSON. Born June 17, 1937 in Jacksonville, NC. Graduate Tenn. AIU. Debut OB 1968 in "Cadillac Dreams," followed by "Land beyond the River," "Voice of the Gene," "Jerico-Jim Crow," "Duet in Black," "Adding Machine," "A Man's a Man," "Cry the Beloved Country," "Mercury Island," "Middle Class Black," "Ceremonies in Dark Old Men," "Murderous Angels," Bdwy bow 1971 in "Two Gentlemen of Verona."

WILLIAMS, TENNESSEE. Born Mar. 26, 1911 in Columbus, Miss. Graduate UIowa. Debut 1972 OB in his own play "Small Craft Warnings."

WILLISON, WALTER. Born June 24, 1947 in Monterey Park, Calif. Bdwy debut 1970 in "Norman, Is That You?," followed by "Two by Two" for which he received a Theatre World Award, "Wild and Wonderful."

WILSON, ELIZABETH. Born Apr. 4, 1925 in Grand Rapids, Mich. Attended Neighborhood Playhouse. On Bdwy in "Picnic," "Desk Set," "Tunnel of Love," "Big Fish, Little Fish," "Sheep on the Runway" "Sticks and Bones," OB in "Plaza 9," "Eh?," "Little Murders," "Good Woman of Setzuan" (LC).

WILSON, LEE. Born Jan. 23, 1948 in Wilmington, Del. Attended HB Studio. Debut 1967 in "Hello, Dolly!," followed by "Here's Where I Belong," "How Now Dow Jones," "La Strada," "Oklahoma!" (LC), "You're a Good Man, Charlie Brown."

Kelly Wood

Aston S. Young

Eda Zahl

Ronald Young

Carol Ziske

WILSON, MARY LOUISE. Born Nov. 12, 1936 in New Haven, Conn. Graduate Northwestern. OB in "Our Town," "Upstairs at the Downstairs," "Threepenny Opera," "A Great Career," "Whispers on the Wind," "Beggar's Opera," Bdwy in "Hot Spot," "Flora, the Red Menace," "Criss-Crossing," "Promises, Promises."

WINDE, BEATRICE. Born Jan. 5 in Chicago. Debut 1966 OB in "In White America," followed by "June Bug Graduates Tonight," Bdwy bow 1971 in "Ain't Supposed to Die a Natural Death" for which she received a Theatre World Award.

WINDUST, PENELOPE. Born in NYC; attended Carnegie Tech. Bdwy debut 1967 in "Spofford," followed by "Elizabeth I."

WINN, KITTY. Born 1944 in Washington, DC. Graduate Boston U. Bdwy debut 1969 in "Three Sisters," followed by "Hamlet" (NYSF).

WINSTON, HATTIE. Born Mar. 3, 1945 in Greenville, Miss. Attended Howard U. OB in "Prodigal Son," "Day of Absence," "Pins and Needles," "Weary Blues," "Man Better Man" "Billy Noname," "Sambo," Bdwy in "The Me Nobody Knows," "Two Gentlemen of Verona."

WINTER, EDWARD. Born June 3, 1937 in Roseburg, Ore. Attended UOre. With LCRep. in "Country Wife," "Condemned of Altona," and "Caucasian Chalk Circle," "Waiting for Godot," Bdwy in "Cabaret," "Birthday Party," "Promises, Promises," "Night Watch."

WINTERS, ROLAND. Born Nov. 22, 1904 in Boston. Attended Boston Sch. of Arts. Bdwy debut 1924 in "The Firebrand," followed by "Who Was That Lady I Saw You With?," "A Cook for Mr. General," "Take Her, She's Mine," "Calculated Risk," "Minnie's Boys," "The Country Girl."

WISEMAN, JOSEPH. Born May 15, 1919 in Montreal, Can. Attended CCNY. Appeared in "Abe Lincoln in Illinois," "Journey to Jerusalem," "Candle in the Wind," "Three Sisters," "Storm Operation," "Joan of Lorraine," "Antony and Cleopatra," "Detective Story," "That Lady," "King Lear," "Golden Boy," "The Lark," LCRep's "Marco Millions," "Incident at Vichy," and "In the Matter of J. Robert Oppenheimer," OB in "Duchess of Malfi," "Last Analysis."

WITHAM, JOHN. Born Apr. 3, 1947 in Plainfield, NJ. Graduate AMDA. Debut 1972 OB in "Two if by Sea."

WOLF, LAWRENCE. Born June 12, 1934 in NYC. Studied at Stella Adler Studio. Debut 1967 OB in "The Experiment," followed by "Narrow Road to the Deep North" (LC).

WOLFE, JOEL. Born Sept. 19, 1936 in NYC. Graduate CCNY. Debut 1968 OB in "Ergo," followed by "Room Service," "The Co-op."

WOOD, KELLY. Born Nov. 10, 1943 in Chicago. Attended San Diego State Col. Debut 1964 OB in "Cindy," followed by "Pequod," "A Gun Play," on Bdwy in "Cactus Flower," "Happiness Is a Little Thing Called a Rolls Royce," "The Sign in Sidney Brustein's Window."

WOODS, JAMES. Born Apr. 18, 1947 Vernal, Utah. Graduate MIT. Bdwy debut 1970 in "Borstal Boy," followed by "Saved" (OB), "Conduct Unbecoming," "Trial of the Catonsville 9," "Moonchildren" for which he received a Theatre World Award.

WOODS, RICHARD. Born May 9, 1930 in Buffalo, NY. Graduate Ithaca Col. Bdwy in "Beg, Borrow or Steal," "Capt. Brassbound's Conversion," "Sail Away," "Coco." OB in "The Crucible," "Summer and Smoke," "American Gothic," "Four-In-One," "My Heart's In The Highlands," "Eastward In Eden," "The Long Gallery," "The Year Boston Won The Pennant" and "In The Matter of J. Robert Oppenheimer" (LC), with APA in "You Can't Take It With You," "War and Peace," "School For Scandal," "Right You Are," "The Wild Duck," "Pantagleize," "Exit The King," "The Cherry Orchard," "Cock-A-Doodle Dandy," and "Hamlet."

WRIGHT, BOB. Born 1911 in Columbia, Mo. Attended U. Mo. Bdwy bow 1948 in "Make Mine Manhattan," followed by "Kiss Me, Kate," "Hit the Trail," "South Pacific" (CC'57), "Tall Story," "Merry Widow" (LC), "Sound of Music" (CC'67), "Man of La Mancha."

WYLER, HILLARY. Born Aug. 15, 1946 in Bklyn. Graduate Northeastern U. Debut 1969 OB in "Trumpets and Drums," followed by "Macbeth," "Oedipus at Colonus" (ELT).

YOHN, ERICA. Born in NYC. OB in "Agammemnon," "Circle of Chalk," "Ascent of F6," "Dream of Love," "Lysistrata," "Middle Man What Now," "Heel of Achilles," "Empire Builders," LCRep's "Yerma," "Caucasian Chalk Circle," and "Danton's Death," on Bdwy in "That Summer, That Fall," "Lenny."

YOUNG, ASTON S. Born June 6, 1930 in NYC. Debut 1965 OB in "The Old Glory," followed by "Outside Man," "Arms and the Man," "Benito Cerino," "Trials of Brother Jero," "Strong Breed," "Man Better Man," "Jamimma."

YOUNG, MADONNA. Born July 16 in Lackawanna, NY. Graduate NYU, AADA. Debut 1972 OB in "DuBarry Was a Lady."

YOUNG, RONALD. Born June 11, 1941 in Tulsa, Okla. Graduate Tulsa U. Bdwy debut in "Hello, Dolly!," followed by "Mame," "George M!," "The Boy Friend," "Different Times."

ZAHL, EDA. Born Nov. 27, 1948 in NYC. Graduate Bennington Col. Bdwy debut 1972 in "The Country Girl."

ZALOOM, JOE. Born July 30, 1944 in Utica, NY. Graduate Catholic U. Bdwy debut 1972 in "Capt. Brassbound's Conversion."

ZANG, EDWARD. Born Aug. 19, 1934 in NYC. Graduate Boston U. OB in "Good Soldier Schweik," "St. Joan" (LC), "Boys in the Band," "The Reliquary of Mr. and Mrs. Potterfield," "Last Analysis."

ZARIT, PAM. Born Mar. 7, 1944 in Chicago. Attended U Denver, Northwestern U. Bdwy debut 1969 in "Promises, Promises," followed by "The Selling of the President."

ZISKE, CAROL ANNE. Born Aug. 5, 1946 in Detroit, Mich. Attended UMich. Debut 1971 OB in "F. Jasmine Addams," followed by "One for the Money" (ELT).

ZORICH, LOUIS. Born Feb. 12, 1924 in Chicago. Attended Roosevelt U. OB in "Six Characters in Search of an Author," "Crimes and Crimes," "Henry V," "Thracian Horses," "All Women Are One," "Good Soldier Schweik," "Shadow of Heroes," "To Clothe the Naked," Bdwy in "Becket," "Moby Dick," "Odd Couple," "Hadrian VII," "Moonchildren," "Fun City."

ZWICK, JOEL. Born Jan. 11, 1942 in Bklyn. Graduate Bklyn Col. Debut 1967 OB in "MacBird!," followed by "Dance Wi' Me."

Spring Byington (1940)

John Chapman (1965)

Maurice Chevalier (1964)

OBITUARIES

LEAH BAIRD, 80, former Broadway, and pioneer film actress, died of anemia in Hollywood on Oct. 3, 1971 after a long illness. Prior to entering films, appeared for 3 years on Broadway with Douglas Fairbanks in "Gentleman from Mississippi," among other plays. Surviving is her husband, former producer Arthur Beck.

HERBERT BIBERMAN, 71, stage and film director, died in NYC of bone cancer on June 30, 1971. Philadelphia born, he joined Theatre Guild in 1928 and directed such plays as "Red Dust," "Valley Forge," "Miracle at Verdun," and "Green Grow the Lilacs," before going to Hollywood. Surviving are his widow, actress Gale Sondergaard, a son and daughter.

JOHN HUNTER BOOTH, 85, playwright and screenwriter, died after a long illness on Nov. 23, 1971 in Norwood, Mass. His plays include "The Masquerader," "Keep Her Smiling," "Like a King," "No Trespassing," and "Brass Buttons." At one time he had five plays running simultaneously on Broadway. In the early '30's he went to Hollywood. A son survives.

RAE BOURBON, 78, night club entertainer and female impersonator, died of a heart ailment on July 19, 1971 in the Big Spring, Tex., prison hospital. He was under a 99 year sentence as an accomplice in murder. Had appeared with Mae West in "Catherine Was Great," and "Diamond Lil." No survivors reported.

ETHEL BRITTON, 57, stage and tv actress, died Feb. 26, 1972 in her NYC home. Appeared in such plays as "Harvey," "Middle of the Night," "Never too Late," and "Best Laid Plans." No reported survivors.

SPRING BYINGTON, 77, stage and screen actress, died in her Hollywood home on Sept. 8, 1971. Born in Colorado Springs, began career with Denver stock company. Made Bdwy debut in 1924 in "Beggar on Horseback," followed by "Puppy Love," "When Ladies Meet," "Weak Sisters," "The Great Adventure," "Merchant of Venice," "Tonight at 12," "Ladies Don't Lie," and "Once in a Lifetime," among others. Went to Hollywood in 1934 and appeared in over 75 movies. Her greatest success was the radio and tv series "December Bride." Surviving are 2 daughters.

REV. THOMAS F. CAREY, 68, director of the Blackfriars Guild from 1941, died in a NY hospital on May 8, 1972. Blackfriars Theatre was among the first off-Broadway experimental showcases, and under Rev. Carey's direction produced over 75 original plays. He was founder of the Blackfriar Institute of Dramatic Arts (now part of Catholic Univ.), and the National Catholic Theatre Conference (now National Theatre Arts Conference).

JOHN CHAPMAN, 71, retired drama critic for the NY Daily News, died Jan. 19, 1972 in Westport, Conn. He joined the Daily News drama staff in 1929 and retired in July of 1971. Had served as president of NY Drama Critics Circle, and edited "Best Plays" yearbooks from 1947 to 1953. He leaves his widow and a daughter.

MAURICE CHEVALIER, 83, France's most popular and best-known entertainer and actor, died in a Paris hospital on Jan. 1, 1972 from cardiac arrest, after fighting a kidney ailment. His career spanned almost 70 years, beginning in cafes, and rising to headliner of revues, and international fame as film star, and singer with straw hat and cane. He brought his one-man show to NY in 1947 and returned successfully several times thereafter through 1966. He was divorced from singer Yvonne Vallee. Several nieces and nephews survive.

GORDON CLARKE, 65, stage and film actor, died in NYC on Jan. 11, 1972 after a coronary attack while at The Lambs Club. Among his stage appearances were "Three Men on a Horse," "The Investigation," "Dylan," "The Best Man," "Arms and the Man," "Three Bags Full," and "The Yearling." His widow survives.

GLADYS COOPER, 82, London-born stage and film actress, died in her sleep on Nov. 17, 1971 in her Henley-on-Thames home in Eng. She had been ill with pneumonia for several weeks. Made her debut in 1905, and reached stardom in 1922. Her first Bdwy appearance was in 1934 in "The Shining Hour," followed by "Othello," "Macbeth," "Call It a Day," "The Chalk Garden," and "Passage to India." She also appeared in "The Rogues" tv series. In 1967 she was made a Dame Commander of the British Empire. From her 3 marriages, two daughters survive.

JEROME COWAN, 74, stage, tv, and film actor, died Jan. 24, 1972 in Hollywood. After burlesque and vaudeville, made Bdwy debut in 1923 in "We've Got to Have Money," followed by "Frankie and Johnny," "Little Black Book," "Marathon," "Both Your Houses," "As Thousands Cheer," "Paths of Glory," "Boy Meets Girl," "My Three Angels," "Lunatics and Lovers," and "Say, Darling," among others. Was in over 100 films, and the "Tycoon" and "Alias Smith and Jones" tv series. Surviving are his widow, former actress Helen Dodge, and 2 daughters.

MAY CRAIG, 83, an actress with the Abbey Theatre Company, died in her native Dublin on Feb. 8, 1972. She appeared on Bdwy, beginning in 1932, in "The Plough and the Stars," "Juno and the Paycock," "Autumn Fire," "Big House," "King Oedipus," "The Well of the Saints," and "Church Street." She leaves 2 daughters and a son.

CHARLIE DALE, 90, deadpan partner of the Smith and Dale vaudeville team, died Nov. 16, 1971 of natural causes in Teaneck, N.J. Their partnership began when Dale (Charles Marks) was 16 and Smith (Joe Seltzer) was 14, and lasted 70 years. They were headliners at the Palace for many years, and made several films in the 1930's. After the death of Mrs. Dale in 1968, he joined Mr. Smith at the Actors Fund Home. A brother and sister survive.

MARGARET DALE, 96, retired Bdwy leading lady, died in a NYC hospital on Mar. 23, 1972. She co-starred with George Arliss, E. H. Sothern, and John Drew, and played character parts until her retirement 25 years ago. Her most memorable roles were in "Disraeli," "The Master," "The Importance of Being Earnest," "The Mummy and the Humming Bird," "The Duke of Killiecrankie," "If I Were King," "Caesar's Wife," "Cradle Snatchers," "Dinner at 8," "The Dark Tower," "The Old Maid," "Tovarich," "The Late George Apley," and "Lady in the Dark." No reported survivors.

DOROTHY DALTON, 78, stage and silent film star, died Apr. 13, 1972 in her Scarsdale, NY home. Her biggest successes were "Aphrodite" and "The Country Wife." After her marriage in 1924 to producer Arthur Hammerstein, she appeared infrequently. A daughter survives.

BLEVINS DAVIS, 68, producer and playwright, died July 16, 1971 in London. His greatest success was as co-producer of "Porgy and Bess" in 1952. Other productions were "Rhapsody," "A Joy Forever," "Skipper Next to God," and "Ballet Ballads." No immediate survivors.

JASPER DEETER, 78, actor, director, producer, teacher, and founder of Hedgerow Theatre in Pa., died May 31, 1972 in Media, Pa., of complications following a fall that resulted in a broken hip. After cremation his ashes were scattered in the garden of his home in Summerdale, Pa. No reported survivors.

BRIAN DONLEVY, 71, Irish-born stage and film actor, died Apr. 5, 1972 of cancer in the Motion Picture Hospital. Made Bdwy debut 1924 in "What Price Glory?," followed by "Hit the Deck!," "Ringside," "Rainbow," "Queen Bee," "Up Pops the Devil," "Peter Flies High," "Society Girl," "Inside Story," "Boy Friend," "Three-Cornered Moon," "The Milky Way," "Life Begins at 8:40." A daughter survives.

CLIFF EDWARDS, 76, stage and film singer-actor, also known as "Ukelele Ike," died in Hollywood on July 17, 1971. After headlining in vaudeville with his ukelele, appeared on Bdwy in "George White's Scandals," "Lady Be Good," "Sunny," and "Ziegfeld Follies." Is credited with selling over 74 million records including "Ja-Da," "Singin' in the Rain," and "When You Wish upon a Star" which he introduced. He was twice married and divorced.

Gladys Cooper (1961)

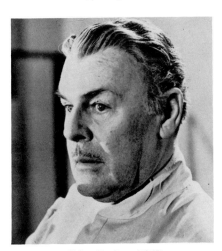

Brian Donlevy (1965)

Cliff Edwards

Thomas Gomez (1952)

Dorothy Greener (1960)

Van Heflin (1960)

PHOEBE EPHRON, 57, co-author with her husband Henry Ephron, of several stage and screen comedies, died in her NYC home Oct. 13, 1971 after a long illness. Her plays include "Three's a Family," "Howie," "Take Her, She's Mine," and "My Daughter, Your Son." Surviving are her husband and 4 daughters.

BILLY GILBERT, 77, stage and screen comedian and director-producer, died Sept. 23, 1971 in Hollywood. Born of theatrical parents, began his career as female impersonator with a singing children's group, subsequently appearing in vaudeville, burlesque, films, tv, and on stage and radio. For 15 years was a Bdwy producer. Probably best remembered as the man of many sneezes. Appeared on Bdwy in "Gypsy Lady," "The Chocolate Soldier," "Buttrio Square," and "Fanny." He leaves his widow, former actress Lolly McKenzie.

THOMAS GOMEZ, 65, stage, film and tv actor, died June 18, 1971 in a Santa Monica hospital after 3 weeks in a coma. NY-born, made debut in 1923 with Walter Hampden in "Cyrano de Bergerac," followed by "Hamlet," "Grand Street Follies," "Caponsacchi," "Richelieu," "Taming of the Shrew," "Idiot's Delight," "The Seagull," "Ladies and Gentlemen," "There Shall Be No Night," "Sherlock Holmes," "Cat on a Hot Tin Roof," "The Visit," and "A Man for All Seasons." No reported survivors.

JACK GOODE, 63, musical comedy performer on stage and film, died from hepatitis in a NYC hospital on June 24, 1971. Made debut 1933 in "Of Thee I Sing," subsequently in "Face the Music," "Ziegfeld Follies," "Pajama Game," "Desert Song," "Bells Are Ringing," and "Hello, Dolly!" Born Irwin Thomas Whittridge in Columbus, O. He leaves his widow, former actress-dancer Renalda Green, and a son.

AL GOODMAN, 81, Russian-born conductor, composer, and arranger for stage and radio, died in a NYC hospital on Jan. 10, 1972 after a long illness. He wrote the score and book for the smash hit "So Long Letty," and was subsequently involved with "Vanities," "Scandals," "Sinbad," "Rio Rita," "Strike Me Pink," "Sons o' Guns," and "The Cat and the Fiddle." A daughter survives.

TOM GORMAN, 63, actor, and writer, died Oct. 2, 1971 of pulmonary embolism in a NY hospital. Had appeared in "The Investigation," "A Shadow of My Enemy," "The Best Man," "Sunrise at Campobello," "Hadrian VII," and "1776." His widow, 2 sons, and 4 daughters survive.

DOROTHY GREENER, 54, actress, singer, comedienne, died Dec. 6, 1971 of cancer in a NYC hospital. Had appeared in "The Girls against the Boys," "My Mother, My Father, and Me," "Come What May," "Razzle Dazzle," "Shoestring Revue," "Leave It to Jane," and "War Games." No reported survivors.

VIRGINIA HAMMOND, 78, Pennsylvania-born stage and film actress, died Apr. 6, 1972 in Washington, D.C. Made debut 1909 in "Arsene Lupin," followed by "What the Doctor Ordered," "The Arab," "If I Were King," "The Famous Mrs. Fair," "Her Temporary Husband," "The Harem," "You Can't Take It with You," "The Man Who Came to Dinner," "Winged Victory," "Craig's Wife," "Life with Mother," and "Crime and Punishment." A son survives.

FRED HEBERT, 60, producer, manager, and director, died Mar. 7, 1972 following open heart surgery in a Newark, NJ. hospital. He had been associated with "Pajama Game," "The Caretaker," "Alfie," "The Flip Side," "Time of the Barracudas," "Donnybrook!," "Coco," and "Twigs." He leaves his widow, a son, and daughter.

VAN HEFLIN, 60, versatile stage, film, and tv actor, died July 23, 1971 in a Hollywood hospital after suffering a heart attack while swimming in his pool, June 6. Oklahoma-born Evan Heflin made Bdwy debut 1928 in "Mr. Moneypenny," subsequently appeared in "The Bride of Torozko," "End of Summer," "Philadelphia Story," "A View from the Bridge," and "A Case of Libel." Divorced from his second wife, former actress Frances Neal, he leaves a son and 2 daughters. After cremation, his remains were scattered over the Pacific.

PERCY HELTON, 77, vaudevillian, stage, and film actor, died Sept. 11, 1971 in a Hollywood hospital. Began career at 3 in vaudeville with his father. Appeared on Bdwy in, among others, "The Return of Peter Grimm," "Young America," "One Sunday Afternoon," "Naughty-Naught '00." Moved to Hollywood in 1937 and appeared in over 200 films. No reported survivors.

LEONARD M. HICKS, 53, actor, died Aug. 8, 1971 of cancer in NYC. Had appeared with NY Shakespeare Festival, and in "The Connection," "My Mother, My Father and Me, "Moondreamers," and "Gloria and Esperanza." No reported survivors.

LIBBY HOLMAN, 65, musical comedy singer and actress, died June 18, 1971, an apparent suicide from carbon monoxide poisoning on her North Stamford, Conn., estate. Famous in the 1920's and '30's as a blues and torch singer, made her Bdwy debut 1925 in "Garrick Gaities," followed by "Greenwich Village Follies," "Merry-Go-Round," "Rainbow," "Ned Wayburn's Gambols," "The Little Show," "Three's a Crowd," "Revenge with Music," "You Never Know," and "Libby Holman's Blues, Ballads and Sin Songs." In later years, often gave folksong concerts for charities. Surviving is her third husband, artist Louis Schanker.

Libby Holman (1954)

HAL JAMES, 58, writer-director for radio and tv, and Bdwy producer, died July 30, 1971 after a stroke in his Westport, Conn., home. Bdwy credits include "Man of La Mancha," "Hallelujah, Baby!," and "Portrait of a Queen." Surviving are his widow, a daughter, and 2 sons.

ROBERT C. JARVIS, 79, director, and former musical comedy actor, died Nov. 13, 1971 in Teaneck, NJ. A veteran of more than 60 years on stage, had played in "The Gingham Girl," "Desert Song," "The Cat and the Fiddle," and "Roberta," among others. Directed Lambertville Music Circus for many years. He leaves his widow, a son, and daughter.

ISABEL JEWELL, 62, stage and film actress, was found dead in her Hollywood home on Apr. 5, 1972. Her Bdwy credits include "Up Pops the Devil," and "Blessed Event" that took her to Hollywood in 1932. No reported survivors.

T. C. JONES, 50, actor, and female impersonator, died Sept. 25, 1971 of cancer in Duarte, Calif. Appeared in "My Dear Public," "Sadie Thompson," "Polonaise," "Jackpot," "Girl from Nantucket," "One Touch of Venus," and "New Faces of 1956" in which he first did his impersonations. Subsequently appeared on Bdwy and internationally in his own musical divertissement "Mask and Gown." More recently had been in films and tv. His widow survives.

Isabel Jewell (1933)

JULIA KELETY, 85, Budapest-born musical and operetta actress-singer, died Jan. 1, 1972 in her NYC home. After moving to U. S. in 1940, appeared in "The Merry Widow," "Joanne of Arkansas," "Two Little Girls in Blue," "Gingham Girl," "Roberta," and "Music in the Air." A daughter survives.

MURIEL KIRKLAND, 68, stage and film actress, died in a NYC hospital of emphysema on Sept. 26, 1971. Bdwy debut 1923 in "Knave of Hearts," followed by "School for Scandal," "Out of Step," "Brass Buttons," "Cock Robin," "Strictly Dishonorable" (that brought her stardom and films), "The Greeks Had a Word for It," "Abe Lincoln in Illinois," "Life with Father," "Inherit the Wind," and "Legend of Lizzie." She leaves her husband, actor Staats Cotsworth.

WILLIAM KROT, 45, stage manager, died in his sleep Dec. 2, 1971 in his NYC home. Bdwy credits include "Camino Real," "Rhinoceros," "Rose Tattoo," "New Faces of 1956," "Fade Out-Fade In," "Flora the Red Menace," "How to Be a Jewish Mother," and "Jimmy Shine." Surviving are his widow actress Carol Raymond, and a son.

Muriel Kirkland (1930)

Jessie Royce Landis (1963)

Paul Lukas (1963)

Diana Lynn (1962)

JESSIE ROYCE LANDIS, 67, stage, film, and tv actress, died Feb. 2, 1972 of cancer in Danbury, Conn. Chicago-born, made Bdwy debut 1926 in "The Honor of the Family," subsequently in over 45 plays in NY and London, including "The Furies," "Command Performance," "Solid South," "Merrily We Roll Along," "Love from a Stranger," "Richard II," "Sing Me No Lullaby," "Love's Old Sweet Song," "Papa Is All," "Kiss and Tell," "Little Women," "Winter's Tale," "Little A," "Richard III," "Someone waiting," and "Roar Like a Dove." She leaves her second husband, Gen. J.F.R. Seitz.

WINDSOR LEWIS, 53, stage manager, and director, died May 15, 1972 in a NYC hospital after a long illness. Credits include "Life with Mother," "Antony and Cleopatra," "That Lady," "The Constant Wife," "Time Limit!," and "One More River." Surviving are his wife, actress Barbara Bel Geddes, and 2 daughters.

JOHN LITEL, 77, stage, film, and tv actor, died Feb. 3, 1972 in Woodland Hills Motion Picture Hospital. After success on Bdwy in "Ceiling Zero," "Irene," "The First Legion," and "Life's Too Short," moved to Hollywood in the 1930's and became a popular supporting player. His second wife survives.

PAUL LUKAS, 76, stage, film, and tv actor, died Aug. 15, 1971 of a heart failure in a Tangier hospital. Budapest-born, made Bdwy debut 1937 in "A Doll's House," followed between films by "Watch on the Rhine," "Call Me Madam," "Flight into Egypt," and "The Wayward Saint." His second wife survives.

DIANA LYNN, 45, stage, and film actress, and pianist, died Dec. 18, 1971 in a Los Angeles hospital after suffering a stroke and brain hemorrhage. Made Bdwy appearances in "The Wild Duck," "Horses in Midstream," "The Moon Is Blue," and "Mary, Mary." Her second husband, Mortimer Hall, and 4 children survive.

FANIA MARINOFF, 81, retired Russian-born actress, died Nov. 16, 1971 in an Englewood, N.J., hospital. Made stage debut at 9 in Denver, subsequently appeared in NY in "Japanese Nightingale," "You Never Can Tell," "Sorceress," "Streets of New York," "Pillars of Society," "The Bride the Sun Shines On," "Christopher Comes Across," "Judgment Day," "Times Have Changed," "Rainbow," "Within the Law," "Arms and the Man," "The Tempest," "Awakening of Spring," "Frank Fay's Fables," "Tarnish," and "The Charlatan." She was the widow of critic-author-photographer Carl Van Vechten.

OLIVER McGOWAN, 64, stage, film, and tv actor, died in his sleep Aug. 23, 1971 in his Hollywood home. Before moving to Calif., had appeared as SHERLING OLIVER in over 20 plays, including "God Loves Us," "The Mystery Ship," "One Way Street," "Cafe de Danse," "The Web," "Invitation to a Murder," "Symphony," "Without Love," and "Magnificent Yankee." No reported survivors.

GEORGE MITCHELL, 67, stage, and film actor, and writer, died in his sleep Jan. 18, 1972 in Washington, DC. where he was in rehearsal. Bdwy debut 1941 in "Tanyard Street," followed by "The Patriots," "Goodbye, My Fancy," "The Day after Tomorrow," "The Crucible," and "The Indians." No reported survivors.

HORACE McMAHON, 64, stage, film, and tv character actor, died Aug. 17, 1971 in Norwalk, Conn. of a heart ailment. Bdwy bow 1931 in "Wonder Boy," subsequently in "Vagabond King," "Man Bites Dog," "Gas," "Sailor Beware," "Battleship Gertie," "Three Men on a Horse," "Red Gloves," "Detective Story," "Say, Darling," and "The Mundy Scheme." Made 135 films, and was Lt. Parker in the tv series "Naked City." Surviving are his wife, actress Louise Campbell, a son, and 2 daughters.

THOMAS W. MOSELEY, 93, actor, and former executive secretary of the Negro Actors Guild, died in NYC on Aug. 17, 1971. Had starred in "In Abraham's Bosom," and appeared in "Stevedore," "Turpentine," "House of Shadows," "The Tree," and "Brown Buddies." His widow, 2 sons, and 2 daughters survive.

LE ROI OPERTI, 75, singer-actor, died after a long illness on June 22, 1971 in a NYC hospital. After 13 years in opera, musicals, and stock in Boston, made NY debut 1920 with Walter Hampden's repertory company in "George Washington," followed by many Shakespearean roles, and "The Servant in the House," "Firebird," "Idiot's Delight," "The Cradle Will Rock," "The American Way," "The Man Who Came to Dinner," "A Kiss for Cinderella," "The Would-be Gentleman," "Madwoman of Chaillot," "Make a Wish," "The First Gentleman," "Time Remembered." No reported survivors.

MICHAEL O'SULLIVAN, 37, actor, was found dead in his San Francisco apartment on July 24, 1971. Cause of death was unknown. Appeared in several regional theatres, and in NY in "Six Characters in Search of an Author," "Tartuffe" for which he received a Theatre World Award, "The Alchemist," "The White House," "It's a Bird, It's a Plane, It's Superman," "Love and Let Love," "The Bench," "A Flea in Her Ear," and "Three Sisters." No reported survivors.

ANN PENNINGTON, 77, dancing star of the 1920's, died Nov. 4, 1971 in a NYC hospital after a long illness. Bdwy debut 1911 in "The Red Widow," followed by six editions of "Ziegfeld Follies," five "George White's Scandals" (in which she danced "The Black Bottom" that swept the country in 1926), "Jack and Jill," "The New Yorkers," "Everybody's Welcome," and "The Student Prince" her last performance in 1943. She was never married, and left no known survivors.

ROBERT H. PORTERFIELD, 66, former actor, and founder-director of Barter Theatre in Va., died Oct. 28, 1971 of a heart attack after being admitted to an Abingdon, Va., hospital with pneumonia. Bdwy debut 1927 in "The Ivory Door," followed by "Mima," "The Dagger and the Rose," "Blue Ghost," "Blind Windows," "Cyrano de Bergerac," "Petrified Forest," "Let Freedom Ring," "Bury the Dead," and "Everywhere I Roam." Opened Barter Theatre in 1933 with a 35c admission "or the equivalent in produce." It is now the State Theatre of Virginia. In 1948 he received a "Tony" for outstanding contribution to the theatre. Surviving are his second wife and a son.

STANLEY PRAGER, 54, stage and film actor, director, producer, died Jan. 18, 1972 while on a business trip to Los Angeles from his native NYC. Acting debut 1942 in "The Eve of St. Mark," subsequently in "The Skin of Our Teeth," "Two on the Aisle," "Two's Company," "Room Service," "Pajama Game." Directed "Come Blow Your Horn," "Let It Ride!," "Bravo Giovanni!," "Minnie's Boys." Appeared in 25 films; directed tv's "Car 54," and "Patty Duke Show" series. His widow, actress Georgann Johnson, and 4 daughters survive.

B. S. PULLY, 61, film and stage actor, and night club comedian, died Jan. 6, 1972 of a heart attack in Philadelphia hospital. He created Big Jule in "Guys and Dolls," and repeated it in the film version. Appeared in over 30 films. He leaves his widow, former dancer, Helen Stone, and a son.

MICHAEL RENNIE, 62, British-born stage, film, and tv actor, died June 10, 1971 of natural causes while visiting his mother in London. A U.S. citizen from 1960, appeared on Bdwy in "Mary, Mary," in over 50 films, and the successful tv series "The Third Man." His mother and a son survive.

RENIE RIANO, age unreported, veteran of Bdwy, vaudeville, films, and tv, died July 3, 1971 in Woodland Hills, Calif., after a long illness. Among her Bdwy credits are "Honey Girl," "Music Box Revue," and "The Man Who Came to Dinner." Moved to Hollywood in 1937 and made over 150 films. Also appeared in tv in "The Partridge Family," and "Mayberry, R.F.D." A daughter survives.

MARGARET RUTHERFORD, 80, stage and film actress for over 40 years, died May 22, 1972 in her Buckinghamshire, Eng., home after several weeks' illness. Appeared on Bdwy in "The Importance of Being Earnest," and "Farewell, Farewell, Eugene." She made over 30 films and received an "Oscar" for "The V.I.P.'s" in 1964. In 1967 was made a Dame of the British Empire. Surviving are her husband, actor-producer Stringer Davis, and 4 adopted children.

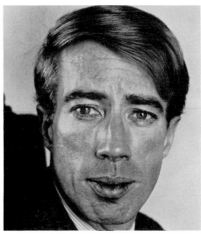

Michael O'Sullivan (1966)

Michael Rennie (1966)

Renie Riano

Margaret Rutherford (1967)

Joseph Santley (1952)

JOSEPH SANTLEY, 81, stage and film actor and producer, died Aug. 8, 1971 in his West Los Angeles home. Attained stardom at 9 in "Boy of the Streets," followed by "From Rags to Riches," and "Billy the Kid." At 21 was starring in musical comedies and became a matinee idol in such productions as "When Dreams Come True," "Betty," "Just Fancy," "Stop! Look! Listen!," "Oh, Boy!," "Half Moon," two editions of "The Music Box Revue," "All Over Town," "Oh, My Dear," and "The Wild Rose." Moved to Hollywood where he acted, directed over 50 films, and produced for tv. His widow, former actress Ivy Sawyer, a daughter, and 2 sons survive.

RICHARD SKINNER, 71, actor, manager, producer, died in NYC Aug. 3, 1971 after a long illness. Made Bdwy debut 1922 in "Hamlet." Became involved with touring Jitney Players, and subsequently with summer theatres. Was co-producer of "Family Portrait," "I Know What I Like," and "Charley's Aunt." He leaves a brother and sister.

RALPH STANTLEY, 58, stage, screen, and tv actor, died May 10, 1972 of cancer in a NYC hospital. Bdwy debut 1944 in "Harriet," followed by "Burlesque," "The Visit," "Call Me Mister," "Tall Story," "Golden Fleecing," "Sing, Muse!," and "What Makes Sammy Run." His mother and sister survive.

JOHN STEEL, 71, tenor star of many "Ziegfeld Follies," and several "Music Box Revues," died June 24, 1971 in a NYC hospital. "A Pretty Girl Is Like a Melody" was written for and introduced by him in the 1919 "Follies." He had been in retirement for several years. Surviving is his widow, former dancer Jeanette Hackett.

COWLES STRICKLAND, 68, teacher, director, and founder of Berkshire Playhouse, died Oct. 20, 1971 of cancer in Washington, D.C., where he taught at American Univ. For Bdwy, he directed "The Patriarch," "Fly Away Home," "Out of the Frying Pan," and "Best Sellers." He was also a director at Washington's Arena Stage. His widow, a son, and a daughter survive.

JAMES TRITTIPO, 43, television art director, and theatrical designer, died Sept. 15, 1971 in Los Angeles. Won 3 "Emmys" for his tv designs, and did the sets for this season's revival of "On the Town." Surviving are his parents, a brother, and a sister.

FRANK TWEDDELL, 76, stage and film actor, died Dec. 20, 1971 in a Guilford, Conn., hospital. Bdwy debut 1923 in "The Devil's Disciple," followed by "Abe Lincoln in Illinois," "Claudia," "Suds in Your Eyes," "Pick-Up Girl," "Strange Fruit," "The Iceman Cometh," "Two Blind Mice," "Mr. Barry's Etchings," "Borned in Texas," "The Golden State," and "All the Way Home." His widow and two daughters survive.

JAMES WESTERFIELD, 58, stage, tv, and film character actor, and summer theatre producer, died Sept. 20, 1971 of a heart attack in Woodland Hills, Calif. Bdwy bow 1944 in "Sing Out Sweet Land," followed by "Madwoman of Chaillot" and "Detective Story" for both of which he received a Drama Critics Award, "Venus Observed," "Wooden Dish," and "Inherit the Wind." He leaves his widow, actress Fay Tracey.

WALTER WINCHELL, 74, former vaudeville song-and-dance man who became a newspaper columnist and newscaster, died Feb. 20, 1972 of cancer in Los Angeles Medical Center. Was critic and drama editor of The Graphic, a tabloid, where his column "Your Broadway and Mine" began. Subsequently transferred to The Mirror and used "On Broadway" as title for his column. Retired in 1965. A daughter survives.

MARY MARSDEN YOUNG, 92, stage and screen actress, died June 23, 1971 of a heart attack in La Jolla, Calif. For 21 years, she and her actor-manager husband, the late John Craig, operated Castle Square Theatre in Boston. Before moving to Hollywood, appeared on Bdwy in "Believe Me, Xantippe," "Hamlet," "The Outrageous Mrs. Palmer," "Dancing Mothers." Was active in films and tv until her retirement in 1968. No reported survivors.

INDEX

271

275

276

277

280

283

285